THE DEATH OF THE MEHDI ARMY

NICHOLAS KROHLEY

The Death of the Mehdi Army

The Rise, Fall, and Revival of Iraq's Most Powerful Militia

Oxford University Press is a department of the
University of Oxford. It furthers the University's objective
of excellence in research, scholarship, and education
by publishing worldwide.

Oxford New York
Auckland Cape Town Dar es Salaam Hong Kong Karachi
Kuala Lumpur Madrid Melbourne Mexico City Nairobi
New Delhi Shanghai Taipei Toronto

With offices in
Argentina Austria Brazil Chile Czech Republic France Greece
Guatemala Hungary Italy Japan Poland Portugal Singapore
South Korea Switzerland Thailand Turkey Ukraine Vietnam

Published in the United States of America by
Oxford University Press
198 Madison Avenue, New York, NY 10016

Library of Congress Cataloging-in-Publication Data is available
Krohley, Nicholas
The Death of the Mehdi Army/The Rise, Fall, and Revival of Iraq's Most
Powerful Militia
ISBN 978-0-19-939625-2

Printed in India on acid-free paper

CONTENTS

LIST OF MAPS AND FIGURES

Chapter 7

Appendix

ABBREVIATIONS

AO	Area of Operations
BCT	US Army Brigade Combat Team
COIN	Counterinsurgency
EFP	Explosively Formed Projectile
ePRT	embedded Provincial Reconstruction Team
FOB	Forward Operating Base
HTT	Human Terrain Team
ISF	Iraqi Security Forces
INP	Iraqi National Police
JAM	*Jaish al-Mehdi* (The Mehdi Army)
JSS	Joint Security Station
MESH	Middle East Strategy at Harvard
NATO	North Atlantic Treaty Organization
NPTT	National Police Training Team
OPEC	Organization of the Petroleum Exporting Countries
SCIRI	Supreme Council for Islamic Revolution in Iraq (which became the SIIC in the post-Saddam era)
SIIC	Supreme Iraqi Islamic Council
UIA	United Iraqi Alliance

PREFACE

The Prose of Counterinsurgency

In a critique of how British officials documented military action in colonial India, the historian Ranajit Guha observed a distinct "prose of counterinsurgency."[1] Their accounts of insurgent activity, and of the operations mounted in response, invariably focused on British actions and interests, Guha noted, to the point that the indigenous people (and the specifics of the insurgency itself) effectively disappeared from the text. Even when an author explicitly declared an intention to detail aspects of insurgency, focus would consistently shift back to a discussion of British concerns, while references to the insurgents were often couched in the dehumanizing vocabulary of nature and disease (for example floods, swarms, plagues). "The rebel has no place in this history as the subject of rebellion," Guha lamented, insinuating that the ethnocentrism underpinning British documentation denied the indigenous people their rightful place in the narrative of their own lives.[2] The British instead took center stage in the historiography of colonial India, constituting an instance of intellectual imperialism that compounded the injustices of the subcontinent's colonial past.

One need not transpose Guha's explanations of racism and deliberate bias (nor subscribe to his interpretation of British colonial history) to acknowledge that a similar phenomenon is at work today in the literature of post-Saddam Iraq. Despite the growth of a sizable canon of texts by men and women with direct experience of the invasion and occupation of Iraq, remarkably little has been written that explores the country in rigorous detail, or that breaks new ground in the study of Iraqi society.[3] On the contrary, the commonality that has united the great majority of books ostensibly written about Iraq since 2003, irrespective of their immediate focus or political tilt, is that they have not, in fact, been about Iraq at all. These books have instead been merely set in Iraq, utilizing the country as a medium for, rather than the subject of, discussion.

Those who have gone to Iraq and had a frontline view of events have returned to write, almost exclusively, about themselves. From personal stories of deployment experiences to assessments of the strategies and tactics employed by the US and its allies, the accounts of those who have navigated the terrain of post-Saddam Iraq have been overwhelmingly self-centered.[4] Occasionally offering potted histories of Iraq, and typically neglecting any detailed examination of the localized dynamics of violence (instead, more commonly dismissing the viability of such exploration by presenting Iraq as hopelessly divided and impenetrably complex), the country and its people have received only token attention from authors whose central focus has lain elsewhere.

This phenomenon can be attributed to a variety of forces. Most immediately, the prevalence of "first-hand" accounts of the post-Saddam era that center on the actions and opinions of each particular author can be attributed to the overriding interests of the authors in question—as well as an understanding of their readers' appetites, which favor stories of harrowing combat experiences and critiques of Western policy over examinations of Iraqi society or history. The contemporary prose of counterinsurgency thus may be understood, in significant measure, as a manifestation of our collective disinterest in Iraq, and our overriding preoccupation with ourselves.

Yet this prevailing focus on the actions and interests of the occupying powers also reflects dominant intellectual trends in academia, the press, and the defense establishment. On the one hand, the notion that the US and its allies made the critical decisions of the post-Saddam era, and that the Iraqis were mere pawns in the games of others, sits neatly within a broader narrative that is widely held among professional observers of the Middle East.[5] If America and its partners were, in fact, "in the driver's seat of history" throughout the invasion and occupation of Iraq, it is only natural that accounts of the period should focus on their actions.[6] On the other hand, in adopting an occupier-centric framework of analysis, authors are following the lead of countless pundits and policy experts, who have written far more about the implications of the war on Western interests and objectives than about Iraq or the Iraqi people. With the

Iraq war occupying a central position in America's political discourse from late 2002 until 2008, those with ground-level experience have been called upon far more to make sense of America and its allies' involvement than to expound on the specifics of the country itself.

Lastly, a more mundane concern merits consideration: namely, the practical reality of occupation, and the limited range of experiences that it offered. Those who deployed to Iraq, as a general rule, did not experience an extended immersion in Iraqi society. Nor were they offered extensive opportunities to interact meaningfully with a broad range of Iraqis. On the contrary, deployment experiences were often profoundly isolating, amounting to intensive and prolonged immersions among one's own kind on insular military installations. Even for those spending significant amounts of time "outside the wire," the barriers of language, culture, armor, and mutual suspicion typically dictated that Iraq and the Iraqis remained distant and inaccessible. The lessons learned and insights gathered by those deployed were thus, above all else, of the self, leading to a body of literature that is understandably introspective.

Nevertheless, however innovative this body of literature may be with respect to its own objectives, and despite of the merits of individual works, overwhelming trends toward introspection and reflection have created severe distortions. First, as self-critique becomes self-absorption, the influence (for good or for ill, depending on one's particular world-view) of the US and its allies' counterinsurgent campaign has been fundamentally overstated, corrupting analysts' ability to understand events or evaluate the effectiveness and wisdom of particular actions. Second, and more insidiously, the sheer volume of military-centric prose that has been produced—examining the efficacy of the tools in the counterinsurgent's arsenal, for example, with emphasis on metrics, methods, and "lessons-learned" from particular operations—has swelled to the point that insurgency has fallen from view.[7] Counterinsurgency—or "COIN"—has become a thing in and of itself, which is discussed and debated without reference to any particular set of specific local circumstances (with best practices that can be adhered to, and solutions that can be applied, irrespective of the challenges they are meant to address).

In a response to this trend, and likewise to the historiographic imbalances detailed above, this book has two main objectives. First and foremost, it is a study of the Mehdi Army's campaign on the margins of eastern Baghdad, which illuminates the social dynamics that shaped the militia's fortunes and, by extension, offers insights into the condition of Iraqi society. In this capacity, it is both a study of war in the neighborhoods of Baghdad, as well as a study of Baghdad's neighborhoods at war.

Second, this book is offered as a primary source for practitioners and students of insurgency and counterinsurgency, in the hope that it might draw attention to imbalances in the literature of the field, and also offer a case study of how an insurgency can be confronted, assessed, and deconstructed by fusing traditional military and intelligence methods with the resources of the social sciences.[8]

INTRODUCTION

"March Madness"

At the end of March 2008, more than a year into the Americans' highly-touted initiative to restore order in and around Baghdad that was known as the Surge, the impoverished Shi'a neighborhoods on the city's eastern periphery erupted in violence. Barrages of rockets were fired westward across the Tigris River toward the Green Zone, which housed the upper echelons of the Iraqi government and the American-led coalition; Iraqi-manned security checkpoints across eastern Baghdad were overrun or deserted; and the numerous neighborhood-level outposts that the Americans had established throughout the area came under heavy fire. Originating from the strongholds of Muqtada al-Sadr and his Mehdi Army militia, this intense and unexpected paroxysm of violence—dubbed "March Madness" by the Americans—appeared to demonstrate the enduring potency of Iraq's so-called Shi'a insurgency.

The outburst in Baghdad came in response to the launch of a large-scale military offensive by the Iraqi government in the southern city of Basra.[1] Shi'a militias hostile to the central government, the Mehdi Army foremost among them, had seized control of Basra following the withdrawal of British forces in 2007. Their control of the city had provided both a sanctuary from which to stage attacks against the Iraqi government and Coalition Forces, as well as access to the revenues generated at Iraq's primary commercial outlet to the Persian Gulf. The Basra offensive, labeled Operation Knight's Charge, was thus orchestrated by Prime Minister Nuri al-Maliki to reclaim the city and restore government rule.[2]

The Basra offensive held deeper significance, however, as it also marked a violent re-escalation of a long-running rivalry between the factions of

Iraq's Shi'a elite (most notable among them the Supreme Iraqi Islamic Council and Prime Minister Maliki's Da'wa Party) and the Sadrist movement, which represented Iraq's demographically-powerful but historically-marginalized Shi'a underclass.[3] Tracing its immediate roots to the 1990s, when Muqtada al-Sadr's father, Mohammed Mohammed Sadiq al-Sadr, mobilized a sweeping grassroots movement of the underclass masses that challenged the power, privilege, and legitimacy of the traditional Shi'a establishment, this bitter intra-Shi'a rivalry became a pivotal axis of conflict after the fall of Saddam Hussein.[4]

In the early years of the post-Saddam era, the two blocs engaged in fierce fighting. The parties of the Shi'a elite aligned themselves with the American-led coalition, thereby ensconcing themselves at the heart of the emerging political order. Muqtada al-Sadr, on the other hand, positioned the Sadrist movement and the Mehdi Army at the forefront of "resistance." A series of bloody clashes ensued during 2003 and 2004, which delineated a class-based schism within Iraq's Shi'a populace. Indeed, while a combination of political opportunism and mutual fear inspired by the rise of fanatical Sunni militants would drive the two into an uneasy partnership in the years that followed, powerful intra-Shi'a tensions persisted for the duration of Iraq's sectarian war.[5] When sectarian violence abated during the course of 2007 and 2008, therefore, and the forces that had forged their unlikely alliance waned significantly, the stage was set for conflict to resume.

Recognizing that the prime minister's assault on Basra marked a declaration of renewed intra-Shi'a war, the Mehdi Army and its affiliates offered fierce opposition.[6] Their counter-attack in Basra broke the initial momentum of government forces and necessitated the infusion of reinforcements and American support. Simultaneous assaults in Baghdad were formidable as well. Significant numbers of Shi'a security personnel stationed in the capital proved of dubious loyalty, either abandoning their posts or turning their rifles on their colleagues; satellite television broadcast the surrender of entire Iraqi units in the Mehdi Army stronghold of Sadr City; the principal Iraqi spokesman for counterinsurgency initiatives in Baghdad was kidnapped; and thousands of the Sadrist movement's supporters took to the streets.[7] American forces in Baghdad (and their remaining Iraqi counterparts) braced themselves for a sustained offensive, which threatened to undo months of hard-fought progress.

However, the escalation of hostilities, while intense, proved ephemeral. Rather than signaling either the start of a revitalized insurgency by the Mehdi Army or the onset of a bloody reckoning between competing demographic subsets of Iraq's Shi'a community, the fury of March Madness gave way to a general rout. In Baghdad, as in Basra and elsewhere across southern Iraq, American and Iraqi forces not only restored control over areas enveloped by violence during the outburst of late March, but they also drove the Mehdi Army from its core strongholds. Prominent militants were captured, killed, or forced to flee to sanctuary in Iran. The militia, once dominant across broad swathes of the country, was battered and discredited to the point that Muqtada announced its wholesale dissolution in June of that year.

The Successes of the Surge Against the Mehdi Army

In the prevailing narrative that has coalesced around the final years of American-led combat operations in Iraq, the dramatic collapse of the Mehdi Army is explained principally as the by-product of Iraqi *realpolitik* and American perseverance and ingenuity.[8] On the Iraqi side, Prime Minister Nuri al-Maliki's decision to break with the Sadrist movement and turn on the Mehdi Army was instrumental in isolating the militia politically. Having made use of the Mehdi Army's fighting prowess to check the onslaught of Sunni militants and achieve a decisive Shi'a "victory" in Iraq's sectarian war, Prime Minister Maliki was sufficiently secure in his position to turn on his enemy-turned-ally-of-necessity.[9] The cold calculations of intra-Shi'a intrigue thus left the Mehdi Army exposed, rendering it all the more vulnerable to the American-led assault that followed.

Accounts of America's role in the Mehdi Army's defeat emphasize both political will and military innovation. First, President George W. Bush's decision to recommit American forces to Iraq via the Surge is widely cited as a critical precondition to the achievements that followed.[10] By allocating additional resources and reaffirming America's intent to bring security and stability to Iraq (and to Baghdad in particular), American forces were well positioned to influence Prime Minister Maliki and to capitalize on the vicissitudes of Iraqi politics. Second, the successes achieved during 2007 and 2008 are commonly attributed to the American military's embrace of the strategies and tactics of counterinsurgency, or "COIN."[11] The Surge did not succeed, goes the argument, by virtue of additional manpower and renewed commitment alone, but because of critical adaptations to the manner in which military operations were conducted.

Breaking markedly from past practices of self-containment on isolated bases (a deliberate strategy that had been built on the premise that the daily presence of foreign soldiers in the lives of Iraqi civilians provoked resentment, thereby stoking the very insurgency that the coalition was attempting to quell), American forces spread out into the neighborhoods of the Iraqi capital and proactively engaged the city.[12] Efforts to kill or capture Shi'a militants were paired with initiatives to restore essential services, meet pressing public health needs, reform the government and the security services, and reinvigorate the economy. This multi-faceted offensive was designed to overwhelm the Mehdi Army, inflicting damage upon its fighters while simultaneously undermining popular support for its insurgent agenda.[13]

Finally, in discussions of the Mehdi Army's own contributions to its downfall, emphasis is commonly placed on the manner in which its internal troubles left it vulnerable to attack.[14] The militia's already disjointed chain of command, for example, made the capture, death, or flight abroad of key leaders particularly destabilizing, while the abuses of its notoriously undisciplined rank and file further eroded its base of popular support. As a result, once betrayed by its notional allies in the Maliki administration, the Mehdi Army was unable to fend off the intensified and recalibrated attentions of the Surge.

Yet, while each of these factors played an important role in the downfall of the Mehdi Army, the circumstances surrounding the militia's collapse require closer inspection. At issue is the scope and speed of its apparent rout, and the fact that it was achieved without the costly and destabilizing violence widely anticipated by observers.[15] From the Basra offensive in late March through the remainder of 2008 there were fierce bouts of fighting, particularly in Baghdad, yet nothing on a scale commensurate with the rivalry that existed between the Sadrist movement and its foes in the Shi'a establishment, or the depth of Sadrist opposition to the American-led coalition.

How then, to account for the Mehdi Army's precipitous decline and ultimate dissolution during the spring and summer of 2008? What caused the apparent implosion of the militia not only as a fighting force, but also as the vanguard of popular insurgency on behalf of Iraq's long-suffering Shi'a underclass? Had estimates fundamentally overstated the power of the Mehdi Army, or the depth of popular support for the Sadrist movement? Did the combination of a shifting political landscape and the counterinsurgency approaches of the American military overwhelm the militia? Alternatively, might the Mehdi Army's seeming collapse have been a coordinated display of strategic patience, with Muqtada and his supporters seeking to avoid direct confrontation in order to fight another day?[16]

A View Beneath the Violence

This book is an attempt to explain the dynamics, and the implications, of the Mehdi Army's collapse. Drawing from first-hand experience in the Tisa Nissan political district of eastern Baghdad between February and December 2008, it presents a neighborhood-by-neighborhood examination of the militia's changing fortunes. Rooted in a study of Baghdad's history, and building upon the experiences and observations of the author, his civilian and military colleagues on a US Army Human Terrain Team, and the American military personnel whom they supported, this book details the Mehdi Army's rise to dominance in Tisa Nissan through the early years of the post-Saddam era—and explains the reasons for its fall during the course of 2008.[17]

The primary research that forms the core of this book is, in many respects, a by-product of the Surge and its accompanying innovations. The Human Terrain System itself (a US Army program developed to harness civilian academic expertise in support of military operations) was an idea that grew from the efforts of the American defense establishment to recalibrate its approach to ongoing wars in Iraq and Afghanistan.[18] With military personnel returning from deployments to both conflicts lamenting a lack of insight into social and cultural issues and citing difficulty in understanding the "human terrain" of the battlefield as a key concern, the Human Terrain System was created to fill this knowledge gap.[19] Had that innovation not taken place, the author, as a civilian, would have been unable to gain the sort of access to frontline American units (and, by extension, to the Iraqi people) that was essential to the work that follows.

Furthermore, the neighborhood-level insights offered herein would likely have been unachievable without both the altered posture of American forces that came with the Surge, as well as the momentum it generated against the Mehdi Army. The decision to break out from the

Figure 0.1: Baghdad's Political Districts

insular Forward Operating Bases (FOBs) that the military had constructed across Baghdad and establish a network of small patrol bases within the neighborhoods of the city greatly increased opportunities for interaction with Baghdadis. Additionally, by pushing militants off of the streets and inserting American and Iraqi forces as the arbiters of law and order, the Surge altered the dynamic between Baghdadis and American personnel. Notions of "winning hearts and minds" aside, the declining local position of the Mehdi Army, the exodus from Baghdad of prominent militants, and the daily presence of American and Iraqi security personnel on the city's streets created an environment that was increasingly conducive to face-to-face interaction.

As American forces pressed deeper into the neighborhoods of Tisa Nissan during the spring and summer of 2008, it was possible to look beneath the violence of the militia's campaign and study the people and territory over which it had ruled. How had the Mehdi Army established itself across Tisa Nissan? How had different elements of the local population responded, and how had the militia's insurgent campaign evolved? What accounted for the Mehdi Army's ability to conquer the district during the initial years of the post-Saddam era, making it an integral part of the militia's expansive domain, only to cede it in a relatively sudden and unexpected fashion? Lastly, what insights might the militia's experience in Tisa Nissan offer into its overall fate, and into the broader dynamics of conflict in post-Saddam Iraq?

Insurgency, Civil Society, and the Death of the Mehdi Army

The toppling of Saddam Hussein presented Muqtada al-Sadr with an extraordinary opportunity. As his martyred father had drawn together the masses of Iraq's Shi'a underclass during the course of the previous decade, instilling a powerful sense of shared pride and solidarity within their battered ranks, Muqtada had the chance to engage a new, democratic Iraq as the head of one of the country's only broadly-based popular movements.[20]

Rebuilding his father's movement around the framework of the Mehdi Army militia, Muqtada launched an ambitious insurgent campaign. The Mehdi Army was to serve as the vanguard of a sweeping popular movement of Iraq's downtrodden Shi'a underclass, which would carry Muqtada to a position of national-level political and clerical power. Sadrist devotees were thus channeled into the militia, fueling its massive expansion into a powerful force on the streets of Baghdad and across much of southern and central Iraq.[21]

However, despite the militia's impressive growth, and irrespective of an enduring affinity to Sadrist ideals among Iraq's underclass Shi'a (for whom Mohammed Mohammed Sadiq al-Sadr remained an object of near-universal veneration), Muqtada ultimately failed to rally a cohesive, mass-based insurgency.

In examining the Mehdi Army's fortunes in the neighborhoods of Tisa Nissan, it appears that this outcome was largely pre-determined by the condition of Iraqi society. With the district's residents ravaged and socially atomized by an array of forces that are detailed in the chapters that follow, civil society in Tisa Nissan was not merely infertile ground for the cultivation of popular insurgency but, in places, toxic. On the one hand, the badly degraded state of civil society effectively precluded the mobilization of what became an increasingly conspicuous "silent majority." Rather than shaping the character of the rekindled Sadrist movement, the great majority of Tisa Nissan's underclass Shi'a residents withdrew into the relative safety of their homes, seeking shelter from the chaos that threatened to consume them. On the other hand, the volatility, radicalism, and proclivity to extreme violence of those who asserted themselves at the militia's core eventually destroyed its reputation.[22] Rather than acting as the advance guard of a coherent popular movement, the Mehdi Army evolved into a disjointed and exceptionally controversial entity that alienated many who might otherwise have actively supported Muqtada's cause.

Consequently, when the forces of the Surge pushed into the neighborhoods of Tisa Nissan, and likewise into "Sadrist strongholds" elsewhere across Iraq, they were not, for the most part, confronted by a popular, mass-based insurgency. Their task, therefore, was not to "win over" a civilian populace that was either fervently loyal to, or solidly integrated within, the militia's campaign. Instead, the challenge facing counterinsurgent forces was to identify and destroy discrete militant networks of dubious local popularity—something that was accomplished with general success, and without an eruption of large-scale violence.

Yet, while the Mehdi Army's general lack of popular support greatly facilitated the advance of the Surge in Tisa Nissan—making the short-term establishment of security in the wake of March Madness significantly easier than it would otherwise have been—the same social forces that undermined the militia's campaign also plagued subsequent counterinsurgency operations. Much as the militia had struggled to rally the district's residents in support of its endeavor, the Americans and their partners in the Iraqi government met with minimal success in mobilizing the populace to sustain hard-fought security gains, revive economic activity, rebuild critical infrastructure, or rehabilitate local governance.

Contrary to the standard narrative of the Surge, the short-term gains in security that were achieved by American and Iraqi forces in Tisa Nissan during the course of 2008 remained largely unconsolidated. With American forces withdrawing from the district in 2009, leaving Tisa Nissan in the hands of an Iraqi government that was both administratively ill equipped and also prejudicially disinclined to address its many woes, the district's future prospects (and, likewise, the long-term efficacy of the Surge) appeared uncertain at best. Similarly, the future direction of Muqtada al-Sadr and the rekindled Sadrist movement also remained unclear—though the crippling limitations imposed by the degraded condition of Iraqi society on any further efforts to rally mass-based action had been made manifestly evident.

Structural Overview

Chapter one sets the stage for the study of the Mehdi Army's campaign in Tisa Nissan by charting the physical growth of eastern Baghdad and the forces that shaped its social development. It begins with a discussion of the mass migrations that, during the middle decades of the twentieth century, brought hundreds of thousands of impoverished Shi'a farmers from southern Iraq to the nation's capital. Through an examination of how these sweeping population movements transformed the city's demographics, creating a massive, continually expanding Shi'a underclass on Baghdad's eastern margins, the chapter traces the evolution of issues that would become central to the ideology of the Sadrist movement. The urban development program of Prime Minister Abd al-Karim Qasim's revolutionary government of the late 1950s and early 1960s receives particular attention, as do the implications of the Iraqi state's increasingly aggressive efforts to engineer social change. The totalitarian rule of the Ba'th Party is then surveyed, with emphasis on its efforts to reshape Iraqi society. The chapter concludes with analysis of the extent to which the Ba'th regime had asserted wholesale dominance over Iraq by the late 1970s, and an examination of the faltering efforts of Shi'a militants to rally the capital's underclass masses against the government.

Chapter Two traces the rise of the Sadrist movement during the 1990s. The chapter begins with a survey of the disastrous policy decisions of Saddam Hussein during the 1980s and early 1990s, which depleted the regime's resources and forced radical changes to its governance strategy. Analysis focuses on how the contraction of state services and broadly-felt economic and social shocks endured under United Nations-imposed sanctions sparked grassroots tribal and religious movements among the Iraqi people—with emphasis on both the questionable authenticity of these "revivals," and the ways in which the regime harnessed and manipulated them.

The rise of Mohammed Mohammed Sadiq al-Sadr, from relative obscurity to the pre-eminent position in Iraqi Shi'ism, is then explained as having been inextricably linked to both the changes underway in Iraqi society and the regime's recalibrated approach to maintaining domestic control. The controversy surrounding Sadr's relationship with the regime is presented (Sadr's supporters argue that he took advantage of the regime's growing weakness to care for Iraq's Shi'a underclass at a time of extraordinary need, while his critics allege he was a regime collaborator who undermined the traditional Shi'a elite to the advantage of Saddam Hussein), as is the way that Sadr built an enormous popular following among Iraq's Shi'a poor. The chapter continues with a discussion of Sadr's ideology, and of how his populist militancy both broadened and deepened class-based divisions among Iraqi Shi'a that would be central to the intra-Shi'a violence of the post-Saddam era. It concludes with an analysis of how his mounting criticisms of the Ba'th regime precipitated his murder in 1999.

The third chapter traces the successes and failures of Muqtada al-Sadr as he attempted to resurrect his father's movement in the aftermath of Saddam Hussein's fall. It begins with an analysis of the Mehdi Army's initial efforts to influence post-Saddam politics by clashing with Coalition Forces and their Iraqi allies, and how Muqtada and his militia became leading symbols of resistance against both foreign occupation and Iraq's emerging political order. The chapter then details how the exigencies of electoral politics and the escalation of sectarian violence induced the Shi'a elite to reach out to the Sadrists, and how the rival Shi'a blocs cooperated to achieve victory in a sectarian war against radical Sunni militants. The process through which the Mehdi Army conquered large sectors of Baghdad in the course of the fighting receives particular attention, as does the way that targeted killing and forced displacement transformed the demographic landscape. The chapter concludes with an analysis of the militia's subsequent fragmentation, set in the context of Prime Minster Maliki's decision to turn on the Mehdi Army and resume intra-Shi'a conflict.

Chapter four introduces the area study at the heart of this work. The chapter begins with an overview of the district's local history. Elaborating on the migratory and urban development processes introduced in chapter one, it surveys the local specifics of the district's creation, settlement, and governance during the second half of the twentieth century. The rise of class-based tensions between the middle class and minority communities nearest to the city's core, and the predominantly Shi'a residents of the district's poorer, peripheral neighborhoods, is a main issue of focus, as is the way that this dynamic fueled the local popularity of the Sadrist movement during the 1990s.

The second section of the chapter examines the local campaign of the Mehdi Army after the fall of Saddam Hussein. The process through which the militia came to dominate the district is surveyed, with a focus on the district's concurrent demographic transformation. Discussion then turns to the encroachment of the Surge into Tisa Nissan, and the limited progress achieved during 2007 and early 2008. The reasons for Tisa Nissan's seeming intractability are examined, as are the ways in which American and Iraqi forces sought to remedy them. The chapter concludes with an analysis of the violence of March Madness, and how the fighting and its aftermath catalyzed major changes across the district.

Case studies of the *hayys*, or sub-districts, of Tisa Nissan are presented in chapters five through seven.[23] Each chapter examines a pair of *hayys* that shared certain commonalities with respect to the localized dynamics of violence, and explores the ways in which aspects of local society shaped the campaign of the Mehdi Army. These chapters begin with a summary of how each *hayy* was perceived by American forces in early 2008, and detail the immediate effects of March Madness. The core of each chapter then traces the overall trajectory of the militia's rise and fall, examining how the Mehdi Army came to dominate the *hayys* in question, how it defended its conquests against the Surge, and the circumstances surrounding its collapse.

The concluding chapter begins by summarizing the effects of Iraqi society's degraded state on the Mehdi Army's ability to rally a popular insurgency in Tisa Nissan. It argues that distinct social characteristics from one area to the next had a decisive effect on the militia's fate, and that the overall condition of the district's "human terrain" had rendered the mobilization of a coherent popular insurgency impossible.

Focus then turns to the manner in which American and Iraqi forces pushed the militia out of Tisa Nissan during 2008. It is argued that the standard narrative of the Surge as a triumph of full-spectrum counterinsurgency, wherein counterinsurgent forces achieved success not merely through force of arms, but also by undermining their enemy through the cultivation of popular support and the inducement of popular participation, bears little resemblance to events in Tisa Nissan. The chapter concludes with a discussion of the wider implications of Iraqi society's degraded condition on the country's future, including the ways in which this has influenced the violence of the post-Saddam era, how it has stunted Iraq's development as a democracy, and how it will continue to enable radical militant groups to exert influence that far outweighs their popularity among the Iraqi people.

1

A CITY TRANSFORMED

THE CREATION OF EASTERN BAGHDAD

The Continuity of Change in Baghdad

Baghdad is a city in flux. Subject to both internal and external pressures, its physical landscape and social fabric have both been altered dramatically since the American-led invasion of 2003. Much of the city has been cleansed along sectarian lines, leaving Shi'a and Sunni families in segregated cantons, while violence has taken the lives of tens of thousands, ruptured families, and provoked the flight abroad of vulnerable minorities and many of the best-educated remnants of a once vibrant middle class.[1] Public infrastructure has also deteriorated, compounding the damage done by episodic bombardment and the withering of state services under international sanctions during the 1990s.[2] Baghdad, as a result, has been stressed to the point of systemic collapse, and its residents brutalized to the point of endemic despair.

This is neither the first nor the most catastrophic incidence of tumultuous reconfiguration in the city's long history. Change, often sudden and deadly in nature, has been a recurring feature in the life of the City of Peace. Labeled a "deathtrap" and a "devourer" of men by one of Iraq's most distinguished historians, Baghdad has been repeatedly ravaged and reshaped by floods, plagues, and foreign invasion.[3] In 1831, the cumulative effect of all three in rapid succession (only a generation after a plague had wiped out "most of the people of Iraq") reduced the city's population from 80,000 to a mere 27,000 over the course of four months, bringing down the ruling regime in the process.[4]

The annals of the city reveal further notable instances of destruction, with the arrival of Hulagu and the Mongols in 1258 and of Tamerlane in 1401 bringing utter devastation and ruin. Estimates of the death toll from the Mongol expedition range into the hundreds of thousands (during which the waters of the Tigris were said to have turned black from the ink of Baghdad's libraries and red from the blood of the dead), and the city's destruction prompted the fall of the Abbasid caliphate and the collapse of an entire civilization.[5] Tamerlane's arrival a century and a half later was likewise a civilization-destroying event, as he is infamously recalled to have slaughtered the entirety of Baghdad's population, leaving behind towering pyramids of human heads.[6]

This chapter addresses a further instance of radical, transformative change in Baghdad's history. Yet, in contrast to the tragedies cited above, this particular episode did not feature the destruction of the city or the decimation of its people. On the contrary, it was the direct result of the explosive growth of both, and the efforts of an increasingly wealthy—and increasingly ambitious—central government to manage and direct those processes.

At the start of the twentieth century, Baghdad was a remote, parochial outpost of the Ottoman Empire, home to only 180,000 people.[7] A century later, however, on the eve of the American-led invasion, it was a sprawling metropolis, home to more than six million Iraqis.[8] Major advances in public health and the development of modern infrastructure had contributed to population increases across Iraq during intervening decades, but Baghdad's grossly disproportionate expansion was not the by-product of prosperity, continuity, or other such benefits of "modernity" writ large.[9] It was instead fueled, above all else, by radical social upheaval and grinding rural poverty that, beginning in the 1930s and continuing well into the rule of the Ba'th regime during the 1970s, drove a series of sweeping population movements that collapsed the poorest elements of Iraq's periphery onto the slums of its capital city.

These migrations, originating along the lower reaches of the Tigris River in Iraq's "Deep South," saw hundreds of thousands of destitute Shi'a men, women, and children of the traditional tribal underclass abandon their homes and relocate to Baghdad.[10] Not only did this fundamentally alter the demographic composition of the city (precise records are unavailable, but it is thought that Baghdad had a Sunni majority until the 1950s), but the stresses generated by uncontrolled mass migration also delineated fault lines in the urban landscape that persist to the present day.[11]

In addition to the changes arising from migration flows, the manner in which Iraq's ruling regimes attempted to manage this phenomenon produced profound and pervasive effects. An understanding of these migrations and their consequences is, therefore, essential to interpreting the events of the post-Saddam era in Baghdad—particularly with respect to a discussion of the city's now vast Shi'a underclass, the significance of the city's physical layout to localized patterns of violence, and the mechanics of the Mehdi Army's urban campaign.

A Countryside in Chaos

The mass migrations that overwhelmed Baghdad during the middle of the twentieth century traced their origins to a social engineering experiment initiated decades before Iraq's creation. By the second half of the nineteenth century, the Ottoman Empire had claimed sovereignty over what was then known as Mesopotamia for over 300 years. Imperial power had long been concentrated in Baghdad and Basra, leaving much of the expansive terrain between and beyond the two cities as the domain of nomadic Arab tribes.[12]

These tribes were organized into a complex and ever-fluctuating system of confederations, the strongest of which operated as portable "states" in their own right, enabling prominent sheikhs to engage Ottoman bureaucrats more as peers than as subjects.[13] Regional politics was thus characterized by a web of intrigue and double-dealing as rival Arab factions attempted to leverage imperial favor against their indigenous rivals, while Ottoman administrators sought to maintain overall control by manipulating these same local divisions to the empire's advantage.

During the latter decades of the nineteenth century, in the context of a broader, empire-wide campaign toward administrative rejuvenation and the restoration of fading prestige, Ottoman officials took action to alter this dynamic.[14] No longer willing to countenance the existence of powerful, independent tribal groups within the boundaries of the empire, the Ottomans set out to shatter their confederations and assert more complete imperial control. This was not to be achieved through force of arms, but through the manipulation of land. Taking advantage of the empire's ownership of the land across much of the region (and the growing financial allure of commercial agriculture), Ottoman administrators alternately induced, compelled, and coerced Arab tribes to abandon their nomadic ways and become farmers.[15] Their objective in doing so was twofold: not only would the ensuing intra-Arab competition over land and water rights sow localized dissent and preclude collective resistance to the Ottomans' rising power, but southern Mesopotamia would also become a commercial engine that would help to power the empire's global revival.

While the scheme was implemented unevenly across southern Mesopotamia (and provoked such unrest as to warrant its eventual suspension), a chain reaction was catalyzed that brought about the near-universal settling of the tribes, the shattering of their war-fighting coalitions, and an extraordinary agricultural boom along the Tigris and Euphrates rivers.[16] It also wrought a host of unintended and unanticipated consequences, which would exert powerful influences over the subsequent course of Iraqi history. These included the fragmentation and corruption of the regional tribal system as a whole, mass conversions among the newly-settled Arab farmers to the Shi'a sect of Islam and, finally, an exodus from the Deep South that saw the region's poorest and most vulnerable flee to Baghdad.

The Degradation of the Tribal System and the Rise of Shi'ism

Irrespective of the turbulence generated by the Ottoman land scheme, the chaotic manner in which it progressed—and the fact that the Ottomans were driven from Mesopotamia by the British during the First World War while the tribes' settlement was still underway—the transition from nomadism to sedentary agriculture gained irreversible momentum.[17] A fundamental transformation of modes of subsistence and patterns of life thus ensued across southern Mesopotamia around the turn of the twentieth century, as nomads became villagers, warriors became farmers, and sheikhs became landlords—causing shocks to the regional tribal order that went well beyond the structural fragmentation desired by the Ottoman government.[18]

On the one hand, despite the widespread fragmentation of tribal structures, the caste-like socio-cultural hierarchy of the traditional tribal system was intensified.[19] Certain areas saw the upper echelons of the traditional social order become powerful landowners (leaving their underclass subordinates as a landless peasantry), while others witnessed fierce competition between relative equals over land and water rights. The net effect was the exacerbation of social prejudices and the intensification of identity-based rivalry.[20] On the other hand, and perhaps more insidiously, dramatic changes also occurred to relations within tribes. As sheikhs took on roles that entailed both authority and responsibilities tied to the regional political economy, their position vis-à-vis their tribesmen was altered. They transitioned, in effect, from serving as their tribesmen's protector and advocate to that of their master and administrator.[21] The incentives and pressures of commercial agriculture thus had a commoditizing effect on sheikh-tribesman relations and, while the balance of power between sheikhs and their tribesmen varied from place-to-place and tribe-to-tribe, the relationship became an increasingly antagonistic one.

Social unrest permeated southern Mesopotamia as a result of the tribal system's structural fragmentation and ethical corruption, prompting a search for a new schema to order the lives of the southern farmers. This search played out haphazardly and informally in the midst of the tribes' sedentarization, and its progression was largely obscured by the political unrest that consumed the region at that time (as mentioned above, due not only to the turmoil generated by the Ottomans' initiative, but also the British invasion in the context of the First World War). It progressed nonetheless, and in doing so it catalyzed a sweeping demographic change that would have extraordinary consequences for the future of Iraq. This was the mass conversion of newly-settled Arab farmers to Shi'ism, which occurred on such a scale as to elevate it to the majority faith in Mesopotamia.[22]

Aided by proximate factors as dramatic as the raids of viciously sectarian Wahabis from the Arabian Peninsula (which motivated the small and heavily Persian Shi'a communities of Najaf and Kerbala to forge alliances with their Arab neighbors), and as mundane as completion of the Hindiyya Canal in 1803 (which made the stretch of the Euphrates River in the immediate vicinity of Shi'ism's holy cities particularly attractive farmland), the emissaries of the Shi'a sect met with extraordinary success as they proselytized across the region. Connecting classic Shi'a narratives of injustice and oppression at the hands of illegitimate leadership to the farmers' recent experiences with both the Ottomans and their own sheikhs (and encouraged at times by Ottoman administrators intent on undermining the tribal system), the Shi'a men of faith who canvassed the growing settlements of southern Mesopotamia offered an appealing new source of leadership and identity to the beleaguered peasant farmers.[23]

Fight or Flight in the Deep South

The dislocations arising from the transition to sedentary farming and the degradation of the tribal order were at their harshest along the lower reaches of the Tigris River, in Iraq's Deep South. There, where Ottoman power had been at its weakest, a narrow cadre of tribal elites established themselves as the guarantors of regional stability.[24] By positioning themselves as the indispensable proxies of the distant central government (a role they would maintain via astute political maneuvering well into the second-half of the twentieth century), they secured control over some of the largest estates in the Middle East.[25] They also assumed tyrannical, feudal-style powers over their vast holdings, while the traditional tribal underclass was relegated to serf status and forced to work under horrendous conditions.

Further compounding the plight of these warriors-turned-serfs, the reach of religious emissaries faded and the palliative influence of Shi'ism appears to have waned significantly as the distance increased from Najaf and Kerbala. To the distant southeast of the holy cities, where the new agricultural order was at its most brutal, Shi'ism made its weakest inroads. A 1947 survey of present-day Maysan and Wasit provinces, for example, failed to find a single mosque—and thus while the farmers of the Deep South nominally adopted the Shi'a faith *en masse*, the spread of Shi'ism failed to provide a structure of social relations that could adequately replace the tribe.[26]

The faith of the Deep South, spread by self-proclaimed holy men of dubious provenance, instead developed as a rough overlay of traditional tribal norms.[27] Couched in the local vernacular and laden with superstitions, magical rites, and the cults of saints, the peasant farmers' faith became a matter of contempt among their higher-class co-religionists elsewhere—adding a further layer to their marginal, underclass status in the new regional order.

Irrespective of the comforts provided by their new faith, conditions on the agricultural estates of the Deep South proved unbearable. The sheikhly elite codified their powers and privileges under the laws of the nascent

Iraqi state (in which the tribal domain was left outside of federal jurisdiction, leaving the southern sheikhs quite literally a law unto themselves), and they further became a powerful constituency in parliament during the 1930s and 1940s. Attempts to challenge their position occurred sporadically into the 1950s—featuring the legislative initiatives of reform-minded politicians as well as militant action by revolutionary communists—yet substantive challenges were consistently thwarted.[28] Conditions continued to deteriorate, and life expectancy for the farmers (who were infamously described as "living pathological specimen" by a visiting British doctor) was measured only in the upper-thirties.[29]

The dislocations arising from the fragmentation of the tribal system, the farmers' appalling quality of life, and the seeming impossibility of material or social improvement created an atmosphere of despair that, from the 1930s onwards, prompted an exodus from the Deep South (and from modern-day Maysan Province in particular). Initial movements were modest enough to be absorbed by Iraq's various urban areas as families, extended families, and "tribal fragments" boarded trucks and buses for passage to a new start in Baghdad, Basra, and other smaller cities throughout the south.[30] Yet by the mid 1940s, it was apparent that a mass migration of extraordinary proportions was underway. Migration levels would accelerate continuously through the decades that followed, with the Iraqi capital emerging as the destination of choice. As a result, not only would Shi'ism rise to majority status in Baghdad shortly after mid century for the first time in the city's long history, but the countryside would also be depopulated to the point of jeopardizing Iraq's agricultural productivity.[31]

Mahallahs, Migration, and Baghdad's Evolving Landscape

While the southern countryside's destabilizing transformation progressed through the first half of the twentieth century, Baghdad was also changing. Ottoman Baghdad had long been home to a kaleidoscope of distinct and discordant communities that were delineated variously along the lines of family, religion, profession, tribal affiliation, ethnicity, and sect. Aspects of one's communal identity dictated sharp social, economic, and political distinctions, and urban society thus shared important structural commonalities with its rural, tribal counterpart.[32]

Just as the tribes of southern Mesopotamia laid claim to physical terrain, the social and cultural forces that segmented Baghdad were manifested spatially on the urban landscape in the form of the *mahallah*, or city quarter.[33] A *mahallah* served as the basic structure of urban social organization, and its residents existed "as a rule… in a world of their own… and seldom if ever took thought of the community at large or of its interests, or had even any real understanding of such a community."[34] Particular kinship groups, religious sects, and professional guilds thus occupied independent sectors of the city that, often surrounded by formidable walls and gates, demarcated the boundaries of their lives.[35] Despite being "diverse" in statistical terms, the identity-based fault lines of Ottoman Baghdad—and the powerful prejudices that upheld them—inhibited intercommunal blending and precluded the development of a shared identity.

By the 1930s and 1940s, however, when migration to Baghdad was intensifying, the boundaries of the *mahallahs* were blurring.[36] The rise of Arab nationalism around the time of the First World War, and the development thereafter of an Iraq-specific conception of identity (which was promulgated aggressively by the Iraqi monarchy following independence in 1932), had powerful influences on the city.[37] In addition to the rise of Iraqi nationalism, intellectual currents of liberalism and radical strands of communism and fascism spread among Baghdad's educated classes.[38] The city was thus in the midst of a transformative period of its own, wherein Baghdadis were attempting to transcend traditional divisions (the categories and values of the traditional past became objects of extraordinary scorn among the budding intelligentsia), while the identity-based clusters at the city's increasingly cosmopolitan core, and the "*mahallah* mentality" that accompanied them, were giving way to a more inclusive urban environment.[39]

Arrival in "The Capital"

The intellectual dynamism evident at the heart of the Iraqi capital did not translate into widespread support for the migrants' plight, however, or into receptiveness to their arrival. On the contrary, the influx of impoverished and illiterate peasants (who were derisively referred to as *shurughis*, or "easterners") was perceived as both a physical and cultural threat. To the elites of the city, and to growing legions of increasingly better-educated Baghdadis with aspirations to elite status, the migrants were crude, ignorant, and dangerously belligerent—anachronistic manifestations of Iraq's backward past. Their appearance in the city prompted responses analogous to the arrival of a plague.[40]

The migrants' initial attempts to erect their distinctive palm-frond and mud-brick huts on open plots of land within the city prompted a backlash.[41] Known as *sarifas*, these simple, portable structures were begrudged as a blight on the cityscape, due not only to their incongruous appearance, but also to the attempts of their inhabitants to tap into the city's already sub-standard infrastructure. Established residents would thus summon the police to disperse migrant settlement clusters, and the majority of new arrivals were barred from the city center.[42] Instead, they were largely relegated to the city's vacant periphery, where sprawling tangles of *sarifas* rapidly accumulated to accommodate what were widely-viewed as "growing and rather menacing hordes" of *shurughis*.[43]

The largest and most notorious concentration of *sarifas* developed on the eastern edge of Baghdad. There, on open terrain just beyond the earthen wall known as "the bund" that protected the city from the devastating floodwaters of the Tigris River, a satellite city grew alongside Baghdad.[44] Despite the fact that this area was prone to catastrophic flooding (and furthermore served as the principal garbage dump for Baghdad proper), the migrants made it their home, incorporating assorted debris into the construction of their *sarifas*. This sprawling slum was given the nickname *al-'asima*, "the capital." By the time of its demolition in 1963 it would stretch for 10 kilometers (through what is now the heart of eastern Baghdad, from the Rusafa Political District southeastward toward Baghdad al-Jadeeda) and house over 25 per cent of the city's population.[45]

Community Beyond the Bund

Visitors to *al-'asima* (and to the smaller settlement clusters like it that could be found around Baghdad's margins at mid century) were struck by the intensity of local destitution.[46] These areas were wholly unplanned and unserviced, lacking plumbing, proper roads, electricity, or any other sort of public amenity. A survey of *al-'asima*, conducted in 1957, found that only 7 per cent had access to even a stand-alone outhouse toilet, and there were no bathing facilities for the slum's 184,000 residents.[47] Multiple families could thus be found crammed into squalid three- to five-room houses (with an average of 5.2 people to a room by one count), which were periodically swept away by floodwaters.[48] Further adding to public health concerns, buffalo herders from the southern marshlands had joined the migration to *al-'asima*, and while they made up only a small fraction of the population, their large herds produced voluminous amounts of waste.[49] The large pits from which mud was exhumed for brick-making thus filled rapidly to overflow with a potent mixture of human and animal excrement (as well as the refuse that continued to be hauled to the area from the city proper), which spilled over onto the paths that weaved haphazardly throughout the dismal, cholera-ridden wasteland.

Apart from its physical characteristics, the social environment of *al-'asima* further contributed to its distinctness from the city center.[50] While the migrants' exodus to Baghdad had been driven by the degradation of the tribal system, the dynamics of migration and subsequent patterns of settlement enabled them to preserve (and, to a certain extent, reconstitute) aspects thereof. Having fled the Deep South in kinship clusters and then found themselves largely unable to penetrate urban society, migrants formed settlements on the open terrain of *al-'asima* that mimicked the structure of the *mahallah*.[51] Building from tribal ties, familial connections, and common geographic origins, these communal encampments became beacons that attracted subsequent arrivals possessing shared kinship markers, serving, in a limited capacity, as incubators for traditional bonds.

Yet, while the migrants' efforts to preserve elements of their tribal past appears to have eased their adjustment to life in *al-'asima*, and the slum developed striking physical and cultural similarities to the villages of the Deep South, an array of forces undermined efforts to recreate a quasi-traditional civil society. It was, after all, to escape the tyranny and predations of their sheikhs that many migrants had fled to Baghdad in the first place, making the large-scale recreation of tribal networks deeply problematic. Furthermore, inescapable dislocations of long-range migration and the realities of urban slum life pulled communal groups apart.[52] Aspiring communal leaders, detached from traditional sources of economic and social power, struggled to remain influential in the lives of their kinsmen, while the search for often scarce and insecure wage labor (or improved material conditions elsewhere in the city) pulled the slums' *mahallah*-like clusters apart.

The *shurughis* cemented a reputation as the "urban nomads" of Baghdad's bleak periphery: illiterate, unskilled outcasts who inhabited a diseased wasteland of open sewers and decrepit huts on the city's margins.[53] While continuing to adhere to the norms and mannerisms of their tribal roots, they were increasingly detached from the kinship networks that had provided a degree of stability in the past.[54] Their Shi'a faith, meanwhile, appears to have afforded little succor. The migrants retained their reputation for irreligiosity (with only one in ten responding that they regularly attended mosque in a 1957 survey), and accounts of the era are silent regarding any actions by the Shi'a religious establishment toward the improvement of their condition.[55] The combination of economic hardship and social decay instead fueled rising crime rates in *al-'asima*, and the slum established a reputation as Baghdad's most dangerous and depraved place—reinforcing popular prejudices against the *shurughis* and the allegedly regressive, violent nature of their traditional values.[56]

Social Justice through Civil Engineering

Migration flows were not the only source of turbulence in Baghdad at mid century. Stoked by political factions hostile to the monarchy (including communists, pan-Arabists, and fascists), the 1940s and 1950s witnessed a barrage of strikes, protests, and deadly riots on the streets of the capital.[57] Capitalizing on mass unrest arising from issues such as the economic shocks that accompanied World War Two, rising economic inequality, and the monarchy's continued close relations with much-despised Great Britain, opposition groups mobilized enormous, volatile crowds. The violence was such that the monarchy imposed martial law for years at a time, and a consensus emerged among contemporary observers that Baghdad was a cauldron of accumulated grievances and unmet expectations that threatened to boil over into revolution.[58]

Nonetheless, an array of forces prevented the migrants from proactively engaging in politics. These included the social and physical barriers that separated them from the city proper; their inability to mobilize effectively due to an absence of unifying social structures; near-universal illiteracy that rendered them politically inarticulate; the fact that many were legally classified as fugitives for having fled the Deep South in violation of debt laws; and, lastly, the simple fact that surveys found the migrants to be generally positive about their lives in Baghdad.[59] However appalling outside observers may have found conditions in *al-'asima*, they marked a significant improvement upon life in the Deep South. Thus, while the contrast between the slums and the concentrations of wealth that developed in other parts of the city sparked resentment among the less fortunate, the migrants were not the latent revolutionary force that some have idealized them as having been.[60]

Despite the *shurughis'* general silence, their squalid condition was politicized by opposition groups like the Iraqi Communist Party as evidence of the injustice of the status quo. While the communists drew their cadre strength principally from the middle classes and laborers of higher socioeconomic strata than the *shurughis*, they proved able to summon enormous crowds of migrants in support of their often violent rallies.[61] The advocacy of the communists also helped to drive public opinion toward a more sympathetic posture vis-à-vis the migrants and, by the mid 1950s, elements of the liberal intelligentsia and professional classes had joined their calls to redress the injustices of the countryside and improve conditions in Baghdad's slums.

The monarchy was at once unable and unwilling to take action, however. First, the sheikhs of the Deep South retained their status as irreplaceable guarantors of order due to the administrative weakness of the Iraqi government. Second, the government deliberately refrained from making infrastructural improvements to *al-'asima* out of fear that such efforts would encourage additional, undesired, migration flows.[62] The slum was thus intentionally left to fester as a deterrent to those contemplating flight from southern Iraq, while the monarchy instead sought to make use of Baghdad's growing social tensions—to wit significant numbers of *shurughis* were recruited into the security services, where their willingness to fire upon crowds of middle class protestors was a valued asset.[63]

The Revolution of 1958 and Qasim's Reforms

On 14 July 1958, members of the Iraqi Army launched a bloody *coup d'état* that toppled the monarchy, bringing sweeping changes to Iraq. Colonel Abd al-Karim Qasim's revolutionary regime was equally outspoken and determined in its pursuit of a more egalitarian, progressive Iraq, and "social justice" comprised a central plank of its platform.[64] In recognition of the appalling conditions in *al-'asima* (and of the widespread support shown by the urban poor during and after Qasim's seizure of power), eastern Baghdad was chosen as a primary focal point of the government's reform agenda.[65]

To improve the migrants' condition, Qasim initiated the wholesale demolition of the decrepit, disease-ridden *sarifas*, and leveled the earthen wall that divided *al-'asima* from Baghdad proper. The bund was replaced by a canal that would control the flooding of the Tigris River (thereby allowing for development on either side, and enabling a dramatic eastward expansion of the city), while the *sarifas* of *al-'asima* were replaced by a grid of modern housing. This new district of the city was triumphantly named *medinat ath-thawra*, or "Revolution City", and along with its sister development called Shula on the western side of Baghdad, it was intended as a symbol of revolutionary Iraq's commitment to its most downtrodden citizens.

Development efforts progressed through Qasim's rule, laying the infrastructural groundwork for modern-day Baghdad. The Army Canal was completed in 1961 and the initial grid of Revolution City was erected a year later, while additional plots of land were distributed to professional and social groups favored by the new regime.[67] The demolition of the *sar-*

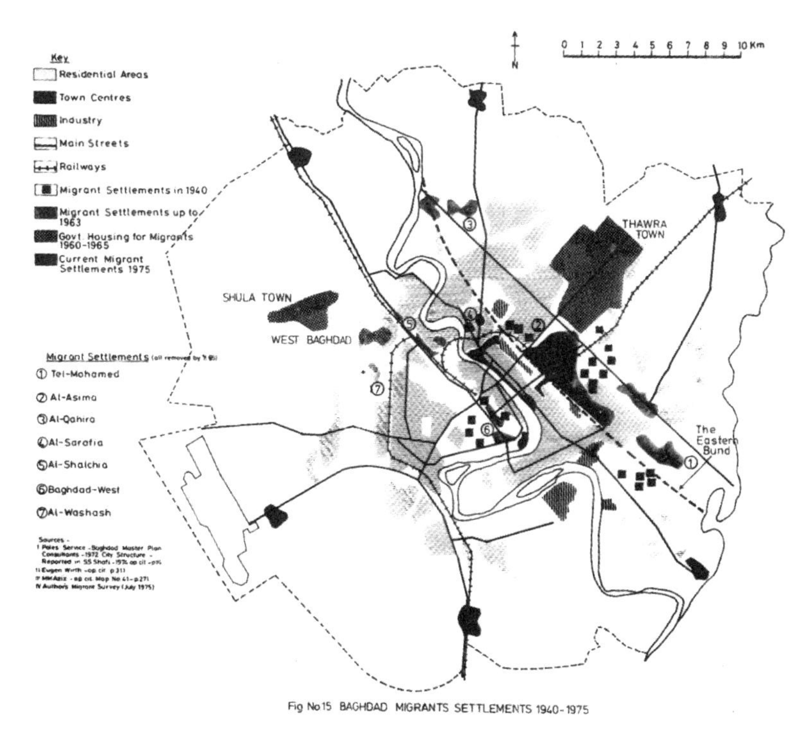

Figure 1.1: Hilmi's Sketch of Migrant Settlements, 1940–1975[66]

ifas also continued steadily through the early 1960s (with their residents being funneled into the new development zones), while the erection of new *sarifas* was prohibited in an attempt to bring migration flows under control.[68] Furthermore, efforts were undertaken to address the root causes of migration, principally through a land reform scheme designed to break up the feudal estates of the Deep South.[69]

From the outset, however, Qasim's urban and rural programmes each met with significant problems. Revolution City was intended to contain 16,000 housing units constructed by the government and Shula an additional 4,000, but administrative shortcomings dictated that, after erecting only 1,000 units in Revolution City alone, construction halted.[70] The rest of the land was instead parceled out vacant (albeit free of charge) to those who applied through the Ministry of Housing. Furthermore, both the homes that were constructed by the government and the plots of land allocated for future building were far too small for the large migrant households.[71] Conditions of dramatic overcrowding swiftly ensued, as the former *sarifa*-dwellers poured into the housing projects and overwhelmed available resources.

The flood of impoverished Shi'a families into Revolution City was made all the more rapid and destabilizing by the catastrophic failure of Qasim's efforts in the south. Not only did the Agrarian Reform Act fail to improve the lives of the peasant farmers, but it also provoked a full-scale agricultural implosion that has been compared to the accomplishments of Robert Mugabe's regime in Zimbabwe.[72] However sincere Qasim's intentions (and however enthusiastically they were celebrated by the recipients of state support), agricultural production collapsed. The resulting economic downturn and general atmosphere of rural chaos was such that, when paired with the growing allure of Baghdad after the regime's highly-publicized construction of modern, subsidized housing, migration levels surged ever higher.[73] Escalating migration flows during the 1960s and 1970s would cause Baghdad's population to explode from 793,000 in 1957 to 3,054,000 by 1975, at which time Revolution City and Shula would contain nearly a third of the city's total population.[74]

Revolution City After Qasim

The decidedly mixed results achieved by Qasim's reforms during his time in power cast doubt over whether he or a like-minded successor could have effectively remedied either the root causes of migration or the social and infrastructural problems it caused in Baghdad. His pursuit of "social justice" appears to have been as sincere as it was celebrated, but irrespective of the wisdom of his reforms, the Iraqi state lacked the administrative capacity to successfully execute initiatives of such magnitude.[75] In any event, he was denied the opportunity to follow through on his initiatives or to address their shortcomings. The horrific street violence and intense political rivalry that had persisted through the course of his reign ultimately consumed him, and he was executed in the course of a 1963 coup, which was launched by the Iraqi Ba'th Party and its allies in the military.[76]

Qasim's killing had far-reaching consequences for Baghdad's swelling Shi'a underclass. Their affection for the fallen prime minister was legendary, and was violently re-emphasized during the coup by the vast crowds that swept inward from the city's margins in his defense. The clashes that occurred between the *shurughis* and the perpetrators of the coup have been counted among "the bloodiest street battles in the history of the country," and they raged on even after Qasim's death became public knowledge.[77] Connections between the Shi'a underclass and the Iraqi Communist Party (and the prominent role of communist leaders in rallying the crowds that emerged from Revolution City and Shula to defend Qasim) worsened the migrants' position in the newly-established order, as the Ba'th were archenemies of the communists. Thus, while the Iraqi Communist Party was subjected to a retaliatory slaughter, Baghdad's Shi'a underclass was regarded as a threat to be contained rather than a target for state assistance, leaving them marginalized yet again in Iraqi politics.[78]

In an ironic distortion of Qasim's vision, Revolution City and Shula thereafter came to stand as monuments to the central government's relationship with Baghdad's Shi'a poor. Rather than testaments to an official commitment to justice and equality, however, the two districts became sprawling, festering reminders of promises unfulfilled, persisting social prejudices, and the continued inability of the state to manage the implications of mass migration. As southern Iraq emptied itself into Baghdad at a continually-accelerating pace, conditions in Revolution City (which had been designed to house only 300,000 people, but by the late 1970s housed an estimated 1.5 million) deteriorated to the point that it was deemed "ready for the bulldozer."[79] Instead of marking a definitive break from the squalid past of *al-'asima*, it inherited *al-'asima's* reputation as the city's poorest, most squalid, and most dangerous place.

The State and Civil Society in Revolutionary Iraq

As Revolution City and Shula swelled uncontrollably through the 1960s and 1970s, Iraq's development as a nation (including both physical, infrastructural growth, and the formation of a coherent Iraqi identity) was also progressing rapidly. Trends in internal migration caused explosive urban growth, technological advancements and industrialization were transforming traditional patterns of life, and an assortment of radical political ideologies were simultaneously interweaving with, and displacing, the identity-based distinctions of the past.[80] These processes were evolving inconsistently and, indeed, at times chaotically, but they nonetheless acquired a collective energy that brought dramatic changes to Iraq.

Nowhere were these changes (or their inconsistent, schizophrenic nature) more evident than in Baghdad. In addition to the sprawling peripheral growth discussed above, major internal renovations were underway that saw widespread demolition in an effort to create a modern cityscape.[81] Infrastructural tumult was also mirrored in the social sphere, where the city's residents were in the midst of varied, often contradictory campaigns to define Iraq's future. The intellectual movements that had coalesced during the latter years of the monarchy, the communists and Pan-Arabists foremost among them, continued to inspire a frenzy of radical ideological activity, while traditionally-defined categories of identity lost ground to the encroachment of modernity.[82]

Yet, from the era of Qasim's rule, a change occurred to the dynamics of Iraq's modernization process. Inspired by radical and extraordinarily ambitious political ideologies, and made possible by surging oil revenues, the Iraqi state attempted to take control of national development. Growing rapidly in size and strength, the government emerged as a proactive agent of change that would use its wealth and power to transcend the past and shape the future. Qasim's bold attempts to restructure both the landscape of Baghdad and the political economy of southern Iraq thus marked early steps in a move toward interventionist governance that, enjoying overwhelming popular support among the Iraqi people, would see the Iraqi state encroach further and further into all sectors of society.[83]

Despite the popularity of statist efforts at civil and social engineering, the rising profile of the government held deeply subversive implications for Iraqi society. Beginning with the much-lauded reform efforts of Qasim, and moving on to the aggressive totalitarianism of the Ba'th regime of the late 1960s and 1970s, civil society fell under siege. In the end, not only would the Iraqi people be rendered dependent upon the state as never before, but the state itself would also either consume or destroy independent social organization almost entirely.

Social Erosion in Revolution City

While the administrative problems that inhibited Qasim's urban reform program and the chaos that arose from his efforts at rural land reform were immediately apparent, there were less obvious—yet no less insidious—consequences to his intrusion into Iraqi society. For Baghdad's Shi'a underclass, including those resident in the city's *sarifa* slums at the time of the coup as well as subsequent migrants to the Iraqi capital, these came in the form of changes to patterns of migration and urban settlement that exacerbated the deterioration of traditional social bonds and accelerated the degradation of civil society.

First, the massive surge of migration that occurred during the 1960s and 1970s witnessed major changes to the patterns of movement. In 1957, a full 98 per cent of *al-'asima's* residents hailed from the Deep South (of whom 87 per cent were from present-day Maysan Province), but the years that followed brought increases in both the number of migrants and their diversity of origin.[84] Although the Deep South continued to provide the majority of new arrivals, the growing allure of Baghdad's housing projects created a powerful draw that, when combined with the collapse of southern agriculture, prompted migration from all across the south. The growing geographical diversity of those surging into Revolution City, Shula, and the city's smaller peripheral slums thus diluted the homogeneity that had facilitated the establishment of communal clusters—while the dramatic increase in the scale of migration flows further contributed to social disarray.[85]

Second, the rise of the government as an increasingly generous provider of largesse (however badly needed, and however gratefully welcomed) further eroded the social capital reserves of civil society.[86] With the state using its oil wealth to offer housing, employment, food, and other essentials to its most needy subjects, the influence of localized communal leadership waned. Tribal sheikhs and other low-level civil society figures had no means to compete with the resources of the government, and as the state took an increasingly active role in the daily lives of the populace, they saw their functional utility disappear.

Third, the demolition of the *sarifa* encampments meant the destruction of the *mahallah*-cum-tribal enclaves that had been established in *al-'asima* and elsewhere.[87] Their residents' relocation to densely-packed grids of tenement houses physically unraveled the communities that had been established in the formerly sprawling slums, thereby undermining the continuity of social bonds. However much Revolution City and Shula marked a structural and sanitary improvement from the *sarifas* of the past, they became vast, overcrowded ghettos where fragments of southern Iraq's dissolving tribal order were collapsed upon one another. Traditional modes of dress, patterns of speech, and social customs persisted, but the structures of traditional society deteriorated apace with their physical surroundings.[88]

Ba'th Party Rule: Reshaping Iraq from Above

Despite the mixed results of Qasim's reform initiatives, the regimes that followed him embraced the role of transformative social engineer with increasing ambition. After a tumultuous decade of coups and counter-coups following Qasim's toppling of the monarchy, the Ba'thists seized power for a second time in 1968.[89] Building from an eclectic ideology that fused elements of the extreme-right and extreme-left, they sought to impose a totalitarian stability on Iraq.[90] Aided in their efforts by an extraordinary boom in oil revenues (which rose tenfold from US$575 million in 1972 to US$5.7 billion in 1974, leaping further to US$26.5 billion by 1980), they would dramatically expand both the size of the state and the scope of its role in society.[91]

In an endeavor that marked a dramatic change in the intensity of state intervention in society (but which also must be acknowledged as having been in keeping with prevailing attitudes toward the writ of the state over society itself), the Ba'th Party sought to resolve, once and for all, the problem of identity- and ideology-based division within Iraq. Rather than using the resources of the state to blend Iraq's disparate array of communal subgroups or to harmonize its competing strands of political thought, the Ba'thist program called for civil and political society to be annihilated in their entirety—and their atomized remnants then drawn into the embrace of the state.[92]

Thus, while the predatory aspects of Ba'th Party rule have attracted the lion's share of attention in accounts of Iraqi history, Ba'thist Iraq was much more than a police state.[93] Its immense security apparatus did not exist merely to stifle political dissent or to eradicate potential threats to the regime. Far more ambitiously, its mandate was to aid in the fundamental restructuring of the social environment from which such dissent or threats might emerge.[94] The extensive capability that the regime developed to surveil, control, and eliminate its citizenry was, therefore, not an end in itself, but rather an element of a broader endeavor that, supported by a powerful propaganda machine and the financial resources of seemingly unlimited petro-wealth, would achieve a complete and final transformation of Iraqi society.

For the ever-swelling Shi'a underclass of Baghdad, Ba'thist governance and oil-fueled prosperity brought both benefits and perils. The Shi'a poor (alongside the rest of their fellow Baghdadis) benefited from the state's growing riches via near-full employment in ballooning government bureaucracies, improved medical care, subsidies on a variety of goods and services, price controls that mitigated against inflation, and an array of welfare benefits.[95] Oil wealth thus enabled the state to feed, clothe, heal, and house the Iraqi people, and as a result, increasing numbers of Iraqis could claim "middle class" status thanks to the Ba'th.[96] The regime's much-touted pursuit of Iraq's modernization (and militarization) likewise evoked widespread popular enthusiasm, and the 1970s have been called a "golden age" in which the country prospered materially while ascending to the pinnacle of the Middle Eastern political order.[97]

Nonetheless, even the most celebrated aspects of Ba'thist prosperity possessed a darker side. The expansion of state bureaucracies, for example, eased the shocks that would otherwise have arisen as nearly one million new migrants poured into Baghdad's slums between 1968 and 1977 (driven by both the allure of growing state generosity and the fallout of yet another ill-conceived attempt at land reform in the south), yet it also furthered the regime's transformative agenda.[98] Taking advantage of popular enthusiasm for government intervention in the economy, the architects of Ba'thist economic policy implemented a program under the guise of "socialism" that was designed to subvert civil society through the creation of endemic dependency.[99] The provision of generous welfare services, employment, and various public amenities was thus not pursued simply for the betterment of the Iraqi people, but instead with the deliberate intent of eradicating independent social and economic capital.[100]

Simultaneously, tribal sheikhs and other traditional leadership figures came under intense, multifaceted pressure. With the welfare state catering to the needs of the populace, the police state aggressively eradicating sources of influence separate from the government, re-ruralization initiatives sending indoctrinated former migrants back into the countryside to "civilize" their peers, land reforms undermining their position in the countryside, and state-run schools and media outlets relentlessly denigrating tribalism as regressive and backwards, the onslaught proved overwhelming.[101]

Furthermore, the Ba'thist offensive against traditional civil society was not limited to the public, communal spheres, but extended into the heart of the family. Saddam Hussein's promotion of women's rights was thus, above all else, a ploy to subvert traditional patriarchal authority, while children were recruited by teachers and Party officials to inform on their parents.[102] Public and private spaces alike were thus filled with the eyes and ears of the regime, to the point that it was widely believed that the government monitored families through their television sets.

The Ba'th, the Shi'a Opposition, and Revolution City

Despite its wealth and power, the Iraqi government remained unable to check migration flows and struggled to manage their implications in the capital.[103] Baghdad's Shi'a slums thus continued to swell, deteriorating further through the peak years of Iraq's oil boom. Employment-related concerns were effectively mitigated through the continued expansion of state bureaucracies, and as in generations past, popular discontent was tempered by the slums' material superiority to life across much of the south, yet the regime nonetheless remained vigilant for signs of unrest.

As such, the efforts of Shi'a militant groups during the 1970s to rally support in Baghdad's slums prompted swift and forceful action.[104] The powers of the government had grown to the point that mass agitation of the sort instigated by the communists in previous decades was inconceivable (forcing radical Shi'a opposition networks like the Da'wa to operate in small, clandestine cells), and the security services were able to isolate and ruthlessly persecute those who attempted to subvert the regime. However, the recruitment initiatives of radical religious factions met with limited success among Baghdad's Shi'a underclass for local reasons as well. The religious devotion of Baghdad's Shi'a underclass remained questionable (despite the Da'wa's reference to Revolution City as its "stronghold of heroes," mosque attendance had fallen to a mere 5.7 per cent by 1975) and the Shi'a underclass had a distant, contentious relationship with Najaf's religious establishment—making the *shurughis* an unlikely base of support for elitist militants seeking Islamic revolution.[105]

At the end of the 1970s, therefore, the Ba'th regime appeared well on its way to the fulfillment of its ideological vision. Its wealth seemed inexhaustible, domestic opposition had been effectively eradicated, and the Iraqi people were tied more closely to the central government than at any time in the nation's history.[106] Saddam Hussein, meanwhile, had taken control of the government in June 1979 after several years of directing events from behind the scenes, and was dispensing a calculated balance of *tarhib wa targhib* (punishment and reward) to reinforce his domestic pre-eminence.[107]

It was at this time of ascendant power, however, that Saddam Hussein made the first of a series of strategic blunders. In response to the advent of the Iranian Revolution, which brought the rise of a millenarian Shi'a regime intent on spreading Islamic revolution into Iraq, Saddam launched a large-scale ground invasion of his neighbor. His particular reasoning remains uncertain, as a case can be made for the invasion as pre-emptive self-defence against the threat posed by revolutionary Iran, or alternatively, as an aggressive effort to assert Iraq's power while the Iranians were still in the midst of revolutionary disarray.[108] Irrespective of his motives, the campaign proved catastrophic. What was intended to be a lightning strike by the Iraqi military became the longest conventional war of the twentieth century, exacting an extraordinary human and material toll on both sides.[109]

Saddam Hussein would attempt to sustain the full edifice of the totalitarian state, and to isolate the Iraqi people from the costs of the war, but this ultimately proved impossible.[110] The balance between terror and reward thus shifted toward the former as the state's resources declined, and Baghdad's Shi'a underclass saw the welfare state contract at a time when the predations of the police—ever vigilant throughout the war for signs of domestic unrest among its Shi'a subjects—remained fearsome.[111] As Revolution City was renamed "Saddam City" in October 1982 (at which time basic infrastructural improvements were made, and cash was distributed to soothe popular discontent), Baghdad's Shi'a underclass saw its fortunes decline further.[112] Confined to increasingly cramped and decrepit tenements on the outskirts of the city, social unrest would simmer through the 1980s—turning the previously apolitical *shurughis* into a growing concern of the regime.

2

THE SANCTIONS ERA

SHIFTS IN CIVIL SOCIETY AND THE RISE OF THE SADRIST MOVEMENT

An Attempted Return to Normalcy

Saddam Hussein and his regime endured the extraordinary costs of war with Iran. At the conflict's end in August 1988, the Iraqi president faced significant challenges—notable among them the need to revitalize a stagnant economy; create jobs to absorb demobilizing soldiers; address the enormous debts incurred during the war's prosecution; overcome significant battlefield attrition of Ba'th Party loyalists; and rehabilitate a badly-damaged oil sector. The situation, however, did not pose an existential crisis for the government.[1] Nor did it prompt Saddam Hussein to alter the core tenets of his methods or ambitions. On the contrary, while the Iraqi regime had been forced to scale back aspects of its totalitarian agenda during the latter stages of the conflict, at its conclusion the Iraqi president emerged determined to quickly reassert his pre-eminence both at home and across the Middle East.

Despite having incurred an estimated 600,000 casualties and accrued debts of US$80 billion, Saddam Hussein had cause for optimism as he worked to reconstitute and reenergize his regime.[2] Iraq's debt burden compared favorably to that of many in the Third World, the country retained vast oil reserves that augured well for its medium- to long-term economic prospects, and his position at the apex of state and society remained secure.[3] Indeed, by the mid 1980s, the cult of personality surrounding Saddam Hussein had grown to eclipse Ba'thist ideology as the centerpiece of Iraqi society, making Saddam Hussein himself the new object of state-mandated devotion.[4]

While Saddam Hussein's position remained secure and his aspirations grandiose, Iraq faced short-term economic problems that required careful and considered care. Iraq's economic model, and the broader governance strategy of which it was a part, relied upon the regime's distribution of the nation's previously inexhaustible oil wealth. With massive outstanding debts, a booming population, and annual revenues of only US$14.5 billion in 1989, the government's resources were insufficient to allow an immediate return to the "normalcy" of the 1970s.[5] Saddam Hussein was thus faced with a dilemma. Desiring to reinvigorate the Iraqi economy without jeopardizing the government's dominance thereof, he would have to radically transform Iraq's fiscal position.[6]

Saddam Hussein's efforts toward that end proved disastrous. Initial attempts at modest austerity through the suspension of an array of subsidies were followed by experiments in privatization and deregulation, all of which precipitated chaos.[7] Inflation soared, shortages of formerly ubiquitous staple goods fueled popular discontent, "entrepreneurs" with ties to the regime accumulated vast and conspicuous fortunes, and a black market economy surged to further distort the marketplace.[8]

Nevertheless, Saddam Hussein's program for Iraq's revival remained centered on the government's continued dominance of the economy.[9] Ambitious and expensive infrastructure projects were thus initiated (ranging from dam building to the construction of an underground metro system in Baghdad), which badly strained the government's finances while failing to rejuvenate economic activity.[10] Furthermore, efforts to solicit external aid proved unsuccessful. The collapse of the Soviet Union deprived Iraq of one of its most reliable benefactors, while Iraq's wealthy Arab neighbors were not only unwilling to forgive the loans they had extended to finance the war against their common Iranian enemy, but were also insensitive to Iraqi requests through OPEC (Organization of the Petroleum Exporting Countries) to collude in raising the price of oil to Iraq's advantage.[11]

By the close of the 1980s, conditions in Iraq were not yet desperate. The government had seen fit to allocate twice the amount for rearmament as it did for reconstruction in the post-war years, for example, and

1990 saw Iraq repay a better than expected US$3.4 billion of its debts.[12] Problems were mounting, however: inflation had surged dramatically, the economy remained stagnant, and simmering unrest within the armed forces prompted a wave of executions.[13]

In response, Saddam Hussein chose to embark on what would prove to be his most disastrous venture to date. Having failed in his efforts to lead Iraq back to prosperity, and unwilling to scale back his ambitions to match his resources, the Iraqi president ordered the invasion of Kuwait.[14] Iraq's neighbor to the south possessed abundant quantities of gold and hard currency that could supply a much-needed stimulus, and also significant oil reserves that would serve as a valuable medium- to long-term revenue source.[15] Its conquest would remedy the regime's problems in a single, decisive strike.

Instead, the August 1990 invasion of Kuwait brought a succession of catastrophes upon Iraq. The invasion itself achieved the remarkable feat of uniting nearly the entire international community against Iraq, while the rout subsequently suffered at the hands of an American-led coalition exacted a devastating toll on both the Iraqi military and national infrastructure.[16] The war's aftermath then witnessed simultaneous uprisings in the Shi'a south and Kurdish north, the suppression of which took tens of thousands of lives and forced the displacement of hundreds of thousands more—leaving Iraq's national unity, and the regime's claim to command the loyalty of its subjects, in tatters.[17] Finally, a further blow was struck by the United Nations, via the imposition of a set of economic sanctions that was unprecedented in scope (and ultimately in duration as well), which would devastate the Iraqi economy and plunge the vast bulk of the populace into poverty.[18]

The damages inflicted on Iraq by Saddam Hussein between 1988 and 1992, which compounded the enormous costs of the eight year war with Iran, catalyzed dramatic changes to both state and society. To the former, the utopian transformative vision of the 1970s (when a seemingly limitless budget had fueled the ambitions of radical ideologues) was replaced by cold pragmatism and the desire to preserve power.[19] Weakened by the consequences of over a decade of disastrous policy decisions, the Ba'th regime as led by Saddam Hussein would no longer seek to transform Iraqi society, but instead to maintain control via the manipulation of its existing features. To the latter, the gradual contraction of the totalitarian state and the concurrent intensification of material and psychological hardship would combine to catalyze changes in Iraqi society. Battered and abused to the point of annihilation, civil society would find space to regenerate—but that process would be compromised and corrupted.

While the Iraqi regime was weakened, it remained ruthless and resourceful. Nascent trends in Iraqi society would not be allowed to develop unchecked in ways that might threaten Saddam Hussein's position, but would instead be co-opted to ensure that their manifestations supported the regime's agenda. With state resources shrinking, Saddam and his associates thus surveyed the domestic landscape for suitable allies to whom they could delegate responsibilities and social forces to manipulate in their favor—and the processes of governmental and societal change thereby became inextricably intertwined. The religious movements, tribal groups, and localized power-brokers that emerged during the following years to fill the space ceded by the previously "omnipotent and omnipresent" state would become defining features of Iraqi society and, bearing the distinct markings of their interactions with the regime, they would exert powerful influences through the final years of Saddam Hussein's rule and beyond.[20]

The "Resurgence" of Tribes and Islam: A Triumph of Tradition?

Saddam Hussein's decision to empower subordinates external to the regime to lessen its administrative burden was a radical yet necessary departure from the methods of rule employed during the 1970s and early 1980s. His choices of tribalism and Islam as the principal frameworks for its implementation made this decision all the more drastic. The social structures and ethical norms of the tribal system had atrophied significantly through the middle decades of the twentieth century, while the prestige of religious leaders and levels of popular religiosity had suffered precipitous declines as well. Tribalism and sectarianism, long-identified as obstacles impeding Iraq's pursuit of modernity, unity, and power, had been attacked and undermined for decades. The sudden rise to national prominence of tribal sheikhs and austere men of religion from the late-1980s into the 1990s was thus a dramatic and unexpected development—the roots and implications of which remain deeply controversial.[21]

One school of thought on the rise of Islam and tribalism in modern Iraq contends that while the Ba'th regime had achieved near-total success in either destroying or consuming all the modern manifestations of civil society (including labor unions, student groups, political parties, and professional and social organizations), it was never able to fully eradicate traditional markers of identity. When the regime's position weakened, the essentialist argument goes, primordial social forces reemerged from the subsoil of Iraqi society to provide order, direction, and comfort to a battered populace. The rise of tribalism and religiosity is thus viewed as the triumph of tradition, and evidence of the persisting power and enduring allure of deeply-rooted cultural and historical forces.

Alternatively, far more immediate and tangible causes may be offered in explanation. The "rebirths" of tribalism and of popular religiosity may be interpreted not as the revival of previously dormant or suppressed forces somehow innate to the Iraqi people, but rather as distinctly modern phenomena: driven by a combination of the regime's deliberate exploitation of the forms and categories of the past, and the mutation of Iraqi society in response to extraordinary economic, psychological, and physical stresses.[22]

In Baghdad, from the city's bourgeois core to its poorer, peripheral districts such as Saddam City, the latter explanation appears far more compelling.[23] Although the tribal and religious movements that swept the Iraqi capital during the 1990s began as grassroots trends in Iraqi society, were couched in the language of the traditional past, and would not have flourished as they did were it not for popular recognition of their historical roots in Iraqi culture, their modern manifestations represented a break from the city's past far more than a return to it.

With respect to rising religiosity, the growing popularity among Sunnis of aggressively radical and explicitly sectarian strains of Islam was unequivocally not a reversion to the beliefs and practices of previous generations. Similarly, the extraordinary fervor with which the notoriously irreligious Shi'a underclass embraced Mohammed Mohammed Sadiq al-Sadr could in no way be construed as a "revival" of Iraqi Shi'ism. The "tribes" that would soon proliferate through the Iraqi capital, meanwhile, would grow not by virtue of a widespread rediscovery of latent traditional bonds or the revitalization of authentic kinship structures among Baghdadis, but rather in the remarkable absence of both.

The Roots of Iraq's Tribal Revival

The process through which tribal sheikhs, networks, and ethics became prominent features of modern Iraqi society began on the country's rural periphery during the war with Iran. Whereas Ba'thist ideology was uncompromising in its condemnation of of tribalism, and the Party had defined itself in no small measure through its disavowal of Iraq's traditional past, administrators had long been pragmatic in their dealings with tribal groups. Thus, while Party ideologues (like the vast majority of their counterparts in educated urban society) viewed sheikhs as "the epitome of backwardness," and tribal loyalties were rhetorically castigated as divisive hindrances to national unity, the offensive against both tribes and tribalism, even during the peak years of Ba'thist totalitarianism, had been only as strong as the localized position of the government.[24]

In urban areas such as Baghdad, where the state was at its strongest and the tribes generally at their weakest, the regime had diligently eradicated independent tribal leadership. In the more remote areas of the countryside, on the other hand, particularly in areas of the south and west where the apparatus of the government was less robust and tribal structures had endured to varying degrees, the Ba'th adopted a policy of empowering the lower echelons of the traditional tribal order at the expense of their social, political, and economic betters.[25] The regime had thereby staved off potential threats from more powerful or respected tribal groups by manipulating enduring traditional divisions; all the while, working to strengthen its powers in a process intended to culminate in the tribes' eventual destruction.[26]

The unanticipated costs of the Iran war halted the planned expansion of the totalitarian state, forcing its contraction from areas of Iraq's periphery and thus altering tribe-state relations. First, while continuing to empower the weak to subvert the strong, the Iraqi government grew increasingly reliant upon tribal proxies to fill important roles in the countryside. Unable to sustain, much less enhance, the full institutional array of the state, the government granted localized powers to trusted tribal clients during the late-1980s. Second, the propaganda apparatus of the regime abandoned core tenets of Ba'thist dogma and began to tout the virtues of Iraq's tribal past in support of the war effort.[27] Thus, despite the fact that official anti-tribal policy enjoyed broad support within the Ba'thist establishment and among the educated urban classes, tribal sheikhs enjoyed a surge of rhetorical support. Third, and equally important, the weakening position of the government during the late 1980s catalyzed grassroots changes in areas affected by the state's contraction. Having spent the duration of its rule devouring Iraqi society and cultivating mass dependency, the government's retreat left a vacuum that tribes and tribalism—with the blessing and encouragement of the regime—began to fill.[28]

The extent to which "tradition" played a determining role in shaping the tribal order that developed thereafter is dubious.[29] While many of the principal sheikhly families of the late nineteenth and early twentieth centuries continued to occupy their traditional domains, none of Iraq's tribes had been preserved in stasis through the intervening decades. Even the most distant, rural reaches of the country had been affected by Iraq's transformative and destabilizing pursuit of modernity, and a large-scale essentialist revival was thus inconceivable. Among Iraq's Shi'a underclass in particular, tribal structures had been corrupted and fragmented by the broad array of forces detailed in the previous chapter, while individual leaders had been relentlessly persecuted and marginalized.

Yet, with the welfare state in decline and the regime empowering its chosen proxies with both official influence and financial resources, traditional authenticity was of secondary concern to the Iraqi people. In an environment of pressing material need, access to patronage and support was vital. When further buttressed by the praises of the official media (and, indeed, by the visible behavior of the regime itself, which took on an increasingly tribal character as Saddam Hussein installed trusted kin in top positions), Iraq's tribal movement became an increasingly prominent feature of the domestic landscape.[30]

The Drivers of a "Resurgent" Islam

The surge in popular religiosity that would ultimately transform Iraq's social and political discourse during the 1990s can be attributed to numerous, interconnected proximate causes: the suffering of the sanctions era, the cumulative dislocations and deprivations of successive wars, the contemporary rise of political Islam across the region, and the collapse and abandonment of the Ba'th Party's "secular" ideology. A key, driving feature behind the rise of religion in public life, however, was the rivalry between the Ba'th regime and prominent Shi'a clerics and laymen who sought to incubate popular religiosity—and to incite armed revolt against the Iraqi government.

The rise of the Shi'a clerical establishment as a rival to the Ba'th regime can be traced to a revivalist trend that began in the seminaries of Najaf during the final years of the Iraqi monarchy. Having faded to a point of near-irrelevance in the lives of a great many Iraqi Shi'a (and having witnessed the anti-religious and anti-elitist Iraqi Communist Party amass an enormous Shi'a following), the elites of the Shi'a establishment began working assiduously during the 1950s to revitalize their faith.[31] Still, while important strides were made (most notably in subverting the Iraqi Communist Party after the fall of the monarchy, at a time when communism appeared poised to assume a powerful role in post-revolutionary politics) religion nonetheless remained marginal to public life.[32]

The ascent to power of the Ba'th regime in 1968 brought unprecedented waves of persecution to the Shi'a religious establishment. Clerics were arrested, murdered, or deported, while agents of the regime penetrated Najaf's seminaries to monitor teachers and students alike.[33] Efforts to engage the masses thus gave way, out of necessity, to clandestine activity—with the Da'wa emerging at the forefront of an assortment of militant networks seeking Islamic revolution and a revival of the faith in Iraq.

The battle between the devoutly secular Ba'th regime and its Shi'a opposition escalated through the 1970s, with the former in firm control. The latter years of the 1970s witnessed sporadic anti-regime protests during religious festivals, yet the prowess of the Ba'thist police state dictated that the general public remained largely passive.[34] Moreover, the extent of popular religious fervor should not be overestimated, as fallout from crippling drought and other economic concerns played vital roles in motivating popular participation in anti-regime activity.[35]

Nonetheless, as noted in the previous chapter, the government felt compelled to redouble its dispensation of terror and reward to its Shi'a subjects during the late 1970s. The security services culled the clerical establishment, while funds were distributed to the Shi'a poor. An additional step was also taken, however, which marked a dramatic break from past practices. Faced with religiously-defined opposition, and sensitive to the fact that its religious message was resonating to some effect, the formerly secular Iraqi regime began to adopt the mantle of religion.[36]

Saddam Hussein, ever the pragmatist in his pursuit of self-preservation, began to define himself and his rule in Islamic terms.[37] The regime dedicated funds to the construction of mosques and the refurbishment of Shi'a shrines and seminaries (while their occupants came under heightened scrutiny), and official rhetoric took an increasingly Islamic turn. The advent of the Iranian Revolution and the ensuing eight years of war, during which time Ayatollah Ruhollah Khomeini continued to decry the fundamental illegitimacy of Iraq's "godless" regime, then prompted further, dramatic amplification of Saddam Hussein's Islamic persona, as the Iraqi leader sought to outflank his religiously-defined opposition at home and abroad.[38]

At a grassroots level, the costs of the war also fueled rising religiosity among the Iraqi people. As battlefield casualties mounted, the Iranians pushed into Iraqi territory, and the welfare state contracted, Iraq began to change from the bottom-up. A spontaneous, popular surge in piety thus intermixed with the increasingly militant Islamic rhetoric of the state to create a push-pull effect, taking Iraq ever further from the secularism of previous decades. The economic shocks that followed the war then added further impetus to both grassroots and government-directed trends toward religiosity, such that by the time of the Kuwait invasion Islam had become "the rhetorical coin of the realm" and Iraqi society was more religious than it had ever been before.[39]

The Transformation of State and Society During the 1990s

The events that followed Iraq's invasion of Kuwait (crushing military defeat, popular uprisings by both Shi'a and Kurdish civilians, and the imposition of sanctions by the United Nations) inflicted extensive damage upon the mechanisms through which the state controlled Iraqi society. First, the failure of the Kuwait invasion and the imposition of sanctions rendered the long-cultivated dependency of the populace a dangerous liability. Iraq's currency reserves were exhausted and oil revenues were minimal, leaving the regime without means to meet the needs of a rapidly expanding population. Second, after the vicious sectarianism and brutal atrocities of the 1991 revolts, even the powerful propaganda apparatus of the state could no longer sustain the notion that Saddam Hussein was the beloved leader of all Iraqis.[40] Iraqi nationalism, having been recast and refocused on the person of Saddam Hussein, was badly damaged. Third, while the security services endured as a fearsome and powerful tool, the regime had struggled to manage the 1991 uprisings. Indeed, although trusted units of the military and intelligence services were responsible for the vast bulk of the killing during the government's counter-offensive in the south, for example, it fell to the regime's tribal clients (who were, of course, themselves Shi'a) to play a decisive role in containing the violence.[41]

Faced with a suffocating sanctions regime, an overwhelmingly hostile international community, fundamentally compromised national unity, rising poverty, a public health crisis that would take the lives of hundreds of thousands, and a significantly weakened state apparatus, the top-down and bottom-up forces that had encouraged the rise of tribalism and religiosity intensified dramatically. The populace turned increasingly to Islam for psychological comfort and to tribes for material assistance. The government, on the other hand, came to rely more and more on its tribal proxies to compensate for its withdrawal from society, and Saddam Hussein tightened his embrace of Islam to align himself with public opinion and re-establish a measure of credibility.[42]

The Flying Sheikhs from Taiwan

One of Saddam Hussein's first high-profile policy decisions following the 1991 revolts was to bring tribalism firmly into the heart of the public order. His tribal clients had proven reliable during the Iran war and, as noted above, Shi'a tribes in particular had been invaluable in the containment of the 1991 uprisings. In recognition of their evident utility, the Iraqi president embraced and empowered them. Saddam Hussein convened a much-publicized gathering of his sheikhly clients in Baghdad, and casting himself in the role of "sheikh of all sheikhs" and the Ba'th Party as the "tribe of all tribes," he presided over ceremonies in which his proxies danced tribal dances, swore loyalty oaths to the regime, and recited traditional poems extolling his virtues.[43] Saddam Hussein also took the additional steps of returning lands that had been confiscated during the reform initiatives of prior decades, and amending Iraqi law to restore sheikhs' traditional rights as patriarchs (most prominently, and controversially, to include their right to kill adulterous female family members).[44]

The surging political prominence of sheikhs provoked significant disdain and dismay, however, to the extent that even the state-run press published critical editorials.[45] Popular stereotypes of sheikhs as backward, ignorant anachronisms persisted, and were famously reinforced by the newly-empowered sheikhs' propensity to spend hours riding the elevators of the Rashid Hotel in Baghdad, captivated by modern technology.[46] Yet, irrespective of the widespread scorn among Baghdadis toward the "flying sheikhs," as they became mockingly known, their influence continued to grow. For, in addition to providing a valuable service to the regime, the contraction of the welfare state and the overall decline of the public sector created a popular need for their services. The sheikhs' position as middlemen between an increasingly weakened regime and an increasingly destitute populace enhanced their status greatly, imparting critical momentum to Iraq's tribal "revival."

The regime's reliance upon tribal proxies to administer Iraq's periphery intensified through the 1990s, despite clear warning signs in the south and west that the strategy held significant dangers. In 1992, for example, a major armed confrontation occurred between competing tribal groups in the vicinity of Kut that left hundreds dead, while by the mid 1990s, the rural margins of the modern-day Anbar Province had become the domain of tribally-defined networks involved in smuggling and organized crime.[47] Nonetheless, the Iraqi regime was either unwilling or unable to exert the power necessary to rein in its unruly clients, and through the course of the decade many established regional fiefdoms and came to control sectors of Iraq's vibrant black market economy. By 1995, 60 per cent of National Assemblymen in the Iraqi government were identifying themselves with tribal names, and the regime established a separate High Council of Tribal Chiefs a year later, granting sheikhs diplomatic passports, land rights, and weaponry.[48]

Tribalism thus permeated the official and unofficial structures that came to dominate Iraq through the course of the 1990s, and what began as a rural, peripheral phenomenon spread into the core of the nation's capital. Yet, while the sheikh-as-proxy strategy appears to have operated with some measure of authenticity on Iraq's periphery, its manifestation in Baghdad was deeply troubled.[49] In the heart of the city, both the structures and the norms of tribalism had been under near-constant attack for generations. The traditional communal clusters of the *mahallah* that had ordered the city's core had been unwound and diluted, while the dislocations of long-range migration and life in urban slums had fragmented tribal bonds among the capital's new arrivals. The city's peripheral zones thus maintained certain cultural affectations of the traditional past, but the city was not home to latent tribal networks that could naturally revive themselves. On the contrary, Baghdad had been subjected to the full force and fury of Ba'thist anti-tribal persecution, whereby not only had the legitimacy of the tribe been badly denigrated but, perhaps more importantly, those individuals who stood out as prospective tribal leaders had also been co-opted or eliminated.

Baghdad's tribalization evolved instead with strong elements of necessity-driven functionalism and cynical opportunism.[50] As the statist economy and the value of the Iraqi Dinar collapsed in tandem, and the government's retreat from society was extended to include the cessation of policing of areas of the capital (leading to sharp increases in crime and violence), Baghdadis were compelled to either resuscitate long-discarded tribal identities or fabricate them entirely.[51] The tribes that emerged in the Iraqi capital during the course of the 1990s were thus not the outgrowth of a sudden resurgence of previously suppressed or obscured kinship bonds, but rather attempts by desperate urbanites to find a measure of security and stability in an increasingly volatile urban environment. "Tribes" thus came to exist in areas of the city where tribalism had long been anathema, and "sheikhs" of dubious authenticity proliferated—often by decree of a regime content to create them when no suitable proxies could be found.[52]

These men, to whom the regime funneled money and granted localized power, and in turn to whom Baghdadis looked for handouts, employment, and protection, were found in increasing numbers as the 1990s wore on. They came to be known collectively as "Taiwani" sheikhs, an epithet that drew equivalence between their fraudulent pedigrees and the origins of the pirated goods from the Far East that came to dominate Baghdad's markets under sanctions.[53] Yet, despite the patent illegitimacy of many urban sheikhs, and the transparent utilitarianism of their tribesmen's newfound allegiances, Baghdad's tribes became indispensable vehicles for localized protection and conduits for state patronage.

Their influence remained controversial, however, and resented by many, for two main reasons. First, many tribes bore a striking resemblance to mafia-style networks, and their sheikhs to distinctly modern urban warlords.[54] Whereas Iraq's resurgent "tribes" were valued for the protection they offered, they were also directly responsible for much of the violence that proliferated. Second, the broader tribal phenomenon of the 1990s saw a debased caricature of the traditional conceptions of honor and vengeance come to Iraq, whereby blood feuds and honor killings became intermeshed with economically- and politically-motivated turf wars.[55] Baghdad thus grew rougher and more violent, with the pseudo-traditional ethics of sanctions-era tribalism reshaping urban culture.[56]

In Search of an Office Cleric

Saddam Hussein's embrace of Islam, and his efforts to co-opt and thereby manage rising religiosity, intensified dramatically in the aftermath of the 1991 uprisings. Rising religiosity had been a notable response to the hardships of years past, and with deprivation and destitution looming on the horizon, the regime attempted to position itself at its vanguard. The regime thus asserted its piety before the populace, via measures such as the prohibition of alcohol in Baghdad's once-vibrant restaurants and bars and the construction of elaborate mosques across the city.[57] The regime's ongoing feud with the United Nations and its Western enemies was also recast in the language of *jihad*, with Saddam Hussein in the role of holy warrior fighting for Islam.[58]

As the government strove to re-invent itself as a beacon of righteous piety, the Iraqi people were turning, of their own volition, to religion and religious institutions.[59] Among Sunnis, growing enthusiasm for Islam was both satisfied and stoked by the religious organizations that flocked to Iraq to mitigate the much-publicized suffering of the sanctions era. These groups, hailing principally from Saudi Arabia and Jordan, brought not only material comfort, but also radical, foreign strands of Islam.[60] Wahabi mosques were thus found in increasing numbers in Iraq, while Salafi movements took root in Baghdad, Mosul, and areas of Anbar Province—most notably the city of Fallujah.[61] It is unclear to what extent the government maintained control over the increasingly radical religious movements that grew thereafter. It has been argued that the rise of militant extremism occurred more in the absence of state supervision than in response to active state encouragement, and Iraqi government documents uncovered after the fall of Saddam Hussein detail how "anyone showing an inclination toward Wahabism was considered an enemy of the state" throughout the 1990s.[62] Regardless, radical Islam spread widely among Iraq's Sunni Arabs.

Rising religiosity posed a far more complicated challenge among the Iraqi Shi'a. It threatened not only to exacerbate popular sectarian hostility in a manner that could provoke unacceptable levels of destabilizing violence, but also to empower figures within the clerical establishment with ties to opposition movements such as the Da'wa and the Supreme Council for Islamic Revolution in Iraq (SCIRI—which would become the Supreme Iraqi Islamic Council in the post-Saddam era). The former had been pursuing a clandestine war against the Iraqi state since the

1970s, while the latter had deployed its Badr Brigade militia of Iraqi Shi'a to fight under Iranian command against the Iraqi Army during the 1980s.

The government's relationship with its Shi'a subjects was at an all time low in the aftermath of the 1991 uprising, wherein mobs of Shi'a youths and their government opponents had traded savage atrocities.[63] The prospect of a popular religious movement taking root among the battered and embittered Shi'a was thus a serious threat, which compelled Saddam Hussein to pursue a course of action that yielded remarkable short- to medium-term success; but which brought with it extraordinarily destabilizing long-term consequences.

Taking advantage of the fearsome internal rivalries that had divided the elites of the Shi'a establishment for centuries (and continuing the regime's established practice of purchasing the loyalty of high-ranking Shi'a clerics, who would thereafter be scornfully referred to by their peers as *ulema al-hafiz*, or "office clerics"), Saddam Hussein installed a man he hoped would be a pliable proxy at the pinnacle of Iraqi Shi'ism.[64]

Sadr and Saddam: A Match Made in Najaf

Mohammed Mohammed Sadiq al-Sadr, the father of Muqtada al-Sadr and the founder of the Sadrist movement, is one of the most polarizing figures in Iraq's history.[65] Born in Iraq in 1943 to a respected Shi'a Arab family with ancestral roots in Lebanon, he embarked on a career as a religious scholar within the seminaries of Najaf at a time when the tattered remnants of Iraq's clerical establishment were attempting to revive their much-diminished position.[66] He studied under the luminaries of modern Shi'ism that congregated in Najaf during the 1960s and 1970s, including the Grand Ayatollahs Muhsin al-Hakim, Mohammed Baqir al-Sadr, and Abu al-Qasim al-Khoei, and among notable contemporaries such as Ali al-Sistani, Mohammed Baqir al-Hakim, and Iranian exile Ruhollah Khomeini.

While his name does not appear in English-language accounts of the Shi'a opposition movements of the 1960s, 1970s, or 1980s, and his clerical career appears to have progressed in relative obscurity, his experience was typical of those who came of age under Ba'thist rule: he was twice arrested during the mid 1970s, allegedly tortured, and then subsequently compelled to maintain a low profile as the Iraqi government turned Najaf into a veritable prison from the late 1970s onwards.[67] His return to prison in 1991 was similarly unremarkable, as Shi'a clerics were rounded up by the hundreds during the course of the government's suppression of the southern uprisings.[68]

In sharp contrast to the fate of numerous peers, however, he was released from prison several months later—after which his career underwent a meteoric ascent. Two narratives compete to account for the events that ensued, each with legions of fiercely devoted adherents. Critics of Sadr allege that he struck a bargain with the regime, where in exchange for government support, he would channel the discontent of the Shi'a masses away from the regime while also attacking its foes in the clerical establishment. Sadr, the story goes, became an agent of the government in order to further his own career at the expense of his more qualified and better established clerical rivals. His supporters, on the other hand, counter with the assertion that Sadr was never a willing agent of the regime. Instead, they maintain, he took advantage of a weakened Iraqi government and manipulated it into enabling him to care for the Shi'a underclass at a time of extraordinary need—something, his followers emphasize, that the elites of the clerical establishment had neglected to do throughout the entirety of Iraq's history.[69]

The details of who was using whom, and to precisely what end, remain contested. What is beyond dispute, however, is that Sadr was released from prison at a time when many of his peers were disappearing into custody, and following the death of the aged Grand Ayatollah Abu al-Qasim al-Khoei the following summer, the Iraqi government orchestrated his elevation to the clerical rank of Grand Ayatollah and installed him at the apex of the clerical establishment.[70]

The Roots of a Controversial Relationship

Irrespective of what transpired between cleric and regime, Sadr held opinions and ambitions that, from the perspective of the government, made him an ideal candidate to assume leadership among the Iraqi Shi'a. Foremost among these was his profound personal hostility to prominent elites within the Shi'a establishment. Sadr was very much a part of the intense rivalries that permeated Najaf's clerical establishment, called the *hawza*, and although the ferocity of its divisions had abated from the heights of the Mesopotamian past (when competing clerics would align themselves with Najaf's *mahallah*-based gangs and rival tribes from the surrounding countryside, engaging in open warfare for control of the city), division, rivalry, and instability remained its defining internal characteristics.[71] Sadr's deep personal animosity toward men such as Mohammed Baqir al-Hakim and Ali al-Sistani (the former tied to the Supreme Council for Islamic Revolution in Iraq, and the latter marked by the regime as an undesirable pillar of Shi'a leadership) was thus likely central to the regime's orchestration of his rise.

Beyond his personal rivalries with opponents of the regime, Sadr possessed views on social and religious issues that would have further endeared him to Saddam Hussein. Prominent among these was his attitude toward the virtues of Iraq's tribal past. In sharp contrast to prevailing attitudes among the clerical elite (where tribalism was generally regarded a regressive social force), Sadr celebrated the norms and values of tribalism. His most famous literary work was a highly controversial effort to reconcile *shari'ah* law with tribal laws and customs, which reflected his view that the tribal, Arab heritage of Iraqi Shi'a was a core component of their national and religious identities (a stance which implied, none too subtly, that clerics of non-Arab heritage such as Ali al-Sistani were not true Iraqis—and thus unfit to lead the Iraqi Shi'a).[72] Sadr's attitude toward tribalism thus served the aims of the regime twice over, as it lent credibility to the government's program of tribal empowerment, while also reinforcing the Arab roots of Iraqi Shi'a identity in ways that undercut Iranian influence.

Sadr was also fiercely critical of the clerical establishment's relationship with the Shi'a underclass. His activist stance on the need to proactively engage the poor marked a two-tiered shift from the practices of the elite. First, Iraq's leading Shi'a clerics had long taken a cautious approach when engaging the public sphere in any capacity. This stemmed, in part, from a strong theological current within Shi'ism known as "quietism," which advocates that clerics distance themselves from the mundane concerns of daily life and focus on the spiritual realm.[73] It was also a reflection of more practical concerns, as the predations of the Ba'th had made such reticence essential. Second, the religious leaders of Iraq's holy cities had developed a reputation for aloofness and elitism in their stance toward the Shi'a underclass. The *shurughis*, with their rough, tribal mannerisms and their occasionally-blasphemous brand of folk religion, were widely regarded by the *hawza* with much the same disdain as was shown by the urbane middle and upper classes of Baghdad.

Having ascended to a position of power, Sadr preached an aggressive, populist line. His views on the necessity of concerted activism, like his allegations regarding the establishment's abdication of its responsibilities vis-à-vis the poor, were uncompromising. He cast the distinction as one not merely between "activist" and "quietist" but, utilizing the vocabulary of warfare, between militancy and passivity.[74] He accused the leading lights of the Shi'a establishment, past and present, not only of having made themselves irrelevant to the lives of Iraq's beleaguered Shi'a through their inaction and timidity, but also of indifference to the suffering of the poor due to class- and identity-based prejudices.[75]

Sadr's populist appeals to the poor, combined with his pro-tribal stance, created powerful synergies with the regime's strategy to empower the lower echelons of the tribal order and undercut the leading figures of the Shi'a elite. His uncompromising stance on activism, on the other hand, meant that not only would he assume responsibility for tending to the Shi'a poor during the sanctions era, but that he would also launch scathing personal and theological attacks on the regime's establishment enemies.[76]

Lastly, Sadr was also a xenophobic Iraqi nationalist. He was fierce in his criticism of Iran, outspoken in attacking Iraq's Israeli and Western enemies, and an ardent proponent of pan-sectarian solidarity among Iraqi Arabs. Each of these positions complemented the regime's official line, which depicted Iran (and its agents within Iraq, members of the Da'wa and clerics of Iranian ancestry prominent among them) as a looming threat, blamed America and its allies for the suffering of the Iraqi people under sanctions, and called for national unity in the face of foreign conspiracies.[77]

Building a Mass Movement

Taking advantage of the regime's support, Sadr (who became known as the "White Lion" in honor of his flowing white beard) created a mass movement of immense proportions. Preaching in the vernacular of the southern underclass as opposed to the classical Arabic favored by his establishment peers, and employing men of humble birth as his emissaries in contrast to the common use of *sayyids* and the kin of the elite, Sadr engaged with the daily struggles of the poor.[78] He was, therefore, the first public figure since Qasim to truly embrace the Shi'a underclass and work toward the betterment of its condition, and his efforts were all the more vital due to the hardships of the era. From the urban slums of Baghdad and Basra to the smaller cities and rural spaces of southern Iraq, the charitable operations of the Sadrists were often the only source of material and spiritual comfort in a time of endemic poverty, hunger, and disease.[79]

Touting the virtue and authenticity of the Shi'a underclass, which was rooted in their tribal, Arab heritage and their long history of suffering, and declaring that the time had come for the *shurughis* to take their rightful place in Iraqi society, Sadr cultivated a massive popular following in places like Saddam City and the Deep South.[80] His ability to tap into deeply-rooted social and economic concerns explained, in large part, how he was able to build such a formidable following among a demographic renowned for its irreligiosity. While the absence of a history of religious sentiment in no way precludes its development—particularly when subjected to stimuli as powerful as those experienced by the Shi'a poor during the 1990s—Sadr's movement was not merely religious.[81] At its core was also a socio-economic message, and one that drew upon grievances that had been building for generations.

Sadr's militant populism lent a distinct current of class warfare to the movement that formed around him. His assertions of identity-based prejudice and quietist impotence on the part of the clerical elite resonated among the destitute Shi'a of Iraq (who had found little help forthcoming from the *hawza* over previous decades), and his attacks on the inauthenticity of his allegedly Persian rivals met with approval among many Iraqi Shi'a (who retained hatred for Iran following the war of the 1980s, in which they comprised the core of the Iraqi Army's enlisted ranks).[82]

His rhetorical assault on the Shi'a elite prompted ardent counterattacks, which featured allegations about his relationship with the regime and accusations of flagrant hypocrisy. While there was undeniable substance to Sadr's critique of the Shi'a establishment as being contemptuous of the underclass and ineffectual in aiding the poor, the fact that he made these charges while operating with the blessing of the regime was not lost upon his critics.[83] Whatever prejudices were harbored within the upper echelons of the Shi'a establishment, and however disinclined the scholarly elites of Najaf may have been to administer to the underclass, any substantive outreach had long been impossible due to the prowess of Ba'thist police. The Hakim family, for example, suffered more than eighty killed during the government assaults of the early 1980s, and by

1992 its surviving members (along with countless other members of the elite) had been driven into exile.[84] Sadr's condemnation of the timidity and inaction of his establishment peers were thus met with fury, as the targets of his vitriol knew full well that Sadr had seen the government's repressive powers first-hand during his many years in Najaf.[85]

Furthermore, in addition to rousing the ire of his establishment peers, the populist militancy of Sadr and his followers provoked resentment among middle and upper class Shi'a. Although the hardships of the 1990s destroyed the economic position of the middle class, the economic parity that came with near-universal impoverishment did not foster a spirit of solidarity. On the contrary, as the "middle class" ceased to exist in any meaningful financial sense, its members clung all the more fiercely to its social and cultural underpinnings.[86] The systemic economic collapse that forced teachers, doctors, and other trained professionals to labor as construction workers or cab drivers (at a time when rough, uneducated sheikhs-cum-gangsters rose to positions of social and economic power) prompted extraordinary frustration.[87] The concurrent rise of a militant populist movement of the Shi'a underclass masses, which proclaimed its explicit intent to surmount them in Iraqi society, caused long-simmering prejudices against the *shurughis* to boil over.

Problematically for the clerical establishment and its middle class followers, prevailing demographic trends were working against them as they sought to hold their ground. Beneath the surface of Iraq's boom in oil wealth and the resulting spread of middle class prosperity to many, the Shi'a underclass had remained a distinct socio-cultural entity. Thus, while the economic position of the *shurughis* improved due to the benefits of state-provided employment and an array of public welfare services, they had remained an identifiable (and continuously expanding) bloc in Baghdad, and in the cities and towns of southern Iraq. Furthermore, as the underclass continued to swell, the middle class began to shrink dramatically as the pressures of sanctions prompted educated Iraqis to flee abroad in growing numbers.[88]

A Monster of its Own Creation

As Sadr's movement continued to grow through the mid 1990s, the pitfalls of the regime's new governance strategy were becoming ever more apparent. In the tribal sphere, the groups that had carved out fiefdoms across the country were proving difficult to manage. Localized disputes raged over control of Iraq's thriving black market, "tribal" networks sought to exert supremacy over the government, while the encroachment of kinship groups into the institutions of the state spread instability through the armed forces that led to violent clashes and assassination attempts against Saddam Hussein.[89]

Sadr, like his increasingly ambitious tribal counterparts, also began to assert his independence. He was well aware that the security services had penetrated his movement and that, as a leading Shi'a cleric, he attracted constant regime attention. Nonetheless, he took an increasingly confrontational stance. Tensions escalated through the second half of the 1990s, as Sadr issued a decree that re-established Friday prayers (an act that held explicitly political connotations, implying a claim to political authority on his own part), and issued statements that included critiques of, and challenges to, the government.[90]

His shift against the regime, and his refusal to comply with Saddam Hussein's subsequent demands for compliance and public support, came at a time of uncertainty for the Iraqi president. Efforts to thwart the work of the United Nations weapons inspectors monitoring Iraq's military programs provoked air strikes in December 1998, which not only exacted a significant toll on the regime's security apparatus, but also sparked a surge in domestic unrest.[91] Unnerved, the Iraqi president ordered a wave of arrests and a spate of executions that included two Grand Ayatollahs—and he demanded that Sadr cease holding Friday prayers and desist from challenging the regime's authority.[92]

Sadr refused, however, and in February of the following year, he and his two eldest sons were murdered as they drove through the streets of Najaf. His death sparked riots in Saddam City, and ill-fated efforts toward a coordinated uprising in various regions of the south that came to be known as the *al-Sadr intifadah*.[93] The riots in Baghdad saw the largest spasm of violence on the city's streets since the toppling of Prime Minister Qasim. But in contrast to the events of 1963, when the *shurughis* had descended upon the city center to defend their champion, violence was contained within the slums. Thousands took to the streets of Saddam City as news spread of the White Lion's martyrdom, and several days of military action were required to pacify the district. Efforts in the south, on the other hand, faltered due to poor coordination—devolving into a series of ineffectual raids by Marsh Arab factions that were party to a long-running feud with the state.

Whereas the retaliatory violence of Sadr's mourners proved ineffectual, the scale of public support that followed his murder showcased both the depth of his admiration within the underclass as well as the breadth of the rift between his supporters and their establishment opponents. Mohammed Baqir al-Hakim, a long-time enemy of Sadr (and blamed by some as complicit in the failure of the *intifadah* for having allegedly withdrawn the promised support of the Badr Brigade), was forced to beat an undignified retreat from funeral services held in Qom, Iran—where he was confronted, accosted, and attacked by members of the crowd.[94] The fact that Hakim had attempted to attend the service was significant in itself, and emblematic of a broader "unseemly scramble" that ensued among Sadr's former critics when they saw the outpouring of popular grief upon his death.[95] Establishment clerics sought to reposition themselves as the martyred cleric's admirers, and his rivals attempted to suppress publications in which they had attacked him as a regime collaborator. Whatever the circumstances of Sadr's rise and the nature of his relationship with Saddam Hussein's government, his martyrdom left his legacy immune to criticism in the eyes of his followers—who constituted an enormous force in Iraq's Shi'a community.

Iraq on the Eve of Invasion

From the time of Sadr's murder until the 2003 invasion, material and social conditions in Iraq decayed further. Vital public infrastructure, the maintenance of which had been neglected during the 1980s and which had suffered serious damage in 1991, was on the verge of total collapse.[96] Problems with the electrical grid, sewage treatment facilities, and water purification systems not only degraded Iraqis' quality of life, but, when taken in concert with shortages in medical supplies and equipment, they also precipitated a public health crisis the extent of which, and ultimate responsibility for, remain controversial.

UNICEF, in an estimate echoed by Denis Halliday (who served briefly as the head of the United Nations' humanitarian mission in Iraq before resigning in protest of what he famously labeled as "genocide"), alleges that one million Iraqi children died as a result of sanctions.[97] Alternatively, a study conducted by Columbia University estimates that between 106,000 and 227,000 children under the age of five died as a result of the 1991 war, the uprisings that followed, and the subsequent hardships of the sanctions era.[98] Arguments also continue over the reasons why such horrific human suffering ensued, with defenders of sanctions asserting that Saddam Hussein deliberately exacerbated the plight of his subjects for political purposes, arguing that the Iraqi president was willing to sacrifice the Iraqi people (and the Shi'a poor in particular) to further the appearance of persecution at the hands of international conspiracies.[99]

Nonetheless, despite the enormous damage inflicted on Iraqi society, sanctions failed to break the hold of the regime. On the contrary, despite its limited resources and compromised legitimacy, popular dependence on the government and its proxies increased significantly during the 1990s.[100] With the economy paralyzed by sanctions and the Iraqi Dinar virtually worthless, official patronage became essential for survival.

In concert with material degradation, Iraqi society also underwent a qualitative shift during the 1990s that statistics on plunging literacy rates and surges in violent crime cannot fully convey. The extraordinary stresses of the era are widely acknowledged to have left Iraq a rougher, angrier, and more volatile place. Civil society, already convulsed by the shocks of modernity and ravaged by decades of predatory governance, was debased and degraded to the point that the Iraqi exiles returning to their home country in 2003 would find it scarcely recognizable.[101] Not only had the education system and the economy effectively collapsed, but so too had their intrinsic value in the eyes of rising generations.[102] A new generation came of age in an environment where destitution, idleness, and want were rampant—and where theft, prostitution, and violence were rife.[103] Corruption, previously confined to the upper echelons of the Ba'th Party and the ruling elite, became both endemic and unremarkable throughout much of society, while "violence and social apathy" emerged as the defining qualities of the decade.[104]

Among the Shi'a underclass, Saddam City emerged as the epicenter of Iraq's misery during the 1990s. "While all of Baghdad suffered during the decade-long era of sanctions," an observer would note after the invasion, "Saddam City suffered the most. Its families are falling apart, its children are malnourished, stunted and ignorant."[105] With the remnants of Sadr's network forced underground after his murder, the district was left to fester.[106] Throughout the rest of the country, on the other hand, the tribal, religious, and criminal groups that had risen to local and regional prominence worked to further consolidate their powers and pursue their ambitions. They, along with the remnants of the White Lion's movement, would emerge among the dominant actors on the political landscape of post-Saddam Iraq, and their rivalries would shape much of the violence in the wake of the American-led invasion.

3

THE CHANGING FORTUNES OF THE REKINDLED SADRIST MOVEMENT

Opportunity Amidst Chaos

As the Americans arrived in Baghdad at the start of March 2003, the city descended into chaos. Crowds surged into the streets to celebrate the fall of the regime, to destroy its most potent symbols, and to take revenge on those who had sustained it. Murals of Saddam Hussein were defaced, his iconic statue in Firdos Square was pulled down, and Ba'th Party functionaries were hunted by their former charges. Looters, meanwhile, ransacked government ministries, museums, businesses, and private homes alike. The heart of the Iraqi capital was thus consumed by a frenzied, destructive burst of activity that, with a mixture of elation, relief, opportunism, and cruelty, brought about the total collapse of public order.

However, the appearance of anarchy created by the wave of thefts, kidnappings, and murders that swept the city obscured the deliberate, directed actions of more coherent forces. Beneath the cover of chaos, numerous groups were maneuvering into position to pursue their own particular agendas on the uncertain terrain of post-Saddam Baghdad.[1]

As the city center burned, one such group emerged unexpectedly on its periphery.[2] In Saddam City, the capital's largest and most notorious ghetto, former associates and devotees of the White Lion took to the streets to provide mundane services such as trash collection, traffic control, and food distribution. "The Sadrists," as they became known, networked through the religious institutions scattered among the district's estimated two million residents and, within a few short weeks, had revived elements of the late cleric's organization and begun the process of rekindling his mass movement.[3] Capitalizing on the still-potent force of the White Lion's legacy among the city's Shi'a underclass, as well as the power vacuum created by the sudden and complete disintegration of the government, the Sadrists claimed the capital's Shi'a slums as their own. Saddam City was renamed "Sadr City" in the White Lion's honor, and the Sadrists, following the model of the Lebanese Hizbullah, proceeded to assume responsibility for the management of schools, medical facilities, and welfare services, as well as the provision of security.[4]

Their ambitions were not limited to the peripheral, impoverished spaces of the capital. On the contrary, the Sadrists aspired to reclaim their martyred namesake's position of pre-eminence within Iraqi Shi'ism, and to ensure that Iraq's long-neglected and much-maligned Shi'a underclass would see its grievances addressed and its ambitions fulfilled in the post-Saddam order. Early attempts to revive the White Lion's grassroots following, and to reconnect his former associates in Baghdad, were thus matched by similar efforts in the cities and towns of southern Iraq. The Sadrists laid the groundwork for what would be a national campaign in pursuit of political power, religious prestige, and social validation.[5]

Yet, while the instability of the invasion's early days enabled the Sadrists to gather themselves and generate a vital measure of initial momentum, their rise proved as unwelcome as it had been unexpected. Core elements of the Sadrists' agenda (and of the manner in which they would pursue that agenda) resulted in an inevitably cold reception by the dominant players of the nascent post-Saddam order.

First, their outspoken and uncompromising belligerence toward the American-led Coalition (a stance that reflected both the ideological heritage of the White Lion, as well as prevailing sentiments within the movement's base) won the Sadrists the enduring enmity of the dominant armed force in Iraq. Second, the legacy of Mohammed Mohammed Sadiq al-Sadr's virulent hostility toward the leading figures, families, and factions of the Shi'a establishment—key elements of which, owing to their cooperation with the invading Coalition, rapidly secured central positions in the emerging political order—ensured the Sadrists' ostracism from the corridors of power. Third, the Sadrists would have to navigate the divisions and prejudices of Iraqi society. Their rise as a movement of the downtrodden Shi'a underclass, with ambitions not only to empower their demographic base, but also to exact vengeance upon those who had oppressed, neglected, and humiliated them in decades past, meant that they would be viewed with hostility and suspicion by many—not least by their "betters" within Iraq's Shi'a community.

Nonetheless, with the White Lion's son, Muqtada, at the resurgent Sadrist movement's helm, and the Mehdi Army militia as its principal organizational body, the Sadrists would become a pivotally influential force in Iraq. They faced an array of formidable obstacles from the outset of their campaign (and they would thereafter acquire additional, powerful foes—Iraqi al-Qaeda foremost among them), but the Sadrists possessed a rare and valuable commodity that would fuel their ascent: the ideological bond that had been forged among the masses of Iraq's Shi'a underclass by Mohammed Mohammed Sadiq al-Sadr.[6] On a national landscape where the populace had been systematically atomized and depoliticized over a period of decades, the Sadrists' ability to build from a genuine, grassroots mass-base was an extraordinary asset. Indeed, the scope of popular enthusiasm for the White Lion's memory was unrivaled by any of the various factions and individuals that sought power in the post-Saddam era, and the Sadrists' ability to mobilize the Shi'a underclass masses would prove decisive in shaping the movement's fortunes.

The Sadrists' Faltering First Steps

The Sadrists' first forays of the post-Saddam era were inauspicious. In their initial effort to reclaim the White Lion's position at the pinnacle of Iraqi Shi'ism, they became embroiled in a controversial murder that cast their enterprise as lawless and prone to savage violence. The provocative manner in which Muqtada then sought to establish his public profile and rally popular support not only reinforced class-based prejudices against the Shi'a underclass, but also alienated broad segments of his father's flock. While the Sadrists' outspoken belligerence against the Coalition and its Iraqi allies earned them significant international acclaim, even this, their greatest early achievement, came with significant caveats. In immediate, practical terms, it led the Sadrists to a series of devastating defeats on the battlefield and intensified domestic isolation. Less vividly, but no less influentially, it also further exacerbated their reputation for recklessness and strategic myopia.[7]

It became evident from the outset, therefore, that the rekindled Sadrist movement would be more radical and more controversial than its predecessor—and that this extremism posed a serious liability to the Sadrists' enterprise. Muqtada's rhetorical ferocity and the Mehdi Army's resolute commitment to "resistance" enabled the Sadrists to rally a sizable contingent of followers, but these same qualities also threatened to undermine the full-scale revival of the White Lion's mass movement. In short, from the earliest moments of the post-Saddam era, the most prominent representatives of the Sadrist movement shaped its character in such a way as to pull it toward the radical extreme of the political spectrum, where it evolved into a potent, yet exceptionally polarizing entity. Extremism would bring advantages, principally via the zeal of their rank and file, but it would also limit their appeal and diminish their potential among the Shi'a underclass at large. As such, after a turbulent year and a half, Muqtada and his colleagues would be compelled to re-evaluate their strategies and seek to refashion their image. They would struggle, however, to alter the distinct persona that had developed around the new iteration of the Sadrist movement.

A Rivalry Resumed

The brutal murder of Abd al-Majid al-Khoei was the first high-profile act of the resurgent Sadrist movement. On 10 April 2003 (only a day after the fall of Baghdad), it announced the Sadrists' violent resumption of the anti-establishment campaign that the White Lion had pursued rhetorically during the 1990s. Khoei, the son of the late Grand Ayatollah Abd al-Qasim al-Khoei (whose death had opened the door for Mohammed Mohammed Sadiq al-Sadr's ascent in 1992), was the scion of a powerful and respected Shi'a family and a consummate insider in Iraq's clerical elite.[8] Having been compelled to flee abroad in response to the persecution of the Shi'a establishment after the 1991 uprisings, Khoei had also become a noted member of Iraq's exiled opposition, earning acclaim as a respected moderate while managing his family's international charitable operations.

From his base in London, Khoei became involved in efforts to prepare for the 2003 invasion. Thereafter, he was among the many exiles who returned to Iraq in concert with Coalition Forces. Arriving in Basra in the early days of the war, Khoei traveled onward to his home city of Najaf. His arrival in Najaf was a contentious act, and emblematic of broader concerns that arose surrounding the return of Iraq's exiled elite.[9] In general terms, the exiles' return in collusion with a foreign invasion force, after years abroad in relative comfort, provoked resentment and accusations of inauthenticity from those who had endured the full duration of Saddam Hussein's rule. More specifically, the aspirations of exiled clerics such as Khoei to resume their traditional dominance within Iraqi Shi'ism posed a serious threat to the Sadrists' ambitions.[10] The arrival in Najaf of Khoei (who was only a few years older than Muqtada, and far more accomplished and respected) was a direct challenge to the Sadrist movement.

Shortly after Khoei's arrival in Najaf, while visiting the shrine to Imam Ali, an armed crowd of Sadrist supporters confronted him and a group of fellow exiles. It remains contested whether what followed was part of a planned attack, or whether events unfolded spontaneously: one account alleges that Khoei and his companions were consumed by a mob that had assembled to take revenge on the facility's Ba'th Party-affiliated caretaker, while another asserts that Muqtada ordered Khoei's death personally.[11] Regardless, the killing was instrumental in shaping initial perceptions of the Sadrists' character. In the dominant narrative that coalesced around the event, the savage murder of a distinguished religious scholar—seized from within one of Shi'ism's holiest sites to be murdered, butchered, and dragged in pieces through the streets of Najaf—was precisely the sort of act to which Muqtada and his ilk were constitutionally inclined. Impressions of the Sadrists as reckless instigators were then reinforced in the days that followed, when a Sadrist mob besieged the Najaf home of Grand Ayatollah Ali al-Sistani, and Sadrist supporters launched a barrage of attacks against returning exiles from the Hakim family as well, marking the initial skirmishes in what would be a protracted war for the seat of Iraqi Shi'ism.[12]

The Penance of the Finalists

Parallel to the rise of tensions in Najaf, pressure mounted on the Sadrists in relation to the looting that was devastating Baghdad. The inaction of the Americans in the midst of the chaos drew widespread criticism, yet resentment also grew regarding the "order" that had been established on the city's periphery. Fairly or not, the Shi'a underclass was blamed for a grossly disproportionate share of the looting, and the anger of many Baghdadis intensified as the Sadrists were perceived to be maintaining control over their home turf while allowing their supporters free rein to pillage the city's core.[13] As the invasion's aftermath proved far more destructive than the fighting that had accompanied the regime's fall, frustrations were captured in the coining of the derisive term *al-hawasim*, meaning "the finalists," in reference to the looters.[14] The epithet was a sarcastic allusion to Saddam Hussein's claim that the defence of Iraq would be *umm al-hawasim*, "the mother of all finales"—and it was applied scornfully to the opportunists who ravaged the city for material gain.

Because of the Shi'a underclass' prominent position within the ranks of the *hawasim*, the eventual issuance of a public appeal that religious leaders assist in the restoration of order and the return of stolen goods cast a spotlight squarely on Muqtada al-Sadr. The young cleric chose not to endear himself to those at the heart of the emerging political order, or to assist in the re-establishment of stability. In one of his first public statements, Muqtada issued what became known as the *hawasim fatwa*. Asserting the fundamental illegitimacy of Saddam Hussein's regime, he declared that any claims to ownership of goods or property were invalid—and that looters were entitled to the fruits of their plunder so long as they paid *khums*, a 20 per cent religious tax on its value, to Sadrist officials.[15]

The most notable result of the *hawasim fatwa* was to confirm popular suspicion as to who had been the principal culprits in the looting, reinforcing prejudices against the city's Shi'a poor. Furthermore, within the backlash that ensued, it became apparent that popular anger transcended socio-economic lines. In an early sign of a generational divide that would exert a strong influence over the development of the rekindled Sadrist movement, many of the older former followers and colleagues of the White Lion were repulsed by his son's actions.[16] Those who had come of age during the 1990s, however, when material deprivation, official corruption, and physical suffering had debased Iraqi society, embraced Muqtada and rallied to his call for radical, aggressive action.

From the outset, therefore, the so-called "sanctions generation" entrenched itself at the heart of the resurgent Sadrist movement.[17] It would be these young men in their twenties and thirties, both clerics and laymen alike, who would be its most active members, and who would fill the ranks of the Mehdi Army militia. Their characteristics, many of which could be observed in Muqtada himself, would define the rekindled Sadrist movement and mark it as something distinct from the White Lion's original initiative.[18] Muqtada would draw upon his father's reputation among the Shi'a underclass, build from the remnants of his father's network, and deploy many of the same rhetorical attacks against his father's former enemies, but the rekindled Sadrist movement became unique in and of itself: it reflected both the personal attributes of its leadership, and the changes that had occurred in Iraqi society during the 1990s.

Defeat in Najaf

The Sadrists cemented a reputation as belligerent outsiders during the first year of the post-Saddam era. In the political sphere, their relentless opposition to Coalition Forces, and to the parties of the Shi'a establishment that were cooperating with the occupation, assured their official marginalization. Likewise, their provocation of instability rendered them widely unpopular among the general population.[19] Rather than softening their stance, the Sadrists embraced their opposition status—forming their own shadow government and growing increasingly militant in word and deed. Thus, while they remained a marginal force in Iraqi politics as the first anniversary of regime change approached (and their Mehdi Army militia was, as yet, similarly unimposing), the Sadrists had fused their anti-occupation and anti-Shi'a establishment views to stake an outspoken claim at the forefront of Shi'a opposition to the new political order.

Despite the Sadrists' limited popularity, their determined agitation attracted the attention of Coalition Forces. With frustration mounting throughout Iraq at the unsatisfactory pace of economic and political reconstruction, and a potent insurgency having developed among Sunni Arabs that had thrown key areas of Anbar Province and Baghdad into turmoil, concern spread over the potential implications of Sadrist incitement. Wary of a Mehdi Army-led "Shi'a insurgency" alongside the so-called "Sunni insurgency," debates raged over the wisdom of either confronting or compromising with Muqtada and the Sadrists.[20]

Such discussions were overtaken by events, as tensions erupted into armed confrontation at the end of March 2004.[21] The immediate spark of the conflagration was a sermon of Muqtada's that proclaimed the September 11 attacks on the United States "a miracle and a blessing from God," prompting the Coalition to take a series of steps against him and his associates. The Sadrists' main newspaper was shuttered for publishing the text, Sadrist political leader Mustapha al-Yacoubi was arrested for his alleged role in the murder of Abd al-Majid al-Khoei, and Muqtada was also named as wanted in connection with the incident.[22]

The Mehdi Army responded with a surge of attacks in and around its operational hub of Sadr City, while Sadrist supporters instigated an uprising across southern Iraq that overwhelmed the contingent of Coalition Forces responsible for the region.[23] Muqtada, meanwhile, fled south to his father's former stronghold in Kufa and then onward to nearby Najaf, where he summoned a sizable force of militiamen from Baghdad to prepare for battle.[24]

The Mehdi Army was routed decisively in the counter-offensive that followed, which saw the American military inflict heavy casualties on it in Najaf (where, in a sign of the potency of intra-Shi'a divisions, the Americans were aided by the tribal allies of Grand Ayatollah Ali al-Sistani).[25] A decision was made to halt operations prior to the full destruction of the Mehdi Army, however, and to allow Muqtada and the remnants of the militia to escape. This course of action averted further destruction of Najaf's venerated religious infrastructure, and brought Coalition Forces a measure of badly-desired stability in southern Iraq at a time when they faced mounting problems with Sunni insurgents in the western city of Fallujah, but subsequent events enabled the Sadrists to gain significant strategic momentum from their tactical defeat.

At issue was a precipitous drop in the already declining popularity of the US-led occupation during April 2004. Major clashes between the Coalition and Iraqi opponents in both Najaf and Fallujah (the latter of which was temporarily besieged by US forces in response to the killing and desecration of civilian security contractors) saw Americans killing Iraqis in large numbers, hardening public opinion against the occupation. The exposure of the Abu Ghraib prisoner abuse scandal immediately thereafter provoked overwhelming outrage, souring Iraqis on the intentions and character of their "liberators." As such, the Sadrists' impeccable record of rejectionism suddenly skyrocketed in value.[26] The ability of the Mehdi Army to have survived the confrontation in Najaf became a victory in its own right that, paired with symbolic gestures such as the Sadrists' delivery of aid to Sunni insurgents in Fallujah, transformed Muqtada and his militia into icons of resistance.

The Sadrists enjoyed a surge of popularity during the summer of 2004, while that of the Coalition declined steeply. Tensions between the two sides re-escalated accordingly, culminating in a second round of heavy fighting in late August. Once again the focal point was Najaf and, once again, the Mehdi Army suffered a decisive, bloody defeat. In contrast to the events of the spring, there were few positives for the Sadrists to take way from the August clash. The fighting ended with Muqtada and his surviving companions yet again being granted safe passage from Najaf, but this was due only to the intervention of Grand Ayatollah Ali al-Sistani.[27] The ceasefire brokered by the White Lion's former archenemy allowed Muqtada and his confederates to escape with their lives, yet its terms barred the Sadrists from the coveted terrain of Najaf's old city, cemented Sistani's dominance over Muqtada, and left the Sadrists' aspirations to clerical pre-eminence in tatters.

An Attempted Course Correction

In the aftermath of the fighting in Najaf, additional setbacks compounded the Sadrists' woes. First, the Mehdi Army's decision to take refuge in and launch attacks upon Coalition and Iraqi units from some of the Shi'a faith's holiest sites provoked popular fury, as significant damage was incurred.[28] Second, with nationwide elections scheduled for January 2005, the Sadrists' continued incitement of Coalition ire at a time when Shi'a parties were well positioned to achieve victory bred frustration. The occupation remained deeply unpopular, but to many Shi'a, "resistance" appeared increasingly counter-productive when electoral triumph was in reach.[29] Third, the Mehdi Army's recklessness prompted Ayatollah Kazem al-Haeri (who had been designated as the official heir to Mohammed Mohammed Sadiq al-Sadr's movement upon his death, and who had been channeling funds to Muqtada from his base in Iran) to sever his relations with Muqtada. This deprived the Sadrists of both a valuable revenue source as well as a claim to clerical respectability, further weakening their position.[30]

The cumulative toll of these setbacks was sufficient to prompt a shift by Muqtada. Looking ahead to the upcoming elections, he withdrew the Mehdi Army from the frontlines of resistance and curbed his rhetoric.[31] The decision to avoid further confrontation enabled the Mehdi Army to regroup, and the Sadrists' subdued stance calmed intra-Shi'a tensions significantly. Yet Muqtada's turn toward the political mainstream, and his simultaneous effort to reform the Mehdi Army, exposed internal problems that would plague the Sadrists in the years to come.

On the one hand, elements of the Mehdi Army rejected Muqtada's pragmatic shift, however incremental, toward moderation. The closing months of 2004 thus saw an internal splintering of factions from the militia's core, which reflected a structural incoherence that extended to its highest levels.[32] On the other, the young cleric's attempt to impose discipline upon the militia's rank and file revealed the staggering scope of the challenge. Although the Sadrists' ability to channel legions of able-bodied young men into the Mehdi Army had been, and would remain, central to the movement's advances, the radicalism and brutality of their most ardent followers vexed efforts at reform.

The internal concerns illuminated by Muqtada's strategic shift were inextricably linked to two emerging trends that would color indelibly the militia's development. The first was the growing scope of Iranian activity in Iraq, and the decision of Iran's Revolutionary Guards to provide training, funding, and weapons to Shi'a militants with whom they shared common objectives.[33] While the Mehdi Army would benefit from Iranian patronage and technical assistance as it sought to improve its capabilities in the wake of 2004's defeats, the militia's organizational integrity would, in the long run, be badly undermined by Iranian intrigue. The Iranian policy of working directly with sub-networks of fighters within the Mehdi Army compromised its chain-of-command, complicating Muqtada's efforts to direct patterns of violence in keeping with his political aims (and confusing efforts of observers to interpret the political significance of Shi'a militancy).[34]

The second force that exerted powerful influence over the militia's development was the rise of sectarian violence within the Sunni insurgency. With radical, aggressively sectarian militant groups like Iraqi al-Qaeda taking an increasingly prominent role in the Sunni insurgency, what began principally as a reaction by elements and clients of the fallen regime to their sudden loss of position transformed into *jihad*, not only against Coalition Forces and their Iraqi allies, but also against Iraq's Shi'a populace at large.[35] The venomous sectarianism of men like the Jordanian, Abu Musab al-Zarqawi, who achieved worldwide infamy as the leader of Iraq's al-Qaeda franchise, thus interwove with the radical strands of Sunni Islam that had developed in Iraq during the sanctions era, giving rise to a devastating, divisive new trend in violence.

The recurrence of spectacular suicide attacks against Shi'a civilians through the course of 2004, and the accompanying, incendiary rhetoric of Sunni militants regarding the elemental illegitimacy of the Shi'a sect, generated a wave of fear, suspicion, and hatred. This surge of intra-Iraqi violence, which was concentrated in Baghdad, also sparked a period of booming growth for the Mehdi Army.[36] The inability of either the Iraqi government or Coalition Forces to secure the capital created desperate demands for protection, and the Mehdi Army grew massively as it emerged as the pre-eminent defender of Shi'a Baghdadis.

The militia's position in the capital was greatly improved as a result, yet both the scope of this growth and the psychological environment in which it took place created problems. On the one hand, rapid expansion exacerbated already severe command and control issues. Thus, while Muqtada was attempting to impose order upon the Mehdi Army at the close of 2004, the militia's surging growth was directly undermining his endeavor. On the other hand, the Mehdi Army's prominent role in counterattacks against Sunnis overwhelmed attempts to redress its reputation for divisiveness and brutality. Instead, the militia's increasingly aggressive role in sectarian violence added a polarizing new element to its already unenviable reputation for viciousness, making it all the more controversial.

The Ascent of the Sadrists

As Muqtada sought to reform the Sadrist movement and rein in the Mehdi Army during the latter months of 2004, the Sadrists' prospects remained uncertain. They had made notable progress in a number of areas, but pressing concerns accompanied their successes. First, while the Sadrists had forced their way, uninvited and unwelcome, onto the field of post-Saddam politics, the Mehdi Army had been decisively bested in its confrontations with Coalition Forces and the Sadrists had been banished from Najaf by their clerical rivals. Second, although the Mehdi Army had seized control over large sections of Baghdad's impoverished periphery (as well as areas of Basra and the Deep South), defining characteristics of the militia—most prominently the radicalism of its core membership and its disjointed, unwieldy structure—undermined efforts to consolidate its gains. The Mehdi Army was thus a powerful street-level force, but its pre-eminence was not paired with the kind of cohesive popular enthusiasm previously enjoyed by the White Lion. Third, while the Sadrists had asserted themselves at the forefront of resistance against a deeply unpopular occupation, the value of that achievement was depreciating. With nationwide elections scheduled for January 2005, the main axis of conflict in Iraq was shifting away from resistance against the Coalition and toward violent, intra-Iraqi competition over the country's future—rendering the Sadrists' rejection of, and ostracism from, the emerging political order a potential liability.

Despite their troubles, the Sadrists were on the verge of a remarkable ascent, the angle and velocity of which would prove greater than Muqtada and his associates could reasonably have anticipated. The reforms and adjustments of Sadrist leadership were instrumental in the successes that ensued, and the assets that they had thus far developed (the Mehdi Army foremost among them) proved invaluable, but forces beyond their control would ultimately shape the Sadrists' fortunes. Indeed, at the root of the Sadrists' rise was the aforementioned shift in the underlying paradigm of conflict in Iraq, whereby fighting between Shi'a and Sunni militants subsumed anti-Coalition resistance as the dominant framework of violence.

This transition was initially problematic for the Sadrists, as they had defined themselves largely through their opposition to the occupation and Sadrist dogma was explicitly non-sectarian. Nonetheless, as sectarian violence intensified, the Sadrists were presented with an array of opportunities for advancement. Capitalizing upon these opportunities, Sadrist politicians would transition from shunned outsiders to powerful insiders in the Iraqi government, the Mehdi Army would expand dramatically to conquer broad swathes of Baghdad, and the city itself would undergo a sweeping demographic transformation that suggested the permanence of the Sadrists' gains.

The Opportunities of the Sectarian War

Sectarian violence—which began as an undercurrent within the Sunni insurgency, gained momentum during the spring and summer of 2004, and then intensified dramatically in the context of the January 2005 elections—altered Iraq's strategic landscape in several ways to the direct benefit of the Sadrists. Most critically, the rise of Iraqi al-Qaeda and the ferocious sectarianism of Sunni *jihadis* compelled the Shi'a elite to put aside their feud with the Sadrists and reach out, however warily, in the name of sectarian solidarity.[37] In the run-up to the January 2005 elections, the Sadrists were welcomed as junior partners into the United Iraqi

Alliance (UIA)—a coalition of religiously-defined Shi'a factions overseen by Grand Ayatollah Ali al-Sistani.

Elections then strengthened the Sadrists' position, as the ballot box enabled them to capitalize on the latent mass base that they had, until that point, rallied with uneven results.[38] However controversial the Mehdi Army's reputation may have been, the Shi'a underclass masses of Baghdad, Basra, and the smaller cities and rural reaches of southern Iraq overwhelmingly backed Sadrists candidates. With the UIA emerging from the elections as Iraq's dominant political grouping (and the Sadrists comprising a sizable electoral bloc in the alliance), the Sadrists' position was thereafter all the more prominent, enabling them to influence the writing of Iraq's constitution, and granting the movement an important measure of respectability.[39]

The intensification of sectarian killing that accompanied the January elections also enabled the Mehdi Army to recast its image and improve its position in Baghdad. While the conduct of Iraq's first nationwide elections since Saddam Hussein's removal marked a notable symbolic achievement, they badly exacerbated sectarian tensions.[40] In protest of what prominent Sunni leaders cited as their unfair persecution by Coalition Forces and their marginalization from the political process, Iraq's Sunni Arabs boycotted the elections *en masse*.[41] Their boycott, combined with the victory of the UIA (which was dominated by radical Shi'a religious parties like the Da'wa and the Supreme Iraqi Islamic Council that possessed strong historical ties to Iran, and also prominently featured the Sadrists, whose Mehdi Army was already infamous for its attacks on Sunnis), had the effect of broadening and deepening Iraq's growing sectarian rift.[42]

Sunni militants responded to the UIA's electoral triumph with a withering offensive in and around the Iraqi capital, featuring beheadings and a wave of suicide bombings that targeted Shi'a religious processions, mosques, and marketplaces.[43] With Coalition Forces deliberately withdrawn from day-to-day policing functions on the streets of the city (as part of a strategy that sought to mitigate popular displeasure with occupation by limiting the presence of foreign soldiers in the daily lives of Iraqis), and Iraqi Security Forces as yet unable to secure the city, the Mehdi Army was presented with an extraordinary opportunity.[44] Its ability to mobilize throngs of armed men—however volatile or predatory—enabled it to set up checkpoints around Shi'a neighborhoods and defend vulnerable public spaces. Furthermore, its notoriety for the persecution of Sunnis helped the Mehdi Army assert itself as a leading exactor of retribution at a time when calls for vengeance were mounting. The same qualities that had previously rendered the militia so controversial were thus found to have a grim, but undeniable utility in countering the onslaught of Sunni fanatics; and the Mehdi Army attracted waves of new recruits as it refashioned itself as Shi'a Baghdadis' indispensable bulwark against the Sunni *jihad*.

The escalation of sectarian violence by Sunni militants also granted the Mehdi Army a valuable reprieve from its conflict with Coalition Forces. Most immediately, with Zarqawi and Iraqi al-Qaeda entrenched at the top of Coalition Forces' threat assessments and the Mehdi Army continuing to check its anti-Coalition activity, the attentions of the militia's most capable adversary were increasingly directed elsewhere. Furthermore, the Sadrists' inclusion within the Iraqi government and their growing importance to Shi'a efforts in the sectarian war conferred additional measures of protection. Iraqi officials shielded the Mehdi Army's fighters from arrest or prosecution and their strongholds were declared off-limits to Coalition Forces, enabling the militia to evolve with greatly diminished interference from the American military.[45]

Victory in the Battle for Baghdad

The Sadrists' rise continued apace with the escalation of sectarian violence through 2005 and into 2006. On the streets of Baghdad, the Mehdi Army grew ever stronger.[46] The steady barrage of Sunni attacks, which were punctuated by spectacular mass casualty events like the Khadimiyah bridge stampede of August 2005 (which saw some 1,000 Shi'a perish when rumors of an impending suicide attack spread panic through a vast crowd of religious pilgrims), enabled the militia both to strengthen its core and expand its membership.[47] The Mehdi Army's lead role in defence of underclass Shi'a strongholds like Sadr City and Shula (which, by virtue of their demographic make-up and their status as the heartland of the militia, became priority targets for Sunni attack) enabled it to attract additional recruits, while the militia's monopoly on service provision and the maintenance of order in Baghdad's Shi'a slums enabled it to cultivate localized popular support.[48]

The Sadrists' rising stature was reinforced by success in the December 2005 elections, in which the movement's political representatives and affiliated candidates secured a formidable thirty-two seat bloc in parliament. As increasingly powerful members of the again-victorious United Iraqi Alliance, Sadrist politicians wielded considerable clout in the protracted post-election wrangling over who would secure the position of prime minister.[49] Indeed, their support for Nouri al-Maliki's candidacy was critical to his eventual success in the contest, and the Sadrists were rewarded with ministerial portfolios that conferred both prestige and valuable patronage opportunities.[50]

As had been the case in the January elections, Iraq's political process also served, yet again, to exacerbate sectarian division to the advantage of the Sadrists. The UIA's victory marked the apparent consolidation of political power by Shi'a religious factions, and sparked a further escalation of sectarian violence. Beginning with the infamous Samarra mosque bombing in late February 2006, and escalating dramatically through the spring and summer to claim tens of thousands of lives and displace over 1.5 million Iraqis from their homes, the scope and intensity of violence rose to previously unseen heights.[51]

While the scale of the killing and the resulting social polarization grew to such levels that observers labeled the conflict a "civil war," the mechanics of violence continued largely unchanged. Rather than a grassroots, popular clash between the city's Shi'a and Sunni residents that featured neighbors taking up arms against one another in a manifestation of long-simmering sectarian divisions, the killing and forced displacement that ravaged Baghdad remained, for the most part, the work of politically-motivated militant networks such as Iraqi al-Qaeda and the Mehdi Army.[52]

In a sign of the structure that underpinned the sectarian war in Baghdad, the conflict became a contest for territory.[53] The violence of 2006 was thus characterized by systematic sectarian cleansing in the name of urban conquest. The Mehdi Army, like its fellow Shi'a in the Badr militia and their mutual Sunni foes, seized control of neighborhoods within the capital by positioning themselves as the benefactors of their local sectarian kin and eliminating civilians of the opposing sect. With its formidable street-level presence, the Mehdi Army achieved great successes in the bloodshed that ensued. Capitalizing on the near impunity with which it could operate owing to the protection of the government, the Mehdi Army led an offensive that pushed Baghdad's Sunni population back into fortified enclaves, claiming broad sections of the capital.[54]

The Transformation of the Iraqi Capital

As mass killing and systematic forced displacement continued into the latter months of 2006, the demographic landscape of Baghdad was radically altered. The city, which had formerly been dominated by the middle class, mixed-sect neighborhoods that developed at its core during the course of the twentieth century, was subjected to a rapid, bloody sectarian segregation.[55] By the close of 2006, the vast majority of eastern Baghdad was exclusively Shi'a (with the exception of the Sunni enclave of Adhamiyyah, and remaining mixed-sect neighborhoods in the heart of the Rusafa political district). On the western bank of the Tigris River, on the other hand, Sunnis were being squeezed into a band of neighborhoods along the terminus of the highway connecting Baghdad to Anbar Province.

The Mehdi Army, having played a leading role in the city's segregation, controlled much of its Shi'a terrain. In its original strongholds of Sadr City and Shula, and in the formerly mixed-sect, poor to working-class neighborhoods around the city's sprawling margins, the militia was firmly entrenched. Its fighters dominated the streets, while Sadrist officials formed a de facto government. Closer to the city center, the militia had also taken possession of a number of formerly mixed-sect, middle class neighborhoods. The militia's position in these areas was contested, as the Badr militia sought to monopolize power in the city center (and Baghdad's middle class Shi'a were broadly hostile to the Sadrist movement), yet the Mehdi Army's gains appeared more durable than might otherwise have been expected.

This was due, in significant measure, to the fact that local demography had been altered in ways that went beyond sectarian realignment. Through the course of the post-Saddam era, rising insecurity and declining living standards had combined to generate outflows of middle class and minority families from Baghdad, thereby continuing the exodus that had begun during previous decades.[56] From the earliest weeks after the 2003 invasion, for example, educated professionals such as doctors and teachers had been targeted aggressively by both kidnappers and politically-minded militants (the latter of whom sought to eliminate the social capital of demographic groups hostile to their particular agendas). Baghdad's Christians, likewise, had found themselves victims of attacks by Muslim militants of both sects, and poorly positioned to defend themselves.[57]

Owing to the layout of Baghdad, the ensuing population outflows caused a gradual hollowing out of the city center, leaving the communities that remained all the more vulnerable to the predations of their enemies and the incursions of outsiders. Critical to the Sadrists' advances, meanwhile, an inward surge of poor Shi'a families was emanating from the city's peripheral slums. The initial years of the post-Saddam era thus saw a small-scale re-enactment of the *shurughi* migrations of the 1940s and 1950s, as clusters of poor Shi'a families from districts like Sadr City and Shula (joined by others from the hinterlands of the capital, and also from southern Iraq where the collapse of the much-relied-upon central government prompted movement to Baghdad) pressed in upon Baghdad's core. Laying claim to the abandoned property of the fallen regime, installing themselves in the homes of the displaced and those who had fled abroad, and erecting ramshackle, modern-day *sarifas* of cinder-blocs, concrete, and scrap metal on open pieces of land, they further transformed the city.[58]

While the scope of these movements was initially modest, the resentment that developed toward these migrants' perceived opportunism was sufficient enough for the pejorative *hawasim*, coined originally in reference to looters, to be scornfully applied to the squatters-cum-settlers. On the one hand, their efforts to rig connections to already compromised water, sewer, and electricity systems further strained critical infrastructure, generating great frustration within adjacent communities. On the other, the rising tide of poor Shi'a, particularly in the mixed-sect neighborhoods near Baghdad's peripheral slums, fostered an environment of identity-based animosity that recalled the 1940s and 1950s.[59] Established residents thus came to view surges in violence and criminality, the accelerating collapse of public infrastructure, and the encroachment of the Shi'a underclass as elements of a single phenomenon—the roots of which could be traced, in the narrative of the besieged middle class, to slums like Sadr City.[60]

As the sectarian war intensified and the Mehdi Army continued its campaign of territorial conquest, the geographic spread of the Shi'a underclass became increasingly politicized. The early flight of middle class and minority families out of Baghdad and the initial flow of *hawasim* into areas adjacent to the capital's slums had progressed with a large measure of spontaneity, but the systematic manipulation of demographics emerged as a key weapon in the Mehdi Army's arsenal.[61] Pressing outwards from districts like Sadr City and Shula, the militia utilized a combination of targeted killing, forced displacement, and intimidation to eliminate or subdue unsympathetic elements of adjoining areas. Supportive members of the Shi'a underclass were thereafter ushered into the area (where they were often joined by displaced Shi'a families of varied socio-economic backgrounds that had been driven from Sunni-conquered areas of Baghdad), establishing themselves on open land or moving into vacated homes.[62] The Mehdi Army not only cleansed broad areas of Baghdad of Sunnis, but also aided in the spread of the Sadrist movement's demographic base.

Betrayal, Exile, and Defeat

By late 2006, the Sadrists were a towering force in Iraq. Muqtada al-Sadr was an influential national figure, Sadrist politicians formed a central component of the Iraqi government, and the movement was the near-exclusive political vehicle for Iraq's burgeoning Shi'a underclass. The Mehdi Army, meanwhile, was larger and more powerful than ever before. The militia had absorbed legions of new recruits, it controlled vast tracts of the Iraqi capital, and its fighters could claim significant credit for having turned the tide of the sectarian war. Furthermore, the demographic changes that had swept Baghdad augured well for the Sadrists' future. Not only was the Iraqi capital more heavily Shi'a than at any time in the city's long history, but the movement's underclass supporters had also grown as a percentage of that Shi'a majority, and expanded geographically as well.[63] From the Sadrists' perspective, therefore, there seemed ample reason to celebrate, and to expect that further successes would follow—and their rising swagger was infamously evident during the December execution of Saddam Hussein, where leaked footage showed the condemned man being taunted with Sadrist slogans as he was led to the gallows.

However, despite the Sadrists' remarkable advances, they faced significant and growing problems.[64] First, while the Sadrists' rise to power (both in government and on the streets of Baghdad) had conferred a broad array of benefits, with power came increased responsibilities, heightened expectations, and intensified public scrutiny. Their successes brought added burdens that they struggled to manage. Second, the Mehdi Army's ascendancy in Baghdad had been matched by both the intensification of its notoriety, as well as the exacerbation of its organizational problems. The militia had grown massively, but it had become all the more controversial and structurally incoherent. Third, impending Shi'a victory in the sectarian war meant that, in the eyes of the dominant players of the Shi'a establishment, the Mehdi Army had served its purpose. The diminishing threat of Iraqi al-Qaeda and the Sunni insurgency (which owed much to the Sunnis' evident defeat in the sectarian war, as well as the associated rise of the Awakening movement that witnessed former insurgents turn on al-Qaeda and seek reconciliation with the government) meant the dissolution of the principal force that had bound the rival Shi'a factions together in the first place.

Beset by a host of internal problems, and confronted by an array of external challenges, the Sadrist movement would experience a precipitous drop in its fortunes. Unable to consolidate their hard-fought gains, the Sadrists found themselves betrayed by their Shi'a establishment rivals and exposed to a devastating American-led offensive. Muqtada would be driven into exile, Sadrist politicians would find themselves outsiders once again, and the Mehdi Army would be routed to the point that Muqtada would be compelled to dissolve it entirely.

The Perils of Success

From the start of their campaign, the Sadrists had positioned themselves as outsiders. This denied them the prestige of official authority and access to the wealth of the state, but it dissociated them from the shortcomings of the Iraqi government and the occupation. Not only were the Sadrists free of blame for the government's inability to restore basic services, establish the rule of law, or revitalize Iraq's economy, but they were also able to cultivate popular support by filling the resulting governance vacuum. Upon their entry into the United Iraqi Alliance, the Sadrists became answerable for the performance of the state. The key role of Sadrist officials in the badly underperforming ministries of Health and Electricity (the former known as the "Ministry of Horrors" among American personnel, in recognition of both the poor standard of care as well as the proclivity of the Mehdi Army to prey upon Sunni patients) thus exposed the Sadrists to mounting criticism.[65] Furthermore, in addition to issues of performance and competency, Sadrist officials proved as prone to corruption as the rest of their colleagues in the Iraqi government.[66] The militant populism and religious austerity of Sadrist rhetoric was compromised by evident hypocrisy, tarnishing the movement's image.

The Mehdi Army likewise struggled to handle the responsibilities that came with the successes of 2005 and 2006. Having seized large sections of the Iraqi capital, the militia presided over millions of Baghdadis who looked to it not only for protection, but also governance. This would have been a daunting task for a well-organized and well-resourced organization. By way of comparison, it was a feat that neither the Iraqi government nor the US-led Coalition had accomplished to any meaningful level of popular satisfaction since the 2003 invasion. For the Mehdi Army, it proved overwhelming.

By 2007 the militia's ranks were dominated by young men in their teens, twenties, and thirties, who were ill-equipped for, and little-inclined toward, the mundane and technical tasks of governance.[67] Furthermore, the abatement of sectarian violence and the cessation of large-scale population transfers deprived the militia of its most important revenue source. While the Mehdi Army had funded itself in part through its control over the informal economy (most notably via the control of gas stations, the distribution of cooking oil, and the sale of electricity from small generators), the assets seized from its victims were an essential funding stream.[68]

The Mehdi Army was faced, therefore, with an extraordinary challenge for which it was neither suited nor equipped. As such, despite the efforts of Muqtada al-Sadr to implement reforms and issue guidance, the militia, as a whole, descended into disorder and predation.[69] The waning months of the sectarian war witnessed a redirection, rather than a cessation, of the militia's martial energies, with militiamen turning their weapons on the Shi'a civilians over whom they presided. Life for many in Mehdi Army-held territory thereafter required running gauntlets of checkpoints staffed by armed youths who became infamous for narcotics-fueled violence, and paying protection money to local strongmen.[70]

The Metastasizing Problems of the Mehdi Army

Far and away the highest-profile element of the rekindled Sadrist movement, the militia was decisively influential in shaping popular opinion toward Muqtada and his associates. As the Sadrists' principle organizational body, the militia was also their most important operational asset. Its reputation and effectiveness were thus paramount concerns, yet efforts to resolve these woes (which began in earnest after the militia's defeats in Najaf in 2004, and remained a top priority through the years that followed), achieved only the most modest of results.[71]

At issue was the inescapable fact that the Mehdi Army's behavior was an authentic manifestation of its membership, and its incoherence a direct by-product of the manner in which it had spread across Baghdad. Having developed from a core of sanctions-generation males and radical junior clerics, and expanded further by enlisting legions of young men (who, in time, were joined by the even more hardened and volatile youths that came of age during the near-anarchy of the post-Saddam era), the Mehdi Army, as an institution, took on their particular attributes. The extreme nature of their rhetoric, the brutality with which they pursued their objectives, and the austere brand of Islamic rule imposed in their wake (often complete with "morality police" in the image of Iran or Saudi Arabia) exerted a formative influence on the militia's identity.

That identity had, in turn, exerted a profound influence over the way Muqtada was able to translate popular affinity for the White Lion's legacy into active support for his agenda. From the initial, polarizing controversy that surrounded the *hawasim fatwa* and the murder of Abd al-Majid al-Khoei to the gruesome atrocities of the militia's sectarian campaign, a self-perpetuating cycle had developed that repelled more moderate elements of the Shi'a underclass while attracting additional like-minded recruits. Efforts, therefore, to curb the militia's most extreme elements and refashion its reputation ran directly against the central current of its development.

The Mehdi Army's growth in Baghdad occurred through the absorption of pre-existing local networks. Taking advantage of the latent base of popular support bequeathed by the White Lion, and drawing further upon the affinity of Shi'a youths for Muqtada and his message, the Mehdi Army mobilized thousands of foot soldiers. In keeping with the best practices of insurgent warfare, the militia "went local"—recruiting not only agents and informants, but also entire operational networks from the neighborhoods that it sought to draw into its domain.[72] Either working out of mosques (which, frequently, were former Sunni mosques that had been seized by the militia) or from Sadrist offices, representatives of the Mehdi Army would recruit from the surrounding area, establishing what amounted to local "franchises."[73]

In so doing, the militia was able to spread quickly across the city and, in the process, acquire troves of valuable intelligence. The increasingly localized and decentralized structure of the militia came at a cost, as the priorities and loyalties of its myriad subcomponents grew increasingly localized as well. The effects of this dynamic were not uniformly negative—indeed, the decentralized nature of the Mehdi Army's expansion allowed for the development of pockets in the city where the Mehdi Army's representatives were tied closely to the local community and enjoyed significant popularity—yet the overall result was deeply detrimental to its strategic coherence.[74]

Mounting External Pressures

In the final weeks of 2006, dramatic changes to Iraq's political landscape brought enormous pressure to bear on the Sadrists and their militia. With Iraqi al-Qaeda in check and Shi'a victory in the sectarian war secured, the rationale for the establishment's alliance with the Sadrists was rapidly collapsing.[75] Furthermore, with the Sadrists appearing potentially vulnerable due to the weaknesses discussed above, and American forces preparing to recommit themselves to Iraq via the Surge, the timing was ideal for Prime Minister Maliki to break with Muqtada, the Sadrists, and the Mehdi Army.[76]

The dynamics of violence in Iraq thus reverted back to that of 2003 and 2004, pitting the Sadrists and their militia against the joint forces of the Coalition, the Iraqi government, and the Badr militia.[77] From January 2007 onward, as Prime Minster Maliki strengthened his association with Coalition Forces, American personnel spread out through the capital in the context of the Surge and initiated a major offensive against the Mehdi Army.[78] The Sadrists' betrayal by their establishment rivals meant that militiamen were no longer able to rely on the protection of the government, and their strongholds were no longer off limits to the Americans.[79] The forces arrayed against the Mehdi Army were such that Muqtada was compelled to order his militia not to counter the offensive, while the young cleric fled to exile in Iran.[80]

As the pressure increased on the Mehdi Army during the spring and summer of 2007, the militia's strengths and weaknesses were clearly defined. In Baghdad, the Mehdi Army was driven from many of the formerly mixed-sect, middle class neighborhoods most distant from its principal strongholds, while the refocused attention of Coalition Forces compelled numerous high-ranking militiamen to seek refuge in the Deep South and Iran.[81] Nonetheless, while the militia's penetration of the city's core proved short-lived, it remained dominant around much of Baghdad's periphery. Indeed, a full year into the Surge, the Sadrists' home turf would still be regarded as impenetrable by the most astute of observers, and the prospect of the Mehdi Army's head-on defeat was widely agreed to be "fanciful."[82]

Yet, however well entrenched the Mehdi Army appeared in areas of the capital and across zones of southern Iraq, the intensification of external pressure badly exacerbated its organizational troubles. With Muqtada absent in Iran (and poorly positioned to quell the dissent that festered in response to his order that the militia not aggressively combat the encroachment of the Surge), the various sub-networks within the Mehdi Army splintered apart.[83] Muqtada's stated strategy of non-confrontation was thus compromised at a vital time, as elements of the militia came into sporadically heavy confrontation with Coalition Forces and the Iraqi government.

The most prominent instigators of violence were the so-called "Special Groups," which took advantage of Iranian technical expertise, financial resources, and advanced weaponry to launch a formidable counteroffensive.[84] The close ties of Special Group leaders with the Mehdi Army, and the consequently indeterminate political motives of their operations, opened the door for a broad policy of retributive targeting by Coalition Forces. Furthermore, the numerous local franchises that had been absorbed into the Mehdi Army during its expansion were unable to mount a coherent response to the advance of the Surge either. The sustained, street-level counterinsurgency operations of the Surge brought the militia's affiliates into direct, daily contact with American and Iraqi units. Faced with the advance of powerful enemies, and lacking an effective organizational hierarchy upon which to call, elements of the militia pursued independent courses of action. Some sought reconciliation with the Iraqi government and worked in concert with local officials to enhance stability and security, others went to ground or fled their neighborhoods, while still others offered violent resistance.

The End of the Mehdi Army?

In August 2007, the Mehdi Army's fortunes took a further downward turn. The militia was engaged in a long-running battle with the Badr militia for supremacy in southern Iraq, and the spring and summer of 2007 brought an escalation of skirmishes and assassinations.[85] These clashes culminated in a major confrontation during the *Shabaniyah* Festival in Karbala, where Mehdi Army fighters traded mortar and machine-gun fire with Badr loyalists (who were uniformed members of the Iraqi Security Forces).[86] With some fifty civilians killed and hundreds more wounded, and public opinion placing blame squarely on the shoulders of the Mehdi Army, Muqtada al-Sadr was compelled to take drastic action. On the day after the fighting, he imposed a unilateral ceasefire on his militia for a period of six months—during which time the Sadrist leadership would attempt, yet again, to enforce internal discipline and rehabilitate the militia's image.

The Mehdi Army's ceasefire, which Muqtada would renew in February 2008, led to a significant drop in violence and a tense stalemate in the Iraqi capital.[87] On one side, Sadrist leaders spent these months attempting to reform and reconstitute the Mehdi Army. Muqtada, still in Iran, continued his religious studies in an effort to elevate his clerical credentials and burnish his credibility. The Sadrist strategy focused on the consolidation of its base and the pursuit of long-term goals, while avoiding direct clashes.[88] Citing the continued hostilities of Special Group cells and elements of the Mehdi Army as immediate justification, however, and remaining intent on the defeat of their outspoken, long-term enemy, American forces continued to take an aggressive line against the Mehdi Army, pushing further into the militia's domain. As a result, Muqtada's ceasefire grew increasingly unpopular within the ranks of the militia, and a major confrontation loomed as 2007 drew to a close.[89]

However, 2008 did not feature a large-scale eruption of violence. Instead, with the exception of March Madness' fleeting turmoil and sporadic clashes in Basra, Baghdad, and elsewhere, the militia suffered a string of crushing defeats. Not only was it driven from the territory that it had captured during the sectarian war, but it was also forced to cede control over the heartland of the Sadrist movement. The scope of its defeats in Baghdad and the Deep South were such that Muqtada ordered the wholesale dissolution of the once-fearsome militia in June, leaving the future direction of the rekindled Sadrist movement in question.[90]

What caused this sudden and unexpected collapse? The external challenges and internal weaknesses raised above are generally cited, with varying degrees of emphasis, as having been the principal forces responsible. However, as argued at the outset of this book, they are ultimately unsatisfying in explaining fully the scope, speed, and style of the Mehdi Army's dramatic implosion during 2008.

Examination of the Mehdi Army's campaign at the local, neighborhood level exposes additional internal problems that were pivotal in the militia's demise. These flaws, detailed in the chapters that follow, were direct by-products of how the militia mobilized the Sadrist movement's underclass Shi'a following, and how it engaged with Iraqi society at large. By mobilizing tens of thousands of young men, the Mehdi Army grew into one of the most formidable forces in post-Saddam Iraq. Yet because of the manner in which this mobilization took place, and the particular qualities of those who became the militia's most conspicuous and powerful representatives, the very process through which the Mehdi Army rose to prominence sowed the seeds of its destruction.

4

TISA NISSAN

DISTRICT OVERVIEW

Area Study Overview

The area study that follows examines six of the ten *hayys*, or administrative sub-districts, of Baghdad's Tisa Nissan political district. These *hayys*: Amin, Beladiyat, Fedaliyah, Kamaliyah, Mashtal, and Shawra wa Umm Jidr, are known collectively, along with the *hayy* of Obeidy, as the area of Tisa Nissan "beyond the Army Canal."[1]

In Arabic, *Tisa Nissan* means "9 April," and the name is a play on words that juxtapose the present with the past. In present terms, the district's name commemorates the day that Saddam Hussein's iconic statue was pulled down in Firdos Square in the early days of the 2003 invasion, signifying the fall of the Ba'th regime. In reference to the past, the name also evokes *Sab'a Nissan*, "7 April," which was the name that the Ba'th regime had bestowed upon one of the district's neighborhoods in a tribute to the date of the Ba'th Party's first congress in 1947.[2]

The Landscape of Eastern Baghdad

The foundation of present-day Tisa Nissan, like that of nearby Sadr City, was laid during Abd al-Karim Qasim's urban development initiative of the early 1960s. As discussed in chapter one, at the time of the coup that brought Qasim to power, the eastern half of the Iraqi capital had long

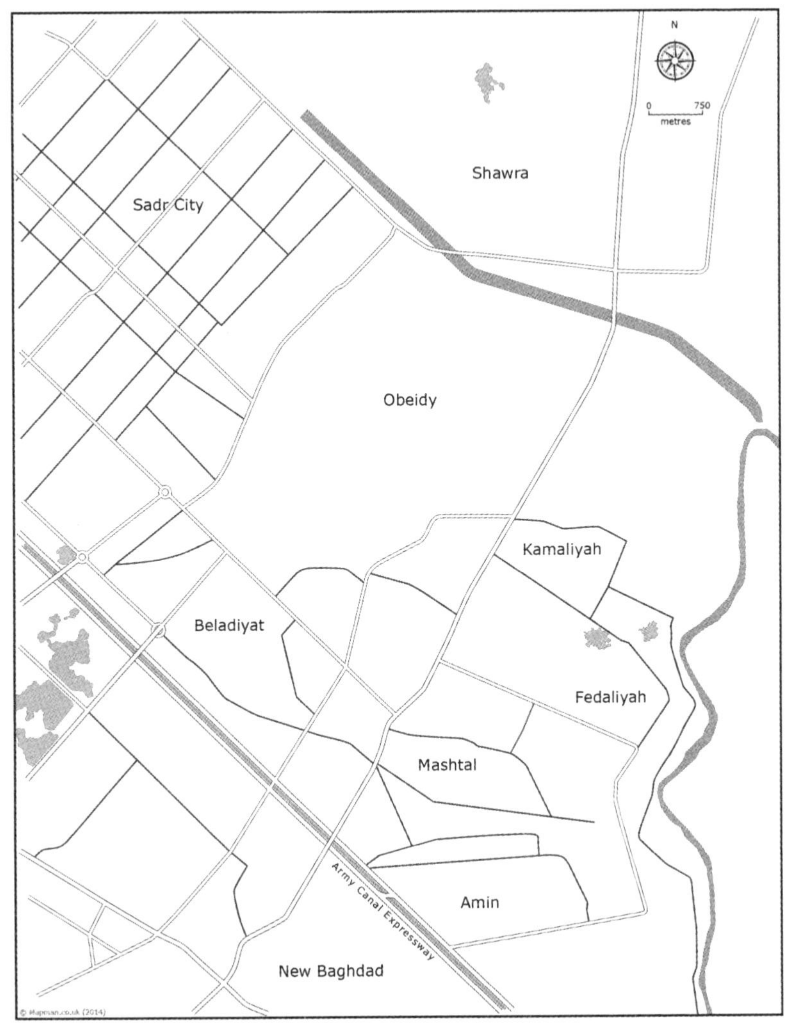

Figure 4.1: The *Hayys* of Tisa Nissan & Surrounding Areas

been contained almost entirely within a small area of the modern-day Rusafa political district. Confined largely to the eastern bank of the Tigris River (stretching from Adhamiyyah in the north to the base of the Karrada Peninsula in the south), and limited from eastward expansion by the earthen flood-protection wall known as the bund, the city was a small fraction of its present size.[3]

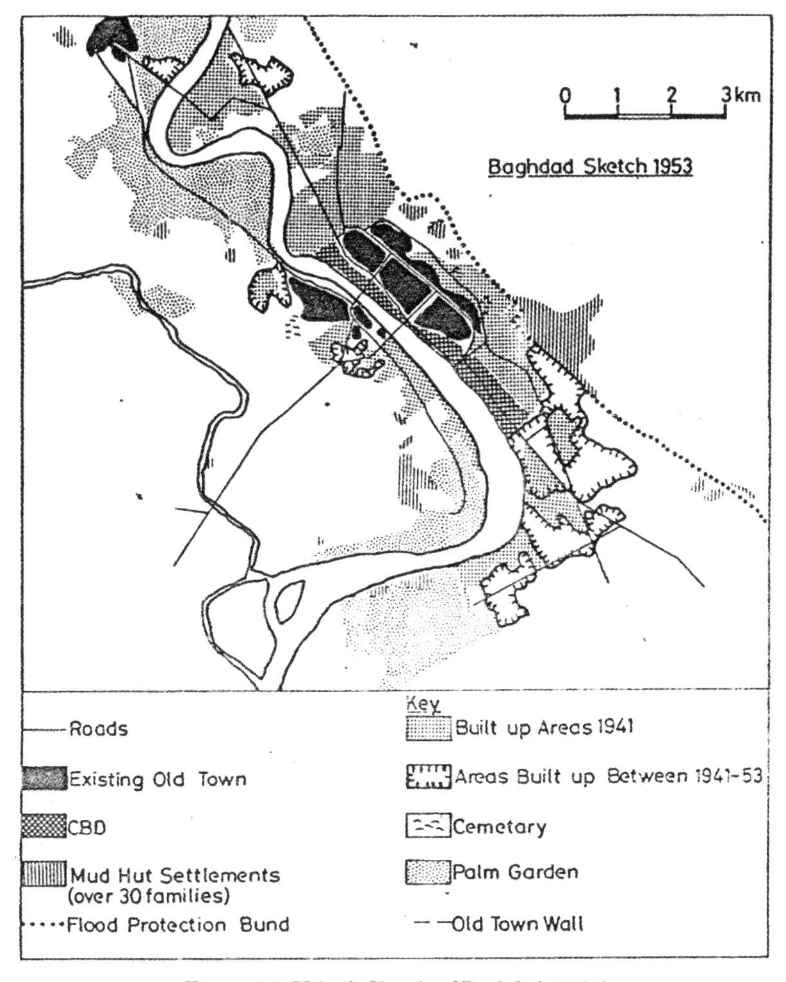

Figure 4.2: Hilmi's Sketch of Baghdad, 1953[4]

The replacement of the bund with the Army Canal, and the relocation to Revolution City of the hundreds of thousands of underclass Shi'a slum dwellers that had erected their *sarifas* just beyond it, opened a broad expanse of land to urban development. Having swelled numerically in preceding decades, quadrupling from 200,000 residents in 1922 to approximately 800,000 at the time of the 1958 coup, Baghdad would now grow geographically as well.[5] What was formerly a cramped, antiquated city began its physical transformation into the sprawling, concrete metropolis of some six million that it was at the time of the 2003 invasion.

The Fundamentals of Planned Development

Whereas initial waves of migration from Iraq's Deep South progressed effectively unregulated through the 1940s and 1950s, with migrant groups establishing settlement clusters on the city's ungoverned margins, Qasim's reforms ushered in a new era of government-directed development. In an effort to bring order to Baghdad's expansion, civil and social engineers sought to proactively manage growth and give structure to the city's modernization. To that end, a schema was developed that blended traditional modes of urban social organization with modern political imperatives, creating what amounted to a reinterpretation of the traditional *mahallah*. The city's growth would thereafter be delineated through the creation of new, identity-based settlement clusters. Yet, in a break from the traditional past, the tribal and religious distinctions that had defined the inward-looking enclaves of Ottoman Baghdad were largely replaced by professional associations and other modern client-groups of the state.[6]

The manner in which the *mahallah* framework was adapted reflected both the self-consciously progressive, transformative ideals dominant within the upper echelons of Iraqi society, as well as the growing ambitions of the Iraqi state. To the former, prevailing intellectual currents within educated society during the mid twentieth century espoused the urgent necessity of transforming Iraqi society from its antiquated, divided past into a modern, cohesive future. The Ba'th Party's rhetoric, for example, concerning the need to create a "new Iraqi man" who could transcend the parochial, regressive forces of tribe and sect, was wholly in keeping with the thinking of the era.[7] The use of an occupation-based framework of social organization to structure Baghdad's growth was thus a way to further the unification of Iraqi society and facilitate the development of a modern Iraqi identity.

With respect to the agenda of the state, the reinterpreted *mahallah* advanced official interests in a more practical way as well. Beginning with Prime Minister Qasim, and continuing through the rule of Saddam Hussein, the Iraqi state sought to radically expand its control over Iraqi society. The state—the size and strength of which grew enormously as oil revenues surged—positioned itself as architect and engineer of social change. Concurrently, the regimes that ruled Iraq after the toppling of the monarchy also grew increasingly totalitarian, culminating in the reign of the Ba'th. With the state thus attempting to dominate society as well as refashion it, government resources were deployed not merely to modernize Baghdad, but also to do so in a manner that reinforced the power of the ruling regime. The distribution (and, conversely, the confiscation) of land within the capital was a way for a regime to consolidate its power, as the loyalty of particular client groups could be cultivated in a manner that simultaneously reaffirmed their dependency.

Through the 1960s and 1970s, eastern Baghdad's development progressed via government-directed construction that featured the allocation of land to favored groups. Present-day Tisa Nissan, like similar

Figure 4.3: Gulick's Sketch of Baghdad's Development, 1965[8]

spaces elsewhere on the city's expanding periphery, was divided and allocated to groups of soldiers, teachers, engineers, municipal workers, doctors, laborers, and factory workers, whereupon residential neighborhoods were founded that blended Baghdadis of various sects, religions, and ethnicities.

In the area between where the bund had been situated and where the Army Canal was dug to replace it, the city's middle class core was expanded outward to the canal's inner edge.[9] Zones of residential and commercial development thus extended Rusafa further eastward, and to the southeast, middle class neighborhoods such as Officer City were established. The commercial hub of Baghdad al-Jadeeda, meaning "New Baghdad," was also erected near the far southeastern corner of the city. New Baghdad was to be the area's primary economic engine, containing a mixture of commerce, light industry, and sizable grids of housing for middle to working class families.

In addition to the extension of Baghdad's core, there was also a major initiative to expand the city beyond the Army Canal.[10] Revolution City was the largest and most ambitious element of this campaign (and one that eschewed the progressive-minded framework that sought to break down the divisions of the past, preferring instead to ghettoize the bulk of the Shi'a underclass), but territory between its southeastern boundary and the Diyala River was targeted for urbanization of a more affluent, integrated variety. Amin, for example, was established during the 1960s as an extension of the working class housing developments and commercial districts of New Baghdad. Moving up the socio-economic scale, Mashtal was also founded as an enclave for middle class families of both sects. Further development along the Army Canal's outer edge then saw the space between Amin and Revolution City (which would become the *hayy* of Beladiyat) allocated to professional groups from the Baghdad city government and various state ministries. By the early 1970s, therefore, the area was progressing toward the sort of integrated, cosmopolitan space that had been envisaged by its creators. Salaried, middle to working class Muslim families of both sects lived side-by-side in southeastern Baghdad's new *mahallahs*, while the area's promising early development attracted a sizable Christian community as well.

The Shifting Terrain of Southeastern Baghdad

Despite efforts to proactively manage Baghdad's expansion during the second half of the twentieth century, numerous forces worked to influence development in ways both unanticipated and undesired by the government. In southeastern Baghdad, the most important of these was the continued escalation of mass migration by impoverished Shi'a families. Although the rapidly-swelling ghetto of Revolution City became the epicenter of migrant settlement, migration flows were by no means confined therein. On the one hand, new arrivals from the Deep South continued to erect *sarifas* on open terrain across eastern Baghdad through the 1960s, despite the government's ban on their construction.[11] On the other hand, migrant families poured into neighborhoods such as Kamaliyah on the city's expanding margins, tilting the demographic composition of poorer, working-class neighborhoods and giving them an expanding *shurughi* profile.

As the neighborhoods of eastern Baghdad developed further through the 1970s, and underclass Shi'a migration flows surged yet again, tensions developed between the residents of middle class, mixed-sect neighborhoods within Beladiyat and Mashtal and the rising tide of impoverished Shi'a on their borders.[12] On one side of the dispute, the residents of eastern Baghdad's planned neighborhoods considered themselves an integral part of the capital's dynamic and growing urban core. The continued influx of underclass Shia migrants into their immediate environs was thus resented as a negative influence on local development. On the other side, resentment grew in kind among the migrants, over their inferior quality of life and the scorn that was heaped upon them. Those residents in the poorer areas of Kamaliyah, like those who settled in growing numbers in areas of Amin and Obeidy, became keenly aware of their poverty in comparison with nearby middle class Baghdadis, and also fully conscious of the prejudices harbored against them.

At the root of simmering tensions in eastern Baghdad was the continued inability of the Iraqi government, even at the peak of its oil-fueled powers during the late 1970s, to muster the necessary combination of focused attention and administrative capacity to see through the development process and effectively manage the repercussions of rural-to-urban migration.[13] The main neighborhoods within Mashtal, Beladiyat, and Amin, like those of Baghdad al-Jadeeda on the inner bank of the Army Canal, had been intended to facilitate an eastward extension of the city's core. However, vital public infrastructure—including the power grid, paved roads, sewers, marketplaces, medical facilities, and schools—was never sufficiently developed to accommodate the growth that ensued. The nuclei of these *hayys* enjoyed fairly reliable infrastructure and essential services, but spaces in their immediate outskirts frequently did not. Furthermore, surges of migration undermined the efforts of social and civil engineers to perpetuate forward-looking middle and working class development in the *hayys* beyond the Army Canal. As impoverished, unskilled Shi'a migrants continued to press into eastern Baghdad, the canal instead came to replace the bund, serving as the dividing line where the core of Baghdad ended, and its underserviced, *shurughi*-dominated periphery began.

An array of grievances accumulated beyond the Army Canal, which intensified as the resources of the state declined sharply from the mid 1980s onwards. With electricity supplies growing increasingly unreliable, schools and medical centers decaying, and crime rates surging, a general consensus developed that the attentions of the government (excluding the ever-present security services) dropped sharply as one crossed the canal.[14]

To residents of more affluent neighborhoods within Beladiyat and Mashtal, this was understood, with significant bitterness, to be the result of the area having become home to high levels of poor Shi'a. As the government was forced to prioritize the recipients of its largesse, the *shurughi* profile of eastern Baghdad left it low on the regime's list.[15] To the area's Shi'a poor, who by the 1980s appear to have constituted a solid majority in Tisa Nissan beyond the Army Canal, eastern Baghdad's neglect was likewise understood to stem from its strong *shurughi* profile.[16] Yet, while the migrants and their descendants had come to the same diagnosis as their more affluent counterparts regarding the root cause of their unsatisfactory material situation, a separate set of emotions followed. For the Shi'a underclass, eastern Baghdad's decay marked yet another chapter in their long-running ill treatment at the hands of the government, and the persistence of social prejudices in Iraqi society.

Economic and infrastructural collapse during the sanctions era further exacerbated social divisions. It also made the rise of Mohammed Mohammed Sadiq al-Sadr all the more polarizing.[17] Sadr's fiery rhetoric of class warfare and underclass empowerment was met with extraordinary enthusiasm among the hundreds of thousands of poor Shi'a who inhabited areas such as Kamaliyah, Amin, Obeidy, and Fedaliyah, while the middle class Shi'a loyal to Ali al-Sistani in Beladiyat and Mashtal were left feeling besieged. The opponents of the White Lion viewed his militant populism, his embrace of rough tribal ethics, his promulgation of low, folk religion, and his celebration of the inherent virtues of Iraqi society's lowest rungs, not merely as a symptom of the broader societal collapse underway during the 1990s, but also as a driver thereof. Critics thus readily situated Sadr's alleged debasement of Shi'ism in the context of the implosion of the economy, the fall of the middle class, the rise of pseudo-tribal violence, and the degeneration of Baghdad itself.

The Fall of Saddam and the Rise of the Mehdi Army

By the time of the 2003 invasion, southeastern Baghdad was structurally decrepit and socially divided. The legacy of centrally-planned growth in the spirit of the *mahallah* remained evident, as the area was home to a collection of distinct development clusters, yet it was not the landscape envisioned by its original architects. Neighborhoods adjacent to the Army Canal offered reminders of the middle class, blended society that the Iraqi state had aspired to create, housing families of educated professionals of both Muslim sects and a sizable Christian community.[18] Local residents' financial position had been degraded to the point that their claim to middle class status was more cultural than economic, however, while the less affluent neighborhoods further toward the city's periphery dominated the terrain. The further reaches of modern-day Tisa Nissan were home to tens of thousands of mostly poor to working class families, a majority of whom were Shi'a that traced their roots in the capital to the migrations of previous decades, and material conditions were, on the whole, deplorable.[19]

The turmoil that followed the 2003 invasion brought waves of violent, destabilizing change that caused a sweeping demographic shift. Multiple, overlapping trends in violence (beginning with the persecution of former Ba'thists, followed by the growth of a booming kidnapping-for-ransom trade, and ultimately the rise of the Mehdi Army), carried the daily threat of violence into the heart of Tisa Nissan's various neighborhoods. The resulting insecurity, combined with the accelerated infrastructural collapse that followed the city government's dissolution, generated an array of responses.[20]

Demographic Change and the Advance of the Mehdi Army

In established middle class and minority neighborhoods in *hayys* like Beladiyat and Mashtal, residents attempted to close ranks and isolate themselves from the surging tide of violence. Nonetheless, rising instability and the precipitous decline in overall quality of life prompted population outflows. Many with the financial means and requisite connections to escape Iraq fled abroad in growing numbers, causing a gradual hollowing-out of the neighborhoods they left behind.

The contraction and flight of middle class and minority groups was accompanied by population inflows, which saw Baghdad's periphery encroach with growing force. Taking advantage of the collapse of law and order, poor Shi'a families moved out of nearby Sadr City into areas of Beladiyat and Obeidy, laying claim to vacant or abandoned real estate.[21] Similarly, open terrain within Shawra wa Umm Jidr and Kamaliyah was claimed by new arrivals from Diyala Province, Sadr City, and other areas further afield, leading to a major boom in unlicensed and unregulated home construction. As the great majority of migrants to the area were Shi'a of modest means, the *hayys* beyond the Army Canal thus saw their demographic profile tilt further toward the core constituency of the Sadrist movement, facilitating the Mehdi Army's growth and expansion through the area.

The transformation of Tisa Nissan broadened in scope and accelerated in speed with the escalation of sectarian violence. As the Mehdi Army spread outwards from Sadr City and expanded across eastern Baghdad from late 2004 onwards, the militia capitalized on the demographic strength of the Shi'a underclass to make strong inroads into the district. Despite faring badly in clashes with the US-led Coalition in and around Sadr City, its growth continued to accelerate. In poorer areas with large Shi'a contingents, the militia recruited local allies and thereby embedded itself at street-level. By 2005, the Mehdi Army had firmly established its position across much of Tisa Nissan beyond the Army Canal, where it went about eliminating resident Sunnis, intimidating Shi'a opponents within the area's few middle class neighborhoods, and furthering the district's demographic realignment.

In areas closer to the Army Canal, where the demographic position of the Shi'a underclass was weaker, the expansion of the Mehdi Army met with heightened resistance from both Sunni militants and resident middle class communities. Amin, for example, which was home to a strong working class Sunni population, became a flashpoint of sectarian violence. The Mehdi Army thus engaged in a protracted, brutal struggle with Sunni militants that persisted into 2007 (which, in keeping with the dynamics of the sectarian war, saw the two sides inflict devastating punishment upon local civilians). Areas of Beladiyat and Mashtal also offered resistance to the Mehdi Army's advances, as their core neighborhoods of middle class and minority families were broadly opposed to the Sadrist agenda. By capitalizing on the steadily weakening position of their local foes, as well as the encroachment of underclass Shi'a families from Sadr City (a process in which the militia played an active role), the Mehdi Army was ultimately able to assert control over the two *hayys*.[22] Sunni families were expelled *en masse*, minority groups were compelled to flee abroad or retreat into fortified enclaves, while the remnants of the

Figure 4.4: Areas of Post-Saddam Settlement in Tisa Nissan

local Shi'a middle class continued, with limited success, to attempt to isolate themselves from the rising tide of violence.

Small pockets of middle class Shi'a and minority settlement endured beyond the Army Canal but, by the end of the sectarian war, the area had been broadly cleansed of its Sunni population and reshaped as the domain of the Shi'a underclass. The Sadrist movement was the political party of choice, while the Mehdi Army was the dominant street-level force. Tisa Nissan, previously a diverse, multi-religious area of Baghdad, now appeared relatively homogeneous—and sat firmly under militia control.

Instability persisted, as sweeping population transfers and associated violence had left much of the area in disarray. Not only had thousands of former residents been killed, forcibly displaced, or compelled to flee, but thousands of new Shi'a families had arrived as well. In addition to the speculative inflows of Shi'a families from Sadr City, Diyala Province, and elsewhere, thousands more had been forcibly displaced from their homes in Sunni-conquered areas of western Baghdad and thereafter sought refuge in Mehdi Army-held Tisa Nissan.[23] The battered remnants of the district's pre-2003 communities thus existed in and among a mixture of opportunistic migrants and forcibly displaced families, and the resulting chaos was manifested in the disastrous state of critical infrastructure. Electricity was only sporadically available (despite the presence of one of Baghdad's largest power installations along the Diyala River in Amin), water and sewage systems had collapsed to the point that cholera became a serious concern, and the city government exercised a negligible influence over broad swathes of the district.[24]

Tisa Nissan and the Surge

At the start of the Surge in early 2007, the *hayys* of Tisa Nissan beyond the Army Canal presented a formidable challenge to American forces, who were centered in Forward Operating Base Loyalty in the *hayy* of Beladiyat. The Mehdi Army's local affiliates were the dominant street-level force from one neighborhood to the next, the militia maintained a strong network of operational nodes (to include particularly important facilities in the Sab'a Nissan neighborhood of Beladiyat and in the *hayy* of Fedaliyah), and local politicians were thought to be tied closely to the Sadrist movement and the Mehdi Army.[25] In addition to facing an organized, armed opposition, Coalition Forces were confronted by a civilian population that ranged, for the most part, from passively skeptical to actively hostile. For, while the area's remaining middle class and minority enclaves welcomed the expulsion of the militia and the restoration of law and order, the underclass Shi'a majority was overwhelmingly Sadrist in its sympathies.

As such, while much of Baghdad experienced a remarkable turnaround as the Americans and their Iraqi counterparts fought to reclaim the city during 2007, with levels of violence plummeting and a sense of normalcy beginning to return to the city's streets, Tisa Nissan stagnated.[26] In central areas of Beladiyat and Mashtal, where key elements of the populace cautiously welcomed the American-led offensive, the militia was dislodged and momentum was generated toward the restoration of order. Nearer to the city's periphery, in areas populated by underclass Shi'a and dominated by the Mehdi Army, the Surge's first year met with sustained resistance. American and Iraqi units succeeded in pushing the militia's rank and file off the streets and onto the defensive in many neighborhoods, yet the terrain remained fiercely contested. Indeed, as the Surge's second year began, the Mehdi Army still appeared well entrenched beyond the Army Canal, the civilian populace remained distant from American forces, and efforts toward the improvement of governance and economic activity had met with minimal results—giving the *hayys* beyond the canal a citywide reputation for intractability and lethal dysfunction. The district's troubles were understood by American forces to come from the confluence of numerous factors, including:

Security	*Development*	*Governance*
– The organized efforts of Mehdi Army fighters to resist the advances of the Surge. – The attacks of Special Group cells on American and Iraqi units. – The localized, neighborhood-level influence of strongmen and gang-style networks affiliated with the Mehdi Army.	– The decrepit state of critical infrastructure. – "Brain drain" and the flight of the educated middle class. – The threat of violence against those engaged in Coalition-sponsored development initiatives. – A strong legacy of government control over economic activity, and resulting	– The Sadrist sympathies of prominent local politicians, and their opposition to the political objectives of the Surge. – Widespread practice of localism and patronage among elected leaders, and an absence of district-wide cooperation toward a "common good."

– Negative attitudes toward Coalition Forces among local civilians, complicating efforts to mobilize popular support for counterinsurgency operations.	systemic paralysis following the government's collapse in 2003.[27]	– The Baghdad municipality's lack of administrative capacity in the district, and its low prioritization of Tisa Nissan.

Three distinct yet interconnected groups were held responsible for the majority of violence against American and Iraqi forces. The first was the Mehdi Army, which continued to launch sporadic attacks against American and Iraqi units in Tisa Nissan, despite Muqtada al-Sadr's August 2007 ceasefire.[28] The Americans and their Iraqi counterparts were pursuing a mixed strategy to manage this group, ranging from efforts to capture or kill prominent militants, to overtures to those deemed potentially reconcilable. Simultaneously, attempts were being made to undermine popular support for the Mehdi Army by demonstrating the ability of Coalition Forces (and, by extension, the Iraqi government) to meet the day-to-day needs of the populace. Programs to spur economic development, re-establish the rule of law, revive civil society, and build the capacity of district- and neighborhood-level institutions of governance were thus part of a broader, non-violent offensive to subvert the militia's position.

The second major threat came from small cells of Shi'a militants who were armed, trained, and funded by the Iranian government. These groups were thought to operate independently of the Mehdi Army's leadership structure, yet their members were commonly known to have either past affiliations with, or continuing ties to, the militia. They were understood not to have substantive local connections in the neighborhoods of Tisa Nissan, but rather to operate locally as a result of several favorable aspects of the terrain.[29] Referred to collectively as "the Special Groups," their ability to execute mortar and rocket attacks on American bases, and to strike American and Iraqi convoys with Explosively Formed Projectiles (a type of roadside bomb that utilized shaped-charge technology to penetrate armor plating) made them the most lethal threat in Tisa Nissan.[30] The threat to American and Iraqi units posed by the Special Groups was addressed militarily: locally-stationed American units patrolled the district on a daily basis, and independent Special Operations Forces were specifically dedicated to their pursuit.[31]

The third source of violence came from armed groups of varying types that were local to the neighborhoods of Tisa Nissan. From the Marsh Arab tribes of Fedaliyah, to the mafia-style criminal networks of Kamaliyah, and the gangs of young men in their teens and twenties found on the streets of Amin, locally-rooted groups with motivations having little to do with national-level politics were instrumental in shaping conditions.[32] Many of these groups maintained both affinity for the ideals of the Sadrist movement and operational affiliation with the Mehdi Army, which complicated efforts to disaggregate "political" violence from "local" violence. American and Iraqi forces were pursuing a mixed strategy to manage these groups similar to that deployed against the Mehdi Army's cadre, combining the targeting of notorious militants with attempts to induce those deemed potentially reconcilable to mitigate their disruptive actions.

While important progress had been made on each of these fronts during the course of the Surge's first year, Tisa Nissan remained unstable and deeply frustrating to American personnel. The Mehdi Army had been forced to cede its claims to core areas of Beladiyat and Mashtal, and it was no longer able to operate with the impunity it had previously enjoyed across the area further toward the city's periphery, yet Coalition Forces were struggling to build on their initial advances. Relations with the district's elected leadership, for example, were deeply troubled. American commanders regarded prominent political leaders with skepticism and suspicion (sentiments that were returned in kind), as their corruption, Sadrist sympathies, and suspected militia ties engendered widespread pessimism over the utility of political engagement.[33]

Attempts to engage civil society and rally popular support from the district's residents, on the other hand, had achieved only the most modest of results. Encouragingly, it was evident that Tisa Nissan's resident population was not coherently united behind the militia, and that the district, as a whole, was not an "insurgent stronghold." Indeed, it was broadly understood among locally-stationed American and Iraqi personnel that the militia's past abuses had generated significant popular displeasure, and that the restoration of order and economic development were widely desired.[34] Nonetheless, efforts to capitalize upon popular discontent languished, and American personnel made frequent, exasperated reference to what they saw as a crippling lack of initiative and an absence of public trust.

March Madness: Challenges and Opportunities

As discussed in the introduction, the final days of March 2008 witnessed an explosion of violence in areas of eastern Baghdad beyond the Army Canal. Not only were rockets launched across the Tigris River toward the Green Zone, but the two Forward Operating Bases maintained by the Americans in Tisa Nissan and the network of smaller patrol bases that had been established throughout the district also came under heavy fire.[35]

As violence subsided, conditions in Tisa Nissan changed dramatically yet again. First, the fighting forced local political leaders and members of the Iraqi Security Forces to display their loyalties.[36] The early successes of Shi'a militants, including the televised surrender of Iraqi Security Forces in Sadr City, the overrunning and abandonment of checkpoints across Tisa Nissan, and the kidnapping of the chief Iraqi spokesman for security efforts in Baghdad, encouraged many to betray their pro-militia sympathies. In the aftermath of the revolt's collapse, therefore, American personnel had a clarified understanding of the district's leadership. The Iraqi Security Forces were thereafter purged of militia loyalists, and the Iraqi National Police, in particular, emerged as a far more effective and reliable force.

Second, the successful counter-attack launched by American and Iraqi forces prompted the flight of prominent militants. The subsequent absence of these individuals degraded the offensive capabilities of the Shi'a insurgency. Sporadic and occasionally intense violence would continue through the course of 2008, associated most prominently with ongoing operations in nearby Sadr City and the counter-offensives of Special Group cells such as the Hizbullah Brigades and Asaib Ahl al-Haqq. Yet overall levels of violence fell significantly.

Third, the aftermath of the Mehdi Army's failed offensive witnessed a recalculation of interests by influential local actors in Tisa Nissan. The declining fortunes of the Mehdi Army and the rising profile of the Iraqi government during the spring and summer of 2008 prompted individuals and groups that had previously aligned themselves with the militia to change course, making areas that had previously been extremely hostile far less so—in some cases, seemingly overnight.

Lastly, beyond changes within the district itself, the operational posture of American forces shifted in important ways. In an effort to capitalize on the Mehdi Army's collapsing position, the spring and summer of 2008 saw major district-wide initiatives to confiscate weapons, restore the presence of the Iraqi government, and re-establish law and order that brought American personnel and their Iraqi counterparts into daily contact with local residents. This was part of a coordinated national campaign against the Mehdi Army and associated Shi'a militants that involved methodical pushes into the Sadrist movement's core sanctuaries, and it granted near-daily access to the neighborhoods of Tisa Nissan (and previously unavailable chances to speak with its residents in an increasingly peaceful environment). As such, the remainder of 2008 offered unprecedented opportunities to examine the *hayys* of one of Baghdad's most troubled areas at ground level, enabling investigation of the localized issues beneath the Mehdi Army's changing fortunes in the midst of its precipitous collapse.

Area Study: Structural Overview

Each of the following three chapters examines a pair of *hayys* from Tisa Nissan beyond the Army Canal. The chapters begin with observations on conditions within the *hayys* and how they were perceived by American forces on the eve of March Madness, along with commentary on the key local issues at that time. Discussion follows the changes that occurred in each *hayy* as a result of March Madness, with an emphasis on how these changes generated insights into the dynamics of the militia's campaign. The core of each chapter then traces the overall trajectory of the Mehdi Army's rise and fall, detailing the localized social forces that shaped its successes and failures.

5

BELADIYAT AND MASHTAL

COMMUNITIES UNDER SIEGE

Beladiyat and Mashtal: A Year into the Surge

In the early months of 2008, core areas of Beladiyat and Mashtal were in the midst of a fragile yet marked trend toward improved levels of security and stability.[1] Central neighborhoods of both *hayys* appeared to have moved beyond the worst of the violence of previous years and were viewed—by Americans and Iraqis alike—as the areas in Tisa Nissan beyond the Army Canal where the Surge had yielded its greatest gains. The local institutions of the Iraqi government were functioning with relative coherence in comparison to neighboring *hayys* to the north and east, attacks against Americans and their counterparts in the Iraqi Security Forces were less common than elsewhere beyond the canal, the Mehdi Army had been driven from the streets, and core segments of the resident population appeared cautiously supportive of, and encouraged by, the progress that had been made. Thus, while Beladiyat and Mashtal continued to face an array of problems and the margins of both *hayys* remained dangerous, they stood out as success stories in an area of Baghdad where success had proven difficult to achieve.[2]

Aspects of the *hayys'* histories, and of local demographics, had been instrumental in the progress made by American and Iraqi forces. The main neighborhoods of Beladiyat and Mashtal had been established as the domain of Baghdad's middle class, housing educated professionals of both

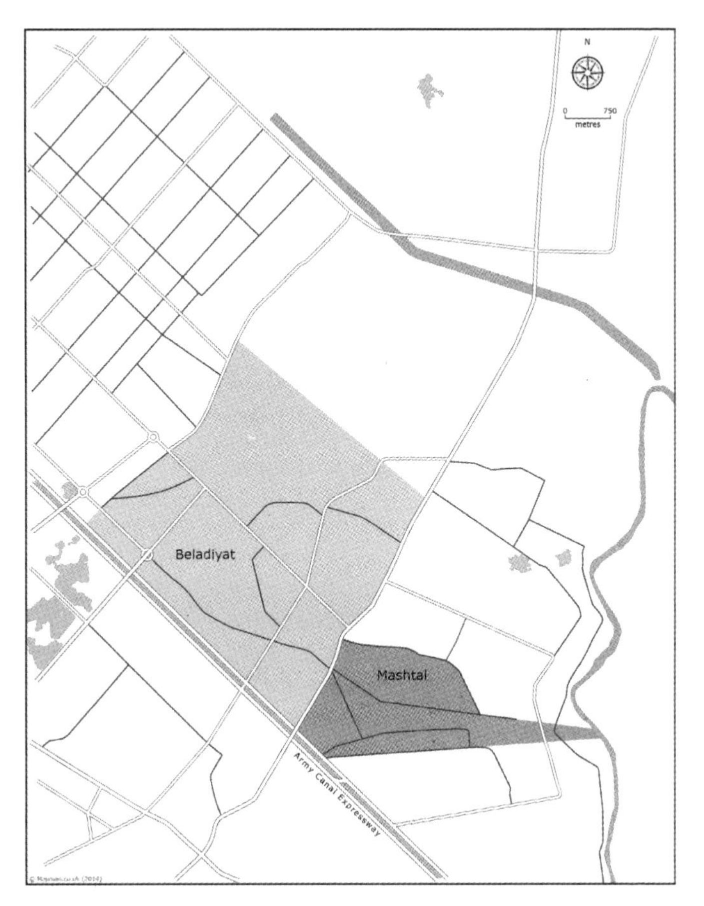

Figure 5.1: *Hayy* Boundaries of Beladiyat and Mashtal

Muslim sects, a sizable Christian minority, and Baghdad's largest concentration of Palestinians. As such, the Mehdi Army had found limited local support, and its advance across the *hayys* had proceeded largely by forcible conquest that featured the methodical eradication of its opponents and sweeping population inflows (into Beladiyat in particular).

While the militia claimed the entirety of both *hayys* within its sphere of influence at the start of the Surge, pockets of localized opposition had remained. When American and Iraqi forces pushed into Beladiyat and Mashtal, offering to re-establish the rule of law, elements of the populace provided support. The militia, facing the redoubled efforts of

American and Iraqi forces, and unable to call upon the support of the two *hayys'* core communities, had been driven back to the margins of Beladiyat and Mashtal. Their main neighborhoods, which had been among the last areas of southeastern Baghdad seized by the militia, were thus among the first that it lost during 2007.

Although significant progress had been achieved during the Surge's initial year and a sense of calm was returning to the *hayys'* main neighborhoods, it was apparent that Mashtal and Beladiyat had been deeply affected by the turbulence and bloodshed of the post-Saddam era. The killing or expulsion of those with ties to the fallen regime, the sectarian cleansing of the vast majority of both *hayys'* Sunni Iraqi populations, the persecution of Christian and Palestinian minorities, the influx of thousands of new Shi'a residents (the majority of whom were of the underclass), and the violent rise of the Mehdi Army had combined to transform the terrain. The neighborhoods of Beladiyat and Mashtal, which had been created with a view to forging a cosmopolitan, forward-looking Iraqi identity, had been Balkanized along lines of faith and class. Furthermore, the physical integrity of both *hayys* had also been degraded, as violence, administrative collapse, and a surge of unregulated construction had pushed already-brittle water, electricity, and sewerage systems beyond the breaking point.

The core neighborhoods of Beladiyat and Mashtal, which had struggled for decades to maintain their middle class identities, had been broken apart and overrun to the point that, even after the threat of the Mehdi Army appeared to have been checked, their recovery remained uncertain. The initial year of the Surge saw a major reduction in violence and encouraging progress toward the revitalization of governance and economic activity, but an array of localized tensions persisted—the most notable of which was between the remnants of pre-invasion middle class and minority communities and the underclass Shi'a families that had moved into the area.[3] With the former viewing the latter as having been intimately complicit in the violence, instability, and infrastructural collapse that had devastated the area, and further hoping to reverse the area's demographic drift into eastern Baghdad's underclass Shi'a periphery, class-based tensions simmered. Although the militia had lost significant ground in the two *hayys*, class rivalry—which had deep roots in the city's history and was enshrined at the heart of Sadrist ideology—threatened not only to hinder the consolidation of progress, but also, potentially, to enable the militia to revive its campaign in the future.

Key Issues in Beladiyat and Mashtal

The post-Saddam era had brought a series of sweeping, transformative changes to the two *hayys*, the most influential and controversial of which had been an influx of *hawasim* and the violent rise of the Mehdi Army. Yet, while it was an article of faith among the *hayys'* middle class and minority communities that the encroachment of the *hawasim* and the rise of the militia had progressed hand-in-hand, the precise nature of the relationship between the Mehdi Army and the *hayys'* new arrivals remained unclear.[4]

To what extent had Beladiyat and Mashtal been venues of popular class warfare? Had the *hayys'* demographic transformation been orchestrated as part of a deliberate campaign of urban conquest, in which the Mehdi Army had mobilized the Sadrist underclass to envelop the most prominent outposts of middle class development beyond the Army Canal? Alternatively, had population flows progressed spontaneously into the two *hayys*, whereupon the new settlements of Sadrist Shi'a had served as a fifth column of sorts, facilitating the militia's inward incursion? Either way, with an eye to the future, might the continued presence of class tensions enable the Mehdi Army to revive its position in Beladiyat and Mashtal?

March Madness in Beladiyat and Mashtal

March Madness witnessed a fleeting surge of violence in Beladiyat and Mashtal. Both *hayys* were home to hotspots of activity, as western areas of Beladiyat were used as launch sites for rocket attacks on the Green Zone and as hideouts for militants, while eastern Mashtal witnessed violence spill northwards from nearby Amin. Nonetheless, patterns of violence tracked well with American forces' understanding of the two *hayys* and the position of Shi'a militants therein. Following the restoration of local order after the revolt's collapse, the attentions of both counterinsurgent forces, as well as those of the *hayys'* resident populations, reverted back to the localized, inter-communal concerns discussed above.

The momentum generated by American and Iraqi forces brought important changes to Beladiyat and Mashtal. American units consolidated their gains by engaging local leadership and establishing a strong street-level presence, and both Iraqi Security Forces and the local elements of the Iraqi government emerged from the clashes with rejuvenated vigor. Improved security and renewed economic activity facilitated interaction between American personnel and local residents, and the diminished threat of retributive violence by militants also made such interactions increasingly safe. Opportunities for Americans to interact with local leaders and ordinary residents proliferated, leading to an array of insights into local conditions.[5]

The Subsoil of Conflict in Beladiyat and Mashtal

The social tensions that underpinned conflict in Beladiyat and Mashtal during the post-Saddam era had deep historical roots. Waves of migration had been crashing upon eastern Baghdad since the 1940s, causing an array of social, economic, and cultural stresses. Despite ambitious urban development initiatives, and enormous state expenditures on an array of welfare services and subsidies, the capital's eastern periphery had been overwhelmed. The Army Canal had thus come to replace the bund as a dividing line between center and periphery on the urban landscape, and an array of class-based grievances emerged that recalled the social frictions of the 1940s and 1950s.

This social divide pitted the city's self-consciously cosmopolitan core against its underclass Shi'a margins, as the denizens of middle class neighborhoods like those in Beladiyat and Mashtal looked on apprehensively at the "growing and rather menacing hordes" of urban poor on their borders.[6] While these tensions were notably lopsided at the outset, with the umbrage of the middle classes outweighing that of their poorer counterparts (who, as noted earlier, found the conditions on Baghdad's margins to be far better than life in the villages and towns they had fled), this dynamic shifted in time.[7] With broad segments of Baghdad's periphery becoming underclass slums, and with socio-cultural prejudices against the *shurughis* persisting through the latter decades of the twentieth century, a reciprocal enmity coalesced among Baghdad's Shi'a poor that was ultimately enshrined at the heart of the Sadrist ideology.

The Foundation of Beladiyat and Mashtal

The position of Beladiyat and Mashtal on the dividing line between Baghdad's middle class core and its impoverished periphery, and the *hayys'* status as focal points for associated class-based tensions, have been discussed in broad terms. However, an understanding of the dynamics and effects of the Mehdi Army's campaign requires a more detailed picture of the *hayys*.

The modern-day administrative *hayys* of Beladiyat and Mashtal are named after the central neighborhoods located within each, which are referred to hereafter as Beladiyat Proper and Central Mashtal.[8] As discussed above, urban planners delineated both during the 1960s, when southeastern Baghdad's expansion was directed along professional and class-based lines. Central Mashtal was founded as a quasi-suburban settlement for middle class families, some of whom had their roots in the Bab Sheikh area of modern-day Rusafa, and it developed through the 1960s as a mixed-sect neighborhood with a sizable Sunni constituency.[9] Beladiyat Proper, on the other hand, was first set aside for workers in the Baghdad municipality, growing steadily through the 1960s and into the 1970s as groups of employees from various government ministries were settled there along with their families.[10] The two- to three-storey homes of these principally residential neighborhoods were of a high standard and local infrastructure was of good quality—particularly compared to contemporary efforts in Amin, Obeidy, and Kamaliyah—and they bore a closer resemblance to neighborhoods below the Army Canal than to those further out toward the city's margins.

The open land in Central Mashtal and Beladiyat Proper's immediate vicinity was likewise developed in the image of urban planners' modernized, cosmopolitan reinterpretation of the *mahallah*. Mu'allimiin was founded in the mid 1960s for teachers and their families, while Old Habibiyyah grew along the border of Revolution City as a home for educated, middle class professionals of mixed sectarian backgrounds. The perceived success of these new neighborhoods attracted increasing numbers of new residents (including a large Christian community that both integrated into the area's main neighborhoods and secured its own dedicated enclave, called Tujar, near the intersection of the Army Canal and Highway 5). Central Mashtal, Mu'allemiin, Beladiyat Proper, and Old Habibiyyah each solidified their respective identities as part of central Baghdad's eastward expansion.

The oil boom of the 1970s brought further development, with infrastructural improvements to existing neighborhoods and the expansion of their residential grids, as well as the creation of entirely new neigh-

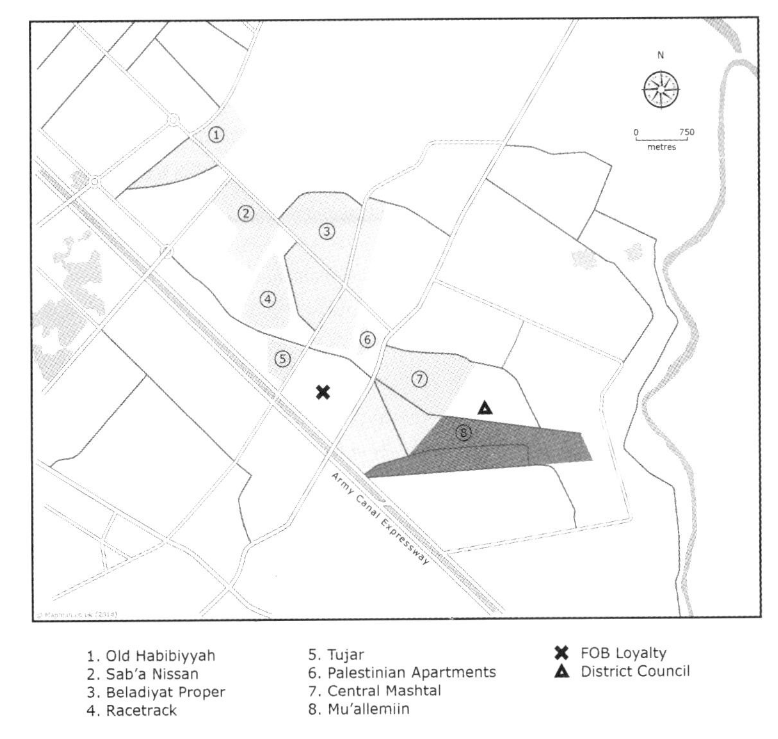

Figure 5.2: The Neighborhoods of Beladiyat and Mashtal

borhoods. Sab'a Nissan was founded to the west of Beladiyat Proper as an enclave for working class Ba'th Party functionaries, for example, while to Beladiyat Proper's southeast (adjacent to the regime's general security complex that would later be the site of FOB Loyalty) an apartment complex was erected into which many of Baghdad's resident Palestinian refugees were relocated.[11] Remaining open terrain was used by the government: the Imam air defence installation was built to the immediate north of Beladiyat Proper, facilities were established for the security services to the north of Mu'allemiin, and a racetrack was built off Beladiyat Proper's southwestern edge for the personal use of Saddam Hussein's family.[12]

The Fault Line between Center and Periphery

The explosive growth experienced in and around Beladiyat and Mashtal did not progress as envisaged by urban planners. Poor Shi'a families continued to migrate to Baghdad in growing numbers through the 1960s and 1970s, and broad areas of eastern Baghdad were overwhelmed by the influx of impoverished migrant families. The residents of Central Mashtal, Beladiyat Proper, and Mu'allemiin thus gradually came to realize that, instead of being the advance guard of the city center's eastward expansion via orderly, state-supported middle class growth, they were now bound within an area of the capital that was being ceded by the government to the city's booming Shi'a underclass.

However, accustomed to a middle class existence, the residents of Beladiyat and Mashtal dug in to defend their position in the city. A siege mentality took root, and when essential services began to contract, and water, sewerage, and electricity infrastructure fell into decay from the mid 1980s onwards, local tensions developed. Traditional social prejudices intermingled with practical grievances about the area's material decline, hardening the divide between eastern Baghdad's outposts of middle class development and the city's ever-growing peripheral slums.[13]

The hardships of the sanctions era intensified both urban decay and social tensions. Local schools and medical facilities atrophied, the salaried middle class saw the value of its savings and the purchasing power of its salaries plummet, and the *hayys'* financial claims to middle class status grew increasingly dubious. Yet, while sanctions may have reduced the economic distance between the underclass and the middle class, the socio-cultural divide between the *shurughis* and their "betters" in Iraqi society was broadened and deepened.[14]

The White Lion was thus able to draw upon the accumulated frustrations and resentments of the Shi'a underclass as it gained strength in the margins beyond Beladiyat and Mashtal. Sadr not only celebrated the virtue and authenticity of the *shurughis*, but also foretold their impending ascent to power and vengeance. To the downtrodden Shi'a poor who rallied to his cause, the White Lion was an empowering figure who provided inspiration during a decade of extraordinary hardship. Among the objects of his ire (most notably the Shi'a devotees of Ali al-Sistani, who were found in abundance in Beladiyat and Mashtal), the rise of the Sadrist movement was met with great concern. Wary of the demographic weight of the underclass, contemptuous of its socio-cultural norms, and fearful of its inward encroachment, the battle-lines between Baghdad's Shi'a underclass and the city's middle class core were drawn ever-more sharply, with Beladiyat and Mashtal on the frontline.

The Contest for Beladiyat and Mashtal

By the time of the 2003 invasion, the neighborhoods of Beladiyat and Mashtal had been battered and degraded by an array of social and economic stresses, yet their foundational identities as the domain of the middle class remained largely intact.[15] The destruction of the Ba'th regime and the collapse of law and order throughout Baghdad unleashed forces that proved considerably more damaging than those of previous years. Waves of violence swept over the *hayys*, beginning with the chaos that wracked Baghdad during the initial invasion, and continuing with the rise of kidnapping networks and criminal gangs during the months that followed.[16] As a host of lethal threats proliferated, the siege mentality that had settled upon local neighborhoods during previous years was intensified dramatically.

The Mehdi Army emerged as the most formidable of these threats. By networking through the underclass Shi'a communities of nearby *hayys* such as Kamaliyah, Fedaliyah, and Amin, and also by riding the surge of population movement that emanated from the southeastern boundary of Sadr City, the militia closed in upon Beladiyat and Mashtal. Having been weakened through the 1980s and 1990s, and then convulsed by the violence and instability that accompanied the fall of the Ba'th regime, the *hayys* were critically vulnerable. The Mehdi Army's subsequent conquest of Beladiyat and Mashtal, while occurring in the midst of the sectarian war and featuring brutal sectarian violence, was thus viewed, by both its architects and its victims alike, more as the climax of a decades-old struggle between center and periphery than a by-product of sectarian tensions among local residents—marking a decisive, and perhaps permanent, victory of the Shi'a underclass.[17]

The Opportunities of Instability and The Encroachment of the Mehdi Army

The Mehdi Army's advance upon Beladiyat and Mashtal began in the immediate wake of the 2003 invasion, with the ravaging of the Ba'thist enclave of Sab'a Nissan. By cleansing the neighborhood of prominent Ba'thists and claiming the small residential grid as its own, the militia established a vital foothold in the *hayy*. Located in close proximity to Sadr City, and situated in the midst of open terrain into which Sadrist

Shi'a began to migrate, the neighborhood became, in effect, a militia-founded colony. From this central location, where a prominent Sadrist university and cultural center was eventually established (and where a key militant node developed), the Mehdi Army projected power throughout the *hayy* and across the Army Canal.[18]

Having established itself in Sab'a Nissan, the Mehdi Army gradually expanded its profile across the western half of Beladiyat. In the northwestern quadrant of the *hayy*, underclass Shi'a emerged from the densely-packed slums of Sadr City to stake claims to open land. Moving through the Ba'th regime's now-abandoned air defence installation, they created a sprawling tangle of modern-day *sarifas*. In the southwestern corner of the *hayy*, a similar population surge occurred. Families pressed eastward out of Sadr City and ensconced themselves in the open areas to the southeast of Old Habibiyyah and Sab'a Nissan, and also on the site of the Hussein family's former racetrack. However, this land, which sat along the Army Canal in close proximity to the city center, was valuable real estate and so it also attracted a more prosperous class of settler. Joining the migrants from Sadr City were significantly wealthier families (many of whom were alleged to have profited either during the regime's decline

Figure 5.3: New Construction in Southwestern Beladiyat, 2008[19]

in the 1990s or in the immediate turmoil of its collapse in 2003) who erected large new homes of their own.[20] The area between Beladiyat's established neighborhoods and the Army Canal thus took on an incongruous feel, as the homes of the wealthy sat side-by-side with the shanties of the poor, crisscrossed by muddy, sewage-strewn pathways and connected by tangled webs of power lines.

While the Mehdi Army actively encouraged migration into Beladiyat, it does not appear that the militia-controlled population flows in any organized, coherent way. The Sab'a Nissan neighborhood seems to have been an exception, as it was thought to be home to a prominent Sadrist "realty office" charged with settling the movement's supporters into properties seized from those that the militia killed or forcibly displaced.[21] On the whole, however, migration into the open areas of the *hayy* appeared to have progressed spontaneously and haphazardly over a period of years. Migrant families from Sadr City, joined in certain areas by wealthier

Figure 5.4: New Construction areas in Beladiyat and Mashtal

counterparts (and, in time, by others fleeing the violence of the sectarian war), made their way into Beladiyat in a prevailing atmosphere of lawlessness and chaos. Upon arrival, they laid informal claim to empty pieces of land, erecting unlicensed homes and tapping into existing infrastructure as best they could.

Despite the apparently limited role of the Mehdi Army in orchestrating migration into the *hayy*, population flows, and the forces that they generated, were instrumental in the militia's advances. The parallel surges of Sadrist Shi'a along the northern and southern borders of Old Habibiyyah enveloped the neighborhood, further solidifying the militia's position in western Beladiyat. The Mehdi Army's subsequent ability to project power from its bases in Sadr City and Sab'a Nissan across areas of migrant *hawasim* settlement enabled it to claim western Beladiyat as its own, and press eastward to the edges of Beladiyat Proper and Tujar.[22]

Across Highway 5, the Mehdi Army's advance progressed in a similarly methodical fashion. Pressing northwards from Amin and southward from Fedaliyah, the militia gradually expanded its influence. Despite the efforts of Mu'allemiin's residents to erect defensive barriers and isolate themselves, a rising tide of violence enveloped the neighborhood—in part, it appears, because of its exposed physical layout, as Mu'allemiin is criss-crossed by numerous avenues that cannot be effectively blocked. The neighborhood thus endured devastating violence, as the partisans of the sectarian war (who, as detailed in chapter six, waged an exceptionally ferocious war for nearby Amin), battled for control of the area.[23] The Mehdi Army's eventual conquest thus came at such a price that not only were local Sunnis largely eradicated and Christians compelled to flee in large numbers, but the neighborhood as a whole also took on a vacant, abandoned feel.

Further to the north, the open area surrounding the District Council facility offered inroads into Central Mashtal that were similar to those provided by the *hawasim* settlements adjacent to Beladiyat Proper. From the early months of the post-Saddam era, waves of opportunistic migrants (coming from as far away as Basra and the Deep South), had claimed its vacated buildings and built their own impromptu, cinder-block *sarifas* on its open land, before being joined in later years by forcibly displaced Shi'a from areas of western Baghdad and Diyala Province who sought refuge from Sunni militants.[24] Like the areas of unlicensed development in Beladiyat, the settlement thereafter offered potential recruits for the militia as well as freedom of movement, opportunities for concealment, and the facilitation of attacks on the District Council headquarters (where American forces were co-located during much of 2007, and where the Iraqi National Police also maintained a regional command center).[25]

Conquering the Cores of Beladiyat and Mashtal

Having established dominance over areas of new settlement in Beladiyat and Mashtal, and having overrun the *hayys'* more vulnerable pre-invasion neighborhoods, the Mehdi Army set upon Beladiyat Proper, Central Mashtal, and the *hayys'* minority enclaves. This brought the militia into conflict with established communities that were generally hostile. Examination of how the militia's advance progressed, and the manner in which its civilian opponents sought to defend themselves, illuminated the underlying dynamics and long-term implications of the Mehdi Army's campaign.

Located on the far side of the Army Canal, in an area of Baghdad where the Mehdi Army emerged as the dominant street-level force of the post-Saddam era, the middle class and minority communities of Beladiyat and Mashtal were forced to mount their own local defences against the violence and instability of the post-Saddam era. A key tactic employed was the erection of physical barriers that blocked access into the neighborhoods, through which residents attempted to create islands of stability. Disabled cars and felled palm trees were used to block roads, and "neighborhood watch" organizations were established.[26] The central neighborhoods of the *hayys* thus took on the look and feel of fortified encampments.[27]

Nonetheless, the militia was able to assert dominance over both Central Mashtal and Beladiyat Proper through a mixture of force and intrigue. With the militia having solidified its position across Tisa Nissan through the sectarian cleansing of surrounding areas of Obeidy, Kamaliyah, and Amin, and having also capitalized on population flows to extend its area of control up to the immediate borders of the *hayys'* core neighborhoods, localized defensive efforts were insufficient protection against its further encroachment. Militants were thus able to overrun both neighborhoods, asserting their influence by eliminating potential opponents.

Furthermore, the militia was able to find an assortment of local allies within Beladiyat Proper and Central Mashtal.[28] From local Shi'a youths for whom Muqtada's agenda held appeal, to those who sought to cultivate the militia's favor in pursuit of personal or familial advantage, to still others who were either driven to sectarian extremes by the atrocities of Sunni militants or who cooperated out of fear of persecution, the Mehdi Army gathered valuable intelligence on its enemies.[29] As a result, most Sunni residents were killed or compelled to flee; Christians retreated to the communal enclave of Tujar or sought refuge abroad; and middle class Shi'a faced an increasingly threatening environment. Despite the fact that the pre-invasion communities of the two neighborhoods remained, on the whole, hostile to the Mehdi Army, and resident Shi'a did not rise up collectively to aid in the targeting of their Sunni neighbors, the militia was able to draw the last bastions of middle class opposition in Tisa Nissan beyond the Army Canal into its sphere of control.[30]

The Christians of Tujar likewise sought to isolate themselves physically from the dangers that proliferated after the fall of Saddam Hussein. Although Iraq's Christian community was a marginal player in the contests for political power that fueled violence in the post-Saddam era, it was nonetheless subjected to an array of threats. Local residents were relatively affluent in comparison to others beyond the Army Canal, and kidnapping and the predations of criminal networks emerged as a major concern. As militant Muslim networks grew increasingly aggressive, Christians found themselves subjected to attacks by both Shi'a and Sunni groups.[31]

The explosion of violence and the mass population movements that followed the Samarra bombing further reinforced the state of siege among Christians. Migration to the open terrain around Tujar had been the source of local tension and unrest since the earliest days after the regime's fall, as the construction of new houses on the site of the racetrack to its northwest, and on what had previously been a public park to the immediate southwest, prompted protests from long-time residents. The surge of additional Shi'a into the area during the spring and summer of 2006 exacerbated these tensions, reinforcing Christian fears of being overwhelmed. For, while relations between local Christians and the Muslim residents of Beladiyat Proper, Central Mashtal, and Mu'allemiin were recalled to have been generally positive (and Shi'a families displaced by sectarian violence elsewhere in the city were said to have been welcomed into vacant homes within Tujar by remaining Christians), the hostility of the Mehdi Army and the encroachment of opportunistic migrants threatened their communal integrity.[32]

Faced with an existential threat, local Christians maintained as low a profile as possible while working to defend their interests through official channels. Christian leaders, wary of accusations regarding their authenticity as Iraqis and fearful of inciting persecution for being seen collaborating with a Western, "Christian" occupier, kept their distance from American forces. Drawing instead upon the resources of the Christian diaspora, both to facilitate overseas migration and to support those who remained behind, local Christians attempted to quietly endure the conflict. Simultaneously, Christian leaders worked through local government institutions to halt unlicensed building on their enclave's periphery, and to roll back the encroachment of post-2003 population flows through appeals to local authorities. Lacking significant influence at higher levels of government, however, and with the rule of law unreliable in post-Saddam Iraq, their efforts met with limited success.[33]

The *hayys'* Palestinian population encountered a separate set of physical threats and social pressures. Whereas local Christians had been an integral part of the social fabric of Beladiyat and Mashtal, the area's Palestinian population had been isolated, concentrated overwhelmingly in the purpose-built apartment complex along Highway 5 that was the Iraqi capital's largest and most prominent Palestinian ghetto.[34] A by-product of the refugee flows created by the 1948 Arab-Israeli war, Baghdad's Palestinian community had never been granted citizenship and its members lacked the legal permissions necessary to own property or make their own way in Iraqi society. Instead, they were relegated to a semi-privileged captivity as wards of the state, and confined to specific residences designated by the government where they enjoyed subsidized rents and an array of benefits that, over time, provoked the resentment of their Iraqi neighbors and landlords.[35]

Having developed significant notoriety as preferred recipients of Saddam Hussein's largesse and as ardent supporters of the Ba'th regime, the 2003 invasion unleashed a torrent of retribution. Across eastern Baghdad, landlords who had been forced to take on Palestinian tenants at fixed rents (and, thereafter, to maintain those fixed rents through the hyperinflation of the 1990s, which reduced the payments of many to the equivalent of a few dollars each month) celebrated the regime's fall by raising rents dramatically or evicting their tenants outright.[36] The Palestinians that had resided in discrete clusters throughout the area were forced to fall back upon the Beladiyat apartment complex, or to attempt to flee the country.

Irrespective of their choice, the plight of Iraq's Palestinians continued to worsen. Those attempting to flee to Jordan found themselves interned in squalid border camps, while those who took refuge in the Beladiyat apartment complex attracted the predations of Shi'a militants.[37] Partisan units of the Iraqi Security Forces, such as the notorious Wolf Brigade, brought steady harassment (and allegations of unlawful detention and torture), while the Mehdi Army paid regular visits to the enclave as well.[38]

The Iraqi government, motivated by lingering animosities from the Saddam era and the sectarianism that came to dominate domestic politics thereafter, took a proactively antagonistic stance toward the country's Palestinians. In October 2005, for example, the Shi'a official from the Ministry of Interior responsible for issues of displacement and migration called for all Palestinians to be expelled to Gaza for their alleged support of terrorism (an allegation that, in the case of the Palestinians of Beladiyat, appears to have been unfounded).[39] Likewise, the processes through which Palestinians were required to renew their residency documents were made deliberately arduous, forcing entire families to run a dangerous gauntlet of checkpoints every two months to re-register with the Ministry of the Interior.[40] Palestinians were thus already living in a state of siege when the Samarra bombing occurred, after which Shi'a attacks escalated to the point that Grand Ayatollah Ali al-Sistani was compelled to issue a *fatwa* explicitly forbidding the killing of Palestinians.[41]

Unlike its Christian counterpart, the Palestinian community of Beladiyat had no meaningful diaspora to fall back on. Having been cut off from the outside world and kept as dependents of the state for decades, Palestinians were isolated and exposed following Saddam's demise. The long-time residents of the Beladiyat apartment complex, and those compelled to seek refuge therein, thus found themselves stranded in a Shi'a district controlled by an aggressively hostile militia force, and governed by a similarly antagonistic new regime. Unable to escape abroad, the Palestinians were pushed into a relationship of necessity with American forces. Irrespective of Palestinians' views of the American military (or resentment over the waves of persecution that had been unleashed upon them by the Americans' removal of their patron), American forces stationed at FOB Loyalty (to the immediate south of the Beladiyat Apartments) proved to be their most reliable source of assistance.[42]

The Reclamation of Beladiyat and Mashtal

As the Surge began during the early months of 2007, the Mehdi Army dominated Beladiyat and Mashtal. The *hayys'* Sunni populations had been largely eradicated, the remnants of their Christian and Palestinian minorities were besieged in narrow enclaves, and the Shi'a middle class was badly battered. Sab'a Nisan was a militant stronghold, Old Habibiyyah and Mu'allemiin had been effectively overrun and overwhelmed, Beladiyat Proper and Central Mashtal were physically degraded and under sustained militia pressure, while the sprawling new settlements in both *hayys*, where Sadrist Shi'a were found in abundance and the Mehdi Army operated with impunity, had further altered the landscape. It thus appeared that the Mehdi Army had firmly conquered Beladiyat and Mashtal, and that the *hayys'* absorption into the city's underclass periphery might well be permanent.

However, as American and Iraqi forces applied heightened pressure to the militia, they exposed weaknesses in its position. Not surprisingly, in Beladiyat Proper and Central Mashtal, and in the minority redoubts of Christians and Palestinians—places over which the Mehdi Army claimed suzerainty, but where it had been unable to rally significant local support—the militia was driven backwards. Yet, the subsequent extension of counterinsurgency operations into areas of western Beladiyat and eastern Mashtal, thought to be under firm militia control, found its apparent strength to be deceptive as well. These were areas where the Mehdi Army had appeared well entrenched, and where its power was thought to have been consolidated. But, from the conquered terrain of Mu'allemiin to the sprawling new settlement zones of both *hayys*, the militia failed to mount a coherent response to the Surge. Instead, its position deteriorated, and examination of where, how, and why this occurred reveal critical insights into the Mehdi Army's overall collapse.

Counterinsurgency in Beladiyat and Mashtal

The local counter-offensive of the Surge began in early 2007, with American and Iraqi forces attacking the Mehdi Army at its weakest points. Focusing initially on areas where the militia was least popular, and where middle class and minority residents anxiously sought the re-establishment of law and order, American and Iraqi forces reclaimed

Beladiyat Proper, Central Mashtal, and the *hayys'* Christian and Palestinian enclaves. After years of violence, uncertainty, and physical degradation, local civilians welcomed, albeit with an abundance of caution and skepticism, the efforts of the American military and the Iraqi government to reinstate governance, revive economic activity, and rebuild critical infrastructure.[43]

American and Iraqi forces then pressed outwards into western Beladiyat and eastern Mashtal. These were areas that the Mehdi Army had conquered decisively, and where local residents, many of whom were Sadrist in their sympathies after the population transfers of previous years, were expected to be far less amenable to the advances of the Surge. Indeed, the momentum of American and Iraqi forces slowed in the face of both armed resistance and popular antipathy, and the militia's enduring presence in western Beladiyat and eastern Mashtal was made evident when they erupted during March Madness.

Although western Beladiyat and eastern Mashtal would remain intermittently lethal to American and Iraqi personnel throughout 2008, the nature of the violence levied against the forces of the Surge betrayed the Mehdi Army's vulnerability. In Beladiyat, the Sab'a Nissan neighborhood was a focal point of militant activity, and exuded a palpable hostility to American personnel that was comparable to hotspots of violence further beyond the Army Canal.[44] It appeared that the Mehdi Army had established itself firmly in the neighborhood. Attempts to displace the militia were thus met with violent reprisals, while efforts to cultivate popular support achieved limited results.[45]

However, the militia's position in the expanses of new development along the northern and southern tiers of Beladiyat, and across the vast bulk of eastern Mashtal as well, proved considerably less formidable. These were areas that had been regarded with extreme caution during the initial phase of the Surge, but as militants fled the area in the wake of March Madness, local dynamics shifted significantly. American and Iraqi forces would encounter sporadic violence in areas of underclass Shi'a settlement in both *hayys*, and the main arteries of Mu'allemiin remained treacherous due to the threat of roadside bombs, but neither eastern Mashtal nor western Beladiyat witnessed coordinated popular resistance on the militia's behalf. On the contrary, an examination of the *hayys'* areas of underclass settlement found a prevailing atmosphere of chaos and uncertainty, where the resident population was preoccupied, above all else, with self-preservation.

A Flawed Narrative of Class-Warfare

As American and Iraqi forces pushed further into eastern Mashtal and western Beladiyat, the Mehdi Army attempted to hold its ground. Groups of Shi'a militants launched mortar and rocket attacks on American and Iraqi facilities, emplaced roadside bombs, and mounted the occasional coordinated assault. Their efforts were sporadic and halting, and failed to check the continued advance of the Surge. The overwhelming majority of the populace, meanwhile, from the battered remnants of Mu'allemiin's pre-invasion population, to the migrants that inhabited the new settlement areas of Beladiyat and the squatter encampment adjacent to the District Council headquarters, withdrew into the relative safety of their homes. There was thus little, if anything, "popular" about the resistance that was encountered.

Close study of the militia's localized resistance to the Surge offered insights into why this was so. In Mu'allemiin, the answer appeared straightforward: having conquered the area during the sectarian war, militants could move freely through the neighborhood to conduct attacks on the forces of the Surge. They could draw little support from remaining local residents, however, whose socio-political sentiments generally mirrored those of their middle class and minority neighbors in Central Mashtal and Beladiyat Proper. Therefore, when pressure intensified on Shi'a militants in the wake of March Madness, with key operatives fleeing the area, levels of violence fell precipitously. The local community thereafter underwent a slow, yet encouraging revival, with displaced Christians returning to their former homes, and the neighborhood's side-streets showing signs of renewed activity.[46]

In the areas of new settlement, on the other hand, where the Mehdi Army had the opportunity to cultivate a broad base of support from a populace that was heavily Sadrist in its sympathies, the militia's weakness appeared to stem from two main factors. The first was the character of the militia itself; developing as it had through the course of the sectarian war, growing increasingly radical and predatory in its actions against local Sunnis, Christians, and Shi'a as well, the Mehdi Army had alienated its ostensible base of support.[47] The nature of the militia's "rule" over these areas in the months that followed the abatement of sectarian violence, and the abuses perpetrated by the young men who filled its ranks—ranging from extortion and racketeering to kidnapping and murder—had significantly soured popular opinion.

The second main factor was the lack of cohesion among the underclass Shi'a migrants themselves. From the impoverished families that had fled the slums of Sadr City for new horizons in Beladiyat, to the geographically diverse and discordant group that descended upon the open terrain to the north of the District Council facility, the Sadrist Shi'a that moved into the two *hayys* were ill-suited to form the backbone of an insurgency.[48] The haphazard process through which migration progressed into Beladiyat and Mashtal, with individual families maneuvering independently to stake claims to desirable terrain, created a disjointed social environment.[49] Faced with the need to secure access to clean water and electricity in the face of fierce opposition from the *hayys'* established communities, and finding themselves in an ungoverned, violent environment where criminal groups and predatory militiamen reigned supreme, the migrants had retreated inwards into the safety of their homes, leaving civil society to languish.

The resulting dearth of locally-rooted social networks or communal groups thus handicapped the Mehdi Army. A key feature of the militia's expansion across Baghdad had been its ability to mobilize elements of the Shi'a underclass, absorbing localized networks of supporters and thereby entrenching itself in new neighborhoods. Weary, battered, fearful, and newly-settled among unfamiliar neighbors on unstable terrain, the Sadrist Shi'a that migrated into western Beladiyat and eastern Mashtal were poorly positioned to play such a role. They provided a permissive environment in which the Mehdi Army could plan, stage, and conduct attacks, and a recruiting pool from which facilitators and other low-level operatives could be drawn, but the underclass Shi'a *hawasim* had ultimately not been able to serve as a "fifth column," or an organized component of the militia's campaign.[50]

Troublingly for the Mehdi Army, the *hayys* had presented prime opportunities to exploit the class tensions at the core of Sadrist ideology and rally support from the newly-arrived Shi'a poor—but the militia appeared to have failed to do so. Part of this failure could be attributed to the predatory nature of the militia itself, as by its actions it had alienated potential supporters. Part also stemmed from the condition of the Shi'a underclass, and the manner in which the atomized state of those who migrated into Beladiyat and Mashtal left Sadrist civilians unable to engage coherently with the militia's campaign. With the exception of the Sab'a Nissan neighborhood (where the militia had imported operatives and supporters, thereby creating a critical level of localized coherence), and areas along the extreme western periphery of Beladiyat that appeared to have been consumed by Sadr City, the Mehdi Army had not built a cohesive base of popular support. In turn, it had been unable to hold its ground when faced with the counter-offensive of the Surge, and had been driven from the *hayys*.

6

KAMALIYAH AND AMIN

RALLYING THE MASSES

Kamaliyah and Amin: A Year into the Surge

At the start of 2008, Kamaliyah and Amin were in turmoil.[1] Home to powerful contingents of the Mehdi Army, and standing, after vicious campaigns of sectarian cleansing, as the domains of the Shi'a underclass, the *hayys* had violently resisted the advances of the Surge. American-led efforts to dislodge the militia had sparked heavy fighting in both *hayys* and, while the militia had been pushed off the streets, further progress remained elusive: violence persisted (not only against the forces of the Surge, but also among local residents), governance was a shambles, essential services and critical infrastructure were mired in disrepair, and residents looked on with emotions that ranged, for the most part, from wariness to outright hostility. As a result, Kamaliyah and Amin were regarded with exceptional frustration by those tasked to patrol and secure them.

Whereas Kamaliyah and Amin inspired similarly negative sentiments among American servicemen, features particular to each *hayy* had created unique sets of local challenges. Kamaliyah, a run-down, semi-urban zone on the margins of Baghdad's eastern periphery, had long been a notorious red-light district. While the Mehdi Army had eradicated the local sex trade when it set upon Kamaliyah's Ba'thist pimps and gypsy prostitutes in the spring of 2003, the *hayy* maintained its decades-old stigma of danger and depravity. From its residents' prominent role in the

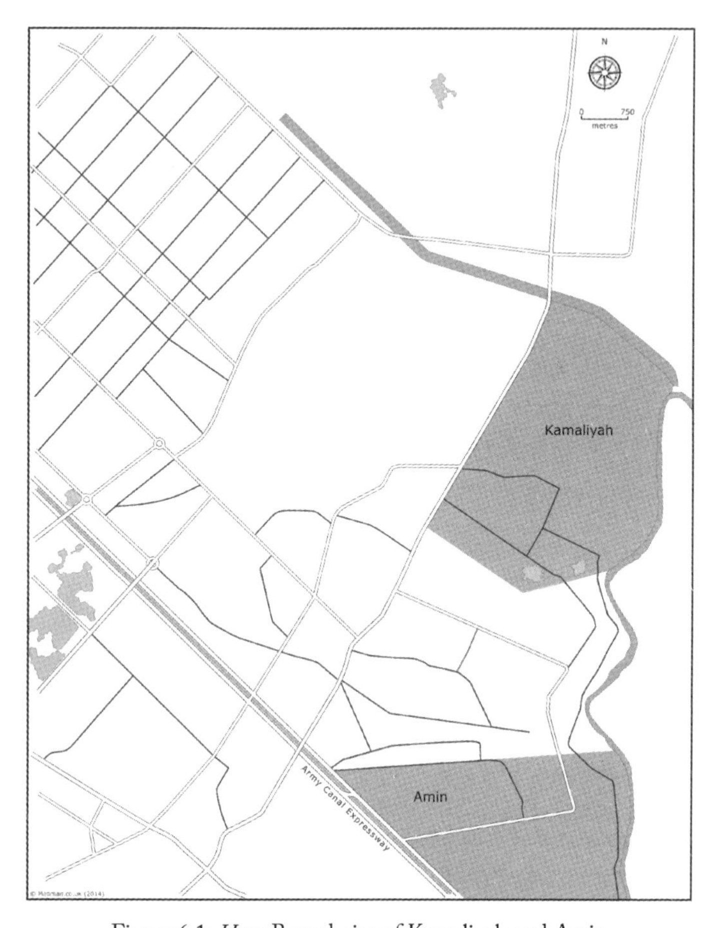

Figure 6.1: *Hayy* Boundaries of Kamaliyah and Amin

post-invasion looting that devastated Baghdad, to the Mafioso-style rule subsequently established by the Mehdi Army's local affiliates, Kamaliyah remained infamous—a condition reinforced by the squalor of its central neighborhood, where a network of knee- to waist-deep open sewers criss-crossed unpaved, potholed streets, emptying into vast, fetid pits.[2] The mention of Kamaliyah among Baghdadis would thus elicit a mixture of amused smirks and solemn warnings, suggesting that the *hayy* demanded both derision and cautious respect. American personnel, on the other hand, frequently referred to the television series "The Wire" and "The

Figure 6.2: Open Sewers in Central Kamaliyah[3]

Sopranos" when trying to explain the mixture of violence, corruption, and suffering that, in their eyes, defined Kamaliyah.[4]

Amin had achieved infamy of a different sort. Having developed through the latter decades of the twentieth century as a densely populated, hardscrabble urban grid that was home to a blend of working to lower class families of both Muslim sects, Amin experienced intense sectarian violence. The Mehdi Army and its Sunni foes waged protracted offensives that featured the bombing of marketplaces, the public execution of civilians, and the burning of corpses tied to utility poles. The Mehdi Army's ultimate victory in that contest had led to the near-elimination of Amin's large Sunni population. The *hayy* thereafter became known as a potent Mehdi Army stronghold where mosques preached a fearsome brand of sectarian Shi'a militarism, gangs of militia-affiliated youths roamed the streets, and Iranian-backed Special Group cells operated extensively.[5]

The forces of the Surge had faced an array of formidable challenges in the two *hayys*. From the gangsters-cum-warlords of Kamaliyah to the

Figure 6.3: The Muhsin al-Hakim Mosque, Amin[6]

sectarian militants of Amin, locally-rooted elements of the Mehdi Army laid firm claim to each. With contingents of youths and young men holding a commanding street-level presence in both *hayys*, and the political sympathies of their populations understood to be overwhelmingly Sadrist, it had been inevitable that the reclamation of Kamaliyah and Amin would be met with sustained resistance. Indeed, the scope of the violence encountered as American forces set up local patrol bases in the two *hayys* during 2007 reflected the fact that the endeavor marked a direct assault on core terrain of the Sadrist movement, which the Mehdi Army would be loathe to concede.

Yet, although Kamaliyah and Amin were in violent disarray, conditions could have been worse.[7] Home to legions of underclass Shi'a, and situated firmly within the Mehdi Army's core territory in eastern Baghdad, Kamaliyah and Amin had presented the militia with prime opportunities to mobilize a mass base of support, and could have been founts of popular insurgency. However, the violence levied against the Surge, and the evident disposition of the *hayys'* civilian populations toward

American-led counterinsurgency efforts, suggested that the Mehdi Army had met with decidedly uneven results. Cadre members of the Mehdi Army, Iranian-backed Special Group cells, and an assortment of local actors attacked American patrols with roadside bombs and small arms fire, and launched mortars and rockets at American facilities, but the residents of Kamaliyah and Amin were not to be found standing shoulder-to-shoulder with the militia. On the contrary, neither *hayy* appeared to offer a united front against the Surge, suggesting that the Mehdi Army's insurgent campaign had somehow gone awry.

Key Issues in Kamaliyah and Amin

It was clear that the Mehdi Army was well established in both *hayys*, and that it had been able to generate fierce local violence. However, neither *hayy* appeared to be home to coherent, popular insurgency. The overwhelming majority of residents in Kamaliyah and Amin, despite being ardent supporters of Sadrist ideals, seemed instead to have retreated into the relative safety of their homes, leaving the Mehdi Army and its local affiliates to confront the encroachment of the Surge.

Was this impression correct? If so, why had the populace not been incorporated into the militia's endeavor? Was the seeming detachment of local residents from the militia's campaign the by-product of disenchantment with the Mehdi Army? Was it a display of pragmatism by a populace that was able to anticipate the militia's impending collapse? Alternatively, were appearances deceptive, and were the *hayys* in fact home to a latent popular insurgency that was exercising strategic patience, and waiting for Muqtada's call to arms?

If the Mehdi Army's insurgent campaign had indeed faltered in Kamaliyah and Amin, why were counterinsurgency efforts also meeting with limited success? Intuitively, it followed that if the militia had somehow alienated the local population, or otherwise failed to root itself in a firm base of popular support, then the *hayys* might be receptive to the overtures of counterinsurgents. Yet, although American and Iraqi forces had achieved significant gains against local militants during the Surge's initial year, both *hayys* remained mired in violence and beset by an array of problems. What could account for the seeming intractability of Kamaliyah and Amin, and for the *hayys'* enduring instability?

March Madness in Kamaliyah and Amin

March Madness enveloped both *hayys* in violence. The American units responsible for Amin and Kamaliyah endured a spike in casualties, Iraqi Security Forces suffered high levels of absenteeism and outright defections to the Mehdi Army, and the *hayys*, like much of Tisa Nissan beyond the Army Canal, descended into chaos.[8] American forces were compelled to engage in heavy fighting in an effort to restore order, while speculation mounted that perhaps the *hayys* had, in fact, been insurgent strongholds all along.[9]

However, as violence abated, conditions in Kamaliyah and Amin improved dramatically. Through the course of the spring and summer of 2008, American forces and their counterparts in the newly-purged Iraqi National Police launched a series of large-scale operations in the two *hayys*. Ranging from cordon and search missions to confiscate illegal weapons to reconstruction-minded efforts to distribute cash grants to small businesses, the forces of the Surge took daily to the streets of Amin and Kamaliyah. The street-level interactions with the *hayys'* residents that ensued offered critical insights into local conditions. While central areas of both *hayys* remained intermittently violent and the threat of roadside bombs persisted, improving trends in security and stability enabled American personnel to gain a significantly improved understanding of the dynamics of the militia's local campaigns.[10]

The Sadrist Movement's Roots in Kamaliyah and Amin

In light of their historical development, there was ample reason to expect that Kamaliyah and Amin would offer strong support to the Sadrist movement, and that the Mehdi Army might rally substantive support in each *hayy*.[11] Established during the 1960s as part of Baghdad's government-directed expansion, Amin and Kamaliyah became prominent venues of migrant settlement in the decades that followed. Located on the capital's eastern edge, near the outlets of major highways that connected Baghdad to rural, agricultural areas beyond, they absorbed tens of thousands of underclass Shi'a migrants and took on *shurughi*-heavy demographic profiles.

Developing thereafter into under-serviced, marginalized areas of the Iraqi capital, they also became focal points for the frustrations and social tensions that were ultimately enshrined in the Sadrist movement. As such, while Amin and Kamaliyah were not homogeneous zones of underclass Shi'a settlement like nearby Saddam City, the Sadrist movement was able to build a strong local foundation during the 1990s. Drawing upon the accumulated grievances of local Shi'a, the White Lion rallied enormous local support. Thus, when Muqtada al-Sadr set out to revive his father's movement in the wake of Saddam Hussein's fall, there was a latent, yet powerful ideological bond among the *hayys'* Shi'a residents upon which he could build.

The Formation of Kamaliyah and Amin

Kamaliyah and Amin grew rapidly during their formative decades, in a development process that was powered by a continually intensifying surge of underclass Shi'a into Baghdad. Amin, sitting at the terminus of the main highway connecting Iraq's Deep South to the capital, was an appealing destination for migrants. Located adjacent to the economic hub of Baghdad al-Jadeeda and home to its own local commerce and light industry, it offered the prospect of nearby employment—and its allure was such that newly-arrived migrants were joined by large numbers of working class Shi'a and Sunni families from other areas of the capital, as well as places further afield. Amin thus became home to a multitude of tradesmen, laborers, and unskilled workers and their families, driving the construction of compact clusters of mostly two- to four-storey residential buildings southward from the *hayy's* original settlement block (along the southern edge of Mu'allemiin) toward the Army Canal.

Kamaliyah, as a remote and especially poor development area on the furthest reaches of eastern Baghdad, offered an affordable escape from the miseries of rural poverty that attracted large numbers of southern Shi'a migrants. Located at the entry point into Baghdad on the highway that connects the Iraqi capital to the rural expanses of Diyala Province, it also absorbed numerous migrants from the mixed-sect, tribal areas northeast of the Iraqi capital.[12] The *hayy's* main neighborhood, referred to hereafter as Central Kamaliyah, thus came to house a blend of poor Shi'a and Sunni families that resided in rudimentary two- to three-storey buildings, while much of the local labor force occupied the lower rungs of the urban economy elsewhere in the city.[13]

Both *hayys* continued to expand through the 1970s and into the 1980s. In Amin, urban development progressed with the establishment of Oil

City along the Diyala River, and the construction of new, purpose-built neighborhoods for veterans of the war with Iran and the families of battlefield casualties.[14] The *hayy* thus consolidated its identity as a blue-collar area of Baghdad that, while housing large numbers of Shi'a migrants and their descendents, was home to a diverse population and could claim connectivity to the city center through its links to nearby Baghdad al-Jadeeda.

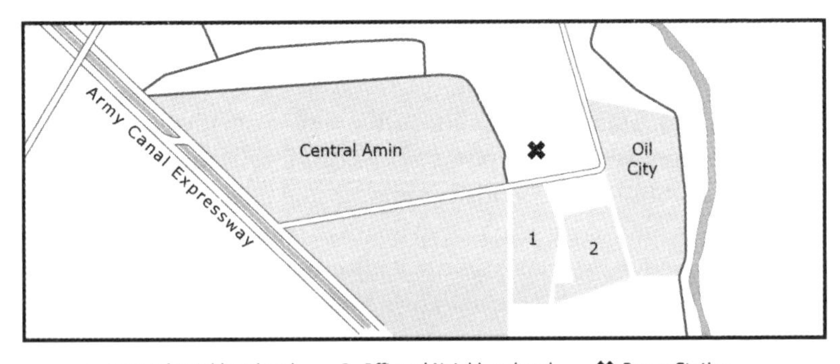

Figure 6.4: Key Areas in and around Amin

Whereas Amin developed into a down-market, yet distinctly urban area that was criss-crossed by broad, paved avenues lined with markets, shops, and light industry, Kamaliyah remained significantly poorer and less developed. Although industrial zones were established to the immediate east of Central Kamaliyah and also further north near the outer canal, the *hayy* remained largely without basic infrastructure such as paved roads and sewers. Despite the poor condition of the area (and the notoriety it quickly acquired for prostitution and criminality), local growth continued.[15] In addition to the expansion of Central Kamaliyah, a series of satellite settlements were established, referred to collectively as Riyasah. Forming, in effect, a ring of suburbs around the main grid of Central Kamaliyah, Riyasah was comprised of the Ma'mun and Mu'awaqiin neighborhoods (which area residents recalled to have been founded in an effort to avoid Central Kamaliyah's squalor), and also incorporated the wealthier, pre-existing enclave of Bustan (where affluent Baghdadi families had built a cluster of large, gated homes in a palm grove along the Diyala River, which provided seasonal refuge from the heat of the city center).[16]

Sanctions and the Sadrist Movement in Kamaliyah and Amin

Although Amin and Kamaliyah developed in different ways, acquiring unique characteristics during their formative decades, the Iraqi government's declining financial position catalyzed a common systemic collapse from the late 1980s. With both *hayys* situated on the capital's eastern margins, home to large numbers of underclass Shi'a and consequently unable to command a significant share of the regime's increasingly lim-

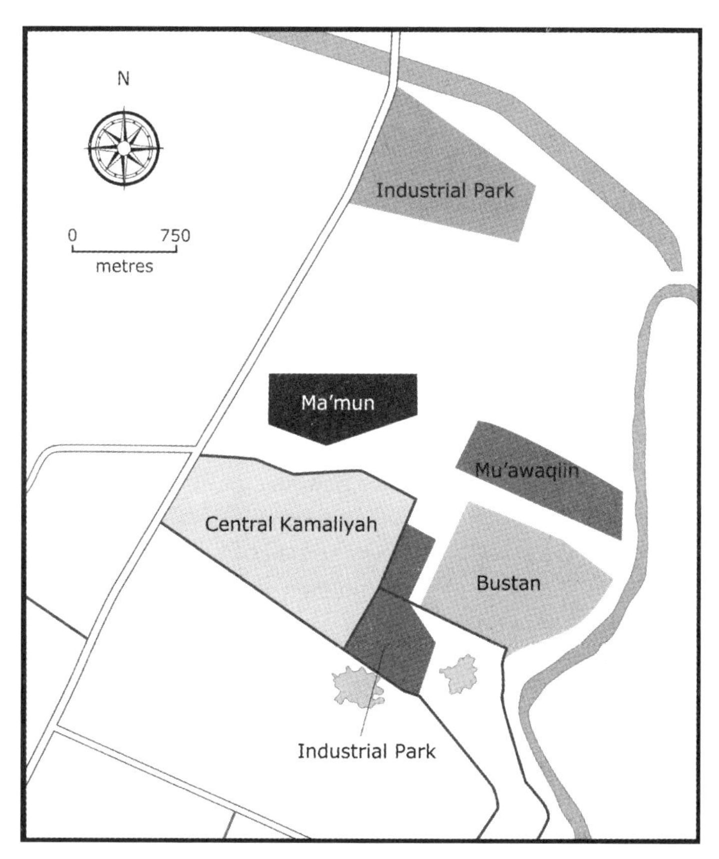

Figure 6.5: The Sub-neighborhoods of Kamaliyah

ited resources, Amin and Kamaliyah fell into disrepair. Surging unemployment, hyperinflation, and the scarcity of staple goods catalyzed devastating economic shocks, while the attentions of the security services were left as the central pillar of governance. Kamaliyah thus deteriorated into a seedy, dilapidated wasteland on the capital's distant edge, while Amin became a congested, decaying urban grid with overcrowded schools, crumbling infrastructure, and an increasingly destitute populace.

As Amin and Kamaliyah suffered the effects of economic collapse, infrastructural degradation, and the retreat of the much-relied-upon state, the "revivals" of tribalism and Islam swept the two *hayys*. In the tribal sphere, with the encouragement of the regime, a contingent of sheikhs emerged.[17] Assuming low-level administrative functions to compensate for the declining capacity of the state, they took on increasingly prominent roles in local society. Yet, while the tribal heritage of the *hayys'* residents suggested that tribalism might provide a natural, authentic replacement for state authority (and the poorer zones of eastern Baghdad were known, like the slums of *al-'asima* before them, as places where the norms and values of the tribal milieu had persisted with relative strength), Amin and Kamaliyah were ill-suited for an essentialist tribal resurgence.

Instead, Amin and Kamaliyah were prime examples of urban areas where the pressures detailed in chapters one and two had, over the course of decades, unraveled tribal structures and degraded tribal coherence. From the corruption of the traditional tribal system that had prompted the mass abandonment of Iraq's rural, tribal regions in the first place, to the dislocations that accompanied long-range migration, to the mixing-bowl effect that ensued as families had maneuvered across the urban landscape in pursuit of work and better housing, the structural integrity of tribal networks had been irreversibly compromised.[18] Furthermore, an array of powerful forces had undermined sheikhly leadership, including the anti-tribal teachings of Iraq's public education system, the state's monopolization of patronage through its control of the economy, and the aggressive predations of Ba'thist totalitarianism.[19] Not only were there no geographically contiguous tribal enclaves evident in Amin or Kamaliyah, but there had also been little prospect of anyone exercising significant social power—tribal or otherwise—without a direct partnership with the government.

With Baghdad's tribal "revival" providing limited, qualified support to the residents of Amin and Kamaliyah, the rise of Mohammed Mohammed

Sadiq al-Sadr appears to have been all the more significant.[20] The White Lion and his emissaries stood pre-eminent among the meager resources available to the Shi'a poor of Amin and Kamaliyah during the 1990s and, in response, the Sadrist movement was met with extraordinary local enthusiasm. Amin thus became home to a well-organized mass following that networked through the religious institutions of its urban grid, while even Kamaliyah—a place not known for its piety—saw the White Lion become an iconic figure.

The 1990s thus witnessed a surge in popular religiosity among the underclass Shi'a of the two *hayys*, as the White Lion united local residents, at least in spirit, with millions of their co-religionists elsewhere in the Iraqi capital and across southern Iraq.[21] Emphasizing their common heritage as Arabs of Iraq's tribal south, and proclaiming their impending empowerment after generations of prejudice and marginalization, he established an ideological movement that would endure beyond his death. Indeed, although his murder and the wave of government repression that followed was sufficient to check the Sadrist threat to Saddam Hussein's regime, the battle-lines of future conflict between the Shi'a underclass and its "betters" in Iraqi society had been drawn.[22]

The Mehdi Army's Struggle in Kamaliyah and Amin

As Muqtada al-Sadr revived the Sadrist movement in the spring of 2003, directing the Mehdi Army on its initial campaign to claim Baghdad's impoverished, Shi'a-dominated periphery, Amin and Kamaliyah became hotbeds of Shi'a militarism. Drawing upon the enduring sentiments of the White Lion's former devotees, and also capitalizing on the resonance of Muqtada's impassioned anti-occupation rhetoric, the Mehdi Army established itself firmly in the two *hayys*. Kamaliyah and Amin may have lacked the demographic homogeneity of nearby Sadr City, where the rekindled Sadrist movement could claim to represent the entirety of the resident populace, but thc milita was nonetheless able to exert a formidable street-level presence.

Having established a firm foothold in Amin and Kamaliyah during the initial year of the post-Saddam era, the Mehdi Army then consolidated its position during the sectarian war by violently cleansing the *hayys* of the bulk of their Sunni residents and asserting itself as their de facto ruler. While the decimation of the *hayys*' Sunni populations and the elimination of organized local opposition left the militia in uncontested control, problems emerged in each area. As the Mehdi Army attempted to govern Amin and Kamaliyah, it became increasingly apparent that the militia's local characteristics were deeply corrosive to the rekindled Sadrist movement's insurgent agenda.

Victory in Kamaliyah and Amin

The Mehdi Army made its presence felt in Kamaliyah and Amin from the earliest weeks of the post-Saddam era.[23] In Kamaliyah, the militia began by targeting noted Ba'thists and eradicating the resident gypsy community, bringing a violent end to the local sex trade.[24] However, the militia's ability to exercise local power by preying upon its enemies did not translate into an ability to establish local order. On the contrary, Central Kamaliyah emerged as a major base of operations for the looters who were pillaging the city center, fostering an atmosphere of criminalized chaos during the months that followed. Thus, while the militia steadily built up its local presence (in large measure by absorbing allies from among the Mafioso-style figures that were active in the area who, in turn, directed gangs of local youths on the militia's behalf), Kamaliyah remained deeply unstable.

The Mehdi Army's beginnings were more structured in Amin, where the chaos of the initial invasion gave way to a more organized and politically purposeful trend in violence.[25] Working through local mosques, the militia raised platoons of young men that played a prominent role in early clashes with the Coalition, giving the *hayy* a reputation for lethality.[26] Concurrently, the Mehdi Army also cultivated popular support among local residents. By providing much-needed welfare services to the public, and reportedly taking an active role in the movement of underclass Shi'a families from Sadr City into the open terrain to the south of Amin's core grid (where two- to three-storey homes were erected in large numbers, gradually filling the area between the *hayy's* pre-invasion grid and the cement factory to the south), the militia steadily strengthened its base.[27]

The explosion of the sectarian war brought sweeping changes to Amin and Kamaliyah. Both *hayys* were home to extreme violence, which culminated in the killing or forced displacement of their sizable Sunni populations and the rise of the Mehdi Army to a position of total dominance.[28] However, the particular dynamics of violence in each *hayy* were deeply influenced by local factors. In Kamaliyah, the chaos of the invasion's early days persisted through the duration of the conflict.[29] Thus, while the local strongmen that served as the militia's proxies led groups of young men on a brutal rampage against resident Sunnis, and mosques such as the Imam Ali on Central Kamaliyah's northwestern edge became central nodes of command and control for a religiously-defined war of attrition against Sunni civilians, Shi'a families found themselves subjected to attacks as well. Indeed, the violence of Kamaliyah's "sectarian" war appears to have been driven largely by localized, material ambitions that evoked the criminality for which the *hayy* was infamous, as homes and businesses that presented attractive targets were plundered irrespective of their owners' sectarian identity.[30]

In Amin, the sectarian war proceeded with greater structure, and greater ferocity. The Mehdi Army's local aspirations were fiercely challenged by Sunni militants, who struck marketplaces and other prominent civilian targets with a campaign of suicide bombings, and beheaded Shi'a civilians. Shi'a militants responded with their own offensive against local Sunnis, leading to a protracted battle that inflicted devastating punishment on the entire population.

As the fighting progressed, several factors combined to generate an atmosphere of singular virulence. First, the gruesome toll of the fighting appears to have had a radicalizing, desensitizing effect on local militiamen, creating a cycle of intensifying fear and hatred that, in turn, spawned further atrocities. Second, the scope and duration of the fighting drew in militiamen from Sadr City and southern Iraq, and Iranian-sponsored Special Group fighters as well.[31] The mosques of Amin, prominent among them the Muhsin al-Hakim, thus came to espouse an exceptionally fearsome brand of internationalized Shi'a militarism, and became not only operational bases and cache sites, but also sources of legitimizing ideology in one of the sectarian war's more ferociously contested venues.[32]

The Perils of Success in Kamaliyah and Amin

Whereas the violence of the sectarian war followed distinct trajectories in Amin and Kamaliyah, it yielded a common outcome. By the start of 2007, both *hayys* sat within a broad arc of eastern Baghdad that was firmly held by the Mehdi Army.[33] Amin and Kamaliyah, effectively cleansed of their Sunni residents, were now integral parts of the militia's greatly expanded domain in the Iraqi capital.

Nonetheless, the Mehdi Army faced significant local challenges. Having positioned itself as the defender and benefactor of the *hayys'* Shi'a residents, and standing as the local representative of the rekindled Sadrist movement, the militia had to govern its conquests. After decades of neglect and decay, however, and the waves of destructive violence and destabilizing population shifts that followed the 2003 invasion, the *hayys* were in a state of near-ruin. Meanwhile, the militia was suffering from severe internal difficulties as well, such that the abatement of sectarian violence did not bring a period of respite that might have enabled the militia to consolidate its gains in preparation for the advance of the Surge.

In Kamaliyah, the problems facing the Mehdi Army were, in many ways, reflections of the *hayy* itself. The strongmen who comprised its local leadership and the gangs of young men that ran the streets of Central Kamaliyah were remarkably ill suited to the responsibilities of governance. Their fighting prowess had been sufficient to drive out Sunni civilians and defend the *hayy* from the incursions of Sunni militants, but they did not instill feelings of security or sectarian pride among the populace at large.[34] Nor were they equipped or inclined to lead the *hayy's* reconstruction. Instead, with the violence of the sectarian war having driven away the owners and operators of local industry, and the final eradication of Sunnis drying up the militia's principal income stream, Kamaliyah degenerated further as the predations of its defenders were redirected inward toward the local population.[35]

While the Mehdi Army remained dominant in Kamaliyah, the populace at large was not effectively mobilized in support of its campaign. On the contrary, there was little evidence of "popular" activity of any kind in Central Kamaliyah, where civil society appeared to be in full retreat. The years of violence, uncertainty, and extensive population turnover that followed the 2003 invasion had prompted local families to withdraw further from its dangerous and decrepit public spaces, seeking sanctuary in their homes—where the cleanliness and order (and occasional concentrations of remarkable wealth) stood in stark contrast to conditions beyond their doors.[36]

Likewise, the Riyasah suburbs and the *hayy's* peripheral zones were far from bastions of popular insurgency. With the exception of Ma'mun (where the militia-affiliated elite was understood to congregate, prompting Americans to view the neighborhood as "the center of all evil in Kamaliyah"), and the three residential blocks to its immediate west along

Highway 5 (which were deeply influenced by the nearby Imam Ali mosque, a hub of militant activity in Kamaliyah and Obeidy), the Mehdi Army did not appear to have integrated into local communities.[37] In Mu'awaqiin and Bustan, local residents had adopted defensive postures. These were neighborhoods that had sought to isolate themselves from the corrosive influences of Central Kamaliyah since well before the 2003 invasion, and thus while Mu'awaqiin appeared staunchly Sadrist, neither area was amenable to the local manifestation of the Mehdi Army.[38]

The thousands of underclass Shi'a who migrated to the open areas on Kamaliyah's northern tier were not mobilized in support of the Mehdi Army either. Coming principally from Diyala Province, families began moving into the area from the early months of the post-Saddam era (with a later, sizable influx occurring in late 2006, when Sunni militants escalated their activities in the Diyala Province), erecting sizable single family homes and creating a sprawling new settlement zone.[39] However, in contrast to events on the southern tier of Amin, where the militia was noted to have been active in both channeling supporters into the area and facilitating their settlement with various service offerings, such efforts appear to have proved beyond the militia's abilities in Kamaliyah.[40] New arrivals were instead left to fend for themselves, and the landscape took on a jumbled, chaotic quality, epitomized by the dense tangles of power lines rigged by local residents that hung over the dirt pathways crisscrossing the area.

Despite Kamaliyah's overall demographic homogeneity after the sectarian war and the prevailing Sadrist sympathies of its residents, the Mehdi Army's dominance was not matched by a strong base of popular support. Efforts to reinforce the militia's position through the predations of local fighters and the deployment of morality police failed to mold Kamaliyah into a more manageable environment (or to impose hard-line Islamic discipline upon local residents), provoking resentment instead.[41] As a result, mosques such as the Imam Ali from which militants operated sat detached and isolated on the terrain, more like fortified fighting positions than integral parts of the surrounding neighborhood.[42]

In Amin, the Mehdi Army's internal difficulties stemmed in part from issues specific to the *hayy* itself, yet more so from the manner in which the *hayy* had been conquered. Victory in the sectarian war had been achieved through the mobilization of local young men, the overarching leadership of religious militants, and the supplementary efforts of Special

Group fighters. Collectively, they had driven Sunni militants from the battlefield and largely cleansed the *hayy* of its Sunni residents. However, the excesses of that process held lingering, deleterious consequences. Not only did the brutality with which local Sunni civilians were dispatched alienate popular opinion, but the character of rule imposed thereafter by militarized local gangs and radical sectarian militants also further undermined the Mehdi Army's support.

As in Kamaliyah, the prominent role of volatile, often predatory young men in the militia's ranks did much to adversely influence popular opinion. Shi'a civilians may have been able to overlook their abuses for so long as they provided much-needed protection from the terror of Sunni *jihadis*, but as the sectarian war cooled, relations soured between the families of Amin and their ostensible protectors.[43] Deprived of the income stream that their now-eradicated Sunni victims had provided, and having been further radicalized by a savagely-fought sectarian battle, the Mehdi Army grew increasingly predatory. The social services that had previously won the militia an important measure of goodwill thus dried up, as young men turned upon their elders and upon the populace at large.[44]

At the same time, the particular brand of Shi'ism that took root in the mosques of Amin also appears to have alienated local opinion. While the populace of Amin had become increasingly devout during the 1990s, the strands of Islam preached in mosques like the Muhsin al-Hakim went beyond the radical populism of the White Lion, entering the realm of internationalized, Iranian-influenced Shi'a militarism. It remained unclear whether this was an outgrowth of locally-grown radicalism or an import of the sectarian war, yet regardless, and despite whatever inspiration it may have provided to Shi'a partisans, it appears to have exceeded the appetite of the local population.

The radical overreach of local militants was evident in the signage that surrounded mosques such as the Muhsin al-Hakim. Although the quantity, quality, and geographic dispersion of militant imagery offered impressive evidence of the militia's power, the content of these images was problematic. Sadrist imagery across Tisa Nissan, and more broadly throughout Iraq, commonly presented Muqtada al-Sadr alongside his father. Muqtada, however young and inexperienced, was displayed to the Iraqi people as the second coming of the White Lion. Often joined by likenesses of Imam Ali and Imam Hussein (in homage to the central figures of the Shi'a faith), and at times Mohammed Baqir al-Sadr (a grand-uncle of Muqtada's who, like the White Lion, was martyred by the former regime), images such as Figure 6.6 sought to emphasize Muqtada's pedigree and burnish the image of the rekindled Sadrist movement.[45]

In Amin, however, a shift occurred that was not observed elsewhere in the district. Figure 6.7, displayed prominently on the main street in front of the Muhsin al-Hakim mosque, depicts Muqtada not only alongside his father and Imam Hussein, but also in the company of leading figures in international Shi'a militarism: Hasan Nasrallah of the Lebanese Hizbullah and Ruhollah Khomeini, the iconic leader of the Iranian Revolution.

Nasrallah's inclusion, while by far the less controversial of the two, was nonetheless troublesome. As the leader of a militarized political party that had dramatically advanced the position of Lebanon's own long-marginalized Shi'a underclass (establishing itself as one of Israel and the West's most formidable foes in the process), the Lebanese Hizbullah was a much-lauded entity on the so-called Arab Street and, as noted in chapter three, a natural model for the Mehdi Army.[46] Yet, while several Shi'a insurgent groups in Iraq appropriated the Hizbullah moniker, the Lebanese Hizbullah's Iranian pedigree made it controversial. Anti-Iranian

Figure 6.6: Typical Sadrist Imagery[47]

Figure 6.7: Sadrist Imagery in Amin[48]

sentiments run strong among many Iraqi Shi'a—particularly among those with memories of Iraq's eight year war with Iran—for whom the rise of Iranian influence over Iraq (and, likewise, over the Sadrist movement) remains anathema.[49]

Whereas the Lebanese Hizbullah's Iranian ties rendered the inclusion of Nasrallah controversial, the addition of Ruhollah Khomenei in Sadrist imagery was extraordinarily provocative. Poor to working class Shi'a such as those in Amin had done much of the fighting, and the dying, during Iraq's eight-year war against Khomeini's Iran. The appearance of Khomeini in Mehdi Army imagery on the streets of Amin (only blocks away from neighborhoods built especially for veterans of the Iran war and the families of the fallen), and the presentation of Muqtada al-Sadr and his father as ideological kin of the leader of the Iranian Revolution, thus offered insight into the Mehdi Army's alienation of public opinion in Amin.[50]

Social Erosion and the Fall of the Mehdi Army in Kamaliyah and Amin

When the Surge commenced in Amin and Kamaliyah, American forces were confronted with an array of daunting challenges. The populations of the two *hayys* may not have been mobilized cohesively behind the militia's campaign, but both areas were home to well-armed, locally-rooted groups that were committed to preserving their hard-fought gains. Furthermore, uneven popular sentiment toward the Mehdi Army did not translate into enthusiasm for the encroachment of American forces or the ascendancy of the Shi'a establishment-dominated Iraqi government. On the contrary, with the anti-Americanism of the White Lion continuing to resonate, particularly in Amin, and with residents of both *hayys* having been neglected and scorned by the post-Saddam political establishment in much the same way as its predecessors in previous decades, the advances of counterinsurgent forces were viewed with extreme skepticism.

Progress in Amin and Kamaliyah thus came slowly, and at great cost. During the initial year of the Surge, American forces pushed local militants onto the defensive and prompted others to flee Tisa Nissan. Efforts to build upon these gains stalled, however. Rather than responding to counterinsurgency initiatives, Amin and Kamaliyah appeared intractable.

Counterinsurgency in Amin and Kamaliyah

Throughout the Surge's initial year, American forces had worked with their counterparts in the Iraqi National Police and the *hayys*' District- and Neighborhood-level government bodies to address security, development, and governance issues in Amin and Kamaliyah. Preliminary efforts to assert influence in the *hayys* witnessed the establishment of small, Company-sized patrol bases to allow American forces to maintain steady local presences, yet the potency of the Mehdi Army dictated that they be located on the peripheries of both *hayys*.[51] An arduous process commenced thereafter, as American units fought to assert themselves within the two *hayys* and restore the writ of the Iraqi government, involving heavy fighting on the *hayys*' streets and repeated attacks on American outposts.

As American forces and their Iraqi counterparts established themselves more firmly in Amin and Kamaliyah, an uneasy stalemate developed. Low-level violence persisted, but by the end of 2007 it appeared that the successful targeting of local militants and Muqtada's calls for a ceasefire were combining to make Amin and Kamaliyah less dangerous.[52]

Nonetheless, efforts to reform governance and spur development achieved limited results. Governance initiatives were hindered by the mutual wariness that underpinned relations with local politicians (whom Americans regarded as ranging from ineffective to deeply corrupt and supportive of the Mehdi Army), and also by prevailing sympathies toward the Mehdi Army within the heavily Shi'a Iraqi National Police unit that was assigned to eastern Tisa Nissan.[53] Development programmes also suffered as a result of the *hayys'* staggering infrastructural and economic problems, and the difficulty in mobilizing effective local leadership or active popular support. Amin thus continued to endure widespread electricity shortages that were particularly embittering for local residents in light of the nearby presence of one of Baghdad's primary power installations, while efforts to remedy Kamaliyah's infamous sewage problem were stalled by violence and contracting difficulties.[54]

The violence of March Madness, which erupted suddenly after an extended lull in activity during the winter of 2007–2008, caused considerable initial concern among American personnel. The ability of the militia and its affiliates to generate heavy violence in both *hayys* betrayed the fragility of gains achieved to date, not only demonstrating the enduring power of local militants over a year into the Surge, but also suggesting that the Mehdi Army's position in Amin and Kamaliyah might be stronger than previously appreciated.[55] As violence abated in the wake of March Madness' collapse, and American forces set about reclaiming Tisa Nissan during the spring and summer of 2008, conditions in Amin and Kamaliyah shifted yet again. The flight of noted Mehdi Army and Special Group fighters and the cessation of hostilities by prominent local militants led to major gains in security.[56] As American forces swept through the neighborhoods of Amin and Kamaliyah, working in partnership with a purged and now much-reformed Iraqi National Police force, they encountered only occasional resistance.[57]

Despite remarkable improvements in security, efforts to address development and governance issues still made limited headway. Local marketplaces enjoyed a resurgence in Amin and Kamaliyah, and many local areas showed encouraging signs of revitalized activity, but the *hayys'* official leadership remained as ineffective as before and crippling infrastructural woes sat unremedied.[58] The installation of a large generator in Kamaliyah's central industrial park failed to spur a local economic revival, for example, while issues of corruption and systemic dysfunction continued to plague the power station in Amin. Indeed, frustration with the slow pace of progress and the perceived ineptitude, impotence, and corruption of local officials reached the point that American forces largely disengaged from the local political system, seeking instead to pursue their objectives by working directly with the *hayys'* residents.

In support of this strategic shift, American personnel sought to identify and cultivate relationships with influential civilians who might assist in the *hayys'* revitalization.[59] Yet this effort, like many others before it in Amin and Kamaliyah, foundered. Moving from neighborhood to neighborhood and house to house throughout both *hayys* during the spring and summer of 2008, no evidence was found of an underlying social order that American forces might leverage in pursuit of their objectives, or of local leaders who enjoyed broadly-based communal influence. The Americans' civil society initiative thus languished—though it did offer important insights into the roots of the *hayys'* intractability.

The Degraded Terrain of Amin and Kamaliyah

At issue was the fact that the badly degraded state of civil society in Amin and Kamaliyah had left the bulk of the *hayys'* populations unable to coherently support either insurgency or counterinsurgency. With the traditional, tribal vestiges of civil society having been worn down by the stresses of migration and modernity, and with the Ba'th regime having methodically eradicated independent local leadership, there was no substantive underlying social order in the *hayys*. Instead, with the state having appropriated and manipulated what little remained of civil society during the 1990s, the fall of the old regime left the populace in a state of extreme atomization.

With the Mehdi Army's insurgent campaign relying heavily upon the ability to expand through the mobilization of local affiliates, the social condition of Amin and Kamaliyah directly influenced its fortunes in both *hayys*. The militia's core membership possessed inherent, defining qualities of its own (embodied most famously by Muqtada al-Sadr and his counterparts in the sanctions generation) but particular features of Amin and Kamaliyah did much to dictate the manner in which the militia developed locally. Both *hayys* were home to tens of thousands of underclass Shi'a who were devoted to the memory of the White Lion, but they were not organized coherently in viable social structures (whether tribal, professional, local, or otherwise). Lacking vital frameworks of organization and trust through which the social, religious, or political sentiments of the masses might be translated into substantive action, ordinary civilians were unable to exert a collective agency that would shape the Mehdi Army's evolution.[60]

There were, however, local networks that were eager and willing to contribute to the Mehdi Army's campaign. In Kamaliyah, an assortment of seasoned gangsters came to the fore, while the mosques of Amin offered a framework from which the militia could build. Furthermore, both *hayys* offered platoons of young men, who responded vigorously to the style and substance of Muqtada al-Sadr's message. The *hayys'* "silent majorities" of ordinary Shi'a families, on the other hand, appear to have remained marginal to the action of the post-Saddam era.[61] Hiding in their homes, they were reduced to looking on in horror at the abuses and atrocities wrought by militants, while lamenting Iraq's descent into sectarian division and bloodshed. Even their homes provided limited shelter, however, as families had been rendered unstable by the pressures and stresses of prior years. With adults in the *hayys* speaking openly of living in fear of their children, the generation gap often noted in the development of the Mehdi Army thus betrayed the degraded condition of communities and families alike.[62]

As a result of the Mehdi Army's encounter with civil society in Amin and Kamaliyah, what might have been a mass-based insurgency of the Shi'a underclass devolved into something far less coherent, and far less formidable. When the Surge advanced upon the *hayys*, therefore, it did not meet with coordinated popular resistance. This simplified American-led efforts to re-establish security, as the task required confronting and attacking distinct militant networks rather than overcoming the active, collective enmity of entire communities. However, the same underlying factors that had corrupted the Mehdi Army's insurgency also undermined counterinsurgency initiatives: just as the bulk of the *hayys'* populations had been unable to shape meaningfully the development of the militia, endemic social atomization (which had been further exacerbated by the violence and forced displacement of the sectarian war) precluded collective action in concert with the Surge.

Thus, despite widespread desire for the rule of law, the rehabilitation of critical infrastructure, and the revitalization of the local economy, the forces of the Surge remained largely unable to mobilize the people of

Amin and Kamaliyah. On the one hand, there did not appear to be any sheikhs or civic leaders able to compensate for the shortcomings of the government by initiating grassroots efforts to administer local neighborhoods or take ownership of development projects on a significant scale.[63] On the other hand, with local residents having been aggressively conditioned over the course of generations to look to the state as the driver of political, economic, and even social action, such endeavors were all the more unlikely to take root.[64]

The continued improvement of security conditions in Amin and Kamaliyah during the summer and fall of 2008 was thus not matched by comparable gains in governance or development. Neighborhood- and District-level institutions remained unable to resolve the *hayys'* many problems, while Baghdad's central administration proved reluctant to allocate funds to such notoriously corrupt and troubled areas of the city.[65] The goodwill achieved through gains in public safety was offset, therefore, by festering discontent over continued problems with essential services, creating an atmosphere of frustration and disenchantment. Indeed, quality of life was sufficiently unsatisfactory to provoke recurring expressions of nostalgia from local residents for the rule of Saddam Hussein.

7

FEDALIYAH AND SHAWRA WA UMM JIDR

TRACTION IN THE REMNANTS OF TRADITION

Fedaliyah and Shawra wa Umm Jidr: A Year into the Surge

In the early months of 2008, the *hayys* of Fedaliyah and Shawra wa Umm Jidr (hereafter referred to as "Shawra") were the areas of Tisa Nissan that were least secured and least accessible to American forces.[1] Fedaliyah was an insular, exclusively Shi'a enclave of Iraq's much-maligned Marsh Arab community, and one of Baghdad's most impenetrable places. This was due in part to the local terrain, which was criss-crossed by a tangled web of narrow, muddy lanes that were impassible by American vehicles. More importantly, however, it was a result of the *hayy's* inhabitants, who had further embellished the Marsh Arabs' centuries-old infamy for belligerence by turning Fedaliyah into one of the Mehdi Army's most important (and most feared) operational centers.[2] Shawra, on the other hand, was a sprawling tract of land that extended northward from Baghdad's outer canal. Forcibly cleansed and conquered by the Mehdi Army during the early years of the post-Saddam era, this remote area had thereafter been largely ignored by American and Iraqi forces—enabling Shi'a militants to establish local strongholds and maintain critical transit routes between militia-held territory in eastern Baghdad and points north-northeast of the city.[3]

The progress seen across much of Baghdad during the Surge's initial year had bypassed both *hayys* almost entirely. Fedaliyah and Shawra sat

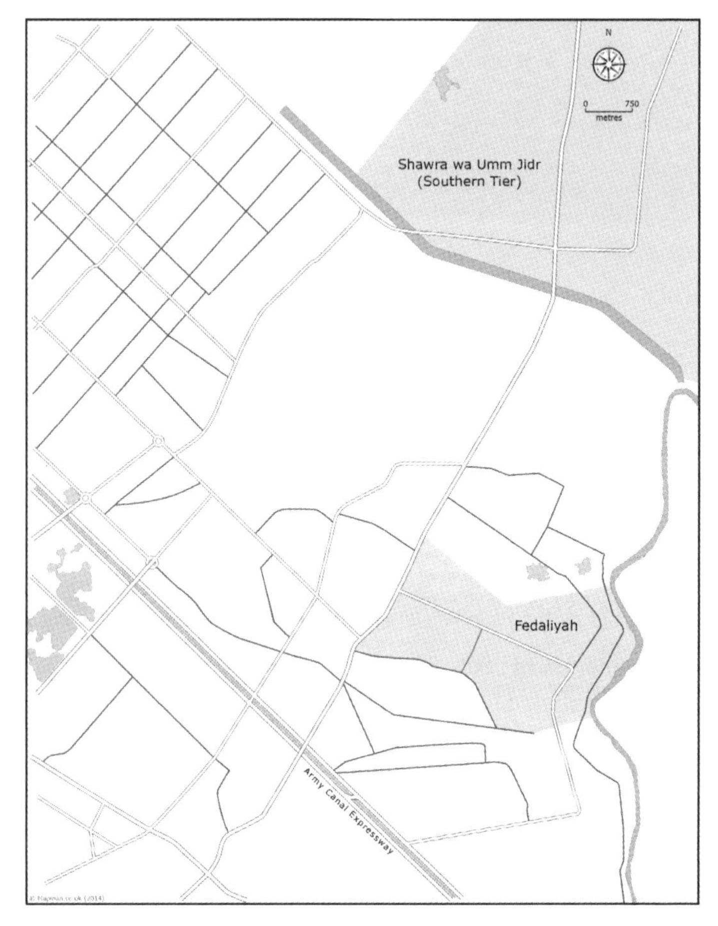

Figure 7.1: *Hayy* Boundaries of Fedaliyah and Shawra wa Umm Jidr

firmly outside the reach of the Iraqi government, and the encroachment of American or Iraqi units was reliably met with violence.[4] Indeed, Fedaliyah and Shawra were sufficiently inhospitable that American personnel had only been able to develop a limited range of first-hand insights into either *hayy*.

Fedaliyah, a place unlike any other in the Iraqi capital, was one that outsiders were eager to discuss, however. The Marsh Arabs of Fedaliyah were infamous in Baghdad, and the free-flowing accounts of Iraqis from surrounding neighborhoods and the ranks of the Security Forces catalogued their proclivity to extreme violence, the remarkable squalor in which they lived (which owed much to the herds of enormous water buffaloes, called *jamoose*, which many locals kept in pens attached to their homes), and their preservation of the austere tribal customs of traditional Marsh Arab society.[5] To enter Fedaliyah (a move roundly discouraged by enlisted personnel of the Iraqi Police) was described as a trip backward in time: its physical landscape, strewn with dilapidated, single-storey houses of mud-brick, cinder-blocks, and sheet-metal, and pockmarked with vast lakes of raw sewage in which herds of *jamoose* would bathe, evoked the long-demolished slums of *al-'asima*.[6] Local patterns of life, on the other hand, revolved primarily around the maintenance of *jamoose*, and were marred by tribal blood feuds and revenge killings that recalled some of the most regressive, anachronistic aspects of Iraq's traditional past.

The trepidation with which outsiders approached Fedaliyah acquired an additional facet in the post-Saddam era, as the *hayy's* Marsh Arabs established an exceptionally potent relationship with the Mehdi Army. Having become passionate devotees of the White Lion during the 1990s, the Marsh Arabs of Fedaliyah, like many of their counterparts in the slums of Basra and scattered across southern Iraq, embraced Muqtada and his militia.[7] Their fervor for the Sadrist cause and their prowess in battle transformed Fedaliyah into a bastion of Shi'a militarism, where

Figure 7.2: Sewage in Central Fedaliyah[8]

the Mehdi Army worked in concert with local tribes to export fearsome violence against American forces, the Iraqi government, and Baghdad's Sunnis as well.

Shawra, while known to contain pockets of strong Mehdi Army support, owed much of its inaccessibility and its unsecured status to its location and size. Situated on Tisa Nissan's northernmost edge, and covering a broad expanse of terrain stretching from eastern Baghdad's outer canal toward the rural, southern reaches of Diyala Province, Shawra had been infrequently patrolled and essentially ungoverned until the force realignment of the Surge. Even then, the allocation of a single Company of American soldiers had only enabled the establishment of a meaningful presence in the Rashad neighborhood in its southwestern corner. Efforts to project power eastward across Highway 5 or northward into the *hayy's* upper tier were inhibited by manpower constraints, the difficulty and danger of movement along local roads, and the strong presence of the Mehdi Army in the immediate vicinity of Joint Security Station SUJ, the patrol base from which most operations were conducted.

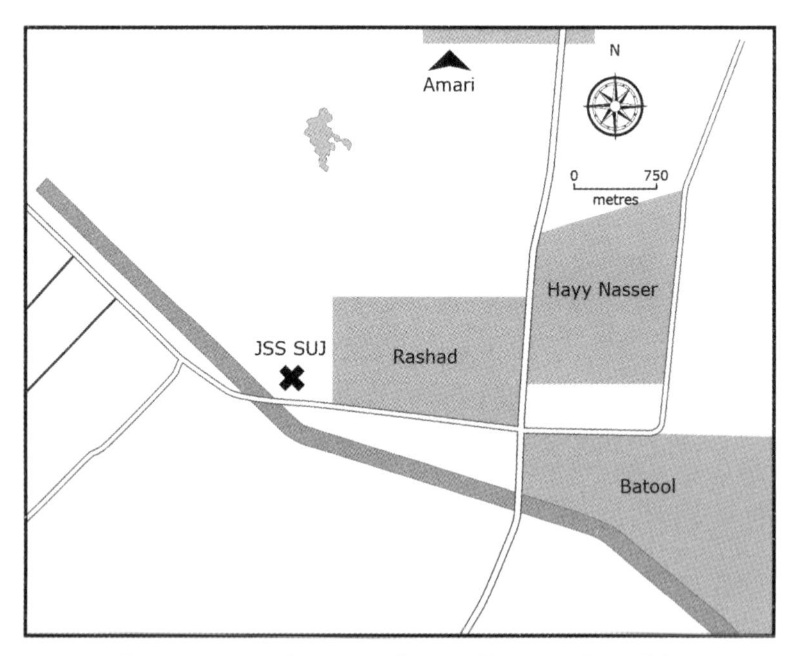

Figure 7.3: Main Settlement Areas in Shawra wa Umm Jidr

Nonetheless, American personnel active in the *hayy* believed that they presided over an area of underappreciated strategic importance. First, the *hayy* was a vital corridor for Mehdi Army and Special Group personnel, who moved men and material through Shawra between militia-held areas of eastern Baghdad and zones north and east of the capital (to include both the sectarian flashpoint of Baquba in Diyala Province, and the Iranian border).[9] Second, the *hayy* was also home to potent local centers of support for the militia. The Hayy Nasser neighborhood in Shawra's southeastern quadrant had offered strong resistance to the Surge, and the *hayy's* northern tier was likewise understood to be under firm militia control. The depth of the militia's position to the north was uncertain, as American and Iraqi forces had only been able to extend a limited presence into the area, yet it was understood that the *hayy's* full reclamation would require significantly more resources than had been available to date.

Key Issues in Fedaliyah and Shawra wa Umm Jidr

In Fedaliyah, local residents were renowned for their ferocity in attacking both American forces and Sunni Baghdadis alike, and the Mehdi Army's local command center was a hub of city-wide militant activity. However, the nature of the militia's relationship with local residents was unclear. How did an insular enclave of Marsh Arabs, shunned by outsiders and broadly reviled across Baghdad, come to host one of the Mehdi Army's most important command centers? Popular prejudices against the Marsh Arabs—who had long-occupied the lowest rung of the traditional tribal hierarchy, and who remained social pariahs in modern Iraqi society—were pervasive and powerful. The centrality of Fedaliyah to the Mehdi Army's campaign was thus remarkable. What had drawn the Mehdi Army to the *hayy*, and what had enabled the militia to achieve a localized operational potency that surpassed its accomplishments elsewhere?

In Shawra, it appeared that a security vacuum had enabled the Mehdi Army and associated Shi'a militant groups to build a strong local presence. However, the exact manner in which the militia had established itself was unknown, as was the nature of its connections to the *hayy's* residents. It was understood that the Mehdi Army's conquest of Shawra had been tied to large-scale population transfers, which saw not only the eviction of local Sunnis, but also the influx of large numbers of Shi'a from Sadr City and elsewhere. How had the militia asserted itself in Shawra, what were the circumstances under which former Sunni residents had been displaced, and how supportive was the resident population of its continued presence? Was the Mehdi Army's evident strength the by-product of substantive popular support, or was it more a consequence of the *hayy's* neglect by American and Iraqi forces during previous years?

March Madness in Fedaliyah and Shawra wa Umm Jidr

Having been effectively inaccessible to American forces during the early months of 2008, Fedaliyah and Shawra were scenes of intense militant activity during March Madness.[10] Furthermore, whereas the weeks that followed saw American and Iraqi forces reassert firm control over much of Beladiyat and Mashtal and make promising early strides in Amin and Kamaliyah, both Fedaliyah and the vast bulk of Shawra remained impenetrable. American and Iraqi forces were compelled to hold Fedaliyah in quarantine, controlling the roads leading in and out of the *hayy* but deigning to enter. In Shawra, on the other hand, American forces were able to re-establish themselves in Rashad, but they met stiff resistance in Hayy Nasser and remained unable to project significant power across the *hayy's* northern tier.[11]

The Mehdi Army thus retained both *hayys* through the spring of 2008, despite enduring major setbacks elsewhere in Tisa Nissan. Yet, as momentum in the district continued to swing in the favor of American and Iraqi forces, Fedaliyah and Shawra were increasingly isolated. Furthermore, the Mehdi Army was in full retreat on the national stage. Large-scale operations pressed into the core Sadrist strongholds of Sadr City and Maysan Province during May and June, inflicting such heavy damage on the militia that Muqtada was compelled to announce the Mehdi Army's dissolution.[12]

In an effort to capitalize on these developments, and to reclaim two of Baghdad's most prominent remaining strongholds of Shi'a militarism, American and Iraqi forces launched major initiatives to seize control of Fedaliyah and Shawra. In Fedaliyah, results came abruptly and unexpectedly. On 22 June, American forces and the bulk of an Iraqi National Police battalion embarked on an intensive, multi-day clearance of the entire *hayy*. Beginning on Highway 5 along the *hayy's* western edge, and pressing eastward to the Diyala River, each home, store, warehouse, and *jamoose* enclosure was searched for weapons and wanted militants. This marked the largest incursion yet into Fedaliyah, and heavy fighting was anticipated—yet the reception afforded by the Marsh Arabs was entirely pacific, cadre militants were found to have fled the area, and the weapons caches thought to be spread throughout the *hayy's jamoose* enclosures proved equally elusive. Not only did the operation progress without hostilities, but local residents greeted Iraqi and American personnel warmly from the doors of their homes, with offers of tea and *jamoose* milk.

Those taking part in the initial clearance of Fedaliyah, and who remained to patrol the area during the months that followed, were thus able to engage regularly with local residents in discussions, moving from house to house across the *hayy*.[13] The Marsh Arabs' altered posture toward the Surge transformed Fedaliyah into one of Tisa Nissan's more inviting areas for ground-level investigation, offering an array of invaluable insights into local conditions.[14]

Efforts to assert control over Shawra, meanwhile, which intensified through the summer of 2008, met with determined, sustained opposition. The operational tempo of American and Iraqi forces was escalated significantly from August onwards, with an additional Company of American soldiers relocating to the *hayy* in September to provide further support. Patrols were thereafter extended beyond the limits of Rashad with greater frequency, challenging militants in Hayy Nasser and meeting with uneven, yet occasionally intense resistance in northern areas of the *hayy*.[15]

Furthermore, as American and Iraqi forces raised their profile in Shawra, displacing militants from its southern tier and projecting influence further to the north, opportunities for sit-down meetings with local leadership emerged as well. On the one hand, the *hayy's* Neighborhood Council was revived after an extended period of dormancy, facilitating regular interactions with Shawra's official leaders. On the other, the gradual abatement of violence was followed by appeals for sectarian reconciliation and the return of forcibly displaced Sunnis, culminating in a series of meetings held among local leaders that were mediated by the Iraqi National Police.[16] American forces were presented with a growing range of venues in which they could meet and develop relationships with prominent local residents, gaining insights into the events that had brought sweeping changes to the *hayy* since 2003.

The Distinctiveness of Fedaliyah and Shawra wa Umm Jidr

From the Mehdi Army's impressive displays of localized strength during the Surge's initial year, to the subsequent durability of its resistance in the months after March Madness, it was evident that the militia had achieved a superior potency in Fedaliyah and Shawra. In both *hayys*, the Surge met with powerful opposition, which was well entrenched in the terrain and proved exceptionally difficult to dislodge. An understanding of the source of this potency, and of how and why the Mehdi Army's insurgent campaign in Tisa Nissan appeared to have reached its greatest heights in Fedaliyah and Shawra, offered potentially powerful insights into the dynamics of its broader fortunes.

Close study of the Mehdi Army's rise and fall in Fedaliyah and Shawra shows that its insurgent campaign was shaped in fundamental ways by the *hayys'* histories, and the manner in which they had evolved during previous decades. While Fedaliyah and Shawra's creation and growth owed much to the same migratory flows and urban development initiatives that drove the overall expansion of Baghdad's eastern periphery, each had acquired distinct social and demographic characteristics that presented the Mehdi Army with critical advantages.

The Foundation and Preservation of Fedaliyah

Fedaliyah was established during the initial phase of eastern Baghdad's government-led expansion, as a dedicated enclave for Marsh Arabs.[17] Groups of Marsh Arabs (and their herds of *jamoose*) had been present among the early waves of mass migration to the Iraqi capital during the 1940s and 1950s. Settling in small clusters in the slums of *al-'asima*, interspersed among the masses of underclass Shi'a migrants, they and their animals acquired an immediate notoriety for their contamination of the landscape.[18] The extraordinary amounts of waste generated by their herds of *jamoose*, and the animals' habit of cooling themselves in vast pits thereof, featured prominently in the accounts of appalled observers as defining features of Baghdad's increasingly wretched periphery; providing ammunition both to those who agitated for reform on the migrants' behalf, as well as to those who bemoaned the corrosive influences of migration on the capital.[19]

There was, therefore, a certain irony in the fact that Prime Minister Qasim's sweeping urban development initiative—which was a fundamentally sympathetic effort to remedy the plight of the migrants, signifying the revolutionary regime's commitment to "social justice" for Iraq's downtrodden Shi'a underclass—raised an existential threat to the Marsh Arabs' position in the Iraqi capital. Requiring space to house their herds and access to ample reserves of food and water, eastern Baghdad's emerging landscape of densely-packed housing blocks was wholly inhospitable. The demolition of Baghdad's decrepit and diseased *sarifas* and their replacement with the modern tenements of Revolution City and Shula was a dramatic initial step toward the betterment of the vast bulk of Baghdad's migrant poor, but it imperiled the Marsh Arabs' traditional way of life.

To remedy the concerns of the Marsh Arabs, a parcel of land far from the city center was designated for their use. The disparate communities of Marsh Arabs that had settled along the city's margins thus relocated with their herds to a plot of land along the Diyala River, forming the nucleus of Fedaliyah. There they established a localized social, cultural, and economic ecosystem all of their own that, through subsequent decades, became a magnet that attracted further Marsh Arab migrants whilst repelling all others.[20]

As eastern Baghdad's growth continued through the 1970s and 1980s, external pressures mounted on Fedaliyah. Its Marsh Arab residents grew infamous for their ties to criminal activity, while their steadfast adherence to rough, traditional customs and pastoral patterns of life inspired near-universal contempt.[21] The neighborhood thus came to be regarded as a blight on the urban landscape that ought to be eradicated, and the accumulation of popular enmity further isolated the Marsh Arabs in Fedaliyah.

During the 1990s, the social prejudices that had long hounded the Marsh Arabs were compounded by waves of aggressive government persecution. With Saddam Hussein waging an all-out war against the Marsh Arabs of southern Iraq (largely in response to the anti-regime actions of Marsh Arab groups, which reached alarming levels during and after the 1991 uprising), Iraq's Marsh Arabs were besieged as never before.[22] Declaring that the "marsh people" were not Arabs, but instead "indistinguishable from" the *jamoose* with which they had allegedly been breeding for generations, the Iraqi government attacked them both rhetorically and physically.[23] Furthermore, the Iraqi government also initiated preparations for Fedaliyah's demolition and the relocation of its residents out of Baghdad across the Diyala River. The Marsh Arabs' enclave in Baghdad, which they had struggled to maintain in the face of great adversity through prior decades, was thus threatened with final destruction; and the violence that emanated from the neighborhood earned it the nickname *shishan*, meaning Chechen, in reference to the brutal insurgency ongoing at that time in the former Soviet Union.

In light of these intensifying stresses, Iraq's Marsh Arabs greeted the rise of the White Lion with great passion. The sustained outreach of Sadrist emissaries (who made deliberate overtures to Marsh Arabs across Iraq, actively cultivating their support) stood in sharp contrast to the neglect and disdain shown previously by the elites of the clerical establishment. As a result, irrespective of their notorious reputation for impiety, the Marsh Arabs of Fedaliyah, like their counterparts across Iraq, embraced the Sadrist movement. Integrating Sadrist ideals into their own long-running struggle for communal preservation, Marsh Arabs emerged among the movement's most fervent and dedicated supporters—a point violently punctuated by their leading role in the retributive anti-regime violence that followed Sadr's murder in 1999.[24]

The Development of Shawra wa Umm Jidr

As a result of Shawra's size and location, its northern and southern tiers evolved in response to two different sets of influences. To the south, along the edge of Baghdad's outer canal, the Iraqi state drove development directly. For the purpose of containing domestic unrest, it was established practice in Iraq to encircle major urban areas with trusted loyalists and government facilities.[25] With the outer canal demarcating the capital's northeastern border, and Highway 5 the key route between Baghdad and points north-northeast, southern Shawra became the domain of the state: three prisons were built (one of which was for women), a regional domestic security headquarters was established, and the ministry of agriculture and other institutions also developed sizable presences.[26]

In conjunction with the proliferation of government facilities, which reached its apex under Ba'thist rule, southern Shawra also acquired a small, heavily Ba'thist residential population. The Rashad neighborhood in particular became home to numerous government officials and, as a result, local infrastructure and essential services were maintained to a significantly higher standard than in surrounding areas (earning the small settlement the nickname "Tikrit," in reference to the hometown of

Saddam Hussein). As such, while Rashad also attracted a collection of relatively poor migrant families of Shi'a from Diyala Province, southern Iraq, and nearby areas of Baghdad, the neighborhood maintained a far more orderly feel than other areas of intensive migrant settlement like Kamaliyah and Amin.[27]

To the east of Highway 5, a modest industrial base also developed during the 1970s and 1980s, with brick factories and textile plants occupying the terrain alongside local government installations. Additional residential growth then occurred in the wake of the Iran war, with the construction of Hayy Nasser, or "Neighborhood of Victory."[28] The neighborhood became home to an assortment of lower to middle class Shi'a and Sunni families (Ba'thists prominent among them) and grew incrementally through the 1990s. Yet southern Shawra remained a lightly populated zone that was dominated by the state.[29]

Along Shawra's northern tier, local growth mirrored developments in the remote, adjoining zones of southern Diyala Province. From the drab, semi-urban settlement of Amari, to the clusters of homes that sprawled further northward along Highway 5, and the small encampments interspersed across the farmland near the Diyala River, northern Shawra was far removed from the administrative attentions and urbanizing influences of central Baghdad. Instead, the area attracted a collection of Shi'a and Sunni tribal and familial clusters, some of which blended together in the area's more dense settlements, and some of which established individual enclaves across the open terrain.[30]

Growing modestly as an offshoot of the major population shifts that occurred from Iraq's periphery toward Baghdad during the mid to late twentieth century (which gave rise to many of the small towns and settlements on the bleak agricultural belt surrounding the Iraqi capital), northern Shawra remained significantly more rural and tribal than much of the rest of Baghdad. Indeed, in a reflection of the extent to which Shawra, as a whole, laid only the most tenuous claim to inclusion within the city, the area was repeatedly transferred administratively between Baghdad and Baquba.[31] Receiving scant attention from authorities in either city, the area remained poor, underdeveloped, and underserviced by the government, with local residents mired in a state of relative neglect and isolation.

Having absorbed substantial numbers of underclass Shi'a residents during the 1970s and 1980s, the Sadrist movement was able to make inroads into Shawra during the 1990s. The area's mixed sectarian composition dictated that support was patchy, yet the Shi'a of Amari and its environs, like others in Rashad and Hayy Nasser, rallied to the White Lion's call. Furthermore, still-vibrant tribal ties between the Shi'a of Shawra's northern tier and their counterparts in the Sadrist strongholds of Iraq's Deep South appear to have facilitated the Sadrist movement's spread through the area, to the extent that the 1990s witnessed the development of a local base of organized support that would endure well beyond the White Lion's murder.[32]

The Mehdi Army's Power in Fedaliyah and Shawra wa Umm Jidr

As Muqtada al-Sadr set about rekindling the Sadrist movement and channeling underclass Shi'a men into the Mehdi Army, Fedaliyah and Shawra presented valuable opportunities. In Fedaliyah, the Marsh Arabs' enduring reverence for the White Lion intertwined with their communal desire for self-preservation (and their aggression and aptitude in battle), yielding formidable results. In Shawra, the militia found not only ardent allies among local Shi'a, but also a target rich environment for the persecution of Ba'thists and the conquest of terrain. As a result, the Mehdi Army enjoyed enormous successes in both *hayys*, drawing them into the urban empire that it carved out across eastern Baghdad's periphery.

However, Fedaliyah and Shawra's significance to the militia extended well beyond what might have been expected. With Fedaliyah an insular enclave of socio-cultural pariahs, and Shawra a marginal, remote region that was broadly regarded as lying beyond the city limits, the *hayys* were, in fundamental respects, unlikely hubs of militia activity. Yet, as the Mehdi Army's insurgent campaign faltered elsewhere, with the militia struggling to translate the Sadrist sympathies of the masses into coherent, substantive support, the *hayys* were found to hold considerable value. As a result of features particular to the human terrain of each *hayy*—which were direct by-products of their unique historical experiences and demographic profiles—Fedaliyah and Shawra proved to be the areas in Tisa Nissan where the militia was best able to rally and sustain potent, locally-rooted insurgency.

The Mehdi Army Comes to Fedaliyah

As the Mehdi Army initiated its insurgent campaign in Baghdad, the Marsh Arabs of Fedaliyah vividly reified stereotypes of their innate belligerence. In Baghdad, as in Basra and across key areas of southern Iraq, Marsh Arabs proved themselves to be among the most eager and capable opponents of Coalition Forces.[33] As such, irrespective of any social prejudices harbored by leaders of the rekindled Sadrist movement, Iraq's Marsh Arabs assumed prominent positions as proxy allies of the Mehdi Army—as the violent behavior for which they had been long derided was found to have great utility on the battlefield.

Fedaliyah's value to the Mehdi Army then rose further during the sectarian war.[34] As a purely Shi'a enclave of passionate Sadrists, and an insular environment that was impregnable by Sunni militants, Fedaliyah offered an ideal sanctuary for Shi'a partisans. The Sadrist office established on the *hayy's* main east-west artery thus became a central command and control center, from which cadre militants oversaw operations citywide.[35]

In addition to providing an unassailable defensive position, Fedaliyah also supplied the Mehdi Army with some of its most fearsome shock troops—as a result not only of the martial aptitude of the Marsh Arabs, but also of the vibrancy of Fedaliyah's local tribal order. In contrast to other areas of Tisa Nissan, where a host of stresses had combined over the course of decades to atomize the population, Fedaliyah possessed a critical measure of internal social order. Its *mahallah*-like homogeneity appeared to have facilitated the preservation of communal integrity, with tribal leaders enjoying significant influence and prestige, while its insularity had helped shield traditional civil society from corrosive external influences.[36] Therefore, when the Mehdi Army sought to rally local support, there were coherent structures that provided traction for offensive and defensive purposes alike.

As a result, previously shunned and scorned Marsh Arabs of Fedaliyah found themselves at the heart of the Mehdi Army's campaign in Baghdad. Social prejudices persisted (and, indeed, appear to have intensified, as the Marsh Arabs' excesses against Sunni civilians provoked accusations of barbarism from even their Sadrist allies), yet the prominence of Fedaliyah as a bastion of Shi'a militarism continued to grow.[37] The combined power generated by the militia and its Marsh Arab kin was such that forcibly displaced Shi'a from middle to working class areas of western Baghdad sought refuge on the *hayy's* northwestern margins, enduring squalid conditions in exchange for guaranteed protection from Sunni militants.[38]

Retaining its importance to the Mehdi Army as sectarian violence abated, Fedaliyah became a key base for resistance against the Surge.

Owing to the formidable capabilities of the Mehdi Army and its Marsh Arab allies, and also the difficulty of maneuvering on the *hayy's* treacherous terrain, the forces of the Surge made little headway.[39] The local Sadrist office instead remained a prominent operational center for Shi'a resistance, the *jamoose* stables and haystacks scattered throughout the *hayy* were thought to conceal a sizeable arsenal, and residents appeared ardently hostile to the encroachment of both the American military and the Iraqi government (which, like its Ba'thist predecessor, regarded the Marsh Arabs with a blend of contempt, concern, and irritation).

Taking Shawra wa Umm Jidr

The Mehdi Army's conquest of Shawra began in the early months of the post-Saddam era. Home to sizable concentrations of Ba'thists and numerous installations of Saddam Hussein's police state, the *hayy's* southern tier attracted the predatory attentions of the Mehdi Army.[40] Successfully eradicating the functionaries of the former regime, the militia was left in de facto control over much of the area—leaving it well positioned to draw strength from, and to proactively influence, the inward surge of Shi'a families from nearby areas of Sadr City, Diyala Province, and other areas within Baghdad.[41]

The early years of the post-Saddam era witnessed hundreds of new homes spring up on the open spaces around Rashad, Hayy Nasser, and Batool, as opportunistic migrants laid claim to the property of the fallen regime and to land that had formerly been vacant. Modern-day *sarifas* of the sort found across northern Beladiyat and throughout much of nearby Obeidy thus proliferated, while larger homes were also built in Batool.[42] Similar to the Mehdi Army's advance into Beladiyat, therefore, the militia was able to entrench itself in southern Shawra by channeling operatives and supporters into the area (to Hayy Nasser in particular, which appeared to have been colonized in much the same way as Sab'a Nissan), and by drawing foot soldiers and facilitators from among the growing pool of underclass Shi'a youths.[43]

As the sectarian war gathered momentum, southern Shawra attracted additional population flows and was drawn more tightly into the militia's embrace. The area's peripheral position, removed geographically from the turmoil that was wracking much of Baghdad and Diyala Province, rendered it an attractive point of refuge for Shi'a families. Migrants of various socio-economic backgrounds thus moved into the area's expansive open spaces in growing numbers, where the Mehdi Army's local power provided protection against Sunni attack. Hayy Nasser also emerged as an important operational center. Located at a strategic position at the entrance to eastern Baghdad, and having attracted a strong contingent of militants, the neighborhood became a key transit node and a sanctuary for fighters—roles that it would retain as sectarian violence abated, and Shi'a militants turned their attentions to combating the Surge.

In northern Shawra, the dynamics of the militia's rise resembled the progression of events elsewhere across Diyala Province's rural expanses. Having been relatively isolated during the early instability of the post-Saddam era (when the main insurgent groups were focused principally on attacking Coalition Forces and disrupting the emerging political order), the area was plunged into chaos by the eruption of sectarian violence. The battle for Baghdad sparked numerous tangential contests for control over mixed-sect areas on the main approaches to the city, and northern Shawra thus attracted the attentions of the conflict's principal antagonists.[44]

The fighting that ensued in northern Shawra involved a web of alliances between nationally-oriented sectarian militant networks and local tribal groups.[45] With the Mehdi Army drawing upon the active support of certain local Shi'a tribes, and area Sunnis alleged to have liaised with al-Qaeda affiliated militants, a series of battles occurred during the summer and fall of 2006 in the region between Amari and the Diyala River.[46] The Mehdi Army and its local allies won a decisive victory, after which the area's remaining Sunnis sought protection from local Shi'a who had abstained from the fighting. Continued pressure from the Mehdi Army and its affiliates ultimately forced the cessation of that support, however. A rout ensued, ending with the disposal of bodies in the nearby landfill and the exodus of approximately 1,000 Sunni survivors to the Taji area north of Baghdad.[47]

Consolidating ties with its allies, the Mehdi Army was thereafter the dominant force in northern Shawra. Furthermore, it appeared that the relationship forged between the militia and its local affiliates created synergies that benefited both parties. For the Mehdi Army, tapping into a localized tribal order enabled it to entrench itself firmly in northern Shawra, providing structure and order to its presence; while for the militia's tribal allies, partnership with the Mehdi Army enabled them to achieve a level of influence that was otherwise unobtainable.[48] With

American and Iraqi forces largely absent from the area, the Amari neighborhood became a key transit hub for Shi'a militants that was strewn with Sadrist imagery, while the familial and tribal connection between residents of Amari and Hayy Nasser further consolidated the *hayy's* stability as a Mehdi Army stronghold.[49]

The Surge in Fedaliyah and Shawra wa Umm Jidr

For more than a year, Fedaliyah and Shawra resisted the advances of the Surge. Drawing upon the strength of its local allies in both *hayys*, and capitalizing on its success in reshaping the terrain of southern Shawra (thus creating a localized base of support), the Mehdi Army mounted formidable, durable opposition to American-led counterinsurgency operations.[50] Indeed, in a vivid demonstration of the exceptional localized strength of Shi'a militarism, the two *hayys* remained beyond the reach of American and Iraqi forces in the wake of March Madness, when Sadrist-inspired resistance was collapsing elsewhere and the Mehdi Army itself was dissolved.

Yet while Fedaliyah and Shawra marked the Mehdi Army's greatest successes in Tisa Nissan, the events surrounding their reclamation suggested that the militia's local achievements required qualification. The ultimate ability of the Surge to penetrate Fedaliyah and Shawra was primarily the result of the Mehdi Army's nationwide implosion (as opposed to the efficacy of local counterinsurgency initiatives), but the sequence of events as American and Iraqi forces entered the *hayys* exposed a vulnerability in the militia's insurgent strategy: the harnessing of dynamic local allies had generated exceptional operational potency, but the militia had not effectively subsumed its proxies' local, communal identities and priorities within its own. As such, the militia's core cadre was left exposed to recalculation and betrayal as its broader fortunes soured, with its local allies pursuing independent strategies of communal self-preservation rather than acting as part of a cohesive whole.

Counterinsurgency in Fedaliyah and Shawra wa Umm Jidr

From the start of the Surge in early 2007 until the summer of 2008, American and Iraqi forces made minimal headway in Fedaliyah and Shawra. In Fedaliyah, the strength of local hostility prevented American forces from establishing a patrol base within the Marsh Arabs' domain. Confined instead to Joint Security Station al-Khansa (located alongside Highway 5 to the north of its intersection with Fedaliyah's main east-west artery), American units and their Iraqi counterparts struggled to project meaningful influence in the *hayy*.[51] Shawra, meanwhile, attracted scant attention from American and Iraqi forces alike. Those stationed at Forward Operating Base Hope in the *hayy's* southwestern corner (later renamed Joint Security Station SUJ) extended only a modest reach into Shawra's sprawling expanse, while Shi'a militants operated with impunity to their immediate west, north, and east.[52]

Both *hayys* reacted violently to the incursions of American and Iraqi patrols, and proved overwhelmingly inhospitable to the non-violent, constructive inducements of counterinsurgency. As such, minimal progress was made before March Madness. Prevailing American views of Fedaliyah were captured in the succinct assessment of a soldier from the infantry Company that had administered the *hayy*, who described it as "a place we go to get in a gunfight," while the vast bulk of Shawra remained inaccessible.[53] Both *hayys* remained in the hands of Shi'a militants, and their prominent roles in the violence that erupted during late March—as well as their continued hostility during the months that followed—were unsurprising to American personnel.

When large-scale initiatives were launched to finally assert control over the *hayys* during the summer and fall of 2008, it was widely understood that this marked an intrusion upon Shi'a militants' strongest remaining fortifications, and that the outcome of these operations might prove decisive to the fate of Tisa Nissan's Shi'a insurgency. The sudden and unexpected transformation of Fedaliyah—from a cauldron of insurgency to a peaceful, permissive environment for Americans—provoked amazement that was at once celebratory and cautious.

On the one hand, the pacification of Fedaliyah marked an extraordinary achievement, as it represented the taming of what had been one of the Mehdi Army's most impenetrable bases of operation. On the other hand, with the *hayy* having been, in effect, "offered up" rather than actively reclaimed, there was a palpable eeriness to Fedaliyah's newfound calm.[54] As American personnel and their Iraqi counterparts attempted to consolidate their gains, most notably through economic support to *jamoose* owners (who claimed to have fallen on hard times when the Ba'th regime's destruction led to the cessation of grain subsidies necessary to feed their herds), those operating in Fedaliyah remained wary of an equally sudden return to violence.[55]

Progress came neither as suddenly nor as dramatically in Shawra. From mid summer onwards, efforts to displace Shi'a militants from Hayy Nasser brought heavy violence to the *hayy's* southern tier. Blocking local roads with burning tires and assorted debris, the remnants of the now-disbanded Mehdi Army (joined by Special Group militants and various local fighters) barricaded Hayy Nasser and fought a protracted battle that continued into the fall. This firmly established the neighborhood as Tisa Nissan's most prominent remaining trouble spot.

The arrival of an additional Company of American soldiers in September and the redoubled attentions of American and Iraqi forces then brought significant pressure to bear at a time when the positions of local militants were increasingly isolated.[56] Violence continued, but momentum shifted decisively against those resisting the Surge, catalyzing changes that resonated across the *hayy*. With a revived Neighborhood Council system providing a framework for discussion, and an increasingly respected Iraqi National Police leadership mediating the process, fighting eventually gave way to highly-charged inter-communal maneuvering. Forcibly displaced Sunni groups worked to orchestrate their return, local Shi'a claiming to have abstained from the violence of previous years sought to endear themselves to American and Iraqi forces, and the militia's local affiliates attempted to protect their interests and retain their hard-fought gains.

The Perils of Segmentation and Localism

Critical to the efforts of American and Iraqi forces, the same social bonds that had made the two *hayys* such prolific founts of popular insurgency also created vulnerabilites for the militia. Home to coherent local groups with overriding local priorities, Fedaliyah and northern Shawra offered sound footing for counterinsurgency. The vitality and cohesion of tribal networks in the two *hayys*, which had been instrumental in lifting the militia to otherwise unattainable levels of operational potency, proved to be a double-edged sword.

At issue was the fact that the relationship between the Mehdi Army's cadre leadership and its local tribal allies was not one of commander and subordinate. On the contrary, rather than resembling the structure of a modern military organization, the dynamic between the militia's core and its local proxies evoked the segmentary tribal confederations of Mesopotamia's traditional past.[57] Fedaliyah's Marsh Arabs and the Shi'a tribes of northern Shawra were eager to fight for Sadrist causes, so long as they remained compatible with their own local, communal objectives. But, as evidenced during the course of the Mehdi Army's rout and collapse during the course of 2008, they were not prepared to sacrifice themselves against a determined foe with superior firepower and strategic momentum.

This was most clearly evident in Fedaliyah, where the sudden change of posture by the Marsh Arabs appears to have betrayed the diverging priorities of local residents and dedicated militants. Evidence accumulated that a significant break had occurred between the general population and the remnants of the Mehdi Army. From a series of murders that were attributed to former militia operatives, to the occurrence of a full-scale tribal battle that brought heavily armed factions out into the streets of the *hayy*, recurrent intra-communal violence within Fedaliyah in the aftermath of its "pacification" suggested that the departure of cadre militants and the cessation of resistance had been contested rather than consensual.

Having struggled for generations to maintain their enclave in Baghdad, the nationwide collapse of the Mehdi Army seems to have compelled local Marsh Arabs to cease their hostilities against the Surge and cultivate ties with their former foes. Their hearts may well have remained with the cause of Sadrist resistance, but the preservation of their traditional way of life (and their very position in the city) required accommodation with a shifting strategic landscape—which was made most evident by the tenacity and seeming desperation with which local *jamoose* owners pursued American officers and civilian personnel for economic support.[58]

In Shawra, several factors contributed to the eventual collapse of resistance against the Surge. In and around Hayy Nasser, there were notable commonalities with events elsewhere in Tisa Nissan. By cleansing the area of its pre-invasion Ba'thist population, overseeing the influx of thousands of new Shi'a residents, and concentrating its operatives in Hayy Nasser, the militia's conquest of the area bore a distinct resemblance to its campaign in western Beladiyat. The militia hub of Hayy Nasser shared much in common with Sab'a Nissan, while the area's broader social landscape—filled with ordinary families who had arrived in haphazard fashion from a broad array of places, and who remained overwhelmingly preoccupied with their own survival—resembled the *hawasim* zones of Beladiyat and the northern tier of Kamaliyah.

In a further echo of events elsewhere in Tisa Nissan, localized resistance to the Surge remained the work of a relative few in southern Shawra.[59] Sadrist sympathies ran strong among local Shi'a, and the area's prolonged neglect left civilians extremely skeptical of the inducements of counterinsurgent forces, but the militia's reputation had suffered from abuses like those witnessed in Amin and Kamaliyah. Morality police terrorized local residents, and the predations of militants left desecrated bodies hanging from football goalposts. Thus, when the forces of the Surge were able to mass in sufficient strength to displace key militants, violence abated significantly and "resistance" imploded.

Along Shawra's northern tier, the inter-communal jockeying that accompanied the collapse of the Mehdi Army evoked aspects of both Beladiyat and Fedaliyah. Like the besieged middle class and minority communities of Beladiyat, Sunni groups that had suffered at the hands of the Mehdi Army sought to redress their grievances through interaction with American and Iraqi forces. The Mehdi Army's former allies, like their counterparts in Fedaliyah, attempted to distance themselves from the violence of previous years and protect their immediate, local interests. With the area's various Shi'a tribal groups bearing varied and contested levels of responsibility for the violence of prior years, and local elders seeking exculpation on the grounds that they, like many others in Tisa Nissan, had been unable to rein in their sons' militant passions, negotiations proved delicate and contentious.[60] Key Shi'a militants were nevertheless compelled to flee northwards into ungoverned areas of Diyala Province or further afield to Iran, leaving Shawra increasingly secure as 2008 drew to a close.

8

INSURGENCY AND COUNTERINSURGENCY ON UNEVEN TERRAIN

Insurgency as a Reflection of Civil Society

At the dawn of of the post-Saddam era, there was great cause for optimism regarding the prospects of Muqtada al-Sadr and the rekindled Sadrist movement. Building on the still-potent legacy of the White Lion among Iraq's underclass Shi'a (who, by virtue of their numerical strength in Baghdad and across key areas of the oil-rich south, were assured pivotal influence in any democratic political system), the Sadrists were presented with a remarkable opportunity.[1] With the potential to become Iraq's only grassroots-supported, mass-based political movement outside of Iraqi Kurdistan, and with their principal rivals in Shi'ism's clerical establishment and the middle and upper classes enduring prolonged periods of decline, the Sadrists were well positioned to realize the White Lion's vision.[2]

However, as evidenced most vividly by the erratic trajectory of the Mehdi Army, the rekindled Sadrist movement struggled to find and maintain its footing. From the outset, this owed much to the fierce opposition of the Shi'a elite and their powerful Western allies. Yet external hostility alone cannot account for the Sadrists' difficulties, or explain the implosion of the Mehdi Army. Irrespective of the strength of the Sadrists' opponents (whose ranks, as noted in chapter three, quickly expanded to include Iraq's powerful al-Qaeda franchise), the Mehdi Army grew massively from 2004 onwards and Sadrist politicians won major victories in the elections of 2005. By 2006, the rekindled Sadrist movement and its Mehdi Army militia were established as a Lebanese Hizbullah-like politico-cum-military force that seemed poised to exert extraordinary influence in Iraqi politics for years to come.

Yet, due to the forces detailed in the preceding chapters, the Mehdi Army's greatest successes sowed the seeds of its demise. In theory, the militia was to be the vanguard of Muqtada's Sadrist resurgence, spearheading a popular uprising of Iraq's downtrodden Shi'a underclass in the name of political, religious, and social validation. In practice, however, the dearth of coherent social bonds among Iraq's underclass Shi'a citizenry precluded the formation of what might otherwise have been a sweeping, popular movement.[3] Instead, the militia came to be dominated by the likes of Kamaliyah's hardened strongmen, the anachronistic Marsh Arabs of Fedaliyah, and the sectarian radicals of Amin—supported by platoons of volatile young men who had come of age in an era of societal collapse, material hardship, and pervasive, vicious violence. The Mehdi Army, which grew by absorbing elements of Iraqi society, was poisoned from within.

Surveying the militia's fortunes across Tisa Nissan, the localized influence of civil society is striking. In Beladiyat and Mashtal, the Mehdi Army faced relatively coherent middle class and minority communities hostile to its advance, which compelled a strategy of peripheral encroachment. The militia thus made inroads into Beladiyat by conquering and colonizing Sab'a Nissan, and by riding a demographic wave of underclass Shi'a migration eastward out of Sadr City. In Mashtal, on the other hand, the militia benefited from its potency in nearby Amin and Fedaliyah, as well as its dominance over the settlement area north of the District Council facility, which enabled an inward advance from the margins of the *hayy*.

While the Mehdi Army was ultimately able to overcome its local opponents and assert its writ over the core neighborhoods of Beladiyat and Mashtal, it could not consolidate its gains. The *hayys'* new settlement areas, which were home to thousands of underclass Shi'a, provided concealment for militants and a modest supply of low-level operatives—but their residents could not be coherently mobilized. Despite benefiting from a prime opportunity to capitalize on the class-based tensions at the heart of Sadrist ideology, the militia's leaders failed to rally the newly-arrived Shi'a poor of Beladiyat and Mashtal in support of their efforts. This was due in part to the negative qualities of the militia's cadre, which repelled many with Sadrist sympathies, but also to the social fragmentation of the Mehdi Army's prospective local base of support and its tenuous position on the local landscape.

In Amin and Kamaliyah, where the White Lion reigned during the 1990s, the Mehdi Army also failed to effectively mobilize its base. Home at the time of the 2003 invasion to large contingents of Sadrist Shi'a, and becoming the near-exclusive domain of the Sadrists' demographic base after the Mehdi Army's brutal campaign of sectarian cleansing, both *hayys* came to sit firmly within the militia's urban empire. As such, the leaders of the militia had numerous opportunities over a period of years to translate popular affinity for Sadrist ideals into substantive, active support for their endeavor. However, owing to the ways in which the *hayys'* histories shaped local society—both by influencing those who came to be the Mehdi Army's most prominent representatives, and by degrading communal bonds that might have otherwise enabled the Sadrist masses to steer the militia's development in a more popular direction—neither Amin nor Kamaliyah fulfilled its insurgent potential. In the end, shared Sadrist sentiments among the *hayys'* residents proved insufficient as an operational framework for the mobilization of insurgency; more substantive, tangible social bonds were needed.[4]

Finally, in Fedaliyah and Shawra, the Mehdi Army enjoyed its greatest successes. The two *hayys* were home to fervent bases of support for the Sadrist cause. They also possessed social structures that enabled the militia to translate popular sentiments into concrete action. In Fedaliyah, this was due to the unique historical experience of the Marsh Arabs in Baghdad, and the resulting operational functionality, and ferocity, of resident tribes. In Shawra, this was likewise due, in part, to local tribal groups' ability to have survived the fragmentary pressures of previous decades, aided further by the Mehdi Army's ability to conquer key areas of the *hayy's* southern tier virtually unopposed, overseeing the establishment of "colonies" on the landscape.

Yet, as noted in chapter seven, the centrality of Fedaliyah and Shawra to the Mehdi Army's operations was compelling evidence of its failures elsewhere. Fedaliyah, home of the much-maligned Marsh Arabs, was an exceedingly unlikely command center for an insurgent movement that cast itself as the vanguard of the underclass Shi'a masses.[5] The prominence of Shawra, particularly in the militia's resistance against the Surge, betrayed the inability of Shi'a militants to hold their ground in more central areas of the capital. Furthermore, with the Mehdi Army unable to fully subsume the local, communal priorities of its affiliates from Fedaliyah and Shawra within its own, there remained the prospect of betrayal as the militia's broader fortunes soured.

Even the militia's most impressive and enduring achievements in Tisa Nissan were thus incomplete, exposing the overall failure of its endeavor in an area of Baghdad that ought to have served as a springboard for further Sadrist advances in the post-Saddam era.

Counterinsurgency on Uneven Terrain

The Mehdi Army's weaknesses in Tisa Nissan created immediate opportunities for the forces of the Surge. As the militia was not at the head of a unified, grassroots movement, the challenges facing American and Iraqi forces were greatly simplified. The principal task of the Surge in Tisa Nissan was not to engage in an abstract contest for the "hearts and minds" of the populace, but rather to identify and destroy discrete militant networks. The inducements and "arguments" of counterinsurgency were of modest relevance to the re-establishment of security in the district, because the civilian population was, for the most part, uninvolved in violence and ill positioned to influence its trajectory.[6]

Benefiting from the fighting prowess of its local representatives and widespread popular skepticism at the advances of the American military and the Iraqi government, the Mehdi Army was able to defend its position in Tisa Nissan with some success during 2007 and early 2008. However, as American and Iraqi forces applied intensifying pressure, the militia was forced further and further onto the defensive.

In the core neighborhoods of Beladiyat and Mashtal, where the bulk of the populace had remained hostile to its presence, the Mehdi Army was displaced in relatively short order. In Amin and Kamaliyah, and in the peripheral zones of Beladiyat and Mashtal, the encroachment of the Surge pushed militants off of streets that they had formerly roamed with impunity. Yet conflict persisted thereafter in these areas, and efforts to spur development and reform governance achieved minimal success. A sporadically violent stasis set in, with Shi'a militants and the forces of the Surge trading blows, and the latter gradually wearing down the former in a protracted battle of attrition.[7]

Lastly, Fedaliyah and Shawra remained insurgent strongholds throughout the first year and a half of the Surge. For so long as the Mehdi Army remained embedded in the local terrain, efforts to reclaim the *hayys* met with fearsome resistance. Indeed, the intensity of violence encountered in Fedaliyah, and the immediate vicinity of JSS SUJ in southern Shawra, rendered the population-centric approaches of counterinsurgency impracticable in both *hayys*. A quarantine was thus established around the former, while operations stalled in the latter.[8]

The stalemate in Tisa Nissan was then broken by a nationwide offensive against the Mehdi Army and its affiliates in the spring and summer of 2008. Launching large-scale military operations in Basra, Baghdad, and the Deep South, American and Iraqi forces inflicted a succession of major defeats on Shi'a militants. The damage incurred by the militia—paired with its incoherent response to the offensive and the evident lack of support it received from the Shi'a underclass as a whole—compelled Muqtada (who likely wished to disassociate himself and his political future from the militia's failings) to disband what had been the Sadrist movement's premier operational entity.

The progression of events on the national stage yielded dramatic results in Tisa Nissan. Within the structures of the Iraqi government, March Madness and its aftermath had an invaluable clarifying effect as to the loyalties of both local politicians and members of the Iraqi Security Forces. Across the district itself, the reactions of different communities were instructive as to the underlying dynamics of violence. In Beladiyat and Mashtal, the declining position of the Mehdi Army and the rising profile of the Iraqi government emboldened the remnants of pre-2003 communities to redouble their efforts at restoring their neighborhoods and reversing the advances of the *hawasim*. In Amin and Kamaliyah, the flight of prominent militants and the corresponding abatement of violence enabled the revival of local markets and a palpable easing of tensions on the *hayys'* streets. Finally, in Fedaliyah, changes to the political landscape appeared to compel the Marsh Arabs to recalculate their interests and radically alter their posture to the Surge, while in Shawra, the cumulative force of counterinsurgent momentum overran Tisa Nissan's last redoubt of Shi'a militarism and prompted a local scramble to readjust to a dramatically changed strategic picture.

However, contrary to conceptions of the Surge as a triumph of full-spectrum counterinsurgency, the fall of the Mehdi Army in Tisa Nissan owed little to popular enthusiasm for either the Iraqi government or American forces. Counterinsurgent forces did not inflict a series of defeats upon the Mehdi Army and its affiliates in the district by winning over the loyalty and support of the Shi'a underclass, inducing its proactive support. On the contrary, short-term security gains were achieved in spite of widespread skepticism on the part of much of the populace toward both the Americans and their Iraqi partners. A great many of Tisa Nissan's residents welcomed the restoration of security after the turmoil of recent years (and localized initiatives to provide clean water, spur economic activity, and rehabilitate critical infrastructure earned a measure of appreciation), but frustration and dissatisfaction prevailed before, during, and after the Mehdi Army's collapse.

To the extent that a battle was fought for the "hearts and minds" of Tisa Nissan's residents, pitting the Mehdi Army against the American military and the Iraqi government, both sides can be said to have lost. Hunkered down in their homes, battered by years of violence and embittered by decades of abuse and official neglect, the residents of Tisa Nissan remained overwhelmingly pessimistic about their current condition and future prospects.

The beleaguered defenders of neighborhoods like Beladiyat Proper, Central Mashtal, and Tujar welcomed relief from the Mehdi Army's encroachment, for example, but their ability to help consolidate the gains of the Surge was limited. Localized communal bonds had been sufficient to mount modestly-effective neighborhood defenses, but residents were ill suited to contribute to a counteroffensive, or to proactively resolve the problems facing the area. The fight against Shi'a militants was instead conducted through the day-to-day operations of American and Iraqi forces, who secured the *hayys'* main neighborhoods before pressing outwards to forcibly drive militants from their peripheries. Local residents subsequently attempted to re-establish governance and improve conditions in their neighborhoods, and the core areas of the *hayys* marked the greatest successes of American-led efforts in Tisa Nissan above the Army Canal. Progress remained unsatisfactorily slow, however, and the increasingly-besieged *hawasim* zones faced mounting persecution; thus stoking class-based tensions and raising the prospect of renewed conflict.

Areas dominated by the Shi'a underclass proved even more challenging. In Amin and Kamaliyah, American and Iraqi forces were unable to consolidate security gains through comparable advances in governance and development. This was not the result of counterinsurgency "malpractice," but rather an inevitable by-product of local conditions.[9] On the one hand, local residents had been steeped in decades of aggressive anti-Americanism (from both Saddam Hussein's regime, and from the White Lion), and had realized decidedly uneven benefits from the Coalition's removal of Saddam Hussein. On the other, protracted neglect and sporadic abuse at the hands of the country's pre- and post-2003 regimes engendered widespread popular enmity toward the Iraqi government. American and Iraqi forces thus faced long odds in their efforts to cultivate popular support.

Irrespective of popular sentiments, just as Amin and Kamaliyah had proven infertile ground for the mobilization of popular insurgency, the *hayys* were not places where "the people" could be leveraged effectively in support of local, grassroots initiatives. Socially atomized, cowed by years of brutal violence in and around their neighborhoods, and conditioned to defer initiative to the central government, the people of Amin and Kamaliyah had been effectively deprived of agency. As a result, their principal contribution to the Surge, like that of their underclass Shi'a counterparts in areas of new settlement across the district, was made through inaction—they abstained from supporting the retreating militia, remaining on the sidelines of the conflict.

Local residents provided valuable intelligence that assisted in the targeting of wanted militants, but this owed far more to the abuses perpetrated by those militants (and localized rivalries that intertwined with the militia's campaign) than to any popular enthusiasm generated by American-funded development projects or the administrative accomplishments of the District Council. The notion that the inducements of counterinsurgency "won over" ardent supporters of the Mehdi Army in Amin or Kamaliyah is thus extremely dubious, as is any suggestion that the Americans rallied substantive, organized popular support in either *hayy*. The motivations that compelled cooperation with the Surge invariably traced their roots to considerations more profound than micro-grants for small businesses or the refurbishment of schools, and in any event, the vast majority of the populace was effectively inanimate from the perspective of counterinsurgents due to the factors detailed in chapter six.

Finally, despite being home to coherent social groups that could be engaged in support of counterinsurgency operations, American and Iraqi forces also struggled to consolidate their gains in Fedaliyah and Shawra. Fedaliyah's Marsh Arabs strove to win the favor of American forces, and likewise to re-engage the Iraqi government in an effort to reinstate feed subsidies for their *jamoose* and preserve their enclave in Baghdad. Little assistance was forthcoming, however. In a dynamic that plagued Tisa Nissan in its entirety, there was little prospect of an Iraqi government that was unable to maintain basic services in the heart of the capital extending substantive support to its eastern fringes—particularly to a community that occupied the lowest rung of the city's social order, and which had been at the forefront of both sectarian and insurgent violence. As such, apart from avoiding a bloody confrontation with American forces, the Marsh Arabs gained only the most modest benefits from their change of tact during the summer of 2008.

Similarly, the tribes of northern Shawra could maneuver amongst one another for local position in the wake of the Mehdi Army's collapse, but with Shi'a militants still active in nearby areas of southern Diyala Province (where the Iraqi government's influence was negligible, and where American forces exercised extremely limited power even at the peak of the Surge), the prospects of durable reconciliation or the return of displaced Sunnis were remote. There was no possibility of the Iraqi government bringing the resources and attention to bear that would be needed to remedy the *hayy's* extensive infrastructural shortcomings, leaving both northern and southern Shawra in conditions of festering squalor.

Across Tisa Nissan, therefore, the dramatic security gains achieved during the spring and summer of 2008 lay in jeopardy at the close of the Surge. With American forces contracting from the district during 2009, the central government either unwilling or unable to extend necessary assistance, the district's local representatives proving inept, corrupt, or simply unable to overcome the extraordinary challenges facing the area, and much of the populace lacking the capacity for independent, collective action, Tisa Nissan faced a bleak future.[10]

Lessons of Tisa Nissan and the Future of Iraq

The fate of the Mehdi Army in Tisa Nissan offers a variety of insights into the future of Iraq—most of them discouraging. On the positive side of the ledger, close study of the local mechanics of violence reinforces the general consensus among observers of the post-Saddam era that sectarian violence was not the by-product of broadly-shared or deeply-seated essentialist hatreds. Neighbors did not turn upon neighbors as previously suppressed animosities percolated upwards from the bedrock of their traditional, primeval identities, leading to sectarian polarization and mass slaughter. Instead, while the turmoil that wracked Tisa Nissan fed off of decades-old grievances (most notably class-based conflict between the Shi'a underclass and its social "superiors"), the violence that devastated the district was not the work of the masses, or a natural outgrowth of latent social forces. For the most part, violence was instead sparked by the calculations of contemporary politics, fueled by the ruthless strategies and tactics of aspirants to power (who rallied support by stoking identity-based fear and division), and further exacerbated by the cynicism of those who viewed the conflict as an opportunity for personal enrichment.

Tisa Nissan's Sunni citizenry was not slaughtered or forced to flee by the collective popular hatred of their Shi'a neighbors, but overwhelmingly by identifiable, and generally narrowly-based groups of militants. Looking ahead to possible sectarian reconciliation within the district, and more widely across the Iraqi capital, this is of paramount importance. Spontaneous, locally-initiated sectarian attacks certainly occurred during the peak years of the sectarian war, the ferocity of the violence perpetrated by the conflict's antagonists was such that ordinary citizens were compelled to seek protection from radical militant groups, and many were naturally swept up in the sectarian fears and hatreds generated by successive, brutal atrocities. Nonetheless, the terrain-conquering focus of the vast bulk of the violence betrayed its planned, deliberate nature—and one should not overstate either the depth of the allegiances that were formed during the conflict or the breadth of popular participation in, or enthusiasm for, sectarian bloodshed.

Wider analysis of the mechanics of sectarian conflict in Baghdad further illuminates this point: Shi'a armies did not engage Sunni armies in the war for the Iraqi capital, soldiers rarely clashed in battle, and "the people" did not take up arms against "the people" on the streets of the city. Hence the occurrence of a war in which tens of thousands perished, and a great many more were driven from their homes, without a single, large-scale confrontation. Instead, politically-aligned militant groups preyed upon civilians and those militants whom they could identify and capture, seizing them from their homes and from checkpoints along city streets to murder them in furtherance of their own agendas.[11]

Discouragingly, however, the same social degradation that undermined the Mehdi Army's insurgent campaign seems to have also presented an insurmountable obstacle to collective action that might have reformed or resisted the militia's extremism, or quelled violence more broadly.[12] Iraq's "silent majority" of ordinary citizens desirous of peace, unity, and stability was not merely silent, but frequently irrelevant to the events of the post-Saddam era in Tisa Nissan. Any optimism generated by the realization that blood appears to be on the hands of a small minority must be tempered by the implications of this observation vis-à-vis the collective impotence of an atomized, post-totalitarian populace. The overriding lesson of the bloodshed of post-Saddam Iraq, particularly with respect to the sectarian war, has thus not been the (allegedly) hopelessly divided state of Iraqi society, but rather the extent to which the myriad fragmentary pressures of Iraq's modern history left the many catastrophically unable to stand up to the few.[13]

While an understanding of the mechanics of killing and forced displacement in Tisa Nissan engenders certain optimism for the prospects of inter-communal reconciliation, events immediately following the withdrawal of American forces suggested the unlikelihood of substantive progress on this front—long before the stunning offensive by The Islamic State of Iraq and al-Sham, or ISIS, brought Iraq to the brink of full-scale sectarian war in the summer of 2014.[14]

First, the Iraqi government proved unable to maintain the pressure that their American allies had previously applied to Sunni militants, enabling Iraq's al-Qaeda franchise to revive itself from near-annihilation and mount successive devastating suicide attacks on Shi'a civilians during 2012 and 2013. With government unable to secure the citizenry, neighborhoods such as Amin, Kamaliyah, and Beladiyat came under repeated attack, as did nearby Sadr City and Baghdad al-Jadeeda.[15] This reignited sectarian tensions among the populace, and invited vigilante retribution by Shi'a partisans.

Second, the Maliki government actively undermined sectarian relations through provocative political acts. The persecution of Sunni Vice President Tariq al-Hashemi (which was initiated the day after American forces finalized their withdrawal, and culminated in a death sentence being levied against the fugitive politician), the security forces' deadly attack on Sunni protestors in Hawijah in the spring of 2013, mass arrest and indefinite detention of Sunni civilians, and the political rehabilitation of Iranian-linked Shi'a militant groups with explicitly sectarian agendas like Asaib Ahl al-Haq (an unabashed Iranian proxy with a long record of sectarian atrocities) fueled anger and mistrust among Sunni Iraqis.[16]

The resulting inter-communal tensions, set in the context of wave upon wave of attacks against Shi'a targets, escalated to the point that, even before the spectacular assault by the Sunni *jihadis* of ISIS, a return to high intensity sectarian violence appeared more likely than durable, meaningful reconciliation.[17]

The continued advance of ISIS, and the group's declaration of an "Islamic State" that encompasses areas of both Iraq and Syria, appears poised to turn the prospect of a sectarian war into reality. One of the most ominous consequences of ISIS (and the staggeringly ineffectual initial performance of Iraqi forces) has been the call to arms within Iraq's Shi'a community, and the government-sanctioned mobilization of Shi'a militias. Not only have Asaib Ahl al-Haq and Kata'ib Hizbullah joined the frontlines, deploying their Iranian-provided arms and expertise alongside the Iraqi military, but Muqtada al-Sadr has resurrected the Mehdi Army as well.

This marks a dramatic reversal of strategy by Muqtada. While he had previously threatened to reconstitute his militia in the years following its dissolution, the official revival of the militia marks a fundamental, and perhaps irreversible break with the political course that Muqtada has charted over much of the past decade.[18] Since as early as 2005, he has been working to refashion his image into that of a respectable Muslim cleric and mainstream political figure. These efforts were redoubled during the course of the Surge, when the internal flaws of the Mehdi Army were so clearly exposed. Muqtada not only dissolved his militia, but also announced the formation of the Mumehidoon—a successor, of sorts, to the Mehdi Army, which would mobilize the Sadrist rank and file for charitable and educational functions.[19]

Throughout this time, Muqtada sought to reposition himself—and the Sadrist movement a a whole—as proponents of national unity and outspoken opponents of the divisive sectarianism allegedly practised by their rivals (former Prime Minister Maliki most notable among them). As prevailing demographic trends all but guarantee Muqtada a position of continued, growing prominence in a democratic Iraq, he seems to have realized that he does not have to take up arms to achieve his objectives. He needs only to bide his time, rehabilitate his image, and ensure that Iraq remains whole. His much-discussed "withdrawal" from politics in the run-up to the April 2014 elections is best understood in this light, as he sought to distance himself from the corruption and underperformance of politicians claiming the Sadrist mantle. [20]

However, Muqtada's strategy appears to have been overtaken by events. With an international army of Sunni *jihadis* pressing southward through Iraq, proclaiming their intent not only to seize Baghdad, but also to destroy the holy Shi'a cities of Najaf and Kerbala, the leaders of Iraq's Shi'a community were compelled to respond.[21] Following the fall of Mosul, Iraq's second largest city, Muqtada announced the mobilization of "Peace Brigades" to defend against ISIS's advance, while even Grand Ayatollah Ali al-Sistani, with his well-earned reputation for moderation, tolerance, and reticence, called upon his followers to take up arms in defense of their nation, their holy sites, and their faith.[22]

Muqtada al-Sadr has declared that his militiamen will operate in a strictly defensive capacity, and he has avoided provocative sectarian rhetoric. However, as Sadrist fighters come into contact with ISIS militants, there is little reason to expect either party to act with restraint. Instead, the Mehdi Army's return to the field of battle portends a second round of full-scale sectarian war in Iraq, which may not merely quash Muqtada's long-running effort to refashion his public image, but also jeopardize the very survival of the Iraqi nation.

APPENDIX

HUMAN TERRAIN MAPPING AND COUNTERINSURGENCY OPERATIONS

Human Terrain Mapping—Operational Context

The area study introduced in chapter four and presented through chapters five, six, and seven draws from the observations and insights of the author, his colleagues on a Human Terrain Team (HTT), and personnel from the US Army Brigade Combat Team (BCT) that was responsible for southeastern Baghdad in 2008.[1] The mission and purpose of Human Terrain Teams, and the origins of the Human Terrain System as a whole, have been discussed in the Introduction (along with references to further reading on the subject). This appendix presents an overview of how the author (who served as a social scientist, and was thus responsible for research design, the overall management of fieldwork, and the analysis and presentation of collected data) and his colleagues conducted the work upon which this book draws—explaining the context in which it was executed, and addressing practical, methodological, and ethical concerns.

The author and his HTT colleagues were attached to the US Army Brigade Combat Team (BCT) responsible for southeastern Baghdad. The BCT, managed overall by the 4th Brigade of the 10th Mountain Division, was responsible for the provision of security, the furtherance of economic development, and the re-establishment of governance in the Rusafa, Karrada, and Tisa Nissan political districts. Military personnel and their various support elements (including an embedded Provincial Reconstruction Team—or ePRT—provided by the US Department of State) worked with their respective counterparts in the Iraqi Security Forces, the political institutions of Tisa Nissan's Neighborhood and

District Councils, the administrative and technical offices of the Baghdad municipality, and local civil society organizations toward those objectives as part of an overall strategy to transfer full responsibility to the Iraqi government during the course of 2008 and 2009.[2]

Upon arrival at Forward Operating Base Loyalty in February 2008, the author and his colleagues were briefed on conditions in these three political districts. Rusafa and the bulk of Karrada were seen to be progressing adequately toward higher standards of security, development, and governance, and had been marked for transition to full Iraqi control in the coming months. Significant challenges remained, including an active Iraqi al-Qaeda presence in a small area of Rusafa and continued Shi'a militant activity in the Zafaraniyyah area of southern Karrada, yet

Figure A.1: Baghdad's Political Districts

trends in stability and security were viewed as generally satisfactory. Tisa Nissan, however, particularly the portion of the district beyond the Army Canal, was singled out as the BCT's primary problem area. It was, in the words of a senior staff officer, "not responding to treatment."[3]

In support of the BCT's efforts to manage the challenges of Tisa Nissan, the HTT was tasked to produce a *hayy*-level "map" of the district's human terrain that would detail the social, economic, political, and cultural forces beneath its seeming intractability.[4] What was it about the *hayys* beyond the Army Canal that left them resistant to the counterinsurgency approaches employed, with apparent success, elsewhere in the BCT's area of responsibility? What were the particular features of local society from one neighborhood to the next that made some areas more violent and unstable than others? In short, why was Tisa Nissan not responding to treatment?

Aspects of eastern Baghdad's history, and the local growth of both the Shi'a underclass as well as the Sadrist movement, provided the substance of several early briefings to BCT staff.[5] The legacy of the *mahallah* system, for example, and the forces that had combined to degrade civil society on eastern Baghdad's periphery during the course of previous decades, were of particular relevance. Additionally, information on the position of the Shi'a underclass in Iraqi society, and discussion of the social forces beneath the rise of the Sadrist movement, helped explain the wariness of the district's population vis-à-vis the overtures of the Coalition and the establishment-dominated Iraqi government.

While the elucidation of relevant aspects of Iraqi history provided useful contextual information on the district's woes, this was insufficient to enable the HTT to make a substantive, sustained contribution to the BCT's day-to-day operations. The level of detail and the depth of local specificity required to engage meaningfully with debates over specific concerns from one *hayy* to the next, made first-hand investigation necessary. The thematic and historical issues outlined in the first two chapters of this book, and the arc of the Sadrists' fortunes presented in Chapter Three, thus served as a starting point from which the examination of Tisa Nissan beyond the Army Canal began.

Operational Methods

A research plan was built in four main phases to produce a human terrain map of the district.[6] First, the author and his colleagues collected the BCT's existing institutional knowledge and perceptions of Tisa Nissan, producing an initial baseline report. Second, the author analyzed this document for information gaps and issues warranting further exploration, which were aggregated into a research plan. Third, the author and his colleagues conducted fieldwork to fill the identified gaps, while also exploring the district for additional, previously undetected or underappreciated issues of concern. Fourth, the results of fieldwork were synthesized into a collection of documents and presentations that detailed prominent aspects of Tisa Nissan's human terrain on a *hayy*-by-*hayy* basis, explaining the operational implications of the district's features.

Phase 1: Baseline Collection and Analysis

The primary purpose of the initial phase was to capture the BCT's cumulative institutional knowledge of Tisa Nissan.[7] How did American military personnel view the district and its resident population? What did they think was happening in the neighborhoods of Tisa Nissan, and why? What was their understanding of the challenges that they had faced either successfully or unsuccessfully in past operations, and how did they see themselves positioned to pursue their stated objectives?

This process ran from mid February to mid March of 2008, during which time HTT personnel worked in pairs to conduct confidential, semi-structured interviews with individuals and small groups of interviewees who had been identified by BCT leadership as possessing potentially relevant information. The HTT began at the top of the BCT's hierarchy with the senior officers on Brigade staff who were responsible for disciplines such as intelligence, operations, and civil affairs, as well as the military and civilian personnel who staffed the ePRT. Interviews ranged from approximately thirty to ninety minutes, with HTT personnel asking open-ended questions to elicit information about what interviewees saw as objective facts, as well as their own personal thoughts and instincts.[8] The team then progressed incrementally down the rank hierarchy to junior officers, non-commissioned officers, and enlisted personnel within the headquarters, until all potentially relevant sources had been exhausted.

Attention then turned to the two subordinate battalions within the BCT that were directly responsible for day-to-day operations in the *hayys* of Tisa Nissan. The district had been bisected along the north-south axis of Highway 5 (the main road connecting Baghdad to the city of Baquba in Diyala Province), with 2/16 infantry battalion responsible for the eastern half, and 2/30 infantry battalion to the west and in Shawra wa Umm Jidr to the north. Following the same approach utilized at BCT headquarters, HTT personnel began by interviewing the Battalion Commanders and their staffs, working downwards through the rank hierarchy until all relevant staff personnel had been interviewed.

Still working in pairs, team members then traveled to each of the outlying Company-level patrol bases that had been established within the *hayys* of Tisa Nissan. Visits to these outposts lasted several days, and served two main purposes. The first priority was to interview the officers, noncommissioned officers, and enlisted soldiers who were the BCT's primary points of contact with the local population—some of whom, due to the Army's system of staggered deployment rotations and the extended tours of the Surge, had been living and working in the district for over a year.[9] Interviews were conducted in a similar fashion as previously, with pairs of HTT personnel meeting with interviewees either alone or in small groups, eliciting information about the local area, its resident population, and notable trends or events that had occurred therein.[10]

The second objective was to conduct an initial reconnaissance of the district. The Company-level patrol bases situated within the district's *hayys* were the points from which the majority of day-to-day operations were conducted, and visits enabled team members to see local neighborhoods first-hand, and observe the types of operations being conducted within. Team members would participate in the various operations underway during the course of their visits to each patrol base, assessing the permissiveness of each area for fieldwork, evaluating potential venues for future engagement, and identifying prospective local sources of information.

Upon completion of this initial phase, the coded, confidential responses of all those interviewed were analyzed and documented in an initial report. This report captured the *hayys* of Tisa Nissan as they were understood by the BCT, and conveyed both prevailing and dissenting opinions held toward local dynamics in each area. These documents were circulated among a selection of BCT personnel for feedback and clarification, made available via the BCT's internal computer network, and briefed to relevant audiences.

Phase 2: Gap Analysis and Research Planning

A gap analysis was then conducted on the baseline assessment, creating a framework for the HTT's investigation of the district.[11] In light of what the BCT knew about Tisa Nissan, and the key features of its human terrain identified thus far, what issues warranted further investigation? What concerns were widely cited as problematic and insufficiently understood? Were there areas in which BCT personnel held conflicting opinions, or where prevailing wisdom appeared to be at odds with notable facts or trends? With these questions in mind, the results of the initial assessment were analyzed, and groups of unanswered questions were generated. These questions were then prioritized for their potential significance to ongoing and future operations, and used to construct a research plan that identified the main areas of focus from one *hayy* to the next.[12]

Phase 3: Fieldwork

Following BCT approval of the research plan in April 2008, the bulk of the team dispersed throughout the *hayys* of Tisa Nissan, where they remained, for the most part, working either alone or in pairs, from April to November of 2008. Embedding at the company level, team members spent between four to eight weeks investigating a particular *hayy*.[13] Findings from the field were periodically relayed back to BCT headquarters, while new information requirements and other taskings were disseminated, in turn, from BCT staff.

Aspects of the HTT's findings, as well as details of the manner in which each particular *hayy* was investigated, are presented in the footnotes of chapters five, six, and seven. Several overarching issues warrant discussion, however, as they pertain to concerns that affected the team's work in its entirety.

Issues to be addressed when conducting research in the midst of an ongoing conflict (one in which the researchers were active participants) were many and varied. How to find and effectively engage potential sources of information; how to vet, assess, and interpret information collected from sources of uncertain reliability or motivation; how to pursue objectivity and impartiality while working in support of, and participating in, military operations; and how to protect sources from harm? With these questions in mind, the HTT adhered to a set of basic principles regarding the challenges of data acquisition, data fidelity, the pursuit of objectivity, and the protection of sources, as detailed below.

1. Data Acquisition

Local conditions within individual *hayys* dictated the investigative methods utilized. Common to all efforts, however, was the practice of HTT personnel to identify themselves as advisors to the American military, and to gain the informed consent of interviewees (a concern that has been raised by critics of the Human Terrain System, principally from the discipline of anthropology).[14] All interactions thus began with team members (who were generally in military uniform, unless working within the confines of an American-controlled facility) explaining their objectives, and conveying that the subsequent conversation was at the discretion of the interviewee. Cognizant, moreover, of the possibility that an interviewee might wish to avoid engaging team members but be uncomfortable breaking off an encounter in the presence of occupying forces, collectors remained sensitive to the possibility of inadvertently "coercing" consent.

Some areas of Tisa Nissan (Beladiyat and Mashtal, in particular) had functioning governmental and civil society institutions, which provided stable venues where team members could develop relationships with Iraqis who, in the course of their professional lives, regularly and voluntarily interacted with American personnel.[15] Within these more stable environments, HTT personnel found an array of sources eager to converse, share their personal stories, and discuss local history, recent events, and the various challenges confronting the district and Baghdad in general. Other areas (such as Kamaliyah and Amin) remained either unstable or inhospitable to American forces, lacking venues where relationships could be developed over a period of time. In these areas, team members were forced to rely upon relatively brief interactions with local residents in their homes and on the streets of their neighborhoods, and to compensate for unsatisfactory depth with a broadened breadth of coverage. This approach was facilitated by the operational posture and tempo commonly assumed by American units in these more violent areas of the district, where American and Iraqi forces maintained a consistent street-level presence through the conduct of patrols. Regular foot-patrols through neighborhoods such as Central Kamaliyah and the core grid of Amin enabled HTT personnel to interact with local residents in their homes, in shops, and openly on the street, in encounters that were, by the spring of 2008, commonplace and unremarkable.[16]

2. Data Fidelity

Serious obstacles confront any attempt to collect, assess, and interpret information gathered in the midst of an ongoing conflict. How effectively, for example, can a uniformed, armed researcher traveling in the midst of a platoon of American soldiers gather accurate information from Iraqi civilians?[17] The potential distortions arising in such an encounter were numerous. There was the prospect of an interviewee trying to avoid confrontation by telling the researcher something brief and non-controversial in the hope of quickly appeasing his or her interlocutor; that he or she might deliberately misinform a representative of the occupying coalition; or that an interviewee might fabricate information in an attempt to leverage American power in a personal or communal dispute.[18] Furthermore, there was the prospect of distortion via self-selection, wherein the proclivity of certain types of Iraqis (either those amenable to the American presence, or desirous to take advantage of it) would dominate reporting and thus skew the research process.

In light of the unavoidability of these scenarios (team members regularly encountered each of the above situations), HTT personnel attempted to remain vigilant for them, and to learn from local attitudes and biases. How and when did different types of individuals react to American personnel in different ways? How did local attitudes appear to shift from one area or situation to the next, or in response to stimuli induced by political developments, military operations, or local events? In short, it was necessary not only to analyze the information provided by a particular interviewee, but also to assess and deconstruct the context in which that information was provided. Several approaches, discussed below, were employed by team members to mitigate the risk of distortions and misperception, including: subject matter control; history as a frame of reference; triangulation of perspectives; resourcelessness; and expectation management.

2.1 Subject Matter Control

Team members avoided lines of questioning connected to controversial or otherwise sensitive issues, such as the specific local operations of the Mehdi Army or the identities of those engaged in violence. Team members structured interviews to avoid these subjects, as the objective was to explore the social forces beneath Tisa Nissan's particular challenges rather than identify or pursue the specific individuals involved. Questioning instead focused on eliciting personal narratives and general observations. Common issues for exploration included the history of a particular neighborhood and the circumstances that led the interviewee to reside there; local perceptions of changing conditions in the district in response to population flows; recollections of various aspects of life during the Saddam era; memories of the turbulence and violence of the sectarian war; and more general questions regarding patterns of life and local realities.

2.2 History as a Frame of Reference

An academic grounding in Iraqi history provided an invaluable resource throughout the HTT's work in Tisa Nissan, as it gave structure to the research planning process, facilitated rapport-building with Iraqi sources during the research process, and proved instrumental in the interpretation of the data collected. Just as an appreciation of the legacy of the *mahallah* system and its modern reinterpretation in eastern Baghdad's growth generated insights into localized patterns of violence, conversations with Iraqi sources could be initiated with reference to relevant historical themes. Long-time residents of poorer areas beyond the Army Canal could thus be engaged in conversation through reference to the memory of Abd al-Karim Qasim and his still-famous efforts on behalf of the city's Shi'a underclass, while conversations with new arrivals to the district could be initiated through reference to the circumstances beneath their movement from Sadr City or Diyala Province. The discussions that followed in either situation could then be evaluated for the manner in which they did or did not track with what might be expected for the residents of a particular area or the members of a particular identity group, as well as for the extent to which current events marked the continuation of, or a break from, major historical trends.

2.3 Triangulation of Perspectives

In an environment where strong socio-cultural biases and multi-directional political and communal rivalries had permeated society, it was useful to track correlations between particular markers of an interviewee's identity and locality and his corresponding views. This amounted to a sort of profiling and held obvious limitations, but observation of the extent to which residents of particular neighborhoods or demographic cohorts tracked with, or diverged from, the dominant views or opinions of fellow in-group members proved useful. To what extent, for example, did remaining long-time residents of a particular middle class neighborhood hold common views on the Maliki government, the Sadrist movement, or life in the post-Saddam era as a whole? What were the defining values or markers of identity around which groups appeared to coalesce? Observations and comparisons of attitudes toward issues or events from one geographic area or identity-group to the next helped illuminate both commonalities and fault lines in the human terrain, enabling researchers to trace patterns and trends.

2.4 Resourcelessness

It was impossible for HTT personnel to portray themselves as "neutral" parties during their fieldwork, or to fully compensate for the ways in which their own identities as Americans affected interactions with the people of Tisa Nissan. Steps were taken to mitigate prominent potential sources of distortion. Whenever possible, researchers avoided conducting research in venues where Iraqis were likely to see them either as conduits for patronage or as tools to be leveraged in pursuit of personal or communal goals. Team members thus avoided initiating interviews while facilitating economic development projects or brokering political arrangements, as these situations were thought to pose higher risks of manipulation and misrepresentation by local interlocutors.[19] By explicitly avoiding the suggestion of quid pro quo arrangements in which sources would provide information in exchange for favorable treatment, team members attempted to limit corrupting influences on their research.

2.5 Expectation Management

A further way that team members guarded against errors in their work was by deliberately limiting their own objectives. The team did not set out to conduct an ethnography of Tisa Nissan, or to create a comprehensive picture of the district and its residents.[20] The reporting produced by the HTT did not—and the analysis contained in this work does not—purport to detail how and why civil society operated in particular ways, or to offer an insider's view of the district. On the contrary, the HTT limited itself to identifying, as self-conscious outsiders with limited access, particular features of the district that appeared to hold relevance to the BCT's pursuit of its objectives.

3. Objectivity

The potential for inherent bias in the conduct of research on behalf of a military force engaged in combat operations was a further concern.[21] Can a research team that is an integral part of one of the main parties to a conflict conduct objective research on the roots and dynamics of that conflict? When investigating trends in violence, and studying the social forces beneath the campaign of the opposition, can one reliably avoid bias against "the enemy?"

One set of issues relates to the prospect of bias on the part of researchers who, owing to their role in support of a military engaged in combat operations, might feel compelled to depict the conflict in a particular light. The underlying assumptions are that researchers may feel pressured to reach conclusions that harmonize with official messaging, or that the military, engaged in political and informational campaigns alongside its conventional operations, might not allow the production of reports or the expression of views that question its strategies and tactics. There would exist, therefore, an array of direct and indirect pressures that could prevent the execution of impartial work.

Working on the margins of eastern Baghdad (and thus far removed from whatever political pressures may have existed within the upper echelons of the military and diplomatic hierarchies resident in the Green Zone and in the vicinity of Baghdad International Airport), the author and his colleagues worked without any pressure, direct or indirect, to alter their reporting. On the contrary, the overriding priority of battlefield commanders and their subordinates was accuracy in understanding the environment in which they were operating—particularly in light of the frustrations encountered up to that point in Tisa Nissan.

A second concern relates to the prospect that research conducted on an ongoing conflict, which is undertaken by active participants in that conflict, will suffer from more personal biases. At issue are the researchers' inherent sympathies toward the main parties involved, particularly those engaged in violence against the researchers and their friends and colleagues. Can members of a Human Terrain Team produce an impartial, dispassionate assessment of the Mehdi Army, when Shi'a militants are actively, and at times successfully, attempting to kill them?[22]

The casualties incurred during the course of the team's work rendered any pretension to genuine neutrality toward the Mehdi Army, Special Group cells, or local militant groups untenable. The HTT attempted to compensate for this bias, however, through the understanding that objective analysis might help avoid future casualties. This approach was understood to be imperfect (with acknowledgment to the methodological tenet that any enquiry will be corrupted by bias if it is conceived and executed instrumentally), yet under the conditions in which the HTT operated, it was the most effective way to pursue objectivity.[23] The production of a nuanced assessment of the district, which accounted for the diverging perspectives of its residents and contextualized the conflicting views of the competing groups therein (be they hostile, neutral, or supportive toward the American military presence), was pursued as an endeavor that might contribute to the successful navigation of Tisa Nissan's challenges.

4. Source Protection

The protection of sources was a central concern of the HTT. Precautionary guidelines were adhered to, therefore, throughout the course of the team's work, as team members sought to ensure that they did not expose interviewees to harm. Formal interviews with Iraqis were conducted in several ways. Prominent political, economic, and civil leaders regularly interacted with American forces, and could thus be engaged openly in semi-public venues such as Neighborhood or District Council buildings and Iraqi Security Force facilities. In other instances, due either to the fear of retribution by militants or, more commonly, personal rivalries among prominent individuals, interviews were conducted privately—typically on American-controlled FOBs and patrol bases.[24] Lastly, where appropriate, mobile phones were used to converse with Iraqi sources, obviating the need for face-to-face meetings.

When gathering information on the streets of Tisa Nissan—accompanying combat patrols, for example, or manning checkpoints along local roads—separate procedures were followed. In such cases true privacy was impossible, so team members interacted with Iraqis in ways designed not to draw undue attention. Brief conversations could be held behind closed doors with members of a family, for instance, during the time it took Iraqi

National Police personnel to conduct a routine search of their home. Alternatively, patrols to assess economic activity afforded opportunities to interact with shopkeepers and their customers. By mid 2008, the residents of Tisa Nissan had grown accustomed to these aspects of the American presence in the district, and relatively brief, semi-public to public interactions between Americans and Baghdadis were unremarkable.

Precautions were also taken in the team's data management and reporting. When interacting repeatedly with a particular source, team members would code their notes to protect their source's identity. Individual team members maintained their own databases of coded source notes, thereby personally ensuring that the confidentiality of their sources was preserved. In instances where collection efforts were conducted through brief encounters on operations within the district, on the other hand, sources were protected through anonymity.[25] Interviews during neighborhood patrols and clearance operations, for example, or at checkpoints where vehicles were stopped and searched for contraband, were conducted without asking for the interviewee's name. Team members identified themselves as advisors to the American military, secured the consent of their interlocutor, and pursued lines of questioning that avoided the elicitation of identifying personal information.

Phase 4: Reporting

Nearing the end of the team's deployment, an updated human terrain map was produced for the *hayys* of Tisa Nissan that reflected the team's findings. Consisting of neighborhood profiles, maps, and thematic papers on various features of the district (including issues such as the condition of tribal structures across eastern Baghdad, and the roots of the Sadrist movement), it was intended as a reference for those who would subsequently serve in Tisa Nissan.

NOTES

PREFACE

1. Ranajit Guha, "The Prose of Counter-Insurgency," in Ranajit Guha and Gayatri Chakravorty (eds), *Selected Subaltern Studies*, (Oxford: Oxford University Press, 1988).
2. Ibid., pp. 70–1.
3. This is not an original observation; similar concerns have been raised by Munson (a former Middle East specialist with the United States Marine Corps), among others. In a statement on his motives for writing *Iraq in Transition: The Legacy of Dictatorship and the Prospects for Democracy*, (Washington: Potomac Books, 2009), Munson observed that, "while numerous studies and histories had been published on Iraq pre-2003, and several high profile books detailing the military and policy aspects of events in 2003 and after were beginning to show up, none explicitly linked Iraq's history and legacies to what was going on in the country post-invasion. What is more, the quickly growing literature on post-invasion Iraq focused on either policy and strategy critique or individual observations of soldiers or journalists. There was a significant gap for someone trying to learn about Iraqi society, culture, and politics in the new era." Interview published on the Middle East Strategy at Harvard (MESH) blog: https://blogs.law.harvard.edu/mesh/2009/08/iraq-in-transition/ His book further engages the issue, lamenting that "narratives in the West have pigeonholed Iraqis as bit players or legions of similarly costumed extras and focused almost exclusively on American officials, soldiers, and policies." Munson, *Iraq in Transition*, p. 6.
4. Examination of online venues such as the *Small Wars Journal* http://smallwarsjournal.com/ where students and practitioners of counterinsurgency congregate to share experiences and offer insights, reveals an abundance of self-criticism and introspection regarding the successes and failures of contemporary counterinsurgency operations (as well as an array of historical studies of counterinsurgency campaigns), but a dearth of substantive, original work on specific insurgencies and the societies from which they have emerged. The "strategic-level bibliography" of Operation Iraqi Freedom provided by the US Army War College's Strategic Studies Institute is similarly skewed heavily toward self analysis at the expense of texts about Iraq itself: http://www.strategicstudiesinstitute.army.mil/pdffiles/of-interest-11.pdf/ Lastly, the very titles of the more popular "first-hand" accounts of events on the ground betray their focus. See, for example, L. Paul Bremer III and Malcolm McConnell, *My Year in Iraq: The*

Struggle to Build a Future of Hope, (New York: Simon & Schuster, 2006); Colby Buzzell, *My War: Killing Time in Iraq*, (London: Penguin, 2005); Rajiv Chandraseskaran, *Imperial Life in the Emerald City: Inside Iraq's Green Zone*, (New York: Knopf, 2006); Peter Mansoor, *Baghdad at Sunrise: A Brigade Commander's War in Iraq*, (New Haven: Yale University Press, 2008); Linda Robinson, *Tell Me How This Ends: General David Petraeus and the Search for a Way Out of Iraq*, (New York: PublicAffairs, 2008); Thomas Ricks, *Fiasco: The American Military Adventure in Iraq*, (London: Penguin Press, 2006); Rory Stewart, *The Prince of the Marshes and other Occupational Hazards of a Year in Iraq*, (Orlando: Harcourt, 2006). Munson's work stands out as one of the only truly Iraq-focused books to be produced by an active participant in the conflict.

5. For a polemical attack on prevailing trends in academia to treat the Middle East as a recipient of modern history (along with allegations regarding the shortcomings of the academic establishment in engaging the practicalities of defense- and foreign policy-related debates), see Martin Kramer, "Ivory Towers on Sand: The Failure of Middle East Studies in America," *The Washington Institute for Near East Policy*, 2001. Fouad Ajami, *The Arab Predicament*, (Cambridge: Cambridge University Press, 1999), p. 39 notes that this perspective is also broadly held among residents of the region, as in their own minds, "Arabs remain the objects of history."
6. In reference to debates over the reasons for improved conditions in Baghdad in 2007 and 2008, Ward's "Countering the Military's Latest Fad," *The Washington Post*, 26 January 2007, attacks the "mythology" of the Surge. "The prevailing interpretations of the surge narrative—even competing ones, which tend to differ mostly over claims of paternity—put Americans in the driver's seat of history," Ward notes skeptically, such that "the assumption seems to be that the United States, its leaders and the tactics it employed are primarily responsible for the events on the ground."
7. Even critiques of the most flagrantly troubled examples of this trend, such as Joshua Rovner and Tim Hoyt, "There is No Checklist for Counterinsurgency," *Foreign Policy—The AfPak Channel*, 18 November 2010 (levied in response to Christopher Paul, Colin Clarke and Beth Grill, "Victory Has a Thousand Fathers: Sources of Success in Counterinsurgency," *RAND Corporation*, 2010) are more inclined to attack the manner in which counterinsurgency is studied and presented, rather than the underlying counterinsurgent-centric paradigm. David Hendrickson and Robert Tucker, "Revisions in Need of Revising: What Went Wrong in the Iraq War," *Strategic Studies Institute*, December 2005, pp. 3–4, offer a useful counterbalance to occupier-centric interpretations of the post-Saddam era, emphasizing how the fundamental qualities of Iraq itself shaped events; while Ollivant, "Countering the New Orthodoxy: reinterpreting counterinsurgency in Iraq," *New America Foundation*, June 2011, also cites the weaknesses of what he terms "military-centric" analysis.
8. Contextual and methodological considerations relevant to the fieldwork upon which this book draws are detailed in Appendix A, while the footnotes of chapters four through seven provide details of how particular insights were gathered (and commentary on the context in which certain issues were investigated).

INTRODUCTION

1. Marisa Cochrane, "Special Groups Regenerate," *The Institute for the Study of War*, 29 August 2008, pp. 10–11, notes that the initial barrage of rockets fired at the Green Zone came on the day before the Basra offensive, presumably in anticipation thereof. The distinctions among the Mehdi Army, the Special Groups, and the locally-rooted armed factions that collectively formed Iraq's "Shi'a insurgency" are addressed in chapters three and four.
2. Rumors of an impending offensive by Mehdi Army and Special Group fighters under the direction of Iran also played a role in prompting Prime Minister Maliki to press the offensive on short notice—notably, without informing American commanders. The operation and its implications are detailed in Marisa Cochrane, "The Battle for Basra," *The Institute for the Study of War*, 31 May 2008; and Anthony Cordesman, "Sadr and the Mahdi Army: Evolution, Capabilities, and a New Direction," *CSIS*, 4 August 2008, pp. 18–20.
3. While the parties and politicians of Iraq's Shi'a elite are by no means a monolithic bloc, an "establishment" can nonetheless be identified—in significant measure through its historical opposition to the Sadrist movement. Discussed in International Crisis Group, "Shiite Politics in Iraq: The Role of the Supreme Council," *Middle East Report*, No. 70, 15 November 2007. Lastly, the Supreme Iraqi Islamic Council, which was originally known as the Supreme Council for Islamic Revolution in Iraq, has undergone several name changes since 2003.
4. On the significance of intra-Shi'a rivalry to the politics of the post-Saddam era, International Crisis Group, "Shiite Politics in Iraq," p. i argues that: "more than sectarian conflict or confrontation between Anbari sheikhs and al-Qaeda in Iraq fighters, [intra-Shi'a rivalry is] likely to shape the country's future."
5. As discussed further in chapter three, intra-Shi'a violence continued between the Sadrists' Mehdi Army and the Supreme Iraqi Islamic Council's Badr militia throughout the sectarian war—both in Baghdad, and across southern Iraq as well.
6. Patrick Cockburn, *Muqtada al-Sadr and the Shia Insurgency in Iraq*, (London: Faber and Faber, 2009), p. 255 observes that the ensuing battles marked "the biggest military confrontation between Muqtada's militiamen and the Iraqi government since… 2004".
7. Ibid., pp. 256–7.
8. Commentators vary in their emphasis on particular factors in the fall of the Mehdi Army, but they almost universally cite the influence of the Surge, Prime Minister Maliki's decision to facilitate American targeting of the Mehdi Army, and damage accrued to the militia's reputation as a result of its misdeeds. See, Kimberly Kagan *The Surge: A Military History*, (New York: Encounter, 2009) for a quasi-official account of US military actions during the Surge that focuses on America's role in events, which argues (p. 197) that "the change in American strategy in early 2007 was the critical variable that made any success possible." For a critique that "parallels but challenges the military-centric conventional wisdom" of the Surge, see: Douglas Ollivant, "Countering the New Orthodoxy." Ollivant (a former US Army officer who oversaw aspects of the Surge's design and execution) emphasizes the importance of Iraqi politics and presents an array of competing perspectives on the abatement of violence in Baghdad. Disagreements between Kagan and Ollivant are expounded in Tom Bowman, "As the Iraq War Ends, Reassessing the Surge," *NPR*, 16 December 2011. Bernard Stancati, "Tribal Dynamics and the Iraq Surge," *Strategic Studies Quarterly*, Summer 2010, provides

an overview of dominant trends in analysis of the Surge among foreign policy and defense establishment experts.

9. Alternatively, it has been argued that Muqtada al-Sadr was complicit in the American-led targeting of the Mehdi Army. Realizing that he could no longer control his militia, the argument goes, and that the abuses of those acting in his name were badly damaging his reputation, Muqtada declared a ceasefire and acquiesced to the street-level persecution of Shi'a militants by American and Iraqi forces. Noted in David Ucko, "Militias, Tribes and Insurgents: The Challenge of Political Reintegration in Iraq," *Conflict, Security & Development*, October 2008, pp. 361–2. The veracity of this theory is dubious yet, even if accurate, it does not explain the remarkably poor performance of the many Shi'a militants who chose to fight against the advance of the Surge.
10. As the Iraq war was the subject of intensive partisan debate in America, evaluations of the Surge and of the credit due to the Bush administration for positive developments in Iraq have remained fiercely contested. Stancati, "Tribal Dynamics and the Iraq Surge," p. 89 notes how "political bickering… caused the public discourse to degenerate into partisan arguments focused on casualty figures and body counts," which complicated the efforts of defense officials and policy experts to assess the Surge's actual efficacy. For examples of the partisan nature of debate, see, Fred Barnes, "How Bush Decided on the Surge," *The Weekly Standard*, 4 February 2008; George Packer, "Obama's Iraq Problem," *The New Yorker*, 7 July 2008; Ed Henry, "Obama Not Planning to Credit Bush over Iraq 'Surge'," *CNN*, 31 August 2010.
11. The extent to which Coalition Forces' adoption of counterinsurgency approaches was responsible for improved conditions in Baghdad during the Surge remains contested, as does the overall efficacy of the strategies and tactics that came to dominate defense establishment circles at the time. See Gian Gentile, "Freeing the Army from the Counterinsurgency Straightjacket," *Joint Forces Quarterly*, Issue 58, 2010, and Celeste Ward, "Countering the Military's Latest Fad: Counterinsurgency," *The Washington Post*, 17 May 2009. Both authors not only dispute underlying assumptions of counterinsurgency theory, but also note that American commanders were employing certain aspects thereof well before the "revolutionary" changes of 2007 and 2008.
12. The rationale for the "super-FOB" approach (FOB being an acronym for "Forward Operating Base," the designation given to the larger American military installations in Iraq) is discussed in David Kilcullen, *The Accidental Guerilla: Fighting Small Wars in the Midst of a Big One*, (London: Hurst & Co., 2009), pp. 124–9, in the context of a wider discussion of how American strategy adapted through the course of the post-Saddam era.
13. The American military's doctrinal guide to counterinsurgency, "Field Manual 3–24, Counterinsurgency" is available online: http://www.fas.org/irp/doddir/army/fm3–24.pdf Among counterinsurgency's most prominent advocates, strategic victory is achieved less through the application of violence, and more by winning the support of the populace amongst whom the insurgency is being waged. Popular support is thus not simply an objective to be pursued as an end in and of itself, but rather something that can serve as a decisive strategic weapon. This notion was captured most famously by General Stanley McChrystal when, as the commanding officer of NATO forces in Afghanistan, he urged his subordinates to "think of counterinsurgency as an argument to earn the support of the people" who would

thereafter isolate insurgents and facilitate conflict resolution. Quoted in Dexter Filkins, "Stanley McChrystal's Long War," *The New York Times*, 14 October 2009.

14. Marisa Cochrane, "The Fragmentation of the Sadrist Movement," *The Institute for the Study of War*, January 2009, provides an overview of the Mehdi Army's structural woes and leadership divides and the manner in which they contributed to its demise.
15. Most notably, see International Crisis Group, "Iraq's Civil War, The Sadrists and The Surge," *Middle East Report*, No. 72, 7 February 2008, pp. i-ii. Only a month prior to the violence of March 2008, the report characterized the "principal strongholds" of the Mehdi Army as "virtually unassailable," warning of disastrous consequences should counterinsurgent forces attack them head-on. Similarly, Adam Goodman, "Informal Networks and Insurgency in Iraq," *Defence Academy of the United Kingdom: Advanced Research & Assessment Group*, April 2008, p. 18, predicted "civil war" if the Surge was used to attempt a decisive defeat of the Mehdi Army. Although Muqtada al-Sadr and the Mehdi Army had endured a series of setbacks through the course of 2007 (which left the former in Iranian exile, and the latter bristling under a unilateral ceasefire imposed in an effort to restore discipline and rehabilitate the militia's tarnished image), the Mehdi Army was still widely regarded as a potent fighting force. Cockburn, *Muqtada al-Sadr*, p. 259 offers the view that the Mehdi Army and the Sadrist movement were in the midst of a resurgence in early 2008: "The movement's reputation among the Shi'a had benefited from the long ceasefire during which the Mehdi Army had been effectively purged and brought more fully under Muqtada's control… In Shi'a areas, particularly in Baghdad, it was losing its reputation as an umbrella for every local warlord and racketeer."
16. Cockburn, *Muqtada al-Sadr*, pp. 138, 263 advances this theory, noting that Muqtada "always had a good sense of timing," with a penchant for "swift retreats, politically and militarily, when faced with an adversary superior in strength."
17. This book does not offer an overview of the broader currents of Iraqi history. It instead explores selected aspects thereof in depth. Readers new to the subject will be able to follow the text without additional reading, but would benefit by consulting Phebe Marr, *The Modern History of Iraq*, (Boulder: Westview Press, 2004) or Charles Tripp, *A History of Iraq*, (Cambridge: Cambridge University Press, 2007) for concise introductions to the country's history. Suggestions for further reading (as well as comments on historiographical issues and points of contention among experts) are presented in the footnotes throughout.
18. The official history of the Human Terrain System is presented online: http://humanterrainsystem.army.mil/htsAboutHistory.aspx and discussed further by the program's founders, in Montgomery McFate and Steve Fondacaro, "Reflections on the Human Terrain System During the First 4 Years", *PRISM*, Vol. 2, No. 4, September 2011.
19. The role of the HTT was, in the verbiage of the Human Terrain System's official literature as presented online, to "conduct operationally relevant socio-cultural research and analysis… in order to enable operational decision-making, enhance operational effectiveness, and preserve and share socio-cultural institutional knowledge." The team's mission was, in other words, to study the battlefield as a social environment, and advise military commanders on how to best navigate the features of its "human terrain."
20. The reasons for, and the implications of, the general absence of popularly-supported political parties in post-Saddam Iraq are discussed in chapter three.

21. The actual numerical strength of the Mehdi Army remained a point of contention throughout its existence. Cordesman, "Sadr and the Mahdi Army," p. 14 notes the difficulty in assessing the militia's exact strength, estimating a core membership of between 25,000 and 40,000 along with an indeterminate number of facilitators drawn from Iraq's several-million-strong Shi'a underclass.
22. It is possible, had Muqtada been able to revive the Sadrist movement under more stable, peaceful conditions, that he might have met with greater success. However, the argument that the Mehdi Army's polarizing radicalism was, fundamentally, a product of the brutal violence that permeated the post-Saddam era is an unsatisfying explanation of the militia's social evolution—principally because the Mehdi Army was one of the most active forces in perpetrating said violence.
23. For the purposes of clarity and readability, the Arabic definite article, "al-", has been omitted from place names and other proper nouns throughout this work. Exceptions come in the form of place-names such as *al-'asima*, "the capital," where the definite article is central to the translated meaning of the name, and in instances where full Arabic names of individuals are used. Reference to Mohammed Mohammed Sadiq al-Sadr thus includes the definite article, while shorthand references are made simply to "Sadr."

1. A CITY TRANSFORMED: THE CREATION OF EASTERN BAGHDAD

1. Exact casualty figures for Baghdad are unavailable, but the death toll across Iraq from 2003 through 2011 has been estimated at 162,000. See the study by the anti-war organization, Iraq Body Count, which is discussed in Dan Murphy, "The Iraq War Death Toll? At least 162,000 and Counting," *Christian Science Monitor*, 2 January 2012, and available online: http://www.iraqbodycount.org/analysis/numbers/2011
2. See: Karsh and Rautsi, *Saddam Hussein: A Political Biography*, (New York: The Free Press, 1991), pp. 258–9; Makiya, *Cruelty and Silence: War, Tyranny Uprising and the Arab World*, (London: Jonathon Cape, 1993), pp. 202–3; Pollack, *The Threatening Storm: The Case for Invading Iraq*, (New York: Random House, 2002), p. 60; and Cortright and Lopez, *The Sanctions Decade: Assessing UN Strategies in the 1990s*, (Boulder: Lynne Riener, 2000), p. 45 for discussion of the effects of American-led bombing of Baghdad during 1991.
3. Quotations from Batatu, *The Old Social Classes and the Revolutionary Movements of Iraq*, (London; Saqi, 2004), p. 15, alongside a chart on plagues, famines, and invasions that have ravaged Baghdad.
4. See: Batatu, *The Old Social Classes*, pp. 235–6 for discussion of the 1831 plague outbreak in Baghdad that was only alleviated by the devastating floodwaters of the Tigris River (killing a further 15,000 people in a single night). The Ottoman army arrived shortly thereafter to capitalize on the chaos, overthrowing the Mamluk government.
5. For an account of the Mongol campaign of Hulagu situated in reference to the events of the post-Saddam era, see: Ian Frazier, "Invaders: Destroying Baghdad," *The New Yorker*, 25 April 2005. The Mongol campaigns are discussed further in Jack Weatherford, *Genghis Khan and the Making of the Modern World*, (New York: Crown Publishers, 2004). Wilfred Thesiger, *The Marsh Arabs*, (London: Longmans, Green & Co., 1964), pp. 92–3 notes that the devastation of the Mongol expedition created systemic socio-political instability in Mesopotamia, which

was remedied by the adoption of the Bedouin Arab tribal system (which, he argues, had previously been alien to the region).

6. For a comparative discussion of the Mongol campaign and that of Tamerlane, see: Michael Hancock, "Scourges of God: A General Comparison of Tamerlane and Hulagu in the History of Baghdad," available online at: www.academia.edu
7. Toby Dodge, *Inventing Iraq: The Failure of Nation Building and a History Denied*, (London: Hurst & Co., 2003), p. 8 and Batatu, *The Old Social Classes*, p. 217 note that Baghdad's obscurity was such that it was a posting to which the Ottoman government exiled its most troublesome (and, often, its most inept) bureaucrats. Hilmi, *Internal Migration and Regional Policy in Iraq*, Doctoral Dissertation, University of Sheffield, 1978, p. 243 cites census figures from 1905 for Baghdad's population.
8. For comparison, New York City had a population of nearly 3.5 million in 1900, which rose to approximately 8 million by century's end. London grew from nearly 6 million in 1900 to approximately 7 million a century later. Cairo's experience was far closer to that of Baghdad, growing from 600,000 in 1897 to 10 million in 2000.
9. Saad Ibrahim, "Over-urbanization and Under-urbanism: The Case of the Arab World," *International Journal of Middle East Studies*, Vol. 6, No. 1, January 1975, p. 31, argues for urbanization in Iraq having been a force against modernization. Observing the plight of the rural poor who took part in similar contemporary migrations across the Middle East, Manfred Halpern, *The Politics of Social Change in the Middle East and North Africa*, (Princeton: Princeton University Press, 1963), p. 86 notes that "for the great majority of peasants, the benefits of the modern age can be summed up by saying that it has become harder to die… more Middle Eastern peasants are probably kept alive to suffer misery than ever before in history."
10. The term "Deep South," which is used throughout this book in reference to modern-day Maysan and Wasit Provinces, was has particular resonance among American audiences, as many of the prejudices associated with the term in an American context can be transferred to discussions of Iraq.
11. Batatu, "Iraq's Shi'a, their Political Role, and the Process of their Integration into Society," in Stowasser, Barbara (ed.), *The Islamic Impulse*, (London: Croom Helm, 1987), p. 209 states that Shi'ism reached majority status in Baghdad for the first time in the city's history around the time of the 1958 coup that toppled the monarchy. Noted also in Sluglett and Farouk-Sluglett, "Some Reflections on the Sunni/Shi'i Question in Iraq," *British Society for Middle Eastern Studies*, Vol. 5, No. 2, 1978, p. 80.
12. Jabar, "Sheikhs and Ideologues: Deconstruction and Reconstruction of Tribes under Patrimonial Totalitarianism in Iraq, 1968–1998," in Jabar, Faleh, A., and Hosham Dawood (eds), *Tribes and Power: Nationalism and Ethnicity in the Middle East*, (London: Saqi, 2003); and Tripp, *A History of Iraq*, (Cambridge: Cambridge University Press, 2007), pp. 8–19, survey the dynamics of the Arab tribal system in Mesopotamia and its relations with the Ottoman Empire.
13. Jabar, "Sheikhs and Ideologues: Deconstruction and Reconstruction of Tribes under Patrimonial Totalitarianism in Iraq, 1968–1998," pp. 73–4 notes that "each strong tribe was a miniature mobile state." Robert Fernea, *Shaykh and Effendi: Changing Patterns of Authority Among the el Shabana of Southern Iraq*, (Cambridge, MA: Harvard University Press, 1970),

p. 25 argues that "except for sporadic attempts at tax collection and pacification, the southern Mesopotamian countryside was for nearly seven centuries the home of largely self-governing tribal groups."

14. Tripp, *A History of Iraq*, p. 13 traces Ottoman efforts toward the "reconquest" of Mesopotamia to the early nineteenth century, though notes that progress accelerated dramatically under the watch of Midhat Pasha from 1869. For a detailed discussion of the land reform schemes enacted during the *tanzimat*, see: Sluglett and Farouk-Sluglett, "The Transformation of Land Tenure and Rural Social Structure in Central and Southern Iraq, c. 1870–1958," *International Journal of Middle Eastern Studies*, Vol. 15, No. 4, 1983; Haj, *The Making of Iraq, 1900–1963: Capital Power and Ideology*, (Albany: SUNY Albany University Press, 1997), pp. 24–39; Jabar, "Sheikhs and Ideologues: Deconstruction and Reconstruction of Tribes under Patrimonial Totalitarianism in Iraq, 1968–1998"; and David Pool, "From Elite to Class: The Transformation of Iraqi Political Leadership," in Abbas Kelidar (ed.), *The Integration of Modern Iraq*, (London: Croom Helm, 1979), pp. 75–84.
15. The tribes of southern Mesopotamia had been gradually settling along the Tigris and Euphrates through the duration of the nineteenth century, but this process was accelerated dramatically by the Ottoman land scheme. The opening of the Suez Canal in 1869 greatly facilitated the export of Middle Eastern commodities to international markets, while the introduction of steamships to Mesopotamia's rivers further drove commercial activity. The Ottoman settlement scheme thus occurred in the context of numerous other developments that made it all the more effective—and also rapid and destabilizing.
16. The inconsistent nature of the scheme's implementation reflected both the varied strength and competency of Ottoman administrators across southern Mesopotamia, as well as differing local conditions with respect to both land usage and inter-tribal relations. See: Batatu, *The Old Social Classes*, Chapter 5; Fahim Qubain, *The Reconstruction of Iraq: 1950–1957*, (New York: Frederick A. Praeger, 1958); and Fernea, *Shaykh and Effendi*, pp. 12–13 for commentary on the variances of land ownership in the south and the resulting differences in settlement patterns and agricultural practices from the lower Tigris to the middle Euphrates.
17. While idealized conceptions of Arab tribes often reference an innate hostility to the encroachment of government authority, the financial allure of agriculture appears to have been a paramount driver of sedentarization—and the tribal revolts that occurred during the process were overwhelmingly not protests against the end of nomadism or the advance of Ottoman power. Sluglett and Farouk-Sluglett, "Some Reflections on the Sunni/Shi'i Question," p. 82 observe that revolts were instead launched principally in response to perceived slights or injustices in the allocation of land rights and the manner in which sedentarization progressed.
18. Jabar, in *Tribes & Power*, pp. 75–6 notes that the rise of the market economy "triggered processes which changed the tribe beyond recognition," and emphasizes the dislocations that ensued as "warrior chieftains were turned into tax farmers." Qubain, *The Reconstruction of Iraq*, p. 86, also cites the social changes that ensued as "warrior tribesmen," became "subservient sharecroppers."
19. Batatu, *The Old Social Classes*, pp. 16, 68–9, and Jabar, "Shaykhs and Ideologues: Detribalization and Retribalization in Iraq, 1968–1998," *Middle East Report*, No. 215, Summer 2001, p. 28,

detail the divisions that existed among tribal castes, which were largely based on modes of subsistence and patterns of life. Haj, *The Making of Iraq*, pp. 32–9 analyses the social implications of sedentarization, whereby "new class relations evolved, with the dominant tribes emerging as the triumphant landed class."

20. Jabar, "Sheikhs and Ideologues: Deconstruction and Reconstruction of Tribes under Patrimonial Totalitarianism in Iraq, 1968–1998," p. 76 notes how, despite the fact that sedentarization unraveled the tribes structurally, it made the social prejudices associated with the former tribal system more rigid and contentious. Nakash, *The Shi'is of Iraq*, (Princeton: Princeton University Press, 2003), pp. 46–8 also addresses the accentuation of divisions among tribal strata as nomadism was abandoned, and how tribal genealogy (whether real or imagined) became increasingly important as actual structures unraveled. Per the phenomenon of social bias intensifying despite the collapse of the very structures that underpinned those biases, there is an observation to be made regarding basic human nature and the proclivity of those seeking to preserve "tradition" in the face of change by clinging to its less tangible vestiges.
21. See: Batatu, *The Old Social Classes*, pp. 63, 73–8, 83–4 for a discussion of how the sheikhs' transition to landlordism involved a social transformation in which they traded socially-derived authority for economically-derived power, and how the sheikhs of the Deep South came increasingly to rely on private militias to assert authority over "their" tribesmen. Gabbay, *Communism and Agrarian Reform in Iraq*, (London: Croom Helm, 1978), p. 27, observes that the tribes were "undergoing disintegration," and that relations between sheikhs and their tribesmen were increasingly commoditized, while Thesiger, *The Marsh Arabs*, p. 203 laments that "the old relationship between the sheikh and his tribesmen had disappeared and both were poorer in consequence."
22. For a discussion of conversions to Shi'ism, see: Nakash, *The Shi'is of Iraq*; Nakash, "The Conversion of Iraq's Tribes To Shiism," *International Journal of Middle East Studies*, Vol. 26, No. 3, August 1994; and Jabar, *The Shi'ite Movement*, (London: Saqi, 2003). Conversions to Shi'ism had begun prior to the reforms of Midhat Pasha, as nascent agricultural settlements developed in the vicinity of Najaf and Kerbala. The settlement process accelerated dramatically with the Ottoman land scheme, however, and this intensified sedentarization is widely-cited in academic literature as the essential precondition for the mass conversions that followed. Nakash, "The Conversion of Iraq's Tribes To Shiism," p. 457, posits that, "an identity crisis among the settled tribesmen" was the critical driver of the process. He further notes on p. 448 that all of the tribes that remained nomadic remained Sunni through the twentieth century. With the recent nature of these conversions in mind, the oft-referenced "primordial" division between Shi'a and Sunni in Iraq, and the similarly popular notion of a timeless legacy of Shi'a persecution at the hands of Sunnis in Iraq (and Mesopotamia before it) are thus, in fundamental respects, nonsense. Nakash, "The Conversion of Iraq's Tribes To Shiism," p. 443 notes that, "there is no evidence that would suggest that the Shi'is were ever close to forming a majority of Iraq's population before the nineteenth or even twentieth century." On the scale of the conversion process, Nakash notes (p. 455) that upon driving the Ottomans from Mesopotamia during World War I, British officials were "dazed by the scope of the conversion."
23. Nakash notes the practice of Ottoman officials to use religious figures to undercut tribal loyalties in *The Shi'is of Iraq*, p. 39 and "The Conversion of Iraq's Tribes To Shiism," p. 452.

24. For a discussion of regional dynamics in the Deep South, see: Mohammed Tarbush, *The Role of the Military in Politics: A Case Study of Iraq to 1941*, (London: Keegan Paul, 1982), pp. 19–30; and Haj, *The Making of Iraq*. Batatu and Dodge, the former in *The Old Social Classes*, p. 99 and "The Old Social Classes Revisited" in Fernea and Louis (eds), *The Iraqi Revolution of 1958, The Old Social Classes Revisited*, (London: IB Tauris, 1991); the latter in "The Social Ontology of Late Colonialism: Tribes and the Mandated State in Iraq," in *Tribes and Power*, and *Inventing Iraq*, Chapter 5, note how the rising power of southern sheikhs (which gathered momentum under the Ottomans and was then consolidated under British rule) marked a significant break from the past. Indeed, the decision of British administrators to empower them as local proxies (due in part, according to both authors, to their romanticized, essentialist views of Arab tribalism) cemented a major shift in regional dynamics. Dodge is particularly critical of the British in this regard, while Batatu, in *The Old Social Classes*, p. 88, observes that "what may have begun as an administrative expedient ended as a political necessity," as there were no practical alternatives to the governance of the southern countryside apart from the empowerment of sheikhs.
25. Sluglett and Farouk-Sluglett, "The Transformation of Land Tenure and Rural Social Structure," p. 497 note that the estates of the Deep South became among "the largest private estates in the whole of the Middle East," and that their owners paid negligible taxes.
26. Batatu, "Iraq's Shi'a, their Political Role, and the Process of their Integration into Society," p. 205 notes that, as of 1947, there was not a single mosque or husseiniyah in modern-day Maysan and Wasit Provinces. Prevailing styles of architecture partially account for this, but the irreligiosity and outright impiety of the farmers in the region was legendary. Thesiger, *The Marsh Arabs*, p. 20 observes of the Deep South around the mid twentieth century that, "few people in these parts bothered to pray at all, and those that did were mostly old men."
27. Batatu is particularly cynical regarding the mechanics of the conversion process, noting in "Shi'i Organizations in Iraq: al-Da'wa al-Islamiyah and al-Mujahidin," in Cole and Keddie (eds), *Shi'ism and Social Protest*, (New Haven: Yale University Press, 1986), p. 186, that the *mu'mins* and *sayyids* that spread the Shi'a faith among the rural poor "specialized in superstition or even quackery and lived off the peasant tribesmen." On the extent to which Shi'ism displaced or otherwise altered traditional tribal values, Nakash, *The Shi'is of Iraq*, p. 6 argues that the "Arab tribal system was encapsulated by Shi'i religion, not permeated by it."
28. On peasant uprisings during the 1950s, see: Haj, *The Making of Iraq*, pp. 36–8; and al-Arif, *Iraq Reborn: A Firsthand Account of the July 1958 Revolution and After*, (New York: Vantage Press, 1982), p. 24. Dann, *Iraq under Qassem: A Political History, 1958–1963*, (Jerusalem: Israel University Press, 1969), pp. 60–1, discusses the communists' contribution to revolts in present-day Maysan and Wasit Provinces.
29. Quotation from the 1955 account of Dr Michael Critchley in the *British Journal of Industrial Medicine*, cited in Warriner, *Land Reform and Development in the Middle East: A Study of Egypt, Syria and Iraq*, (Oxford: Oxford University Press, 1962), p. 115. Gabbay, *Communism and Agrarian Reform*, p. 29, notes the life expectancy of southern farmers ranged from thirty-five to thirty-nine years between 1921 and 1958.
30. Hilmi, *Internal Migration*, p. 265, notes that until the late 1930s, Iraq's cities were able to absorb much of this migration "in the existing urban fabric," but that peripheral slum developments were notable in eastern Baghdad by the early 1940s. Batatu, "Shi'i

Organizations in Iraq: al-Da'wa al-Islamiyah and al-Mujahidin," p. 188, notes that migration progressed from the 1930s "in great waves, sometimes emptying whole villages." Warriner, *Land Reform and Development*, p. 153, observed "ten lorry loads a day" leaving modern-day Maysan Province for Baghdad in the 1950s. The term "tribal fragments" comes from Tarbush, *The Role of the Military in Politics*, p. 25. Gabbay, *Communism and Agrarian Reform*, p. 41, notes that, "in Iraq, migration had always been a family affair from the outset, implying a determination never to return no matter what conditions were found at the other end of the journey."

31. Thesiger, *The Marsh Arabs*, p. 203 notes the concerns of southern sheikhs (to whom Thesiger was generally sympathetic) regarding their dwindling labor supply. Fernea, *Shaykh and Effendi*, p. 23, writing in the 1960s, noted that if migration flows were not reversed "the *muwaddafin* (government administrators) will soon have to one to serve but each other" in the rural south.
32. See: Batatu, *The Old Social Classes*, pp. 8–10, 16–22, for a discussion of the rigidity of social divisions in both urban and rural spaces, whereby "Iraq consisted to no little extent of distinct, self-absorbed, feebly interconnected societies," where a "strong spirit of localism" prevailed. The similarities between rural and urban social organization in Ottoman Mesopotamia are discussed in Batatu, *The Old Social Classes*, pp. 8–10, and also by the famous Iraqi sociologist Ali al-Wardi in "A Study of The Society of Iraq." Noted in Gulick, "Baghdad: Portrait of a City," p. 251, who also compares the martial aspects of the tribe with the urban gangs that often formed along *mahallah*-based lines.
33. The *dira* is the land to which a tribe lays claim. It can have both fixed properties (such as the particular plot of farmland that a semi-nomadic tribe regularly cultivates) as well as transient, spatial qualities (i.e., the ever-moving buffer zone that a nomadic tribe lays claim to as it moves across the desert). Like their rural counterparts, urban social units were also in constant competition for prized territory. Gulick, "Baghdad: Portrait of a City in Physical and Cultural Change," *Journal of the American Planning Association*, Vol. 33, No. 4, 1967, p. 251, traces the movement of identity-based communities in Baghdad during the first half of the twentieth century.
34. Batatu, *The Old Social Classes*, p. 19.
35. Charles Issawi, "Economic Change and Urbanization in the Middle East." in Lapidus (ed.) *Middle Eastern Cities: A Symposium on Ancient, Islamic and Contemporary Middle Eastern Urbanism*, (Berkeley, University of California Press, 1969), pp. 107–8, notes the prevalence of walls and barriers among communities in what he refers to as "Muslim cities" like Baghdad. This schema of institutionalized division was further reinforced by the Ottomans' *millat* system, which allowed minority communities such as Christians and Jews to administer their own neighborhoods and maintain independent education systems.
36. Gulick, "Baghdad: Portrait of a City," p. 246 notes that the *mahallah* framework was dominant in Baghdad at the turn of the century and that, while its barriers were blurring, the traditional names of these enclaves were still in use during the 1957 census.
37. Batatu, *The Old Social Classes*, pp. 22–3, notes the rise of nationalism and the weakening of the city's kaleidoscopic divisions in response to an array of factors including British occupation; and Tripp, *A History of Iraq*, pp. 26–7, addresses the rise of Arab nationalist thought (itself an outgrowth of Turkish nationalism in key respects, as well as the influences of the

First World War). See: Makiya, *Republic of Fear: The Politics of Modern Iraq*, (Berkeley: University of California Press, 1998), pp. 152–160 and William Cleveland, *The Making of An Arab Nationalist: Ottomanism and Arabism in the Life and Thought of Sati' al-Husri*, (Princeton, Princeton University Press, 1971), on the work of Sati al-Husri in furthering Arab nationalism via public education.

38. Gabbay, *Communism and Agrarian Reform*, p. 48; Haj, *The Making of Iraq*, pp. 82–98; Marr, *The Modern History of Iraq*, p. 45; Israel Gershoni, "Rethinking the Formation of Arab Nationalism in the Middle East, 1920–1945: Old and New Narratives," in James Jankowski and Israel Gershoni (eds), *Rethinking Nationalism in the Arab Middle East*, (New York: Columbia University Press, 1997), pp. 18–9; and Dann, *Iraq Under Qassem*, pp. 12–6, survey the development of increasingly radical political movements from the 1930s to the 1950s (which, in the account of the latter, is emphasized as having been confined to a narrow stratum of elites). Batatu, *The Old Social Classes*, p. 391 notes of the 1920s and 1930s that "political extremism progressively gained force… and moderation became anathema."
39. The "*mahallah* mentality" is Batatu's phrase, *The Old Social Classes*, p. 19. Batatu also comments on pervasive urban disdain for rural, tribal society.
40. The "migrants as plague" metaphor would become reality, with outbreaks of smallpox in the city's migrant slums prompting panic in the winter of 1956–1957. Noted in Phillips, "Rural to Urban Migration in Iraq," *Economic Development and Cultural Change*, Vol. 7, No. 4, 1959, p. 420, who conducted a survey of Baghdad's peripheral slums in early 1957.
41. Hilmi, *Internal Migration*, p. 276, notes the propensity of Baghdad's residents to summon the authorities to eradicate migrant settlements. Thesiger, *The Marsh Arabs*, p. 205, observes "many… left their villages to escape the tyranny of the sheikhs. But in Baghdad or Basra they encountered the police." Gulick, "Baghdad: Portrait of a City," p. 252, further notes that the migrants were "feared and resented" by established residents.
42. Hilmi, *Internal Migration*, pp. 271–7, observes that not all migrants were excluded from the city, and that some (predominantly on the west side of Baghdad) managed to maintain a foothold on open lands and establish legal ownership of property, going on to achieve economic success.
43. Warriner, *Land Reform and Development*, pp. 172–3. Her comment was made in reference to the accumulation of similar slum encampments on the outskirts of cities and towns across the South, but the sentiment was equally applicable (if not more so) to conditions in Baghdad. Dann, *Iraq Under Qassem*, p. 5, notes of the final years of the monarchy: "an uprooted, unassimilated human flotsam accumulated on the outskirts of every sizable town, consisting of declassed, unskilled peasants."
44. The creation of the bund, and its vital role in the growth of Baghdad on the eastern bank of the Tigris River, is discussed in Hilmi, *Internal Migration*, pp. 265–6, and Gulick, "Baghdad: Portrait of a City," p. 249.
45. Hilmi, *Internal Migration*, pp. 269–71, estimates that at the time of *al-'asima's* destruction it contained 20,000 *sarifas*. Population percentage estimate from al-Madfai, "Baghdad," in Berger (ed.), *The New Metropolis in the Arab World*, (Bombay: Allied Publishers, 1963), p. 59, who was the Director General of Planning and Design for the Ministry of Municipalities. He observes that *sarifas* came to constitute 44.6 per cent of Baghdad's housing supply by the time of Qasim's coup, housing some 250,000 people.

46. Batatu, *The Old Social Classes*, p. 49, notes the "somber wretchedness" of the slums, while Hilmi, Warriner, and Phillips all express personal shock at the living conditions endured by the migrants.
47. Survey detailed in Phillips, "Rural-to-Urban Migration," p. 417, who noted of the toilets, "the object is clearly privacy rather than sanitation." Population figures from Hilmi, *Internal Migration*, p. 266. The population of the migrant slums in 1957 was thus greater than the entire population of Baghdad a half-century earlier.
48. Figures cited in Hilmi, *Internal Migration*, p. 277. Phillips, "Rural-to-Urban Migration," p. 420, references the devastating flood of 1954. The city administrators welcomed the flooding of the Tigris, as not only did it sweep away the accumulated waste in *al-'asima*, but it was also hoped to act as a deterrent to the slum's continued growth.
49. Hilmi, *Internal Migration*, pp. 278–85, notes the unique contribution of the Marsh Arabs to the squalor of *al-'asima*.
50. Ismael al-Arif, *Iraq Reborn*, p. 21, observes of the migrants that "they brought with them to the large towns and cities their traditional customs and their tribal solidarity, which kept them aliens in an industrial society. They remained villagers in urban surroundings." Fuad Baali, "Social Factors in Iraqi Rural-Urban Migration," *American Journal of Economics and Sociology*, Vol. 25, No. 4, October 1966, p. 361, further notes the continued use of tribal dispute resolution mechanisms.
51. Bassam Tibi, "The Simultaneity of the Unsimultaneous: Old Tribes and Imposed Nation-States in the Modern Middle East," in Philip Khoury and Joseph Kostner (eds), *Tribes and State Formation in the Middle East* (Berkeley: University of California Press, 1990), p. 142, notes a broader trend in rural-to-urban migration across the Middle East wherein "Those who... cannot be absorbed [into the heart of urban life] rely on their ethnic-tribal kin groups as reference groups; they can survive only through maintaining the network of prenational tribal loyalties and ties." Hosham Dawood, "The 'State-ization' of the Tribe and the Tribalization of the State: the Case of Iraq," in *Tribes and Power*, p. 117, notes how urban migration "threw tribal members on the connections of their *hamoula* and their house." T.H. Greenshields, "'Quarters' and Ethnicity," in G.H. Blake and R.I. Lawless, *The Changing Middle Eastern City*, (London: Croom Helm, 1980), p. 133, notes how "anchor" communities formed in Baghdad's slums, which subsequently drew in additional migrant kin. Hilmi, *Internal Migration*, pp. 500–4, observes how migrant communities developed around bonds of common kinship and geographic origin in the Deep South. Hilmi also notes the doctoral research of Aziz on p. 317, who alleged that tribal leaders had reconstituted their power somewhat during the mid 1960s due to the dynamics of migration and settlement—though Hilmi questions the veracity of this claim, noting his own research in 1975 "point[ed] out clearly the deterioration of the position of tribal chiefs."
52. The 1940s and 1950s were a time of price shocks and rampant economic insecurity for many in Baghdad and, with the massive influx of migrants having flooded the labor market, wages were depressed and job security meager. On the labor-market and financial prospects of the migrants, see: al-Madfai, "Baghdad," p. 60; Atheel al-Jomard, "Internal Migration in Iraq," in *The Integration of Modern Iraq*, p. 117; Sluglett and Farouk-Sluglett, *Iraq Since 1958*, p. 34; Batatu, *The Old Social Classes*, pp. 136–8; Phillips, "Rural-to-Urban Migration," p. 414. Furthermore, al-Madfai, "Baghdad," p. 58, notes how the architectural qualities of the *sarifas* facilitated easy movement within the city.

53. Halpern, *The Politics of Social Change*, p. 85, coins the term "urban nomad," calling him "uprooted, displaced, and superfluous, with no fixed place in society."
54. See the work of Jabar, "Sheikhs and Ideologues: Deconstruction and Reconstruction of Tribes under Patrimonial Totalitarianism in Iraq, 1968–1998," p. 78, on how "tribal ethos or culture, rather than tribal organization, persists in [urban] spaces and keeps [migrants] bound together." Phillips, "Rural-to-Urban Migration," pp. 420–1, notes "the breaking of family and tribal ties by their different employment and higher money incomes," but that "they maintain many of their folkways." Gulick, "Baghdad: Portrait of a City," pp. 251–2 cites the work of al-Wardi on the difficulties encountered by migrants as they attempted to preserve traditional ties.
55. Statistics from Hilmi, *Internal Migration*, p. 454. Sluglett and Farouk-Sluglett, *Iraq Since 1958*, p. 193, and Batatu, "Shi'i Organizations in Iraq: al-Da'wa al-Islamiyah and al-Mujahidin," pp. 184–6, discuss the religiosity of the migrants. The Shi'a faith was in a period of steep decline across Iraq at mid century, and the religious elites of Najaf and Kerbala were focused primarily on reinvigorating their seminaries and reviving popular religiosity among the elite. Batatu, "Shi'i Organizations in Iraq: al-Da'wa al-Islamiyah and al-Mujahidin," p. 188, observes that it was not until the 1960s that the Shi'a elite paid notable attention to the urban poor.
56. Baali, "Social Factors", p. 362, notes the prevalence of criminality in the slums at mid century, which he attributes to "the low level of living and the ignorance prevalent among the dwellers." Gulick, "Baghdad: Portrait of a City," p. 251, cites al-Wardi's observations of how "undesirable elements" eroded communal solidarity in the city's slums.
57. Haj, *The Making of Iraq*, pp. 82–98, examines the development of political parties from 1940–1958 and the ways that economic hardship fueled popular unrest, with a focus on the economic dislocations of World War II. See: Batatu, *The Old Social Classes*, Chapter 17, for a discussion of economic hardship as fuel for political unrest in the 1940s and 1950s, and Chapter 22 on the *wathbah* riots of 1948 that left hundreds dead.
58. Marr, *The Modern History of Iraq*, p. 61, notes that the "last decade of the old regime was a study in contrast," and argues that material conditions played a key role in driving political disturbances. Qubain, *The Reconstruction of Iraq*, p. 30, observes that economic hardship and the concurrent rise of extreme leftist political movements hostile to both the monarchy and its British patron led to "a race between reform and revolution." William Roger Louis, "The British and the Origins of the Iraqi Revolution," in *The Iraqi Revolution of 1958*, p. 45, likewise states that, among British observers, "it was an article of faith… that a race was taking place between development and revolution," between 1956 and 1958. Haj, *The Making of Iraq*, p. 79, notes that martial law was imposed between 1948 and 1952.
59. Phillips, "Rural-to-Urban Migration," pp. 418–9, summarizes the findings of her fieldwork. She emphasizes the migrants' general satisfaction with their significantly improved material conditions in *al-'asima*, while also noting the various factors that rendered them largely apolitical.
60. Tareq Ismael, *The Rise and Fall of the Communist Party of Iraq*, (Cambridge: Cambridge University Press, 2007), p. 313, alleges the creation of a "proletarianized peasantry" prior to the 1958 coup. This appears fundamentally untrue, yet the ability of the ICP to mobilize large crowds of impoverished Shi'a after the 1958 coup, when the party would briefly

establish itself as an informal arm of the revolutionary regime, seems to have prompted ICP admirers to exaggerate its achievements in later years. Hilmi, *Internal Migration*, p. 281, offers a more reasoned assessment of the migrants' economic condition and its implications for the politics of the era. Also, see: Gabbay, *Communism and Agrarian Reform*, for reference to how the anti-British themes of the ICP were pivotal in the party's ability to rouse the Shi'a underclass (as opposed to the popularity of Marxism, or any genuine adherence to communism among the overwhelmingly illiterate underclass).

61. The Iraqi Communist Party has received extensive academic scrutiny, driven both by strong leftist currents among Iraq specialists and by Cold War era concerns. See: Batatu, *The Old Social Classes*, for the most comprehensive (and largely sympathetic) treatment of the ICP. Gabbay, *Communism and Agrarian Reform*, offers a useful counterbalance that presents the ICP as a fairly narrowly-based, elitist party of educated urbanites.
62. Phillips, "Rural-to-Urban Migration," p. 420, notes official government concerns, which would be proven wholly justified in subsequent years.
63. See: Batatu, *The Old Social Classes*, pp. 134–8, on the divisions between the migrants and their economic betters, and the former's incorporation into the security services. Phillips, "Rural-to-Urban Migration," p. 420, notes that basic steps were taken to create roads in *al-'asima* after the 1956–7 smallpox outbreak, but that nothing substantive was achieved.
64. See: Dann, *Iraq Under Qassem*, pp. 63–4, for a discussion of Qasim's genuine commitment to "social justice," and the observation that he was "haunted" by the poverty of his countrymen. In reference to Qasim's legacy, Khadduri, *Republican Iraq: A Study in Iraqi Politics Since the Revolution of 1958*, (London: Oxford University Press, 1969), pp. 154–5, notes the near-mythical status of Qasim among Baghdad's urban poor.
65. Majid Khadduri, *Republican Iraq*, p. 51, and Batatu, *The Old Social Classes*, pp. 804–805, discuss the mutilation and public desecration of Crown Prince Abdullah and Nuri al-Said, and the celebratory riots by mobs of migrants that accompanied Qasim's coup (in which the residents of the slums descended upon the city center in a looting rampage that necessitated the imposition of martial law). Gabbay, *Communism and Agrarian Reform*, p. 121, also cites brutal violence in the Deep South, featuring "unprecedented acts of terror and destruction" by the peasant farmers against their socio-economic betters. Nicholas Thatcher, "Reflection on US Foreign Policy towards Iraq in the 1950s," in *The Iraqi Revolution of 1958*, p. 71, notes how the residents of *al-'asima* "poured into the streets" during the coup.
66. Map showing the chronological development of Baghdad from 1940 to 1975 from Hilmi, *Internal Migration*, p. 268.
67. Dann, *Iraq Under Qassem*, p. 149, discusses Qasim's use of land as a tool to secure the support of influential elements of the military and government bureaucracy, which had been established practice under the monarchy. Al-Arif, *Iraq Reborn*, p. 23, and Tripp, *A History of Iraq*, p. 50, note the monarchy's use of land as, in the words of the latter, "a way of purchasing social order."
68. Continued migration flows were recognized as a major problem in Baghdad during the early 1960s. Not only was the construction of *sarifas* officially prohibited but, in a sign of how contentious the issue was and the extent to which Qasim's regime wanted to demonstrate its achievements, it was made illegal to even photograph them. Discussed in Baali, "Social Factors," pp. 363–4.

69. Gabbay, *Communism and Agrarian Reform*, pp. 109–17, and Batatu, *The Old Social Classes*, pp. 836–7, discuss Qasim's land reform scheme, which was based upon Egyptian efforts to achieve similar ends in 1952. Contrary to suggestions that Qasim was a radical (or, indeed, a communist), Gabbay argues compellingly that his reforms had modest aims and "the dominant approach... was one of tolerance rather than incitement."
70. See details in Hilmi, *Internal Migration*, p. 293, who notes that demand was such that all the land was claimed "within a few weeks."
71. Hilmi, *Internal Migration*, pp. 407–11, discusses overcrowding, observing that average household size among the residents of Revolution City in 1975 was 7.7 people, and that the homes built averaged 3.3 people per room.
72. Hilmi, *Internal Migration*, pp. 115, 473, 517, notes that farmers in the Deep South continued to face feudal injustice and terrible conditions after the 1958 Agrarian Reform Act. Batatu, *The Old Social Classes*, p. 955, discusses the failures of the scheme, and Marr, *The Modern History of Iraq*, p. 99, compares its effects to Zimbabwe.
73. Gabbay, *Communism and Agrarian Reform*, p. 116, notes that the government sought to force those farmers that had been given land grants to remain in the south, and that residents of Baghdad's slums were offered parcels of land outside of the capital to induce them to return to the countryside. Clawson, "Iraq's Economy and International Sanctions," in Baram and Rubin (eds), *Iraq's Road to War*, (London: MacMillan, 1994), p. 70, notes that Qasim's rule marked the beginning of a phase in Iraq's history where economic policy was dictated by ideological objectives as opposed to economic ones, wryly observing that "Iraq was a food exporter for 3,000 years, until after the 1958 land reforms and the subsequent Ba'th actions to reinforce state control over the economy."
74. Hilmi, *Internal Migration*, p. 243, charts Baghdad's growth.
75. However much the ideological outlook of the Iraqi government changed after the monarchy was overthrown, the administrative institutions of the government remained largely intact. Warren Adams, "Reflections on Recent Land Reform Experience in Iraq," *Land Economics*, Vol. 39, No. 2, May 1963, p. 200 (who taught at the Iraqi College of Agriculture), argues for continuity between the regimes, noting that the executors of policy "faced many of the same problems, tried similar solutions and very likely shared much of the same administrative machinery" in their efforts to combat Iraq's most pressing challenges. Iraq had been suffering from administrative sclerosis for decades, and the body tasked with spending Iraq's oil revenue had long been unable to spend the money allocated to it. Hilmi, *Internal Migration*, pp. 101–2, also comments on the severe institutional and administrative problems encountered by the revolutionary government.
76. Batatu, *The Old Social Classes*, and Dann, *Iraq Under Qassem*, catalogue the violence that persisted through Qasim's rule. Qasim had survived an earlier assassination attempt in October 1959, in which a young Saddam Hussein played a central role.
77. Makiya, *Republic of Fear*, pp. 58–9, references the fighting, noting that stories circulated that Qasim was not dead, but would instead soon return from occultation like the *mehdi* of Shi'a lore. Continued resistance prompted the architects of the coup to display Qasim's corpse on television as definitive proof of his demise. Batatu, *The Old Social Classes*, p. 978, references the battles fought between the Shi'a underclass (led, he notes, by members of the Iraqi Communist Party) and the coup's supporters in the Ba'th Party and the Iraqi military.

78. Batatu, *The Old Social Classes*, p. 897, discusses the scope of popular support for the communists in the early months of Qasim's rule, but derisively notes that the vast majority were "July 14th Communists"—implying they were fair weather fans of the party due to its perceived position of prominence in the new order and its ties to the much beloved Qasim. Nonetheless, as the Ba'th subjected the ICP to an "unending year of horror" in 1963, "the districts that had risen against them were treated as enemy country" as well. Batatu, *The Old Social Classes*, p. 988.
79. Quotation from Hilmi, *Internal Migration*, p. 411, who also observes, on p. 141, that, "the modern era of 1957–1975 showed a continuous rise of the rural-urban migration volumes to an alarming scale of unprecedented dimensions." Sluglett and Farouk-Sluglett, *Iraq Since 1958*, p. 248, estimate that the slums of Baghdad absorbed 990,000 new arrivals between 1968 and 1977. W. Thom Workman, *The Social Origins of the Iran-Iraq War* (London: Lynn & Rienner Publishing, 1994), p. 79, notes the discrepancy between Revolution City's intended capacity and its actual population by the mid 1970s.
80. For an example of the complex interweaving of past and present in Iraqi society at mid century, see: Batatu *The Old Social Classes*, pp. 403–424, 481–2, who notes how family ties, as well as the lingering bonds of the *mahallahs*, shaped the formation of modern ideologies. In reference to the city's growth and infrastructural development from the mid 1940s onwards, Batatu, *The Old Social Classes*, p. 35, presents census data that shows Baghdad's population nearly quadrupled between 1922 and 1957. Qubain, *The Reconstruction of Iraq*, p. 30, notes that the scope of associated development prior to the boom of the revolutionary era "has had no parallel in the history of the country since the golden age of the Abbasid Caliphate." Warriner, *Land Reform and Development*, p. 181, notes the "chaos" of urban development and the pursuit of modernity at mid century, as does al-Madfai, "Baghdad." On the incongruities of this process, Warriner, *Land Reform and Development*, p. 175, laments the absurd phenomenon of "sheikhs in Cadillacs" and their "tribesmen in buses."
81. On the infrastructural condition of Baghdad in the 1950s, see: Warriner, *Land Reform and Development*, pp. 121–5, and pp. 181, 175, for a sharp critique of the incongruities of "development," and "change without direction or purpose"; while Gulick, "Baghdad: Portrait of a City," p. 253, observes the city center was modernizing at the expense of traditional social structures. Al-Madfai, "Baghdad," p. 62, details the shortcomings of urban planning in Baghdad.
82. Marr, *The Modern History of Iraq*, pp. 65–6, further notes how the cycle of political violence and repression under the late monarchy fostered rising radicalism, and that "centrist" moderates remained marginalized from popular discourse. Batatu, *The Old Social Classes*, p. 426, notes how the "corrosion" of traditional values among the newly-educated was central to the rise of modern ideological movements. Warriner, *Land Reform and Development*, pp. 182–3, critiques the attitudes prevalent among the educated elite at mid century, noting that the "young bureaucrat just back from California with a degree in economics has apparently learnt nothing but contempt for his fellow countrymen." Dann, *Iraq Under Qassem*, pp. 5–6, likewise writes derisively of the new intelligentsia as being "cut off from or contemptuous of the traditions of their forefathers, often presenting a façade of Western culture which they had not really absorbed." See Abdul-Salam Yousif, "The Struggle for Cultural Hegemony during the Iraqi Revolution," in *The Iraqi Revolution of 1958*, for a more sym-

pathetic analysis, and observations on how the toppling of the monarchy ushered in an era of broadened political activity and a "democratization of culture"—while specifically noting (p. 189) that new intellectual currents "cut across *mahallahs*... and districts" of the city.

83. On the prevalence of strong popular support for transformative governance across the Middle East, see: John Waterbury, "The Growth of Public Sector Enterprise in the Middle East," in Haleh Esfandiari and A.L. Udovitch (eds), *The Economic Dimensions of Middle Eastern History: Essays in Honor of Charles Issawi*, (Princeton: The Darwin Press, 1990), pp. 255–6. Mohsen, "Cultural Totalitarianism," p. 7, observes how Iraqi regimes after the 1958 coup embraced the "mass culture" ideology of Eastern Europe, wherein "the masses were seen as an object whose consciousness could and should be manipulated by the state." Gareth Stansfield, *Iraq: People, History, Politics*, (Cambridge: Polity, 2007), pp. 92–8, traces the rise of totalitarian governance in Iraq from the 1958 coup onwards.
84. In 1957, Phillips, "Rural-to-Urban Migration," p. 413, found that 87 per cent of *al-'asima's* residents came from present-day Maysan Province and 11 per cent from Wasit Province. Hilmi, *Internal Migration*, p. 336, 381, notes that the percentage of migrants from Maysan Province fell to 53.5 per cent by 1975, and that non-migrant families moved into Revolution City and Shula as well, reflecting the fact that the squalor of Baghdad was not limited to the former *sarifa* settlements and, as such, the new development zones were initially attractive to many.
85. Hilmi, *Internal Migration*, p. 401, notes that by 1975, new arrivals to Revolution City were motivated increasingly by financial incentives and significantly less by the desire to join kin.
86. Hilmi, *Internal Migration*, p. 552, observes how the government's provision of goods and services undermined traditional bonds among the poor.
87. Hilmi, *Internal Migration*, p. 565, observes that the two main results of Revolution City and Shula's creation were the acceleration of migration to the city and the alteration of settlement patters away from *mahallah*-style kinship clusters. Gulick, "Village and City: Cultural Continuities in Twentieth Century Middle Eastern Cultures," in *Middle Eastern cities*, p. 149, raised concerns at the time over the implications of the migrants' forced relocation, expressing doubts over the survival of migrant communities.
88. Jabar, "Sheikhs and Ideologues: Deconstruction and Reconstruction of Tribes under Patrimonial Totalitarianism in Iraq, 1968–1998," p. 78, notes that the numerical grid that was originally created to delineate Revolution City was replaced by the *hamoula*-level names that reflected local residents' tribal heritage. Rather than marking the continuity of substantive tribal bonds or the perseverance (or reconstitution) of a broader tribal order in the district, it appears that this was driven by nostalgia and affinity to traditional identities, which the author terms as "cultural tribalism."
89. On the political instability of Iraq at mid century, Makiya, *Republic of Fear*, p. 22, observes that "between 1958 and 1968 there were more than ten coups and attempted coups, two armed rebellions, and a semi continuous civil war against the Kurds."
90. See Makiya, *Republic of Fear*, for a detailed exposition on, and deconstruction of, Ba'thist ideology. Rooted in the writing of chief ideologue Michel Aflaq, Ba'thism was a romantic, mystical ideology that attempted to fuse aspects of pan-Arabism, statist socialism, and fascism. Zuhair al-Jazai'iri, "Ba'thist Ideology and Practice," in Hazelton (ed.), CARDI,

Iraq since the Gulf War: Prospects for Democracy, (London: Zed Books, 1994), p. 34, further examines its ideological heritage in German romanticism.

91. Oil revenues listed in Sluglett and Farouk-Sluglett, *Iraq Since 1958*, p. 172, and Workman, *The Social Origins of the Iran-Iraq War*, p. 104.
92. Makiya, *Republic of Fear*, p. 141, notes succinctly that "their programme is not to win over the masses, but to change them." Makiya's account of Ba'thist Iraq remains the most illuminating and thought-provoking of the resources available on the era, particularly with regard to its implications for Iraqi society. See: Hannah Arendt, *The Origins of Totalitarianism*, (San Diego: Harcourt Brace, 1973), Chapter 11, on how social atomization renders a populace all the more susceptible to the inducements of totalitarian governance. The dislocations of Iraq's chaotic transition to "modernity" (from mass migration, to industrialization, to ideological turmoil) may thus be seen to have paved the way for the rise of totalitarian governance—which, in turn, furthered that same atomization. Makiya, *Republic of Fear*, p. 203, and Stansfield, *Iraq*, p. 79, both emphasize the relevance of Arendt to the study of Iraq, with the former arguing of the Ba'th that "they appealed largely to atomized and disrupted individuals, or to those who felt threatened by the rootlessness brought on by population growth, urbanization, modernization, and the assault of large-scale demographic changes on a traditional way of life." For a contrasting view that draws upon troves of Iraqi government documents seized after the American-led invasion of 2003, see: Joseph Sassoon, *Saddam Hussein's Bath Party: Inside an Authoritarain Regime*, (Cambridge: Cambridge University Press, 2012), pp. 5–6. While conceding that the Ba'th "systematically penetrated every stratum of society," Sassoon argues that Ba'thist Iraq did not meet the criteria for "totalitarianism" due to an alleged lack of bureaucratic and administrative centralization.
93. Pollack, *The Threatening Storm*, pp. 115–22, provides an overview of the various overlapping security organizations used by the Ba'th, which employed some 500,000 Iraqis (excluding the Army).
94. The growth of the security services and the resulting complicity of the general population in the enforcement of Ba'thist rule was an important objective of the Ba'th. Makiya, *Republic of Fear*, p. 32, notes that by 1980 "one-fifth of the economically active Iraqi labour force (about 3.4 million people) were institutionally charged during peacetime with one form or another of violence." Makiya, *Republic of Fear*, p. 66, notes that the most brutal excesses of the Ba'th occurred after the regime had eliminated its principal political rivals and firmly-established its dominance over Iraq. Violence was thus not perpetrated simply to establish the party's control, but rather to transform the citizenry. See: Arendt, *The Origins of Totalitarianism*, p. 422, for a discussion of totalitarianism and the proclivity of state terror to reach its apex after the opposition has been decisively defeated.
95. Batatu, "Iraq's underground Shi'a Movements: Characteristics, Causes and Prospects," *Middle East Institute*, Vol. 35, No. 4, Autumn 1981, p. 4, notes that the daily minimum wage for unskilled labor grew substantially from 1973, while price controls checked inflation, yet conditions remained difficult for the urban poor. Sluglett and Farouk-Sluglett, *Iraq Since 1958*, p. 248, estimate that some 265,000 of the 990,000 migrants that came to Baghdad between 1968 and 1977 wound up employees of the state—overwhelmingly in superfluous, "non-productive" roles created to absorb surplus labor.
96. Jabar, "The War Generation in Iraq: A Case of Failed Etatist Nationalism," in Potter and

Sick (eds), *Iran, Iraq and the legacies of War*, (New York: Palgrave Macmillan, 2004), p. 126, argues that by 1980 the "middle classes" would account for half of Iraq's urban population, due directly to the distribution of oil revenues.

97. See Karsh and Rautsi, *Saddam Hussein*, p. 121, for the observation that Saddam "knew all too well that fear was not enough to secure absolute power; that if he were to stay at the helm for an indefinite period of time… the Iraqi people had to be made to love and adore him… He was to become Iraq." Shadid, *Night Draws Near*, (New York: Picador, 2005), pp. 24–5, further observes that the 1970s were a time when Iraq's "newfound wealth radiated Iraqi culture, influence and power across the region." Said K. Aburish, *Saddam Hussein: Politics of Revenge*, (London: Bloomsbury, 2000), p. 160, likewise observes in an otherwise critical biography of the Iraqi President that all Iraqis enjoyed significant improvements to their material lives throughout the 1970s. Sluglett and Farouk-Sluglett, *Iraq Since 1958*, pp. 231–9, chart economic growth during the 1970s, featuring a dramatic rise in GDP and a surge in wages for both skilled and unskilled labor. For contrary views, see Isam al-Khafaji, "The Parasitic Base of the Ba'thist Regime," in CARDRI, *Saddam's Iraq: Revolution or Reaction?* (London: Zed Books, 1989), pp. 82–4, who attacks the idea that the Ba'th presided over an economic boom in the 1970s, noting that huge disparities of income developed and that inflation surged in keeping with state spending. Alnasrawi, *The Economy of Iraq: Oil, Wars, Destruction & Development and Prospects, 1950–2010*, (London: Greenwood Press, 1994), p. 97, also comments that "labor shortages, stagnant agriculture, rising urban population, persistent inflation, rising dependence on foreign consumer goods (especially foodstuffs), and rising dependence on oil" characterized the era. Karsh and Rautsi, *Saddam Hussein*, p. 91, note that "inefficiency, waste, mismanagement and corruption" poisoned efforts to spend Iraq's oil revenues effectively.
98. The Ba'th Party's land reform program was enacted in May 1969 in an effort to further undermine the position of rural sheikhs, leading to a major drop in production and revolts in modern-day Maysan Province. Detailed in Baram, "Neo-Tribalism in Iraq: Saddam Hussein's Tribal Policies, 1991–1996," *International Journal of Middle East Studies*, Vol. 29, No. 1, 1997, p. 3.
99. The irrelevance of economic theory to Ba'thist conceptions of socialism was captured by chief party ideologue Michel Aflaq: "when I am asked to give a definition of socialism, I can say that it is not to be found in the works of Marx and Lenin. I say: socialism is the religion of life and of its victory over death." Recorded in Alnasrawi, *The Economy of Iraq*, p. 59. Karsh and Rautsi, *Saddam Hussein*, p. 90, note similarly how "socialism was not a coherent body of ideas" to the Ba'th, "but rather a catchword to win the support of the masses." Critically, Ba'thist socialism was not concerned in any meaningful way with the "re"-distribution of wealth to create economic equality. Its goal was, instead, the large-scale distribution of oil revenues—which would make the state the ultimate patron of the populace, and prevent individuals or groups external to the state from exerting socio-economic influence. See: Batatu, *The Old Social Classes*, pp. 1116–20, for contemporary observations on how "social power" was a deliberate target of Ba'thist economic policy in the 1970s, and how the government was becoming ever more able "to determine the direction of social change."
100. Makiya, *Republic of Fear*, pp. 41, 44, observes how "Party, state, and even civil society were

merging into a single, great, formless mass," and that "the Ba'th developed a novel approach to the problem of hostility and alienation from the state: they turned the people into its employees." Mohsen, "Cultural Totalitariansim," pp. 9–10, observes similarly that the Ba'th Party maintained lists of "financially independent and politically non-aligned intellectuals" who were silenced or brought into the service of the state.

101. Baram, "Neo-Tribalism in Iraq," pp. 1–2, notes that the Ba'th were explicitly anti-traditional in their ideology, particularly as party ideologues were urbanites with strong biases against the rural tribal system. Hilmi, *Internal Migration*, pp. 577–81, discusses the re-ruralization initiatives of the Ba'th that sought to return indoctrinated migrants to the countryside where they would serve as "a nucleus for socialism," and facilitate "the elimination of tribal tradition and [the] dominance of backward norms and convictions."
102. Makiya, *Republic of Fear*, pp. 77–8, quotes a Saddam Hussein speech given to the Ministry of Education: "To prevent the father and mother from dominating the household with backwardness, we must make the small one radiate internally to expel it. Some fathers have slipped away from us for various reasons, but the small boy is still in our hands and we must transform him." Karsh and Rautsi, *Saddam Hussein*, p. 93, argue that the promulgation of women's rights was a ploy to undermine families and insert the state—and by extension the regime—in the position of the family as the ultimate locus of loyalty. Karsh (pp. 176–7) notes that the state deliberately sought to make the Ba'th Party the parent figures of Iraqi children. "You must encircle the adults through their sons," Saddam Hussein is quoted as declaring, "you must place in every corner a son of the revolution, with a trustworthy eye and a firm mind who received his instruction from the responsible center of the revolution."
103. Hilmi, *Internal Migration*, pp. 904–5, notes that into the mid 1970s, the Ba'thist apparatus was not robust enough to keep migrants from leaving the south, or to prevent their incursion into Baghdad. Discussions of the comprehensiveness of Ba'thist totalitarianism thus must be qualified by an assessment of the administrative capabilities of the Iraqi state. Put crudely, shortfalls in administrative competency dictated that irrespective of its aspirations, Ba'thist Iraq would never realize its totalitarian ambitions—much as the Iraqi government would remain unable to muster the institutional capacity to spend its surging oil revenues well into the 1980s. Noted in Alnasrawi, *The Economy of Iraq*, p. 81.
104. Batatu, "Iraq's Underground Shi'a Movements"; and Jabar, *The Shi'ite Movement*, offer detailed overviews of the Shi'a opposition movements that grew through the 1960s and 1970s.
105. The fact that the Da'wa was an offshoot of elitist currents in the Shi'a establishment that harbored extensive social prejudices against the *shurughis* (examined in Jabar, *The Shi'ite Movement*, p. 75), suggests strongly the Da'wa's appellation for Revolution City was far more an expression of intent (or, more likely still, a public relations slogan) than a reflection of reality. Batatu, "Iraq's Underground Shi'a Movements," and Batatu, "Shi'i Organizations in Iraq: al-Da'wa al-Islamiyah and al-Mujahidin," offer further detail. Mosque attendance figures from the survey of Hilmi, *Internal Migration*, p. 454. The religiosity of the urban poor (and, equally importantly, their attitude toward Islamist movements such as the Da'wa) remains controversial. The Shi'a religious establishment was held in low regard among the *shurughis* (a sentiment that was returned in kind), as a result of generations of

neglect and the actively hostile stance of the clerical establishment toward underclass interests. Clerical elites had been outspoken opponents of both the Iraqi Communist Party and Qasim's southern land reform scheme, for example, while social prejudices persisted. Nonetheless, as noted by Batatu; Nakash, *The Shi'is of Iraq*, p. 132; and Sluglett and Farouk-Sluglett, *Iraq Since 1958*, p. xxi, radical Shi'a groups did make notable headway in their recruiting efforts, and observers widely attribute this to the same social dislocations and material hardships that had prompted affinity to communism in previous generations.

106. Makiya, *Republic of Fear*, p. 265, notes that "by the late 1970s the Ba'thi state was wealthier and stronger than any state has ever been in the modern history of Iraq." Batatu, *The Old Social Classes*, pp. 1116–20, observed the rise of the Ba'thist state during the 1970s, noting how, by 1977, "the social power of private large-scale property [had been] uprooted," while "side by side with this, the government has grown enormously in the life of the people." These achievements should nonetheless be qualified by an appreciation of the regime's administrative mediocrity, as noted above. Owing to enduring organizational and capacity-related limitations, aspects of Ba'thist "totalitarianism" would remain aspirational as opposed to actual.

107. Terms discussed in Batatu, "Shi'i Organizations in Iraq: al-Da'wa al-Islamiyah and al-Mujahidin," p. 195. Tripp, *A History of Iraq*, pp. 206–26, and Karsh and Rautsi, *Saddam Hussein*, pp. 85–7, detail Saddam's formal assumption of power, having controlled the state from behind the scenes since the mid 1970s.

108. The enthusiastic response of the remnants of Iraq's Shi'a opposition to the Iranian Revolution, and the popular resonance of their subsequently emboldened statements and actions against the Ba'th regime, gave Saddam Hussein legitimate cause for concern. Ayatollah Ruhollah Khomeini's seizure of power in Tehran was met with outspoken praise by Shi'a elites in Iraq and by a renewed Da'wa terrorist campaign as well—which, as noted in Efraim Karsh, *Essential Histories: The Iran Iraq War, 1980–1988* (London: Osprey Publishing, 2002), p. 13, killed some twenty Ba'thist officials and nearly took the life of Vice President Tariq Aziz. See: Sluglett and Farouk-Sluglett, *Iraq Since 1958*, pp. 256–7, for Grand Ayatollah Mohammed Baqir al-Sadr's attitude (and overtures) toward Khomeini. The domestic crackdown that ensued was paired with lavish expenditures on mosques and shrines for the Shi'a, the open distribution of money to the poor in Revolution City, and overtures that won the support of high-ranking Shi'a clerics. The crackdown not only devastated the Da'wa and drove its remnants into Iranian exile, but also saw the execution of Grand Ayatollah Mohammed Baqir al-Sadr (the intellectual inspiration of the Da'wa and the most likely figure to have assumed a Khomeini-esque role in Iraq). Jabar, *The Shi'ite Movement*, p. 234, notes that "this was the first execution of a Grand Ayatollah in the modern history of the Middle East." Cockburn, *Muqtada al-Sadr and the Shia Insurgency in Iraq*, (London: Faber and Faber, 2009), p. 53, notes that after the execution in April 1980, "Saddam appeared to have won a total victory over the Shia radicals in Iraq"—meaning that the invasion of Iran was launched after domestic threats had been contained. Sluglett and Farouk-Sluglett, *Iraq Since 1958*, pp. 256–7, like Makiya, *Republic of Fear*, p. 270, and Tripp, *A History of Iraq*, p. 223, argue that Saddam approached the conflict from a position of confidence and strength. Karsh and Rautsi, *Saddam Hussein*, Chapter Six, argue that Saddam entered the conflict reluctantly in response to a significant, growing threat from Iran.

109. For a concise overview of the conflict, see: Karsh, *Essential Histories*.
110. Sluglett, Farouk-Sluglett and Stork, "Not Quite Armageddon," pp. 27–8, discuss Saddam Hussein's "guns and butter" strategy.
111. See Karsh and Rautsi, *Saddam Hussein*, pp. 153–6, for a discussion of domestic expenditures as being driven by concerns over public support for the war, and that Iraq had already suffered nearly 100,000 dead by the time the Army was driven from Iran in 1982; Frederick Axelgard, *A New Iraq? The Gulf War and Implications for US Policy*, (New York: Praeger, 1988), p. 28, discusses the terrible performance of Iraqi Shi'a troops during the initial offensive into Iran; and Jabar, "The War Generation in Iraq: A Case of Failed Etatist Nationalism," p. 127, likewise notes the prevalence of "deliberate capitulation" by frontline Iraqi soldiers. Isam al-Khafaji, "Iraq's Seventh Year: Saddam's Quart d'Heure?" *Middle East Report*, No. 151, March–April 1988, p. 35, attacks the notion of high morale within the Iraqi Army, citing the actions of the Punishment Corps charged with executing poorly-performing commanders and enforcing loyalty; while Karsh and Rautsi, *Saddam Hussein*, p. 155, also note morale issues within the Iraqi Army.
112. Sluglett, Farouk-Sluglett and Stork, "Not Quite Armageddon," p. 24, notes that the name change took place in October 1982—in recognition, perhaps, of Saddam Hussein's growing discomfort with the word *thawra* (revolution), being spoken among the Shi'a masses at a time when Iranian forces were advancing into Iraq. Batatu, "Shi'i Organizations in Iraq: al-Da'wa al-Islamiyah and al-Mujahidin," p. 198, asserts that the Ba'th paved streets and installed plumbing in areas of Saddam City to mitigate the growth of Islamic radicalism and Da'wa support. See: Batatu, "Shi'i Organizations in Iraq: al-Da'wa al-Islamiyah and al-Mujahidin," p. 184, on the neglect of Revolution City under Ba'thist rule, and the theory that the district's streets had long-remained unpaved due to speculation that large oil deposits lay beneath.

2. THE SANCTIONS ERA: SHIFTS IN CIVIL SOCIETY AND THE RISE OF THE SADRIST MOVEMENT

1. Makiya, *Republic of Fear: The Politics of Modern Iraq*, (Berkeley: University of California Press, 1998), p. xii, notes, "The system that had reached perfection on the eve of the Iraq-Iran war remained intact all throughout it… At no point… was the Iraqi president's authority inside Iraq and among Iraqis (excluding the Kurds) threatened during the 1980s." Sluglett and Farouk-Sluglett, *Iraq since 1958: From Revolution to Dictatorship*, (London: IB Tauris, 1998), p. 280, observe that Iraq's economic position was "certainly bad… but not desperate." Kiren Aziz Chaudhry, "Consuming Interests: Market Failure and the Social Foundations of Iraqi Etatisme," in Kamil Mahdi (ed.), *Iraq's Economic Predicament*, (Reading: Ithaca Press, 2002), p. 245, further notes that the "Ba'thist state upheld its populist pact with consumers during the war with Iran, while systematically undercutting all independent forms of social organization." Al-Jabbar, "Why the *Intifada* Failed," in Hazelton (ed.), *Iraq since the Gulf War: Prospects for Democracy, CARDI*, (London: Zed Books, 1994), p. 100, takes a more alarmist stance regarding the position of the regime, but points out nonetheless that although the "regime was in crisis, so was the opposition."
2. Amatzia Baram, "The Iraqi Invasion of Kuwait: Decision-making in Baghdad," in Baram

and Rubin (eds), *Iraq's Road to War*, (London: MacMillan, 1994), p. 6, notes that Iraq suffered an estimated 200,000 killed and 400,000 wounded, while some 70,000 remained captive in Iran as prisoners of war. Karsh and Rautsi, *Saddam Hussein: A Political Biography*, (New York: The Free Press, 1991), pp. 202–3, cite Iraq's debt burden, while Sluglett and Farouk-Sluglett, *Iraq Since 1958*, p. 272, estimate the total cost of the war to Iraq at nearly US$453 billion. For reference, Alnasrawi, *The Economy of Iraq: Oils, Wars, Destruction & Development and Prospects, 1950–2010*, (London: Greenwood Press, 1994), p. 100, calculates that Iraq's total oil revenues from 1931 to 1988 totaled only US$179.3 billion, making the bill for the war some 254 per cent of Iraq's cumulative historic oil rents. Per the year-to-year funding of the war, Alnasrawi further notes that annual GDP in Iraq averaged US$48.1 billion, while the annual cost of the war was US$50.2 billion—104 per cent of the total.

3. Clawson, "Iraq's Economy and International Sanctions," in *Iraq's Road to War*, p. 72, notes that Iraq's debt burden was less formidable than that of Turkey, Egypt, Argentina, or Brazil.
4. See: Karsh and Rautsi, *Saddam Hussein*, pp. 76–9, 202–3, and Sassoon, *Saddam Hussein's Ba'th Party: Inside an Authoritarian Regime*, (Cambridge: Cambridge University Press), Chapter 6, on the increased personalization of Saddam Hussein's rule during the course of the war. Baram, "The Ruling Political Elite in Bathi Iraq, 1968–1986: The Changing Features of a Collective Profile," *International Journal of Middle East Studies*, Vol. 21, No.4, 1989, pp. 460–1, discusses the marginalization of party figures and their replacement by kinsmen and trusted associates of Saddam. Baram notes the declining academic credentials of government functionaries, moving away from MDs and PhDs toward "those of a much more plebian birth" as Saddam installed his personal allies in key positions. International Crisis Group, "Iraq Backgrounder: What Lies Beneath," *Middle East Report*, No. 6, 1 October 2002, pp. 6–7, further comments on the decline of Ba'thist ideology during the course of the war, arguing that Party ideology had lost its relevance by the mid 1980s.
5. Alnasrawi, "Economic Devastation, Underdevelopment and Outlook," in *Iraq since the Gulf War*, p. 78, notes that Iraq's population grew by a staggering 34 per cent between 1980 and 1989. This represented the continuation of ongoing growth trends, as well as the results of a regime-sponsored fertility campaign during the war. Sluglett and Farouk-Sluglett, *Iraq Since 1958*, pp. 280–1, note that by the end of the war, the Iraqis were thoroughly dependent upon the state for their material wellbeing, making population growth a looming liability.
6. Noting this dynamic, Peter Sluglett, "The International Context of Iraq from 1980 to the Present," in Emma Nicholson and Peter Clark (eds), *The Iraqi Marshlands: A Human and Environmental Study*, (London: Politicos Publishing, 2002), p. 246, observes that "the 'desperateness' of Iraq's financial position was more an expression of Saddam Hussein's priorities than an objective fact."
7. The failures of the government's economic policies in the late 1980s are detailed in Karsh and Rautsi, *Saddam Hussein*, pp. 202–7; Baram, "The Iraqi Invasion of Kuwait: Decision-making in Baghdad," p. 8; Chaudhry, "Consuming Interests: Market Failure and the Social Foundations of Iraqi Etatisme," in Mahdi (ed.), *Iraq's Economic Predicament*, (Reading: Ithaca Press, 2002), Kiren Aziz Chaudhry, "Economic Liberalization and the Lineages of the Rentier State," *Comparative Politics*, Vol. 27, No. 1, October 1994, p. 15.
8. The growth of the informal economy is discussed in Alnasrawi, "Economic Devastation, Underdevelopment and Outlook," p. 81; International Crisis Group, "Iraq Backgrounder," p. 10.

9. The dominance of the regime over the new "capitalist" private sector is noted by al-Khafaji, "A Few Days After: State and Society in a post-Saddam Iraq," p. 80; and Karsh and Rautsi, *Saddam Hussein*, p. 92, who argue that economic liberalization was essentially a political strategy as opposed to an economic one, with the objective of creating a "national bourgeoisie" dependent upon the regime. Hanna Batatu, "State and Capitalism in Iraq: A Comment," *MERIP Middle East Report*, No. 142, September–October 1986, p. 12, finds no evidence that the ostensibly private economic actors who emerged during this time (principally as government contractors) possessed "any genuine autonomous social power."
10. Discussed in Clawson, "Iraq's Economy and International Sanctions," p. 72, who notes that major infrastructure projects consumed US$30 to US$50 billion of the state budget in 1989–1990.
11. See: Karsh and Rautsi, *Saddam Hussein*, pp. 206–7 for further details.
12. Sluglett, "The International Context of Iraq from 1980 to the Present," p. 246, states that from 1988 to 1989 the regime's rearmament expenditures were double that of reconstruction efforts (including the construction of celebratory monuments and palaces). Clawson, "Iraq's Economy and International Sanctions," p. 71, discusses Iraq's debt repayments, noting that oil revenues were rising again at the close of the 1980s. Stansfield, *Iraq: People, History, Politics*, (Cambridge: Polity, 2007), p. 122, emphasizes the role of Iraq's prioritization of military expenditure in its deteriorating fiscal position.
13. Kiren Aziz Chaudhry, "On the Way to Market: Economic Liberalization and Iraq's Invasion of Kuwait," *Middle East Report*, No. 170, May–June 1991, p. 14, observes that the economic chaos led to unrest of the sort that "not even the experienced repressive apparatus of the Ba'th Party could guarantee political stability." See: Karsh and Rautsi, *Saddam Hussein*, pp. 207–8; Baram, "The Iraqi Invasion of Kuwait: Decision-making in Baghdad," p. 8; and al-Jabbar, "Why the *Intifada* Failed," pp. 102–3, on purges of the officer corps, which had grown increasingly independent from the institutions of the regime during the final years of the war (something Saddam Hussein had allowed in the name of improving performance on the battlefield).
14. Iraq's dubious historical claim to its southern neighbor notwithstanding, Kuwait had attracted significant Iraqi ire for perceived transgressions beyond its refusal to either forgive Iraq's war debts or cooperate in driving oil prices higher. Kuwait had been deliberately exceeding OPEC-mandated production quotas and thereby suppressing the price of oil (a policy that cost Iraq billions in lost revenue), and was also accused of "slant-drilling" to steal from oil fields within Iraq. For discussion over the motives behind Iraq's invasion of Kuwait, see: Clawson, "Iraq's Economy and International Sanctions," pp. 71–3 (who attacks the notion that the invasion was in response to sudden economic desperation, instead suggesting it was a considered, deliberate act); Karsh and Rautsi, *Saddam Hussein*, pp. 207–8 (who emphasize Saddam's domestic vulnerability at the time); Long, *Saddam's War of Words: Politics, Religion and the Iraqi Invasion of Kuwait*, (Austin: University of Texas Press, 2004), Chapter 2 (who provides a broad overview of contributing factors) and also Pollack, *The Threatening Storm: The Case for Invading Iraq*, (New York: Palgrave MacMillan, 2004), p. 331, and Chaudhry, "On the Way to Market," p. 14 (who emphasize systemic economic concerns). Jabar, "The War Generation in Iraq: A Case of Failed Etatist Nationalism," in Potter and Sick (eds), *Iran, Iraq and the legacies of War*, (New York: Palgrave Macmillan, 2004), p. 131,

notes the opinion of exiled Iraqi officers that the war was conceived to keep the military occupied, and avoid the need to demobilize additional soldiers.

15. Tripp, *A History of Iraq*, (Cambridge: Cambridge University Press, 2007), p. 242, argues that the conquest of Kuwait was intended as a first step toward a broader exercise of Iraqi power over the Gulf states and Saudi Arabia, which would assert Iraqi dominance in the region and further assist in its economic revitalization.
16. Baghdad in particular suffered severe damage (notably to the electricity grid and water treatment facilities), which surpassed the cumulative effects of the entire Iran war. See: Karsh and Rautsi, *Saddam Hussein*, pp. 258–9, on the damage inflicted by the six-week air campaign.
17. For detailed accounts of the 1991 uprising in southern Iraq, as well as its suppression (and the way in which both badly inflamed sectarian tensions), see Human Rights Watch, "Endless Torment: The 1991 Uprising in Iraq and its Aftermath," June 1992, Chapter 3; Jabar, *The Shi'ite Movement*, pp. 269–70; and al-Jabbar, "Why the *Intifada* Failed," pp. 106–8.
18. David Cortright and George Lopez, *The Sanctions Decade: Assessing UN Strategies in the 1990s*, (Boulder: Lynne Riener, 2000), pp. 8, 40–1, note that Iraq was "in a class by itself as the longest, most comprehensive, and most severe multilateral sanctions regime ever imposed," and offer a list of the various UN Resolutions passed with respect to Iraq. Pollack, *The Threatening Storm*, p. 55, observes that the architects of the sanctions regime expected Saddam Hussein to fall quickly from power, and that they were intended only as a short-term strategy.
19. Cockburn, *Muqtada al-Sadr and the Shia Insurgency in Iraq*, (London: Faber and Faber, 2009), p. 107, observes that, as a result of war damage and sanctions, Iraq's annual oil revenue fell to US$400 million in 1992—leading to the regime's "inability to buy off dissent." Revenues would not rise significantly until the 1995 "Oil for Food" scheme enabled Iraq to sell US$1 billion of oil every ninety days to fund humanitarian needs. Detailed in Agustin Velloso De Santisteban, "Sanctions, War, Occupation, and the De-development of Education in Iraq," *International Review of Education*, Vol. 51, No. 1, 2005, p. 60.
20. Phrase from Jabar, "Sheikhs and Ideologues: Deconstruction and Reconstruction of Tribes under Patrimonial Totalitarianism in Iraq, 1968–1998," in Jabar and Dawood (eds), *Tribes and Power: Nationalism and Ethnicity in the Middle East*, (London: Saqi, 2003), p. 89. Nicholas Haussler, "Third Generation Gangs Revisited: The Iraq Insurgency," MA Thesis, US Naval Postgraduate School, 2005, p. 41, details how the social changes of the 1990s were instrumental in shaping the networks at the heart of post-2003 violence, as does Munson, *Iraq in Transition: The Legacy of Dictatorship and the Prospects for Democracy*, (Washington: Potomac Books, 2009), Chapter Two. See also: Khafaji, "A Few Days After: State and Society in a post-Saddam Iraq," pp. 78–80, for the prediction that the war to oust Saddam Hussein would be far simpler than the task of managing the various "interest groups" that had emerged and staked out claims to various geographic areas and sectors of the economy during the 1990s.
21. For detailed analysis of Saddam Hussein's shifting attitudes toward tribalism, see Baram, "Neo-Tribalism in Iraq," and Jabar, "Sheikhs and Ideologues: Deconstruction and Reconstruction of Tribes under Patrimonial Totalitarianism in Iraq, 1968–1998."

International Crisis Group, "Iraq Backgrounder," pp. 20–1, offers a concise, though strongly essentialist, overview of the rise of tribalism in modern Iraq. In regard to Saddam's embrace of Islam, Long, *Saddam's War of Words*; Ofra Bengio, *Saddam's Word: Political Discourse in Iraq*, (Oxford: Oxford University Press, 1998), especially Chapters 13 and 14; and Jabar, "Clerics, Tribes, Ideologies and Urban Dwellers in the South of Iraq: the Potential for Rebellion," in Dodge and Simon, *Iraq at the Crossroads: State and Society in the Shadow of Regime Change*, (Oxford: Oxford University Press, 2003), offer detailed accounts. Sami Zubaida, "The Rise and Fall of Civil Society in Iraq," *Open Democracy*, 5 February 2003, provides a useful overview of the evolution of civil society in modern Iraqi history, charting the rise of Islam and tribalism in the 1990s.

22. The work of Jabar explores both sides of this argument and details the processes through which tribalism came to re-take a central place in Iraqi society in the 1980s and 1990s. "As Ba'th party organization weakened," Jabar notes, "primordial networks were reinvigorated to fill a social void." Jabar, "Clerics, Tribes, Ideologies and Urban Dwellers in the South of Iraq: the Potential for Rebellion," p. 172. Nonetheless, Jabar, p. 101 notes "there is no clear concept of what a tribe is in late twentieth-century Iraq after almost a century and a half of continuous decomposition."
23. For a contrasting view from the canon of counterinsurgency, see M.W. Shervington, "Small Wars and Counter-Insurgency Warfare: Lessons From Iraq," MA Thesis, Cranfield University Department of Defence Management and Security Analysis, 2005, pp. 67, 99, for the assertion that "at the turn of the millennium, Iraq's society had changed little from its heady days of 1920," and that "the tribe is the one common denominator that links the vast majority of Iraqis together regardless of political or religious persuasion." Essentialist arguments are also advanced, albeit with nuance, in the unfortunately-titled: David Ronfeldt, "In Search of How Societies Work: Tribes—The First and Forever Form," *RAND Corporation*, December 2006.
24. Quotation from Baram, "Neo-Tribalism in Iraq," p. 1, who further notes the regime's "flexible" approach to the eradication of tribes.
25. Detailed in Baram, "Neo-Tribalism in Iraq,", pp. 3–4, observing that the policy of manipulating tribal rivalries was used most notably in the present-day Anbar province, where the tribal order was said to be particularly vibrant and where dominant families and tribal groups had retained their traditional positions. Prominent tribes such as the Jabbur and the Shammar Jarba thus saw their lands confiscated and distributed to weaker rivals. Jabar, "Shaykhs and Ideologues," p. 31, notes how this approach was followed in southern Iraq as well, where the lower echelons of the tribal order (the Marsh Arabs, for example) were made proxies of the state to undermine their traditional superiors.
26. Both Baram, "Neo-Tribalism in Iraq," and Jabar, *The Shi'ite Movement*, and in "Clerics, Tribes, Ideologies and Urban Dwellers in the South of Iraq: the Potential for Rebellion," argue that the empowerment of tribal subordinates during the course of the war with Iran was viewed as a temporary measure, and that the regime's objective remained the wholesale atomization of the populace.
27. Baram, "Neo-Tribalism in Iraq," p. 1, observes that with his tribal policies of the 1990s, "Saddam Hussein altered the Ba'th Party's most central tenets of faith." Baram traces the changing posture of the Ba'th vis-à-vis Iraq's tribes as progressing from outright hostility

and the pursuit of tribal destruction during the 1970s, to the desire to co-opt and manipulate sheikhs as necessary allies during the 1980s, to the use of tribal proxies as "legitimate partners for power-sharing" in the 1990s. See: Jabar, "Sheikhs and Ideologues: Deconstruction and Reconstruction of Tribes under Patrimonial Totalitarianism in Iraq, 1968–1998," p. 90, for a discussion of how government rhetoric about Iraqis' common tribal heritage was used to support the war effort.

28. Per the independent authenticity of the tribal structures that emerged, one must question how and why this could have occurred. Essentialist arguments aside, tribal structures and their leaders would have had to have either avoided or resisted the numerous fragmentary pressures of the twentieth century—and also either avoided or reached an arrangement (and the latter is far more likely) with the Ba'th. Hence, it would seem that the prospects for pure, independent sheikhly authenticity were slim, save for extremely low-level bonds among groups able to remain off Ba'thist radar.

29. Dawood, "The 'State-ization' of the Tribe and the Tribalization of the State: the Case of Iraq," in *Tribes and Power*, p. 119, observes continuity among tribal networks in the "Sunni Triangle in northwestern Iraq"; while Baram, "Neo-Tribalism in Iraq," p. 4, states that the "old cores" of the tribal system endured in the countryside. Jabar, "Sheikhs and Ideologues: Deconstruction and Reconstruction of Tribes under Patrimonial Totalitarianism in Iraq, 1968–1998," pp. 76–7, notes how the spread of public education undermined traditional structures, even in rural areas. On the changing structures (and norms) of the tribal system, Baram, "Neo-Tribalism in Iraq," p. 22, notes the flexible, fluid nature of tribalism—though observes that such "flexibility" can only extend so far, before the underlying validity of the entire enterprise is compromised.

30. On the tribalization of Saddam Hussein's regime, both Baram and Jabar discuss how the Iraqi president embedded his familial and tribal kin within the institutions of the state to strengthen his personal position. Jabar, "Sheikhs and Ideologues: Deconstruction and Reconstruction of Tribes under Patrimonial Totalitarianism in Iraq, 1968–1998," p. 71, describes this practice as "etatist tribalism," which was used "to enhance the political power of a certain fragile and vulnerable state elite." Sluglett and Farouk-Sluglett, *Iraq Since 1958*, pp. 93–4, trace this phenomenon to President Arif's creation of the Republican Guard in the mid 1960s, which was placed under the control of his tribal kin. See: Charles Tripp, "After Saddam," *Survival*, Vol. 44, No. 4, Winter 2002–03, pp. 25–6, for a discussion of *ahl al-thiqa* (people of trust), whom Saddam Hussein embedded in key positions in the government and economy.

31. Sluglett and Farouk-Sluglett, *Iraq Since 1958*, pp. 195–9, discuss the formation of the Association of Najaf Ulema in 1958 and the later emergence of the Da'wa as part of a campaign to counter endemic "atheism" in Iraqi society. Batatu, "Iraq's Underground Shi'a Movements: Characteristics, Causes and Prospects," *Middle East Institute*, Vol. 35, No.4, Autumn 1981, pp. 5–6, notes of the formation of Shi'a revivalist movements: "they were moved by a growing sense that the old faith was receding… that the belief of even the urban Shi'a masses was not as firm… and that the *ulama* were losing ground and declining in prestige and material influence." Batatu, *The Old Social Classes and the Revolutionary Movements of Iraq*, (London: Saqi, 2004), pp. 999–1000, notes the phenomenon of young men from elite clerical families joining the Iraqi Communist Party.

32. Detailed in Jabar, *The Shi'ite Movement*, pp. 95–127, 199–215.
33. Tripp, *A History of Iraq*, p. 195, notes the Ba'th regime's early persecution of the Shi'a establishment, and of the Hakim family in particular.
34. Popular unrest and anti-regime agitation led by Shi'a factions, or otherwise defined in explicitly Shi'a terms (along with the response of the government, which included the execution of opposition figures and noted clerics, mass deportation of Iraqi Shi'a to Iran, and also major expenditures on religious infrastructure and public welfare for the Shi'a masses) are detailed by Batatu, "Shi'i Organizations in Iraq: al-Da'wa al-Islamiyah and al-Mujahidin" in Cole and Keddie (eds), *Shi'ism and Social Protest*, (New Haven: Yale University Press, 1986); and Jabar, *The Shi'ite Movement*.
35. Discussed in Jabar, *The Shi'ite Movement*, pp. 209, 228–33.
36. On the extent to which the regime's embrace marked a break from past practices, see: Tripp, *A History of Iraq*, p. 195, for a discussion of the Ba'th's initially-vicious response to religiously-defined challenges from Shi'a factions, wherein "the government abandoned its earlier pretense of respect for Islamic values," removing Islamic education from the national curriculum and attacking its foes in word and deed.
37. Detailed in Long, *Saddam's War of Words*, pp. 62–9, who surveys how the rhetoric of the Iraqi state, and of Saddam Hussein in particular, changed over time in response to rising Shi'a religiosity. Long argues for Saddam's "instrumental" use of Ba'thist ideology, noting that he was willing to deviate from the Party line whenever necessary.
38. Karsh and Rautsi, *Saddam Hussein*, pp. 144–5, discusses Saddam's reaction to the advent of the Iranian Revolution. Batatu, "Iraq's Underground Shi'a Movements," p. 7, notes that the regime spent 24 million Iraqi Dinars on shrines, mosques, and other religious causes in 1979. Long, *Saddam's War of Words*, pp. 65, 70, notes that Islamic rhetoric escalated in response to the Iranian revolution, and then surged further after battlefield setbacks like the loss of the Faw Peninsula to the Iranians in 1986 (with Saddam Hussein making the *hajj* to Mecca at the end of that year and Iraqi military units, operations, and weapons systems being given Islamic names).
39. Quotation from Long, *Saddam's War of Words*, p. 82, who notes that it was at this time that *Allahu akbar* (God is great) was emblazoned on the Iraqi flag. Baram, "The Iraqi Invasion of Kuwait: Decision-making in Baghdad," p. 18, also notes the Islamicization of regime rhetoric.
40. Atrocities were not solely the work of counterinsurgent forces during 1991. Marr, *The Modern History of Iraq*, (Boulder: Westview Press, 2004), p. 242, observes that the rebels were "unruly, unorganized, and at points almost as brutal as the regime." Detailed in Human Rights Watch, "Endless Torment"; al-Khafaji, "State Terror and the Degradation of Politics," pp. 16–17; and emphasized by Makiya, *Cruelty and Silence: War, Tyranny, Uprising and the Arab World*, (London: Jonathan Cape, 1993), p. 90.
41. Whereas Juan Cole, *Sacred Space and Holy War: The Politics, Culture and History of Shi'ite Islam*, (London: IB Tauris, 2005), p. 180, posits that "probably a majority of shi'ites joined the ranks of the opposition in the fateful spring of 1991," it appears certain that the assessment of Pollack, *The Threatening Storm*, p. 49 (that "probably fewer than 100,000" took part) is far closer to the truth. Baram, "Neo-Tribalism in Iraq," pp. 8–9, and Dodge, *Inventing Iraq: The Failure of Nation Building and a History Denied*, (London: Hurst & Co., 2003),

p. 162, note that many southern sheikhs viewed the revolt with caution, attempting to position themselves, above all else, on the winning side (prompting "resentment and exasperation" among opposition leaders, in the words of Baram). Baram, "Neo-Tribalism in Iraq," p. 7, notes the Ba'th Party apparatus "proved a near-total failure" in the suppression of the Shi'a revolt, while al-Khafaji, "State Terror and the Degradation of Politics," p. 17, states that the regime's cultivation of proxies and informants from among the lower echelons of the southern tribal order—who, in turn, owed their material and social position entirely to the state—were paid off handsomely during counterinsurgency operations. Makiya, *Cruelty and Silence*, p. 100, describes how the government's retaking of Samawah, the last southern town to fall after the uprising, came only "after local tribal leaders switched their allegiances back to the government." Ofra Bengio, "Iraq's Shi'a and Kurdish Communities: From Resentment to Revolt," in *Iraq's Road to War*, p. 61, likewise describes how Saddam Hussein purchased the loyalty of key southern sheikhs to cut the momentum of the Shi'a uprising.

42. Munson, "What Lies Beneath: Saddam's Legacy and the Roots of Resistance in Iraq," MA Thesis, US Naval Postgraduate School, 2005, p. 9, notes, "as the power of the state weakened due to war and sanctions, Saddam increasingly relied on ruthless and personally-profiting security officials, powerful tribes, organized criminals, and religious leaders to ensure stability and loyalty in key areas." Marr, *The Modern History of Iraq*, p. 297, notes that the regime's official "faith campaign" began in 1994.
43. See Jabar, "Shaykhs and Ideologues," p. 31; Baram, "Neo-Tribalism in Iraq," pp. 11–8.
44. Discussed in Baram, "Neo-Tribalism in Iraq," p. 20, who observes that the new regime-tribe relationship amounted, in important respects, to a return to pre-1958 conditions with Iraq's rural, tribal domain under its own legal regime. Also noted by Jabar, "Sheikhs and Ideologues: Deconstruction and Reconstruction of Tribes under Patrimonial Totalitarianism in Iraq, 1968–1998," p. 93. Karsh and Rautsi, *Saddam Hussein*, p. 94, observe that Saddam's reputation as a "liberator of women" was voided as a result.
45. Noted in Baram, "Neo-Tribalism in Iraq," p. 17.
46. Stories detailed in Cockburn, *Muqtada al-Sadr*, p. 122. The educated elite had long been contemptuous of rural tribal sheikhs, as alluded to by Batatu, *The Old Social Classes*, p. 115, who refers to them as "an eminently unlettered class."
47. Baram, "Neo-Tribalism in Iraq," pp. 17–8, describes the Kut engagement, which featured artillery and other military-grade weapons and left 266 dead and 422 wounded. Jabar, "Sheikhs and Ideologues: Deconstruction and Reconstruction of Tribes under Patrimonial Totalitarianism in Iraq, 1968–1998," p. 97, comments on the quasi-tribal raiding parties that made the road from Baghdad to Amman (via Anbar Province) exceptionally treacherous. Whereas the Shi'a tribes of southern Iraq appear to have focused primarily on competition with one another for regional power, Sunni tribes (which were deeply-embedded in the upper echelons of the Iraqi military and security services) were more active in anti-regime intrigue. Pollack, *The Threatening Storm*, pp. 68, 75, notes an assassination attempt against Saddam Hussein by Ubaidi tribesmen in December 1993, and discusses the May 1995 revolt in Ramadi launched by Dulaimi tribesmen.
48. Percentage from Marr, *The Modern History of Iraq*, p. 263. Jabar, "Sheikhs and Ideologues: Deconstruction and Reconstruction of Tribes under Patrimonial Totalitarianism in Iraq,

1968–1998," pp. 95–6, details the benefits that came with membership in the tribal council. Keiko Sakai, "Tribalization as a Tool of State Control in Iraq: Observations on the Army, the Cabinets and the National Assembly," in *Tribes and Power*, pp. 148–151, notes that candidates in the 1989 National Assembly elections had begun to run in remarkable numbers on their tribal credentials—a practice that had been banned during the 1970s in an effort to downplay tribal loyalties. He notes, however, that this had been limited to Sunni candidates and that southern Shi'a did not adopt the practice at that time.

49. Noted in Marr, *The Modern History of Iraq*, p. 263; and Baram, "Neo-Tribalism in Iraq," p. 15, who expresses contemporary surprise at the emergence of tribes in central Baghdad. Jabar, "Sheikhs and Ideologues: Deconstruction and Reconstruction of Tribes under Patrimonial Totalitarianism in Iraq, 1968–1998," p. 94, observes the difficulty encountered by Saddam Hussein in his search for suitable tribal proxies in urban areas, where "the disintegration of actual tribes and clans has reached such a point that any real reconstruction was too difficult to achieve."
50. Distilled by al-Khafaji, "A Few Days After: State and Society in a post-Saddam Iraq, pp. 80–1, who notes "the chiefs and their supposed tribe-members use [the rise of state support for tribalism] in a very pragmatic way—one which does not signify a genuine sense of solidarity." Khafaji observes that "Kinship relations have been used to solidify interest groups," but these groups "do not express more generalized social relations… kinship is a means to cement interest groups… but it is not the basis of those groups."
51. Makiya, *Republic of Fear*, p. xv, notes that, throughout the 1990s, "law and order were collapsing in Baghdad." Jabar, "Sheikhs and Ideologues: Deconstruction and Reconstruction of Tribes under Patrimonial Totalitarianism in Iraq, 1968–1998," pp. 97–9, likewise addresses surging criminality across Iraq—for which tribal groups were in large measure responsible.
52. Cockburn, *Muqtada al-Sadr*, p. 122, observes "where there were no sheikhs to cultivate, or where they were hostile to the regime, new ones were appointed."
53. Term noted in Jabar, "Sheikhs and Ideologues: Deconstruction and Reconstruction of Tribes under Patrimonial Totalitarianism in Iraq, 1968–1998," p. 94, and Cockburn, *Muqtada al-Sadr*, p. 122. The *taiwanii* designation was still used widely by Baghdadis as of 2008, to designate what American personnel referred to simply as "fake sheikhs."
54. Jabar, "Shaykhs and Ideologues," p. 48, laments the rise of "tribal gangsterism."
55. Baram, "Neo-Tribalism in Iraq," p. 14, notes the resurgence of mutated tribal conceptions of justice, to include honor killings, as well as the rising use of inter-tribal mediation in place of the increasingly inoperative state judicial system.
56. See: Shadid, *Night Draws Near*, (New York: Picador, 2005), p. 26 on the rise of *reef*, or "country," ethics during the sanctions era, and observations on the ruralization (and, in the eyes of those who cherished Baghdad's dynamic urban heritage, the debasement) of Baghdad's urban culture. Baram, "Neo-Tribalism in Iraq," p. 21, further notes how "the village conquered the city" as the regime's rough, rural proxies gained increasing power.
57. Jabar, *The Shi'ite Movement*, pp. 271–272, discusses the regime's rising religiosity during the early 1990s.
58. Long, *Saddam's War of Words*, chapter five, offers extensive textual analysis of the speeches of Saddam Hussein and other Ba'thist officials, tracing the rise of religious rhetoric.

59. Jabar, *The Shi'ite Movement*, pp. 271–2, also notes the rise of popular religiosity after the disasters of 1991. "Fear, dislocation, uncertainty, and social ills drove masses into the warmth of religious charities and fraternities," in a process further fueled by simultaneous surges in crime and prostitution. Hashim, *Insurgency and Counter-Insurgency in Iraq*, (Ithaca: Cornell University Press, 2006), pp. 110–111, discusses the revival of Islam during the sanctions era.
60. Munson, "What Lies Beneath," p. 45, notes the radical nature of the networks that came to operate in Iraq. Allawi, *The Occupation of Iraq: Winning the War, Losing the Peace*, (New Haven: Yale University Press, 2007), p. 182, points to the growth of Saudi-financed Wahabism as having been a key driver of deteriorating sectarian relations in Iraq through the 1990s.
61. Hashim, *Insurgency and Counter-Insurgency*, p. 25, notes the rise of Salafism in Fallujah during the 1990s, arguing that the intensity of religious radicalism occurred in tandem with the decreasing power of state surveillance.
62. Quotation from Sassoon, *Saddam Hussein's Ba'th Party*, p. 261, who further notes the regime's hostility toward (and concern over) trends in Saudi-funded fanaticism. Hashim, *Insurgency and Counter-Insurgency*, p. 26, argues that the development of these radical groups fostered unrest and levels of sectarianism that were contrary to the interests of the regime, and that their proliferation was an undesired consequence of the sanctions era rather than a deliberate initiative. For a differing view, see: Makiya, *Republic of Fear*, pp. xxx-xxxi, on Saddam's deliberate cultivation of sectarian tensions as a divide and rule strategy. The encouragement of sectarian tensions was a double-edged sword, which the Iraqi government appears to have used with caution as its resources weakened. Baram, "Neo-Tribalism in Iraq," pp. 18–20, notes that Saddam Hussein's emphasis on Arab tribalism as a core tenet of Iraqi identity was, at least in part, an effort to bridge sectarian divisions in the wake of the 1991 uprisings.
63. Human Rights Watch, "Endless Torment"; and Makiya, *Cruelty and Silence*, pp. 91–2, discuss the chaos of the revolt. Makiya notes how the brutality of Shi'a insurgents was a factor in deterring Army units from joining the uprising. The looting, he observes, "was on a scale that is impossible to exaggerate"—something attributed to the collapse of "public morality."
64. The term *ulama hafiz* is discussed by Batatu, "Shi'i Organizations in Iraq: al-Da'wa al-Islamiyah and al-Mujahidin," pp. 196–7, and Batatu, "Iraq's Underground Shi'a Movements," p. 7. Batatu traces the term to the British occupation of Iraq during the First World War, noting that it was standard practice of Iraqi regimes (which were typically Sunni) to procure the support of Shi'a clerics. Ajami, *The Foreigner's Gift: The Americans, the Arabs and the Iraqis in Iraq*, (New York: Free Press, 2006), p. 98, references the term *marja' al-sulta*, or "jurist of the regime." Jabar, *The Shi'ite Movement*, pp. 171–9, discusses the *marja'* system as one of institutionalized instability, rivalry, and division, which created ample opportunity for outsiders to manipulate its members. Nakash, *The Shi'is of Iraq*, (Princeton, Princeton University Press, 2003), p. 261, also discusses the divisions and rivalries that have long dominated the seminaries of Najaf.
65. For purposes of clarity and brevity, Mohammed Mohammed Sadiq al-Sadr will hereafter be referred to simply as "Sadr," while his son Muqtada al-Sadr will be referred to as

"Muqtada." This has the added benefit, moreover, of re-emphasizing that the former was the founder of the Sadrist movement and the man after whom Sadr City is named.

66. Biographical details on Sadr's life drawn from Cockburn, *Muqtada al-Sadr*; Ajami, *The Foreigner's Gift*; International Crisis Group, "Iraq's Muqtada al-Sadr"; and Allawi, *The Occupation of Iraq*.
67. International Crisis Group, "Iraq's Muqtada al-Sadr," p. 3, states that Sadr was "largely unknown" before he was elevated to the rank of Grand Ayatollah and granted control of Najaf's seminaries by the Ba'th regime.
68. See: Human Rights Watch, "Endless Torment," for details of the government's campaign against clerics, which featured both the targeting of individuals and the physical destruction of Najaf, Kerbala, and other seats of Shi'a religious influence.
69. Discussed in Cockburn, *Muqtada al-Sadr*, Chapter Seven; Ajami, *The Foreigner's Gift*, pp. 93–8: International Crisis Group, "Iraq's Muqtada al-Sadr," pp. 3–4. Cockburn takes the line that Sadr took advantage of the regime, and was not a willing agent thereof. Allawi, *The Occupation of Iraq*, pp. 54–61, is similarly generous regarding Sadr's relationship with the regime, though he does concede that the regime "gave him control over the Najaf seminaries." Cochrane, "The Fragmentation of the Sadrist Movement," *The Institute for the Study of War*, January 2009, p. 9, takes a harsher line; while Jabar, "Clerics, Tribes, Ideologies and Urban Dwellers in the South of Iraq: the Potential for Rebellion," p. 171, notes that Sadr was "a handpicked government appointee."
70. Grand Ayatollah al-Khoei had been the *marja' mutlaq*, or "supreme object of emulation" among Iraqi Shi'a. His death left a vacancy at the apex of the Shi'a establishment, which the regime was able to fill by using its physical strength and financial resources to install a chosen successor at the head of Najaf's seminaries. This maneuver was aided by the fact that, as Cockburn, *Muqtada al-Sadr*, pp. 97–8, notes, most of Khoei's prospective successors were "dead, imprisoned or scattered."
71. See: Juan Cole and Moojan Momen, "Mafia, Mob and Shiism in Iraq: The Rebellion of Ottoman Karbala 1824–3," *Past and Present*, No. 112, August 1986; Nakash, *The Shi'is of Iraq*; and Peter Heine, "Zghurt and Shmurt: Aspects of Traditional Shi'i Society," in Faleh Abdul Jabar (ed.), *Ayatollahs, Sufis and Ideologues: State, Religion and Social Movements in Iraq*, (London: Saqi, 2002), pp. 37–8, on the dynamics of politics in pre-Iraqi Najaf and Kerbala. Cockburn, *Muqtada al-Sadr*, pp. 101, 123, compares the intrigue of Najaf's religious seminaries to the novels of Trollope. Shadid, *Night Draws Near*, pp. 228–9, also emphasizes Sadr's rivalry with Sistani, with the former mocking the latter's Persian accent; while International Crisis Group, "Iraq's Muqtada al-Sadr: Spoiler or Stabilizer?" *Middle East Report*, No. 55, 11 July 2006, pp. 3–4, discusses Sadr's tenuous relationship with his establishment peers.
72. Sadr's *Fiqh al-Asha'ir* is discussed in Mahan Abedin, "The Sadrist Movement," *Middle East Intelligence Bulletin*, Vol. 5, No. 7, July 2003; Cockburn, *Muqtada al-Sadr*, pp. 122–3.
73. International Crisis Group, "Iraq's Shiites Under Occupation," Middle East Briefing, 9 September 2003, provides a concise overview of the quietist/activist issue. In questions regarding the place of religious leadership in the public sphere, distinction between "activist" and "quietist" traditions among Shi'a clerics and the practice of *taqiyya* (concealment) are core issues. The former concerns the extent to which clerics involve themselves in the

political and material concerns of their followers, while the latter is the notion that one's opinions or identity can be concealed in the prudent pursuit of survival. Decades of state-persecution in Iraq rendered the practice of *taqiyya* essential among those working in opposition to the government—particularly during the Ba'thist era—while quietism emerged as the dominant trend among Shi'a clerics in Iraq in response to both similar political pressures and the evolution of theological scholarship.

74. International Crisis Group, "Iraq's Muqtada al-Sadr," p. 2, observes Sadrist references to "field-based" clerical operations and the militancy of Sadr's rhetoric.
75. On the rivalry that developed between Sadr and his establishment peers, International Crisis Group, "Iraq's Muqtada al-Sadr," p. 5, states that "the tribal world was split in two" along lines of class and regional affinity by the Sadr-Sistani rivalry, with the wealthier and better-respected tribal groups in the vicinity of Najaf and Kerbala along the Euphrates giving their allegiance to Sistani, and the poorer, less prestigious groups of the Deep South and the region's urban slums aligning with Sadr. Cockburn, *Muqtada al-Sadr*, pp. 112–3, notes that the followers of Sistani would prevent Sadr's emissaries from using mosques to network and deliver sermons.
76. International Crisis Group, "Iraq's Muqtada al-Sadr," p. 1, discusses the ferocity of Sadr's personal attacks, and the manner in which he actively sought to instill mass disrespect of his establishment foes.
77. His virulent anti-Americanism was of particular note in this regard, as it reflected prevailing sentiments among Iraqi Shi'a stemming from America's betrayal during the 1991 uprisings. Discussed in International Crisis Group, "Iraq's Muqtada al-Sadr"; International Crisis Group, "Shiite Politics in Iraq," *Middle East Report*, No. 70, 15 November 2007; and Cochrane, "The Fragmentation of the Sadrist Movement," p. 10.
78. Sadr's efforts to connect with the Shi'a underclass are discussed in Cockburn, *Muqtada al-Sadr*, pp. 112–4; and Allawi, *The Occupation of Iraq*, pp. 57–8.
79. On the scope of material suffering in the Iraqi capital, Pierre-Jean Luizard and Joe Stork, "The Iraq Question from the Inside," *Middle East Report*, No. 193, March–April 1995, p. 21, note food riots in Baghdad's Shi'a slums.
80. International Crisis Group, "Iraq's Muqtada al-Sadr," p. 5, notes how social connectivity arising from historical migration patterns between Saddam City and the modern-day Maysan Province aided in the spread of Sadr's movement.
81. See Batatu, "Iraq's Underground Shi'a Movements," for discussion of the circumstances surrounding the rise of Shi'ism (and of militant activism) among the urban poor from the 1970s onwards. Also, see: International Crisis Group, "Iraq's Muqtada al-Sadr," p. 3, for anecdotal evidence of continued irreligiosity in the Deep South until the rise of Sadr, who, in many respects, appears to have "introduced" local Shi'a to the core tenets of their faith.
82. See Batatu, "Iraq's Underground Shi'a Movements," p. 8, for popular historical affinity among Iraqi Shi'a toward Arab clerics as opposed to their Persian counterparts—a phenomenon that was intensified by the war with Iran.
83. His allegation that the late Grand Ayatollah Abd al-Qassim al-Khoei had been a regime collaborator, noted in International Crisis Group, "Iraq's Muqtada al-Sadr," p. 3, was thus particularly provocative. Moreover, in contrast to the freedom with which Sadr was able to operate across Iraq, Tripp, *A History of Iraq*, p. 265, notes that Sistani was under "effective house arrest" by 1994.

84. See: International Crisis Group, "Shiite Politics in Iraq," p. 3, for statistics on Hakim casualties.
85. International Crisis Group, "Iraq's Muqtada al-Sadr," p. 3, discusses the strength of his rhetorical attack on his peers and predecessors. Allawi, *The Occupation of Iraq*, pp. 58–9, notes the accusations leveled by the Hakim family and those affiliated with the Shi'a establishment concerning Sadr's ties to the regime.
86. Jabar, "The War Generation in Iraq: A Case of Failed Etatist Nationalism," p. 135, notes "with the collapse of oil rentierism, the salaried middle strata lost its middle class status, but not the longing for it," and thereafter were left "impoverished and humiliated." Chaudhry, "Consuming Interests: Market Failure and the Social Foundations of Iraqi Etatisme," pp. 233–4, observes "since 1990, the Iraqi middle class has been wiped out… functions of the state have been relegated to recreated 'tribal' hierarchies; and large segments of the bourgeoisie holding dinars have been reduced to penury." This created exceptional resentment, alluded to in Munson, "What Lies Beneath," pp. 37–8, who observes the rise of uneducated strongmen on the streets of Baghdad during the 1990s, who held sway over the eviscerated, yet far better educated, former middle class.
87. Munson, *Iraq in Transition*, p. 40, states that sanctions "forced up to 63 percent of professionals to find employment as labourers," while many families were displaced from their middle-class neighborhoods by the criminalized and regime-connected *nouveau riche*.
88. Al-Khafaji, "State Terror and the Degradation of Politics," p. 21, notes the exodus of educated professionals that began in 1991, with Jordan the top destination.
89. Discussed by Sakai, "Tribalization as a Tool of State Control in Iraq," pp. 156–8. The major uprisings against the state were pursued by Sunni factions based in the present-day Anbar Province, marking the fallout of the regime's attempt to integrate tribal networks into the military and security services. The most threatening of these was a revolt by Dulaimi tribesmen in Ramadi in May 1995 that saw the government briefly lose control of the city. See: Baram, "Neo-Tribalism in Iraq"; and Jabar, "Sheikhs and Ideologues: Deconstruction and Reconstruction of Tribes under Patrimonial Totalitarianism in Iraq, 1968–1998," for further insight. Graham-Brown, "Sanctioning Iraq: A Failed Policy," *Middle East Report*, No. 215, Summer 2000, p. 11, notes how the rise of tribal factions active in the black market stoked inter-communal rivalry, and how the failure of the government to maintain its dominance of society led to the proliferation of divisive factionalism.
90. International Crisis Group, "Iraq's Muqtada al-Sadr," p. 4, explains the political implications of Friday prayers, and how Sadr's move represented a challenge not only to the Iraqi regime, but also to the clerical leadership of the Iranian government. See: Cockburn, *Muqtada al-Sadr*, pp. 124–5, for the argument that relations between Sadr and the regime soured from 1996 onwards.
91. Pollack, *The Threatening Storm*, pp. 89–93, discusses the period in question, arguing that Saddam "panicked" in the aftermath of Operation Desert Fox in December 1998 (which came on the heels of the September 1998 passage of the Iraq Liberation Act by the US Congress that explicitly called for regime change). Also worrying to the regime, the state largesse that had mitigated popular discontent among the Shi'a underclass had largely dried up—leaving the Shi'a poor not only better organized and more unified than at any time previous (due to Sadr's efforts), but also increasingly aggrieved at their material condition.

92. In keeping with the accusatory, acrimonious spirit of the *hawza*, Sadr's critics asserted that he played a role in the regime's execution of Grand Ayatollahs Ali al-Gharawi and Murtada Burujurdi. Noted in Allawi, *The Occupation of Iraq*, p. 59. Cockburn, *Muqtada al-Sadr*, pp. 129–130, recounts an attempted uprising in and around Nasiriyah, in southern Iraq, launched by Sadrist supporters in response to the government's mounting crackdown.
93. International Crisis Group, "Iraq's Muqtada al-Sadr," p. 5, notes that major police action was required to suppress the riots in Saddam City. Cockburn, *Muqtada al-Sadr*, pp. 133–4, recounts the events of the *al-Sadr intifadah*. A former Iraqi Army officer (interviewed in March 2008 at Joint Security Station SUJ on the northeastern corner of what was by then known as Sadr City) related the story of how the district was encircled by the military, and Sadrist leaders were summoned to a meeting where its complete destruction was threatened unless unrest ceased.
94. Story detailed in Cockburn, *Muqtada al-Sadr*, pp. 133–6.
95. Quotation from Cockburn, *Muqtada al-Sadr*, p. 119.
96. Karsh and Rautsi, *Saddam Hussein*, pp. 258–9, and Graham-Brown, "Sanctioning Iraq," p. 9, on the deterioration of public infrastructure in Baghdad. Jabar, "The War Generation in Iraq: A Case of Failed Etatist Nationalism," p. 133 notes that the Gulf War had a far greater effect: "the extensive nature of the first war was surpassed by the intensive nature of the second."
97. See Graham-Brown, "Sanctioning Iraq"; Cortright and Lopez, *The Sanctions Decade: Assessing UN Strategies in the 1990s*, (Boulder: Lynne Riener, 2000), Pollack, *The Threatening Storm*; and Voices in the Wilderness, "Myths and Realities Regarding Iraq and Sanctions," in Anthony Arnove (ed.), *Iraq Under Siege: The Deadly Impact of Sanctions and War*, (London: Pluto Press, 2000), for the controversy surrounding the human costs of the sanctions regime and debate over the apportioning of blame. Mohammed Ali, John Blacker and Gareth Jones, "Annual Mortality Rates and Excess Deaths of Children under-Five in Iraq, 1991–1998," *Population Studies*, Vol. 57, No. 2, July 2003, pp. 219–220, note that the suffering was concentrated in southern and central Iraq.
98. Cited in Pollack, *The Threatening Storm*, pp. 137–8.
99. Pollack, *The Threatening Storm*, p. 74, asserts that the Iraqi government "had the funds to address these humanitarian problems," and that the consensus in the American intelligence community was that Saddam Hussein deliberately exacerbated the impact of sanctions. See p. 86 for the observation that medical supplies and infant formula were smuggled out of Iraq to be sold in Jordan and the Gulf states, and that the regime's priority was its financial position (and its ability to purchase the loyalty of its proxies) rather than public health. See also: Amatzia Baram, "The Effect of Iraqi Sanctions: Statistical Pitfalls and Responsibility," *Middle East Journal*, Vol. 54, No. 2, Spring 2000 for further critique of the regime's role in exacerbating (and exaggerating) the popular effects of sanctions. Christopher Foote, William Block, Keith Crane, and Simon Gray, "Economic Policy and Prospects in Iraq," *Federal Reserve Bank of Boston*, Public Policy Discussion Paper 04–1, 4 May 2004, p. 9, cites the estimate of the US General Accounting Office that US$4.4 billion was misappropriated or stolen from the Oil for Food program.
100. The intensification of popular dependency on the government—despite its badly-dimin-

ished resources—is discussed in Sluglett and Farouk-Sluglett, *Iraq Since 1958*, pp. 280–1. Pollack, *The Threatening Storm*, p. 135, notes how ration cards became a tool of social control for the regime. International Crisis Group, "Iraq Backgrounder," p. 10; and Haris Gazder and Ather Hussein, "Crisis and Response: A Study of the Impact of Economic Sanctions in Iraq," in *Iraq's Economic Predicament*, pp. 49–50, likewise discuss the criticality of hand-outs to survive the era and the resulting need to cultivate official favor. Allawi, *The Occupation of Iraq*, p. 129, observes a rising "culture of dependency" throughout the 1990s.

101. Discussed in Allawi, *The Occupation of Iraq*, p. 127.
102. See International Crisis Group, "Iraq Backgrounder," p. 10; and Munson, "What Lies Beneath," p. 36 for shifting attitudes toward education. De Santisteban, "Sanctions, War, Occupation," pp. 64–5, notes a drop in female literacy from 87 per cent in 1987 to 45 per cent by 1995 and an overall drop in literacy from 80 per cent in to 58 per cent.
103. See: Pollack, *The Threatening Storm*, p. 132; Munson, "What Lies Beneath," pp. 36–7; Makiya, *Cruelty and Silence*, pp. 204–6; Graham-Brown, "Sanctioning Iraq," p. 10; and Hussein al-Shaharistani, "The Suppression and Survival of Iraqi Shi'is," in *Iraq Since the Gulf War*, pp. 137–8, for discussion of the social climate of the 1990s. De Santisteban, "Sanctions, War, Occupation," p. 66, cites a 1999 UNSC panel report on social collapse within Iraq.
104. Quotation from Jabar, "The War Generation in Iraq: A Case of Failed Etatist Nationalism," p. 134, who further observes, "the rates of violent crime were doubling by seasons, rather than years." Ayad Rahim, "Attitudes to the West, Arabs and Fellow Iraqis," p. 190, notes of the Iraqis during the 1990s: "vengeance lurks in people's hearts, waiting for an opportunity to explode." Cockburn, *Muqtada al-Sadr*, in *Iraq since the Gulf War*, p. 109, writes of "a generation filled with hate."
105. Quotation from Hashim, *Insurgency and Counter-Insurgency*, p. 253. Pollack, *The Threatening Storm*, p. 192, argues (citing the work of Baram) that the Shi'a poor suffered disproportionately because they were furthest from the institutions of state patronage.
106. Cochrane, "The Fragmentation of the Sadrist Movement," p. 11, traces continuity between the upper echelons of Sadr's movement to the group that would emerge active in the Mehdi Army after the 2003 invasion.

3. THE CHANGING FORTUNES OF THE REKINDLED SADRIST MOVEMENT

1. Apparent chaos concealed numerous, coordinated operations. Allawi, *The Occupation of Iraq: Winning the War, Losing the Peace*, (New Haven: Yale University Press), pp. 144–5, notes emergence of "death squads" during the summer of 2003 to pursue teachers, journalists, politicians, and other former regime elements. Al-Khalidi and Tanner, "Sectarian Violence: Radical Groups Drive Displacement," *The Brookings Institute, University of Bern Project on International Displacement*, October 2006, p. 9, further observe the efforts of the Badr militia to murder Sunni military officers and academics (allegedly at the behest of Iran). Hendrickson and Tucker, "Revisions in Need of Revising: What Went Wrong in the Iraq War," *Strategic Studies Institute*, December 2005, pp. 11–4, suggest that Coalition Forces would not have been able to stop the looting, even if they had attempted to do so.

2. Due to the closed nature of Iraqi society during the sanctions era, the rise of the Sadrist movement was poorly-appreciated outside of the country. The rise of the Sadrists in the aftermath of Saddam Hussein's removal, therefore, not only took outside observers by surprise, but also much of the country's exiled elite. Noted in International Crisis Group, "Iraq's Muqtada al-Sadr: Spoiler or Stabilizer?" *Middle East Report*, No. 55, 11 July 2006, p. 7.
3. Cockburn, *Muqtada al-Sadr and the Shia Insurgency in Iraq*, (London: Faber and Faber, 2009), p. 146, notes that the Sadrists controlled 90 per cent of the district's mosques after only a few months. Per population figures in Sadr City, estimates vary widely in the absence of reliable census data, ranging from 1 million to 2.5 million. Allawi, *The Occupation of Iraq*, p. 267, estimates the population of the district at 2.5 million, noting that Saddam City would be the second-largest city in Iraq if it were counted separately from Baghdad. He further observes that some one-third of all Baghdadis lived in the slum (based on an estimate of the city's population slightly above 6 million).
4. Sadr City is often thought (mistakenly), to be named after Muqtada al-Sadr. For example, see: Sassoon, *Saddam Hussein's Ba'th Party: Inside an Authoritarian Regime*, (Cambridge: Cambridge University Press, 2012), p. 182. This is an error that risks prompting observers to overstate popular reverence for the White Lion's son.
5. Eric Herring and Glen Rangwala, *Iraq in Fragments: The Occupation and its Legacy*, (Ithaca: Cornell UP, 2006), p. 14, note that in the wake of the US-led invasion, Sadrist militants quickly established themselves in Najaf and Kufa.
6. International Crisis Group, "Iraq's Muqtada al-Sadr," p. 7, references the early successes of the Sadrists, but also emphasizes the chaos that surrounded their attempts to revive the White Lion's movement. Indeed, there was not a latent, mass-based "Sadrist movement" to be revived, but instead a broadly-shared set of ideas and sympathies among the martyred cleric's former devotees. There was, therefore, much work to be done in re-mobilizing and organizing the movement's base.
7. Discussed in International Crisis Group, "Iraq's Muqtada al-Sadr," pp. 8–9.
8. The details of Abd al-Majid al-Khoei's life and death are drawn from the al-Khoei Foundation website: www.al-khoei.org; Michael Wood, "Abdul Majid al-Khoei," *The Guardian*, 12 April 2003; "Abdul Majid al-Khoei," *The Economist*, 17 April 2003; Jabar, *The Shi'ite Movement in Iraq*, (London: Saqi, 2003), pp. 23–4; and Cockburn, *Muqtada al-Sadr*, pp. 149–58.
9. For further discussion of the tensions surrounding the return of the clerical elite, see: International Crisis Group, "Shiite Politics in Iraq," *Middle East Report*, No. 70, 15 November 2007; and Cochrane, "The Fragmentation of the Sadrist Movement," *The Institute for the Study of War*, January 2009, p. 13. These tensions were broadly applicable in the case of more secular politicians, as Iraqis were skeptical of the authenticity and intentions of those who had endured the hardships of the 1990s.
10. International Crisis Group, "Iraq's Muqtada al-Sadr," p. 21, notes Sadrist aspirations vis-à-vis Najaf's old city, and that the establishment of a strong presence there was an "ultimate objective" of the movement.
11. The controversy surrounding Khoei's murder is referenced in International Crisis Group, "Iraq's Civil War, The Sadrists and the Surge," *Middle East Report*, No. 72, 7 February 2008,

p. 9; Cockburn, *Muqtada al-Sadr*, pp. 149–58; Munson, *Iraq in Transition*, pp. 96–7; and Jabar, *The Shi'ite Movement*, pp. 23–4.

12. The siege of Sistani's home, and its relief by the intervention of his tribal allies from the surrounding countryside, is described in Cochrane, "The Fragmentation of the Sadrist Movement," p. 13. Popular suspicion regarding the Sadrists' encroachment upon Najaf during the summer of 2003 was such that many blamed them for the assassination of Mohammed Baqir al-Hakim in a car bombing in August of that year—despite the fact that the attack was officially attributed to Sunni militants. Discussed, along with general commentary on hostilities against the Hakim family, in Allawi, *The Occupation of Iraq*, pp. 171–3.
13. Conflicting accounts have been offered on the looting of Baghdad. The Shi'a poor are likely scapegoated at the exclusion of others in the popular imagination, yet they appear to have been notably active. See International Crisis Group, "Iraq's Muqtada al-Sadr," p. 9, for discussion of popular attitudes toward the role of Sadr City residents in the looting. Cockburn, *Muqtada al-Sadr*, pp. 146, 162, mentions the crowds that emerged from the slum to loot the city center, though the author's source asserts that the Sadrists themselves disapproved of the looting. Shadid, *Night Draws Near*, (New York: Picador, 2005), p. 26, notes the anarchy that followed the fall of the government was expected by Baghdadis, who had watched the rise of rural, tribal ethics and the debasement of civil society during the 1990s. Jabar, *The Shi'ite Movement*, p. 23, cites the role of Ba'thist officials intent on destroying evidence of their crimes.
14. Cockburn, *Muqtada al-Sadr*, p. 163, discuss the roots of the term. *Hawasim* is also translated as "decisive," with the implication that the battle between Saddam's forces and the US-led Coalition would be the decisive, final battle of their long-running rivalry.
15. International Crisis Group, "Iraq's Muqtada al-Sadr," p. 8, discusses the "famous" edict and its polarizing effects, as does Cockburn, *Muqtada al-Sadr*, p. 163.
16. International Crisis Group, "Iraq's Muqtada al-Sadr," p. 8, addresses the generational divide among supporters of Muqtada, observing that he often pitted fathers against their sons. Cockburn, *Muqtada al-Sadr*, p. 147, notes the uncouth, anti-intellectual qualities of the rekindled Sadrist movement, declaring that "Muqtada was more reliant than his father on the impoverished urban masses, people whom his opponents denounced and feared as a dangerous, criminalized mob."
17. The size of this "generation" also merits consideration, in light of the explosive population growth detailed in the previous chapters. Munson, "What Lies Beneath: Saddam's Legacy and the Roots of Resistance in Iraq," MA Thesis, US Naval Postgraduate School, 2005, pp. 32–3, cites World Bank figures stating that Iraq's population grew from 13 million in 1980 to 23.3 million in 2000.
18. See: International Crisis Group, "Iraq's Muqtada al-Sadr," pp. 8–9, 18, on Sadr as the archetype of his followers, a discussion of his attraction of the lowest social stratum that had followed his father, and the ignorance and fanaticism of his followers (some of whom revered Muqtada as the actual Mehdi, creating a quasi-divine personality cult around the young cleric).
19. See International Crisis Group, "Iraq's Muqtada al-Sadr," p. 10, for commentary on the Sadrists' early actions, and observations that their popularity fell markedly in late 2003.

20. For further discussion of this period, see: Bremer, *My Year in Iraq*, which is referenced critically in International Crisis Group, "Iraq's Muqtada al-Sadr," p. 11.
21. See International Crisis Group, "Iraq's Muqtada al-Sadr," p. 11; and Allawi, *The Occupation of Iraq*, pp. 270–2, for a discussion of the events leading up to the spring confrontation in Najaf.
22. The management of the Khoei murder became a highly-politicized affair, as the threat of prosecution of Muqtada and his closest associates would be wielded for years as a political weapon designed to punish or incentivize certain behaviors from the Sadrists.
23. Shadid, *Night Draws Near*, pp. 442–3, quotes Major General Martin Dempsey, who cited the fighting in the capital as "the biggest gunfight since the fall of Baghdad." Herring and Rangwala, *Iraq in Fragments*, p. 28, count 800 killed by Coalition Forces in nine weeks of fighting in and around Sadr City. See George Packer, *The Assassins' Gate: America in Iraq*, (London: Faber and Faber, 2006), pp. 322–3 for observations on the performance of the "paper army" of European forces stationed across the south, where the weakness of Coalition Forces played a significant role in the uprising's initial success.
24. Cockburn, *Muqtada al-Sadr*, p. 5, states that many of the militants that fought in Najaf were from Sadr City. On p. 153, however, he notes that the Sadrists did draw in local recruits from among Najaf's urban poor (indeed, the Sadrists' local base had been evident since their participation in Khoei's murder). For further background, see: Batatu, *The Old Social Classes and the Revolutionary Movements of Iraq*, (London: Saqi, 2004), p. 752, on the long legacy of "oppressive wealth and dire poverty" in Najaf and associated class-based tensions—which had enabled the Iraqi Communist Party to build a formidable local following in the 1950s and 1960s, and which were central to the eventual local rise of the Sadrist movement. Hashim, *Insurgency and Counter-Insurgency in Iraq*, (Ithaca: Cornell University Press, 2006), p. 262, observes how the unfamiliarity of militiamen from Sadr City with the urban terrain of Najaf undermined their effectiveness in the fighting.
25. The contribution of Sistani's tribal allies is noted in Packer, *Assassins' Gate*, p. 324. As had been made evident during the initial siege of his home during the April 2003 invasion, the rivalry between Sistani and the White Lion that had polarized the tribal domain of southern Iraq was revived with the rise of the rekindled Sadrist movement. International Crisis Group, "Iraq's Muqtada al-Sadr," p. 17, notes that the lower echelons of the tribal order that had been recruited into Saddam Hussein's paramilitary forces and used to check the power of their tribal "superiors" were later drawn into the Mehdi Army.
26. International Crisis Group, "Iraq's Muqtada al-Sadr," p. 11, cites poll data from May 2004 showing that 81 per cent of Iraqis had a "better" or "much better" opinion of Muqtada than they had three months earlier.
27. The rising threat of Sunni sectarianism and attacks on Shi'a civilians appears to have been a central motivator in the decision of Sistani and the Shi'a elite to spare Muqtada and avert the destruction of the Mehdi Army in Najaf, as it was recognized that the militia would be a useful ally in the sectarian war that was then gathering momentum. Alternatively, Allawi, *The Occupation of Iraq*, p. 325, argues that the primary concern among the Shi'a elite, and the reason for the preservation of the Mehdi Army, was over the growing power of then-Prime Minster Iyad Allawi, whom the author alleges was attempting to create a secular police state that might marginalize the influence of the Shi'a clerical establishment.

28. The *wadi al-salam*, or "Valley of Peace", cemetery on the western edge of Najaf was a major venue of fighting that sustained particularly heavy damage. Furthermore, the inexperience of Mehdi Army fighters was evident in their difficulty handling munitions—leading to a number of destructive explosions in the religious sites they used as caches and firing positions.
29. In the run-up to the January elections, leading Shi'a politicians and members of the clerical establishment made frequent reference to the circumstances surrounding Iraq's formation under British occupation in the aftermath of World War I. As the British were preparing to leave Mesopotamia and transfer authority to the Arabs, prominent Shi'a clerics and Shi'a tribes of southern Mesopotamia instigated a brief, though costly, uprising against the British. Historiography of the period attributes the ensuing ostracism of the Shi'a clerical establishment and the broader marginalization of Shi'a Arabs from the nascent Iraqi government to this ill-advised revolt—and it was thus viewed as a mistake that Shi'a leaders sought to avoid repeating, particularly as the rejectionism of the Sunni insurgency opened the door for wholesale Shi'a dominance of the government.
30. Noted in Cochrane, "The Fragmentation of the Sadrist Movement," p. 15.
31. Discussed in International Crisis Group, "Iraq's Muqtada al-Sadr," pp. 10–16.
32. Qais al-Khazali, a former associate of Muqtada's father, was among the most prominent defectors at this time. For a discussion of Khazali's career, see Cochrane, "Special Groups Regenerate," *The Institute for the Study of War*, January 2009, pp. 3–4; and Kagan, *The Surge: A Military History*, (New York: Encounter, 2009); pp. 167–8.
33. For discussion of Iranian involvement in Iraq with respect to both the development of the Mehdi Army and the rise of Special Groups, see: Kagan, *The Surge*; Cochrane, "Special Groups"; Cochrane, "The Fragmentation of the Sadrist Movement"; and International Crisis Group, "Iraq's Civil War, The Sadrists and the Surge."
34. Popular hostility among Sadrists toward Iran is noted in International Crisis Group, "Iraq's Muqtada al-Sadr," p. 16. As alluded to in Cockburn, *Muqtada al-Sadr*, pp. 209–10, the particular dynamics of the relationship between the Iranians and Muqtada al-Sadr remain controversial. Cockburn's source (presumably a Sadrist seeking to dissociate the movement from Iran) asserts that Muqtada opposed Iranian involvement in the Mehdi Army, but that the disorganized nature of the militia and the desire of its fighters to gain access to funds (and, as time progressed, to increasingly-advanced weaponry) enabled the Iranians to subvert his authority. Kagan, *The Surge*, pp. 167–8, engages this issue further in reference to the uncertainty over the relationship between Muqtada and Qais al-Khazali, a Sadrist militant who worked closely with Iran, as does Goodman, "Informal Networks and Insurgency in Iraq," *Defence Academy of the United Kingdom: Advanced Research and Assessment Group*, April 2008, pp. 9–10.
35. For a discussion of the Sunni insurgency and its roots in the developments that occurred within Iraqi society during the sanctions era, see: Munson, *Iraq in Transition*, Chapters Five and Six. See also, Goodman, "Informal Networks and Insurgency in Iraq," pp. 2–6, on the Islamicization of the Sunni insurgency and the relationships between Ba'thists and radical Islamic movements in Iraq that trace back to the 1990s. Hashim, *Insurgency and Counter-Insurgency*, Chapters Two and Three, provide an overview of the Sunni insurgency's evolution.
36. Shadid, *Night Draws Near*, p. 308, and Cockburn, *Muqtada al-Sadr*, pp. 170, 179, cite the

March 2004 *'ashura* bombings by Iraqi al-Qaeda, which killed 270 people and wounded a further 570, as a major early recruiting boost for the Mehdi Army. Vali Nasr, *The Shi'a Revival: How Conflicts Within Islam Will Shape the Future*, (New York: W.W. Norton, 2007) p. 262, notes how "Shia militias… were often the only forces defending Shia neighbourhoods against Sunni extremists' car bombs."

37. Intra-Shi'a rapprochement is discussed in International Crisis Group, "Iraq's Muqtada al-Sadr," pp. 12–5. Muqtada's turn toward moderation in the wake of the Mehdi Army's defeat in Najaf (and, likewise, the establishment's perception that he had been chastened in the process) was an important precondition of the pan-Shi'a alliance, but it was by no means sufficient to precipitate it.
38. Irrespective of their early missteps and their polarizing radicalism, the Sadrists remained the dominant political vehicle for Iraq's Shi'a underclass. In a testament not only to the enduring legacy of the White Lion, but also to the persistence of social prejudices within the Iraqi elite, the rekindled Sadrist movement was effectively unchallenged in its claim to represent this sizable constituency. The only notable challenges to the Sadrists' position as the political face of the Shi'a underclass came from offshoots of the White Lion's former movement that rejected Muqtada's claim to leadership (such as the Fadhila Party, whose influence was confined largely to Basra and its environs), and narrowly-based, locally-rooted factions such as the Marsh Arabs' Iraqi Hizbullah.
39. As noted in International Crisis Group, "Iraq's Muqtada al-Sadr," p. 15, the exigencies of elite-level *realpolitik* brought further advancement to the Sadrists, as Prime Minister Ibrahim al-Ja'afari and his colleagues in the well-connected, yet exceptionally narrowly-based Da'wa Party cultivated ties with the Sadrists in order to balance the growing clout of their establishment peers in the Supreme Iraqi Islamic Council.
40. The ways in which Iraq's transition to democracy served to exacerbate identity-based division is emphasized throughout Munson, *Iraq in Transition*. See also: Ucko, "Militias, Tribes and Insurgents," pp. 352–4; and Herring and Rangwala, *Iraq in Fragments*, pp. 142, 150–5.
41. On Sunni perceptions of marginalization during late 2004 and early 2005, Herring and Rangwala, *Iraq in Fragments*, p. 36, note the contrast between Coalition Forces' "effective truce" with the Mehdi Army after the August clash in Najaf and their annihilation of Fallujah in November, giving Sunnis the impression that they were being singled out for persecution.
42. Goodman, "Informal Networks and Insurgency in Iraq," pp. 11–12, alleges continued strong ties between the Supreme Iraqi Islamic Council and Iran.
43. Detailed in International Crisis Group, "The Next Iraqi War? Sectarianism and Civil Conflict," *Middle East Report*, No. 52, 27 February 2006, which notes (p. i) "2005 will be remembered as the year Iraq's latent sectarianism took wings, permeating the political discourse and precipitating incidents of appalling violence and sectarian 'cleansing'". Casualty figures for 2005 are charted at Iraq Body Count: http://www.iraqbodycount.org/analysis/numbers/year-three the Brookings Institution's Iraq Index: http://www.brookings.edu/saban/iraq-index.aspx and in Cordesman, "Iraq: Creating a Strategic Partnership," *CSIS*, "Third Review Draft," 2 February 2010, pp. 12–8.
44. Herring and Rangwala, *Iraq in Fragments*, pp. 38–41, discuss Coalition Forces' emphasis

on behind-the-scenes training for Iraqi Security Forces and quick-impact raids during 2005, when the prevailing wisdom was that foreign forces should minimize contact with the Iraqis as to avoid stoking resentment. Further worsening the plight of ordinary Baghdadis and inflaming sectarian enmity, Shi'a elements of the Iraqi Security Forces embarked on a campaign of intimidation, kidnapping, and murder that targeted Sunni militants and civilians. Members of the Supreme Iraqi Islamic Council's Badr militia were well-integrated into the Ministry of the Interior, and they transformed the police, in particular, into a decidedly partisan force. See: Kagan, *The Surge*, p. 6, for discussion of SIIC's (Islamic Supreme Council of Iraq) Bayan Jabr, who took over the Ministry of the Interior in February 2005 and is widely alleged to have established Shi'a death squads within its uniformed ranks.

45. In exchange for the Sadrists' support for the government, Sadr City was declared off limits to Coalition Forces during 2006 and 2007. Cordesman, *Iraq's Insurgency*, Vol. 1, p. 345, notes Prime Minister Maliki's condemnation of a US-led raid into Sadr City in August 2006.
46. International Crisis Group, "Iraq's Muqtada al-Sadr," p. 15, notes that Iraqi government and Badr officials conceded that the Mehdi Army was the dominant force on the streets of Baghdad by the end of 2005.
47. As noted in Cordesman, *Iraq's Insurgency*, Vol. 1, p. 191, Zarqawi's declaration of "total war" against Iraq's Shi'a community in the immediate aftermath of the stampede was a further, significant driver of sectarian fear and a recruiting boon to the Mehdi Army.
48. The continued inability of the government to control the city and administer its poorer neighborhoods meant that the power vacuum that had initially opened the door for the Sadrists' rise persisted through the years that followed. Irrespective of the Sadrists' relationship with the central government, their local-level representatives remained effectively uncontested as service providers and neighborhood-level administrators in underclass Shi'a areas of Baghdad.
49. Discussed in International Crisis Group, "Iraq's Muqtada al-Sadr," p. 14. Sadrist influence was a subject of much media discussion at the time, with Muqtada al-Sadr commonly referred to as a "kingmaker" in recognition of his influence in mediating disputes within the government.
50. In keeping with their attempt to retain "outsider" credibility and avoid active cooperation with Coalition Forces, the Sadrists eschewed high-profile posts in the ministries of defence and interior—instead focusing on social service-oriented positions that enabled them to buttress their grassroots support. Discussed in International Crisis Group, "Iraq's Muqtada al-Sadr," p. 14.
51. Iraq Body Count: http://www.iraqbodycount.org/analysis/numbers/year-four noted at the time that by "every available indicator the year just ended (March 2006–March 2007) [was] by far the worst year for violence against civilians in Iraq since the invasion." Contrary to common assertions that the February bombing of the Samarra mosque was an atrocity that "sparked" the sectarian war, Kagan, *The Surge*, pp. 8–9, notes that rates of civilian casualties rose only 3 per cent from March to April. There was thus a spasm of spontaneous retributive violence against Sunnis in the immediate wake of the bombing but, as noted by Kagan, the conflict did not reach its peak until several months later (in response to an array of political

events, notable among them the formation of the Maliki government in May, the reorganization of Iranian-sponsored Shi'a militant cells shortly thereafter, and the killing of Zarqawi in June).

52. See: al-Khalidi and Tanner, "Sectarian Violence," p. 9, for the observation that the "violence is neither spontaneous nor popular" and that opinion among Iraqis was that there was not a civil war in progress "as long as neighbours are not killing their neighbours." Kagan, *The Surge*, p. 3, asserts that, "violence in Baghdad in 2006 did not emerge from the antipathy between Sunni and Shia neighbours, or from a cataclysmic terrorist attack, but rather from an armed political competition between extremist groups." Goodman, "Informal Networks and Insurgency in Iraq," p. 1, likewise observes that the violence of the sectarian war was not driven by popular antipathy between the sects. "Rather, sectarianism has been a weapon used to further [political] groups' strategic and policy interests. In that sense, sectarianism has served primarily as a weapon of asymmetric warfare in Iraqi politics." For a contrasting view, see: Kilcullen, *The Accidental Guerilla: Fighting Small Wars in the Midst of a Big One*, (London: Hurst & Co., 2009), p. 122, who argues "the killing was a mass social phenomenon, driven from the bottom up rather than from the top down."
53. Cordesman, *Iraq's Insurgency*, Vol. 1, p. 265, notes that forced displacement of the Shi'a was a key strategy of Sunni militants. Allawi, *The Occupation of Iraq*, p. 447, traces the forced displacement phenomenon to late 2004, when Sunni militants expelled Shi'a from areas of western Baghdad in order to make room for families fleeing the US-led offensive on Fallujah.
54. International Crisis Group, "Iraq's Civil War, The Sadrists and the Surge," pp. 2–4, examines the Sadrists' "classic civil war strategy" and the manner in which they seized territory across the city. While units within the Iraqi Security Forces were active in the persecution of Sunnis, a subtle shift took place. The personnel of the Supreme Iraqi Islamic Council's Badr militia (who were well-entrenched in the officer corps of the security services, and who had been prominent in the extra-judicial targeting of Sunni militants as well as the persecution of Sunni civilians during 2005) distanced themselves from the uniformed offensive. On the decision of Badr and the main Shi'a parties to abstain from the worst of the sectarian war's atrocities (allegedly in the name of maintaining good relations with Coalition Forces), see Allawi, *The Occupation of Iraq*, pp. 449–50. Both the Mehdi Army and Badr were complicit in atrocities against Sunni civilians under the cover of the Iraqi Security Forces, and Kagan, *The Surge*, pp. 18–21, notes how Coalition Forces' reliance on the ISF to "hold" areas after clearance operations during 2006 enabled Shi'a militants to further their sectarian objectives and, likewise, drove Sunni civilians closer to radical militants.
55. Bigio and Scott, "Internal Displacement in Iraq: The Process of Working Toward Durable Solutions," *The Brookings Institute, University of Bern Project on International Displacement*, June 2009, pp. 1, 13, estimate that 2.6 million Iraqis were displaced internally by mid 2009, with a further 2 million overseas, and note that 83 per cent of those displaced from a home in Baghdad relocated to another area of the city.
56. See Cordesman, *Iraq's Insurgency*, Vol. 2, pp. 663–6; Tripp, *A History of Iraq*, pp. 288, 309, and Allawi, *The Occupation of Iraq*, pp. 376–8, on the targeting of educated professionals and the resulting "brain drain" in Baghdad. Surging criminality in Baghdad was a major factor in the exodus that occurred, and Cordesman, *Iraq's Insurgency*, Vol. 1, pp. 118–23, cites statistics from the Baghdad morgue that showed 60 per cent of the killings in the city during 2004 were "gunshot wounds… unrelated to the insurgency."

57. See Cordseman, *Iraq's Insurgency*, Vol. 1, p. 333, on the flight of middle class and Christian families in 2006. The Camp Sarah neighborhood, for example, which was a generations-old Christian enclave at the base of the Karradah Peninsula, appeared largely vacant by 2008.
58. Imagery of the Tisa Nissan district on Google maps was updated in the spring of 2012. The contrast between the new imagery (which appears to date to some time in late 2011) and that which it replaced (which dated to May 2004) shows the enormous scale of population movement and new construction on the margins of Sadr City.
59. The legacy of the *hawasim fatwa* further tied the rekindled Sadrist movement to the destabilizing changes that swept Baghdad, particularly in the minds of the movement's middle class and minority opponents. This class-based tension transcended sectarian lines, as it brought middle class Baghdadis of various sects and faiths into conflict with the Shi'a poor. Furthermore, while this dynamic was notably powerful in areas adjacent to Shi'a underclass strongholds (such as the *hayys* of Beladiyat and Obeidy), migrations reached further afield to areas such as central Zafaraniyyah in Baghdad's southeastern corner, and onward as far away as Najaf.
60. This was a recurring theme in conversations with middle class Baghdadis during fieldwork in 2008. The Mehdi Army's conquest of middle class areas of the city drew upon long-running themes of class-based tension, as well as the motif of underclass triumphalism embedded at the core of the White Lion's movement. As poor Shi'a families pressed inwards upon the center of the Iraqi capital, a symbiotic relationship thus developed between the Mehdi Army and the *hawasim* whereby each built from the advances of the other. As such, while the Mehdi Army enjoyed a period of massive growth in Baghdad in response to the escalation of sectarian violence, the militia did not become a cohesive, grassroots force that united Shi'a Baghdadis in the spirit of sectarian solidarity or that spread by virtue of its surging popularity.
61. While the role of forced evictions and depopulation is broadly acknowledged as having been central to the Mehdi Army's expansion across Baghdad, the complementary role of population transfers into the areas seized by the militia has attracted less attention. The dynamics of this process in Tisa Nissan are detailed in the chapters that follow. Al-Khalidi and Tanner, "Sectarian Violence," p. 29, note the phenomenon of "fake" displacement, whereby the influx of underclass Shi'a into contested areas was orchestrated to improve the local position of the Mehdi Army.
62. International Crisis Group, "Iraq's Muqtada al-Sadr," p. 20, cites Sadrist officials stating that the resettlement of displaced Shi'a was a central focus of the movement's non-military wing. Cockburn, *Muqtada al-Sadr*, p. 220, cites anecdotal evidence of Sadrist "realty" offices in the business of placing Shi'a families in homes seized from militia opponents. Reports of such offices in Tisa Nissan are detailed in the following chapters.
63. As discussed in the conclusion, census data is unavailable for post-Saddam Baghdad. Nonetheless, with the flight of middle class and minority families, and the devastation of the city's Sunni population during the sectarian war, it is a certainty that the Shi'a underclass has risen as a percentage of the city's population since 2003 (at which time they had likely comprised at approximately half of the city's 6 million residents).
64. Cochrane, "The Fragmentation of the Sadrist Movement," pp. 23–41, provides an overview of the Mehdi Army's "remarkable reversal of fortunes" in the context of the Surge, which

"stemmed from internal divides that were exacerbated by external pressures." International Crisis Group, "Iraq's Civil War, The Sadrists and the Surge," p. i, argues that the Sadrists were "victims of their own success," and that their accomplishments exposed them to mounting pressures that they were ill-suited to manage.

65. Sunni interviewees displaced from Beladiyat and Mashtal (interviewed in April 2008 on Forward Operating Base Loyalty) made numerous references to the educational and managerial shortcomings of Sadrist "technocrats" in both ministries, blaming underperformance on the ineptitude of those in charge, who were alleged to possess only high school diplomas. International Crisis Group, "Iraq's Civil War, The Sadrists and the Surge," p. 4, provides anecdotes of Sadrist officials without high school diplomas in ministerial roles.
66. International Crisis Group, "Iraq's Civil War, The Sadrists and the Surge," pp. 2, 7, discusses the reputation of Sadrist officials for corruption, and the Sadrists' struggles to perform effectively in the political realm. Herring and Rangwala, *Iraq in Fragments*, pp. 130–2, discuss broader issues of corruption in the post-Saddam state.
67. For discussion of the rising prominence of ever-younger militants due to the battlefield attrition of more seasoned Mehdi Army commanders, see al-Khalidi and Tanner, "Sectarian Violence," p. 10; and International Crisis Group, "Iraq's Civil War, The Sadrists and the Surge," p. 9, which also catalogues growing resentment among Iraqi Shi'a in response to the abuses suffered at the hands of the militia.
68. International Crisis Group, "Iraq's Civil War, The Sadrists and the Surge," pp. 6–7, discusses the prominent role of plunder in financing the Mehdi Army, and further observes how sectarian cleansing became a major financial operation that drew in the unemployed and those desirous of quick riches. Cordesman, *Iraq's Insurgency*, Vol. 2, p. 373, cites UN statistics that 45,000 were being displaced each month at the end of 2006, making displacement and asset seizure a booming industry.
69. The day-to-day realities of life under the Mehdi Army's "protection" had long provoked significant levels of dissatisfaction, featuring the domineering presence of religious radicals and a strong undercurrent of criminal activity such as extortion and theft. Shadid, *Night Draws Near*, pp. 214–5, notes early worries over life under Sadrist rule. Cordesman, *Iraq's Insurgency*, Vol. 2, p. 411, comments on the largely unsuccessful efforts of Muqtada to establish order within the militia during the latter months of 2006.
70. Drug abuse among militiamen is noted in al-Khalidi and Tanner, "Sectarian Violence," p. 11, and was still widely alleged by Iraqi Security Force personnel and residents of Tisa Nissan during 2008.
71. For discussion of attempts to reform the Mehdi Army, see International Crisis Group, "Iraq's Civil War, The Sadrists and the Surge," p. 8; Cochrane, "The Fragmentation of the Sadrist Movement," pp. 16, 25–6. Cordesman, *Iraq's Insurgency*, Vol. 2, p. 411, traces Muqtada's renewed efforts to regain control of the movement and the Mehdi Army to the autumn of 2006, by which time it was widely evident that the Sadrists' reputation was suffering badly from the abuses of Mehdi Army fighters.
72. The particular and varied implications of this approach are examined in detail in the chapters that follow. Discussed also in International Crisis Group, "Iraq's Civil War, The Sadrists and the Surge."
73. Al-Khalidi and Tanner, "Sectarian Violence," p. 12, discuss the common use of mosques as

nodes of violence in the sectarian conflict. Allawi, *The Occupation of Iraq*, p. 449, also notes the Mehdi Army's "franchise"-driven growth.

74. Such localism, and the resulting variation in character of the Mehdi Army, was evident during the course of 2008 when subcomponents of the militia were assessed and engaged individually by American forces, who attempted to differentiate between "good" and "bad" elements of the militia. Noted throughout the course of fieldwork in 2008 (when American commanders emphasized the need to work cooperatively with what they referred to as "good JAM"), and referenced in Bing West, *The Strongest Tribe: War, Politics, and the Endgame in Iraq*, (New York: Random House, 2008), p. 353.
75. Sectarian violence continued nonetheless, and Kilcullen, *The Accidental Guerilla*, p. 125, notes that December 2006 was the peak month for sectarian killing with an average of 125 dead each night (50 per cent of whom were in Baghdad). Nonetheless, Shi'a forces had claimed a decisive strategic victory by this time, and the violence marked, for the most part, the consolidation of gains as opposed to efforts at further conquest.
76. See Cochrane, "The Fragmentation of the Sadrist Movement," p. 22 for a discussion of Prime Minster Maliki's calculations. The survival of the pan-Shi'a alliance was made all the more unlikely by Maliki and his establishment peers' ties with the US-led Coalition. The closing months of 2006 witnessed American officials applying heavy pressure to the Maliki administration to break with the Sadrists and confront the Mehdi Army (while Muqtada and his associates replied in kind with public demands for the Coalition's withdrawal from Iraq). Noted in Cordesman, *Iraq's Insurgency*, Vol. 2, pp. 380–1. Cordesman, *Iraq's Insurgency*, Vol. 2, pp. 409–11, also notes that by mid 2006 the American military regarded the Mehdi Army as a greater threat than al-Qaeda to its interests and to stability in Iraq.
77. Tensions between the Sadrists and the Shi'a establishment had remained evident throughout the course of the sectarian war: the Mehdi Army and the Badr militia had clashed over competing claims newly-cleansed "Shi'a" areas near Baghdad's middle class core, battled for influence in the cities and towns of southern Iraq, and jockeyed for influence within the ranks of the Iraqi Security Forces. The escalation of their antagonism, which occurred in a rough correlation to the abatement of sectarian violence, was a strong indicator that the pan-Shi'a coalition would dissolve as the overriding threat of Sunni militants faded. Cochrane, "Special Groups," p. 12, notes the rise of intra-Shi'a violence across southern Iraq during 2007.
78. As noted in Cochrane, "Special Groups," p. 4, the initial phase of the Surge was focused principally on the defeat of the Iraqi al-Qaeda in an effort to capitalize on the momentum generated by the Awakening. Operations against the Mehdi Army nonetheless progressed in Shi'a areas of the city, becoming a central focus by late 2007.
79. Noted in Tina Susman, "Security Crackdown Widens to Shiite Slum," *Los Angeles Times*, 5 March 2007.
80. The reaction of Muqtada and the Mehdi Army to Operation *Fardh al-Qanoon*, also referred to as the Baghdad Security Plan, is detailed in Kagan, *The Surge*, pp. 54–9. For a discussion of Muqtada's motivations in fleeing Iraq, see: Cochrane, "The Fragmentation of the Sadrist movement," p. 25, who emphasizes both Muqtada's fears of capture by Coalition Forces and of threats from within the Mehdi Army. Cockburn, *Muqtada al-Sadr*, p. 238, offers an assortment of alternative theories, including Muqtada's desire to distance himself from the abuses being perpetrated by the militia.

81. Cochrane, "Special Groups," p. 18, notes that Maysan Province was a point of refuge for Mehdi Army and Special Group fighters fleeing Coalition offensives in Baghdad and Basra. International Crisis Group, "Iraq's Civil War, The Sadrists and the Surge," p. 22, notes how the flight of wealthy militants to areas of the Deep South generated a localized surge in real estate prices.
82. International Crisis Group, "Iraq's Civil War, The Sadrists and the Surge," pp. i-ii.
83. Efforts to mount a coherent response to the Surge featured the creation of the "Golden Brigade" of the Mehdi Army, a unit of cadre loyalists tasked with forcibly disciplining rogue militiamen. Discussed in Cochrane, "The Fragmentation of the Sadrist Movement," pp. 25–6. Cordesman, *Iraq's Insurgency*, Vol. 2, pp. 598–603, and Cochrane, "The Fragmentation of the Sadrist Movement," pp. 25–7, offer detailed breakdowns of the divisions within the Sadrist movement and its militia.
84. For an overview of the Special Groups, see: Cochrane, "Special Groups." Cochrane, "The Fragmentation of the Sadrist Movement," p. 27, discusses documents captured by Coalition Forces during the capture of Qais al-Khazali revealing that the Iranians (via the Revolutionary Guards' Quds Force) were supplying Special Group cells with US$750,000 to US$3 million per month.
85. International Crisis Group, "Shiite Politics in Iraq," p. 20, notes the numerous assassinations of SIIC representatives and Sistani-affiliated clerics during the summer of 2007. Intra-Shi'a tensions are also addressed in Munson, *Iraq in Transition*, pp. 219–20. International Crisis Group, "Iraq's Civil War, The Sadrists and the Surge," p. 12, discusses the intensity of the Mehdi Army's rivalry with Badr.
86. The Kerbala clash was instructive as to the broader dynamics of the Mehdi Army—Badr rivalry. Badr personnel embedded in the Iraqi Security Forces were charged with protecting the Imam Ali shrine, and they came into conflict with Mehdi Army militiamen who sought to assert control over the venue. The clash thus possessed political, economic, and religious connotations. The battle and its implications are discussed in Cochrane, "The Fragmentation of the Sadrist Movement," p. 29.
87. The extent to which the Mehdi Army, however disorganized it was, adhered to the truce imposed by Muqtada surprised many. Noted in International Crisis Group, "Iraq's Civil War, The Sadrists and The Surge," p. 17.
88. Cockburn, *Muqtada al-Sadr*, p. 259, argues that, "the movement's reputation among Shia had benefited from the long ceasefire during which the Mehdi Army had been effectively purged… In Shia areas, particularly in Baghdad, it was losing its reputation as an umbrella group for every local warlord or racketeer." Observations in Tisa Nissan during 2008 (detailed in the chapters that follow) run overwhelmingly contrary to this assertion.
89. Following remarkable successes against the Sunni insurgency during 2006 and 2007, the Mehdi Army and associated Shi'a militant groups became the primary target of the Surge. Heightened violence was thus widely anticipated during 2008 by American military personnel, as the limited time horizon of the Surge dictated that the Mehdi Army would have to be confronted and defeated before the end of that year.
90. The dissolution of the Mehdi Army and the efforts of Muqtada to channel elements of his base into social service-oriented organizations is detailed in Cochrane, "The Fragmentation of the Sadrist Movement," p. 37, along with commentary on the ways in which the military,

religious, and political elements of the rekindled Sadrist movement fell into dispute and disarray during the latter phase of the Surge. On the militia's collapsing strategic position during the fall of 2008, see: Sabrina Tavernise, "A Shiite Militia in Baghdad Sees its Power Wane," *The New York Times*, 27 July 2008; and Bill Roggio, "Mahdi Army Decimated During Recent Fighting," *Long War Journal*, 26 June 2008.

4. TISA NISSAN: DISTRICT OVERVIEW

1. Obeidy has not been included in the area study, as various constraints precluded the conduct of fieldwork in the *hayy*. Collective reference to this area of Tisa Nissan as "beyond the Army Canal" was common practice in Baghdad, as the canal is a prominent feature on the urban landscape and the neighborhoods beyond it share a broad set of common characteristics.
2. The Ba'th Party's first congress was held in Syria, on 7 April 1947. The *Sab'a Nissan* neighborhood was established for low-level Ba'th Party functionaries in the *hayy* of Beladiyat, and is discussed further below and in chapter five.
3. As evident in maps of Baghdad dating prior to the twentieth century, Adhamiyyah was originally an independent city that was absorbed into Baghdad during its massive twentieth century expansion.
4. Sketch of Baghdad in 1953 from Hilmi, *Internal Migration and Regional Policy in Iraq*, Doctoral Dissertation, University of Sheffield, 1978, p. 264.
5. Population figures from Batatu, *The Old Social Classes and the Revolutionary Movements of Iraq*, (London: Saqi, 2004), p. 35.
6. Profession was the dominant organizational framework of the new *mahallahs*, though class-based distinctions remained (and, indeed, were inextricably tied to an occupation-based system). The system thus shared much in common with the traditional *mahallah*, which had also featured professional and guild-based ties as a prominent organizational feature.
7. Ajami, *The Arab Predicament*, (Cambridge: Cambridge University Press, 1999), p. 44, offers a broader discussion of prevailing notions in the Middle East during the second half of the twentieth century regarding region-wide efforts at "the destruction of tradition and the creation of the future." The Ba'th Party's embrace of the "New Iraqi Man" as an ideological concept is discussed in Karsh and Rautsi, *Saddam Hussein: A Political Biography*, (New York: The Free Press, 1991), p. 123; and Fatima Mohsen, "Cultural Totalitarianism," in Hazelton (ed.), CARDI, *Iraq Since the Gulf War: Prospects for Democracy*, (London: Croom Helm, 1979), pp. 15–6.
8. Sketch of Baghdad showing its expansion by 1965, from Gulick, "Baghdad: Portrait of a City in Physical and Cultural Change," *Journal of the American Planning Association*, Vol. 33, No. 4, 1967, p. 247.
9. The former path of the bund remains visible in satellite imagery of the city, as a major urban artery now runs where it once stood (the Mohammed al-Qasim Expressway on Iraqi maps, which was known as "Route Brewers" to Coalition Forces).
10. The history of Tisa Nissan's development, which is explored in greater detail on a neighborhood-by-neighborhood basis in the chapters that follow, is drawn from conversations

with long-time local residents and members of the Iraqi Security Forces held between February and November 2008 at various venues across the district. The particulars of the fieldwork process are further detailed in the Appendix, while localized specifics are addressed in footnotes throughout this and subsequent chapters.

11. Noted by Gulick, "Baghdad: Portrait of a City," p. 252. "In 1965," he observed, "there were still numerous [*sarifas*] outside the Bund, and there were quite a number of infiltrators in the built-up portions of the section called New Baghdad."
12. Class-based social divisions between members of the Shi'a underclass and their fellow Baghdadis were evident throughout the course of fieldwork in Tisa Nissan. Chapter five details the localized tensions in Beladiyat and Mashtal, where the dividing line fell, in effect, between the edges of the city's middle class core and its impoverished periphery.
13. Hilmi, *Internal Migration*, pp. 904–5, observes that during the mid 1970s the government lacked the administrative capacity in Baghdad and in southern Iraq to control migration. The police were unable to control the flow of families, for example, while the administrative apparatus was insufficiently robust to deter movement via the restriction of work permits or other such means.
14. The decrepit state of critical infrastructure prior to the 2003 invasion and the area's long-running neglect was a recurring theme during discussions throughout Tisa Nissan, to include the more affluent and centrally urban *hayy* of Baghdad al-Jadeeda. Crime levels were a more localized phenomenon, as detailed in the chapters that follow.
15. Thus, to the middle class clusters of the area, the very same phenomenon that had been at the root of the area's decline during previous decades was now blamed for the government's neglect in a time of particular need, fueling class-based tensions. These frustrations were made explicit in conversations with residents of Beladiyat and Baghdad al-Jadeeda during the spring and summer of 2008. They attributed the unsatisfactory quality of local schools and medical facilities to the high concentrations of underclass Shi'a in the district—and the government's corresponding neglect.
16. Reliable census-style data is unavailable, but the accounts of long-time residents of Beladiyat and Mashtal made common, corroborating reference to the rising tide of underclass Shi'a in the area and a resulting demographic shift.
17. As discussed in chapter two, rather than uniting Baghdadis in commonly-shared suffering, the rapid impoverishment of middle class families through hyperinflation and the contraction of government bureaucracies fueled heightened social tensions. The fault lines between the core neighborhoods of Beladiyat and Mashtal and the underclass areas further beyond the Army Canal were thus broadened and deepened as the 1990s progressed, with socio-cultural distinctions rising in prominence as economic distinctions faded.
18. The Christians of the area were found mostly within clusters that echoed traditional *mahallah*, yet many families had integrated into nearby mixed-sect, middle class neighborhoods as well.
19. Absent reliable census figures, population estimates are given in rough terms. Nonetheless, Tisa Nissan was widely acknowledged to possess a Shi'a majority at the time of the 2003 invasion, with a total population estimated by Coalition Forces to be in the vicinity of 1.5 million.
20. The story of the Mehdi Army's rise in Tisa Nissan, which is detailed in the chapters that

follow, is drawn from conversations with long-time local residents and members of the Iraqi Security Forces held at various locations across the district between February and November 2008. Key sources included Sunnis exiled from Mashtal, interviewed by the author on FOB Loyalty in April 2008; political and civil society leaders from Beladiyat, interviewed by A. Roosendaal on FOB Loyalty in April and May 2008; and ordinary residents of Amin, Kamaliyah, and Fedaliyah, interviewed in their homes and places of business by the author and J. Makeur throughout the summer and fall of 2008.

21. As detailed in chapter five, underclass Shi'a "squatters" were joined by more affluent Shi'a "prospectors," who seized valuable land along the Army Canal in Beladiyat and erected sizable homes on what had formerly been vacant, government-owned land.
22. Likewise, as noted in chapter three, the decision of American forces to pull back from day-to-day policing functions and the official protection offered to the militia by virtue of the Sadrists' rising political clout (and the militia's penetration of the security services) further facilitated the Mehdi Army's advance across Tisa Nissan.
23. Many of the Shi'a families who sought refuge in Tisa Nissan were of middle class background. With the city center offering little open land, and with Tisa Nissan emerging as a "safe zone" under militia control, Shi'a with limited sympathy for the Mehdi Army moved into the area.
24. Cholera was reported in the Oil City neighborhood of eastern Amin during the spring of 2008.
25. This assessment of Tisa Nissan in the context of the Surge is drawn from the introductory briefings provided to the author and his HTT colleagues in February 2008 by American military personnel from the Brigade Combat Team (BCT) led by the 4th Brigade of the US Army's 10th Mountain Division, which oversaw the district at that time. Practical aspects of these briefings, and of the district-wide survey conducted immediately thereafter by the HTT, are presented in the Appendix. The District Council of Tisa Nissan had a citywide reputation for corruption and inefficiency, to the point that, as discussed in chapter six, American commanders largely disengaged from the district's official leadership during the second half of 2008. This decision was particularly remarkable in light of Coalition Forces' broader emphasis on "partnering" and "capacity building" to build up the Iraqi government in preparation for the Surge's conclusion—but was widely agreed by commanders on the ground to be appropriate in light of local conditions.
26. For an account of American operations in Tisa Nissan during 2007, see: Finkel, *The Good Soldiers*, (New York: Sarah Crichton Books, 2009). The work chronicles the fifteen month deployment of 2–16 Infantry Battalion to the eastern half of Tisa Nissan (which began at the start of the Surge, and ended in the midst of March Madness).
27. American personnel met with sustained frustration in efforts to stimulate economic growth, and a perceived lack of initiative on the part of ordinary Baghdadis attracted significant comment. Mansoor, *Baghdad at Sunrise: A Brigade Commander's War in Iraq*, (New Haven: Yale University Press, 2008), p. 154, offers a representative opinion, lamenting Iraq as "the ultimate entitlement-driven society," and observing that efforts to wean Iraqis off of government handouts "was like forcing them to kick a drug habit." Packer, *The Assassins' Gate: America in Iraq*, (London: Faber and Faber, 2006), p. 144, offers further anecdotes. Steven Metz, in the Foreword to Munson, *Iraq in Transition: The Legacy of Dictatorship and the*

Prospects for Democracy, (Washington: Potomac Books, 2009), p. x, similarly notes the "pervasive lack of initiative" encountered by American forces in Iraq. Munson, Iraq in Transition: The Legacy of Dictatorship and the Prospects for Democracy, (Washington: Potomac Books, 2009), p. 2, introduces his work by describing the Iraqi people as having been "atomized and cowed into inaction."

28. Finkel, *The Good Soldiers*, p. 139, reinforces the observations shared by BCT staff in February 2008, noting that violence continued in Tisa Nissan through the course of 2007, irrespective of Muqtada's "ceasefire."
29. Because of the manner in which American units were dispersed throughout Baghdad (and their limited presence in Sadr City in particular), Tisa Nissan was an attractive targeting environment for Shi'a militants. Benefiting from a network of local facilitators within the district's neighborhoods (which provided both safe houses and low-level operatives); convenient access to and from Sadr City; and ingress/egress routes to the north and east (leading onward to Iran), Tisa Nissan was an ideal venue for militants to launch IED, rocket, and mortar attacks against American forces. Mid-ranking officers of the 4–1 Iraqi National Police Brigade (interviewed by the author at the INP headquarters co-located at the District Council facility in September 2008) reinforced this understanding of violence in Tisa Nissan, alleging that much of the violence levied against the Surge came from Shi'a militants foreign to the area, who had been trained in Iran or in southern Iraq before coming to the district (where they would be given an area familiarization and basic logistical support by local facilitators).
30. Explosively Formed Projectiles, or "EFPs", were introduced to Iraqi Shi'a militants by Iranian advisors. They utilize technology similar to that of rocket propelled grenades, whereby projectiles of molten copper are fired directionally through their armored targets. Weapons caches discovered by American and Iraqi forces from early 2005 onwards found large numbers of EFPs with Iranian markings, though cruder versions were also fabricated within Iraq. Discussed in Cochrane, "The Fragmentation of the Sadrist Movement," *The Institute for the Study of War,* January 2009, pp. 19–20.
31. Separate from the Brigade Combat Teams that were charged with the management of day-to-day counterinsurgency operations in particular areas of Baghdad, Special Operations Forces were organized into Task Forces dedicated to the pursuit of particular high-value targets (the leadership of the Iraqi al-Qaeda, for example, or that of Special Group networks such as Asaib ahl al-Haq). Ollivant, "Countering the New Orthodoxy: Reinterpreting Counterinsurgency in Iraq," *New America Foundation*, June 2011, p. 6, notes the divergence between so-called "landowning" BCTs and the Special Operations units that were exclusively dedicated to targeting militants.
32. See Haussler, "Third Generation Gangs Revisited: The Iraq Insurgency," MA Thesis, US Naval Postgraduate School, 2005; and Max Manwaring, "Street Gangs: The New Urban Insurgency," *Strategic Studies Institute*, March 2005, on commonalities between urban insurgency and the actions of street gangs.
33. The fact, for example, that the District Council representative who headed the security committee for Tisa Nissan made much of his being an uncle to Muqtada al-Sadr was indicative of the general atmosphere in official circles. Enmity toward Tisa Nissan's political establishment was by no means limited to American personnel, as fieldwork would highlight

widespread dissatisfaction among Iraqi sources (including politicians themselves, members of the security forces, and ordinary civilians alike).

34. Interviews conducted by the author and R. Kent during February and March 2008 with the junior officers and enlisted personnel who undertook the vast bulk of day-to-day operations in Tisa Nissan, some of whom had over a year of experience in the district, found remarkably nuanced views of the local civilian population. Interviews were conducted on Forward Operating Bases Loyalty and Rustamiyah, and at the various patrol bases that had been established throughout the *hayys* of Tisa Nissan. Details of the interview process are provided in the Appendix.
35. See Finkel, *The Good Soldiers*, Chapter 12, for an account of March Madness in the eastern half of Tisa Nissan.
36. This was noted with significant satisfaction by senior leaders in the 2–16 Infantry Battalion, who anticipated that the spasm of violence (which occurred during the final days of their deployment) would have a valuable clarifying effect (discussions with battalion command elements, FOB Rustamiyah, March 2008). Finkel, *The Good Soldiers*, p. 248, notes rampant defections by members of the Iraqi National Police battalion responsible for eastern Tisa Nissan during March Madness, while associated aspects of the revolt's aftermath vis-à-vis the purge of Iraqi Security Forces are noted in Michael Gisik, "Troops Arrest Eight Iraqi Police Officers," *Stars and Stripes*, 17 May 2008. Discussion of "corruption" and "disloyalty" within the ranks of the Iraqi National Police must be qualified by an understanding of the threats levied against its members. As the 4–1 National Police Brigade drew many of its personnel from Shi'a areas of Baghdad, militants met with considerable success in intimidating or coercing policemen to desert during March Madness (an occurrence that reached high into the INP's hierarchy, as a Battalion Commander had his children kidnapped by the militia).

5. BELADIYAT AND MASHTAL: COMMUNITIES UNDER SIEGE

1. An initial assessment of Beladiyat was carried out during early March by the author and A. Roosendaal in conjunction with American military personnel from 2–30 Infantry Battalion. A similar survey of Mashtal was conducted in mid March by the author and R. Kent in conjunction with American military personnel from 2–16 Infantry Battalion.
2. By early 2008, core areas of the two *hayys* shared more in common vis-à-vis security and stability with middle class areas below the Army Canal such as Muthana and those of the Rusafa political district than the other neighborhoods beyond the Army Canal. While problem areas remained within the *hayys*, particularly in western areas of Beladiyat adjacent to Sadr City, American commanders highlighted the core neighborhoods of Beladiyat and Mashtal as bright spots within an otherwise deeply-troubled district.
3. The fragility of the progress achieved by early 2008 was a central point of emphasis among American military personnel at the Company level, who had extensive first-hand experience in the *hayys*. The comparative nature of the "successes" gained in both *hayys* thus requires emphasis, as does the fact that senior personnel on BCT staff (who took a broader, comparative view of Tisa Nissan in its entirety, and of eastern Baghdad as a whole) were generally more enthusiastic regarding conditions in Beladiyat and Mashtal.

4. Members of the *hayys'* middle class and minority communities were adamant in their accounts of the interconnectedness between the rise of the Mehdi Army and the encroachment of the *hawasim*, and prominent local leaders were intent on rolling back the advances of the *hawasim* after the militia's expulsion. However, a critical indicator that cast doubt on the militia having led a mass-based invasion of Beladiyat or Mashtal was the relative weakness of the Mehdi Army's anti-Coalition insurgent campaign in the two *hayys*. Areas of new settlement that were home to large numbers of Sadrist Shi'a were more dangerous to American and Iraqi forces than the *hayys'* core neighborhoods but, as discussed in greater detail below, there was little evidence of a coherent civil-military campaign by the Mehdi Army in either *hayy*. On the contrary, while certain specific areas were notably lethal, Beladiyat and Mashtal were, on the whole, palpably less hostile than militia-dominated areas further beyond the Army Canal.
5. Fieldwork in Beladiyat was led by A. Roosendaal in conjunction with personnel from 2–30 Infantry Battalion and with the support of J. Hubbard between April and July 2008. Fieldwork in Mashtal was led by the author in conjunction with personnel from 1–66 Armor Battalion with the support of A. Roosendaal and J. Makeur, initially during April and again between August and October 2008. The primary means by which Beladiyat and Mashtal were investigated was through sit-down meetings held under controlled conditions, called "Key Leader Engagements" in the parlance of the American military. With a contingent of local communal leaders and elected officials meeting regularly with American personnel, HTT personnel were able to speak repeatedly with prominent individuals and cultivate personal relationships. Sources engaged in these meetings included elected representatives from the Neighborhood Council system, self-identified local "tribal" leaders, officers from the Iraqi Security Forces, as well as Sunni politicians and civil society leaders who had been forcibly exiled from the two *hayys*. Interviews and informal discussions were conducted at local government facilities, at patrol bases jointly manned by Iraqi and American personnel, and at FOBs Loyalty and Rustamiyah, covering topics such as the historical development of the two *hayys*, personal narratives on life during the Saddam era, perspectives on the violence that had affected the area since 2003, and the dynamics of relations among the *hayys'* various communities. To balance the perspectives of the local elite with the views of ordinary residents, and also to engage segments of the population that were under- or un-represented in venues where American personnel conducted sit-down business, interviews were supplemented with fieldwork in the neighborhoods of both *hayys*. HTT personnel accompanied joint American-Iraqi operations that were conducted throughout Beladiyat and Mashtal, holding conversations with residents in their homes, on the streets, and in places of business (and also through interactions with Iraqi Security Force personnel) that elicited new perspectives. By combining the top-down perspectives of local leaders with the bottom-up views collected during street-level interactions and observations—which were further supplemented by the insights and opinions of interviewees from other areas of Tisa Nissan—a comprehensive picture of the *hayys* was developed.
6. Phrase quoted from Warriner, *Land Reform and Development in the Middle East: A Study of Egypt, Syria and Iraq*, (Oxford: Oxford University Press, 1962), pp. 172–3.
7. Phillips, "Rural-to-Urban Migration in Iraq," *Economic Development and Cultural Change*, Vol. 7, No. 4, 1959 p. 421, observed of Baghdad at the middle of the twentieth century that

the resentment was notably stronger within middle class communities adjacent to areas of the *sarifa* settlement—as established residents were more aggrieved about the effects of migration on their quality of life than the migrants were with the squalor of their condition.

8. Local residents would not recognize these terms, as the names "Beladiyat" and "Mashtal" are used to refer both to the *hayys* in their entirety and also to the main neighborhoods from which they take their names. The modifiers added here, like that used to distinguish Central Kamaliyah from its surrounding "satellite" neighborhoods in chapter six, have been employed for the purpose of clarity. An alternative would have been to use the numerical designations for each of the district's administrative *mahallahs* (*mahallah* is the lowest unit of urban administrative organization, falling beneath the *hayy*, as political districts are divided into *hayys*, which are in turn divided into numbered *mahallahs*), but this added unhelpful complexity to the text. Nonetheless, it should be noted that a resident of the neighborhood referred to herein as "Beladiyat Proper" would self-identify either as living simply in Beladiyat, or as a resident of "*mahallah* 738" or "*mahallah* 730."
9. Information of the founding and development of Mashtal (in Arabic, "greenhouse") was drawn primarily from sit-down interviews on FOB Loyalty in April 2008 with exiled Sunnis, and from recurring discussions with the *hayy's* elected representatives through the course of the spring and summer.
10. The history of Beladiyat (in Arabic, "municipal administration") was drawn from sit-down interviews with elected leaders and civil society figures from Beladiyat Proper, also conducted on FOB Loyalty during April 2008. Employees of the ministries of the Exterior, Commerce, and Finance were recalled to have comprised sizable local constituencies.
11. As discussed in further detail below, Palestinian refugees resident in Iraq were kept as wards of the state, and were not free to choose where they lived.
12. Naming the air defence installation "al-Imam" appears to have been a further example of the regime's attempt to pander to its Shi'a subjects by utilizing religious nomenclature and imagery for the implements of war.
13. Interestingly, the dividing line between Beladiyat and Mashtal and the poorer areas of southeastern Baghdad beyond the Army Canal was by no means rigid. On the contrary, the two *hayys* stood as accessible rungs of upward socio-economic mobility to those who achieved economic success upon migration to Baghdad—whereas the tonier neighborhoods on the inner side of the Army Canal remained largely inaccessible. There thus appears to have been an element of insecurity to local social tensions, as those who had "made it" fought to preserve their gains.
14. It remained unclear to what extent the sanctions-era *nouveau riche* penetrated Beladiyat and Mashtal. As noted by Munson, *Iraq in Transition: The Legacy of Dictatorship and the Prospects for Democracy*, (Washington: Potomac Books, 2009), p. 40, distortions to the Iraqi economy (featuring, among other phenomena, the collapse of the educated middle class and the rise of regime-connected racketeers) prompted physical movement among neighborhoods in Baghdad. The neighborhoods of Beladiyat and Mashtal, among the more geographically and culturally accessible of Baghdad's middle class enclaves to rising Shi'a families, would have been likely venues for such controversial population shifts, where "rags-to-riches Iraqis were seen as profiteers and criminals by the middle class professionals whose neighborhoods they had taken over."

15. It was unclear whether Old Habibiyyah survived the 1990s with its identity intact. Fieldwork opportunities in the neighborhood were limited due to access constraints, and key insights were instead gathered during interviews conducted at Checkpoint 17—a traffic control station run by the Iraqi National Police along Highway 5 immediately south of the outer canal. Several current and former residents of the neighborhood spoke adamantly about Old Habibiyyah's middle class roots, claiming that they and their families were well educated. Unspoken, yet clearly implied throughout these conversations, was bitterness over the Mehdi Army's conquest of the neighborhood and its contemporary reputation as having been absorbed into Sadr City.
16. The well-known middle class neighborhoods of Central Mashtal and Beladiyat Proper, as well as the Christian enclave of Tujar and Mu'allemiin, emerged among the more attractive targets for kidnappers in southeastern Baghdad. Their socioeconomic profiles rendered them tempting targets of opportunity, while their physical position on the periphery of the city center—removed geographically from the strongholds of potential protectors such as the Badr militia (which was, for all intents and purposes, the militia of the Shi'a middle class), left them exposed and vulnerable.
17. As blended neighborhoods where middle class Shi'a and Sunni families had coexisted for decades, Beladiyat Proper, Central Mashtal, Mu'allemiin, and Old Habibiyyah were neither hotbeds of latent sectarian hatred, nor founts of sectarian violence. Thus, while high levels of ostensibly "sectarian" violence (perpetrated, for the most part, by the Mehdi Army) brought sweeping change and extensive bloodshed to the area, the violence does not appear to have been the outgrowth of localized sectarian divisions.
18. Mehdi Army and Special Group operatives were known to move regularly within the triangle that linked western Beladiyat, southeastern Sadr City and areas beneath the canal in Tisa Nissan and Rusafa. International Crisis Group, "Iraq's Civil War, The Sadrists and the Surge," *Middle East Report*, No. 72, 7 February 2008, p. 3, notes that the Mehdi Army was able to project power into nearby Muthana, which had long been a mixed-sect, upper-middle class neighborhood. Kagan, *The Surge: A Military History*, (New York: Encounter, 2009), pp. 41, 176, notes that Muqtada al-Sadr's spokesman Sheikh Abd al-Hadi al-Darraji was arrested in Beladiyat, and that the Ministry of Education workers kidnapped by the Mehdi Army in November 2006 (the fallout from which was central in the Sadrists' withdrawal from the Maliki government) were held in Beladiyat as well.
19. Higher-end housing construction in southwestern Beladiyat. Photo by A. Cecil, January 2008.
20. Allegations on the sources of the more affluent settlers' wealth came from long-time residents of Beladiyat Proper and from sources within the Iraqi security forces. The former were openly and unapologetically biased against the wealthier strand of *hawasim* and, as such, their allegations must be qualified—yet in light of the extremely limited range of methods through which wealth could have been accumulated from the 1990s onwards, it is likely they were substantively correct.
21. The existence of militia-affiliated "realtors" was a phenomenon that drew significant attention from American and Iraqi forces (not only in Beladiyat, but also across Tisa Nissan in areas where sectarian violence had been particularly intense), but this was difficult to formally substantiate. Direct enquiry into whether particular residents had been aided by the militia

in their relocation to the open spaces and confiscated houses of the *hayy* was impracticable, but the picture of migration to the area as having been piecemeal and largely uncoordinated was nonetheless supported by first-hand investigation of new settlement areas, which found a pervasive absence of localized social order or broader organization of any sort.

22. Additionally, the migrant settlements that developed on the borders of the *hayy's* remaining outposts of middle class and minority settlement caused major infrastructural strain, as water, sewerage, and electricity systems succumbed to rising demand. This not only pressured the militia's opponents in the two neighborhoods, degrading their quality of life and pushing them further onto the defensive, but also caused localized class-based tensions to flare. The same population movements that facilitated the militia's march across Beladiyat thus also reinforced its underlying message of class vengeance, potentially strengthening the Mehdi Army's position by enabling militants to rally support through calls for class-warfare.
23. Like Beladiyat Proper and Central Mashtal, Mu'allemiin was an established, mixed-sect and multi-religious neighborhood where inter-communal relations were recalled to have long been positive. Its residents were not prime actors in the inter-communal violence of the post-Saddam era, as the principal networks involved (the Mehdi Army and Iraqi al-Qaeda) commanded limited local support. Noted in conversations with Sunnis displaced from Central Mashtal, held on FOB Loyalty in April 2008.
24. The "squatter camp" was canvassed over a two day period in August 2008, during which time a broad cross-section of the area was interviewed. The area had been populated incrementally during the five years since the fall of Saddam Hussein, and was home to Shi'a from all over southern Iraq, Diyala Province, and other areas of Baghdad. Situated well within the Mehdi Army's sphere of control, it had been seen as a "safe" area for Shi'a fearful of Sunni militant attack.
25. In a pattern similar to that seen in Beladiyat, the infrastructural stresses generated by local construction created fierce tensions with adjacent areas of Central Mashtal and Mu'allemiin, thereby reifying Sadrist rallying cries. As in Beladiyat Proper, established residents of Central Mashtal and Mu'allemiin were deeply resentful of the infrastructural degradation caused by their new neighbors. Echoing the disputes of prior decades between the city's middle class core and its migrant periphery, local residents blamed the new arrivals for degrading their quality of life, and for importing crime and violence.
26. Locally-rooted groups dedicated to neighborhood defence were noted in Tujar and Beladiyat Proper. Physical barriers were observed in Tujar, Beladiyat Proper, Central Mashtal, and Mu'allemiin. Access constraints to Old Habibiyyah prevented close study of the use of barriers in that neighborhood.
27. As noted above, similar efforts met with less success in the more geographically-exposed neighborhood of Mu'allemiin. During the course of fieldwork, numerous blocked-off side streets were evident where miniature cul-de-sacs of stability had been created; yet the neighborhood, as a whole, possessed an abandoned, vacant feeling in mid 2008. The Mehdi Army moved freely throughout Mu'allemiin, launching attacks on the District Council facility to its north and on American units that moved regularly along the east-west artery (known to American personnel as Route Florida) that ran from Highway 5 to the District Council facility, and onwards to the patrol base from which operations in Mashtal and Amin were conducted.

28. Stories of the militia's local operations during sectarian war, though difficult to corroborate individually, shared common patterns. Discussions with Iraqi Security Force personnel, with local leaders from within Beladiyat, and with Sunnis exiled from both *hayys* painted a broadly consistent picture of the dynamics of violence.
29. Al-Khalidi and Tanner, "Sectarian Violence: Radical Groups Drive Displacement," *The Brookings Institute, University of Bern Project on International Displacement*, October 2006, studies the dynamics of violence in mixed-sect areas similar to Beladiyat and Mashtal. As the core neighborhoods of Beladiyat and Mashtal were home to relatively well-established communities, the sectarian violence endured was recalled to have been particularly personal and intimate. Individual accounts of the violence were impossible to verify, yet an array of themes were commonly cited. In the early phase of post-Saddam violence, during which the Mehdi Army defined itself through its opposition to American occupation, the militia was able to develop local contacts who shared its anti-occupation sentiments. As the sectarian war took shape, the threat of violence compelled others to collaborate in the militia's targeting of Sunnis, Christians, and middle class Shi'a, as neighbors were forced to betray one another in order to save themselves. Alternatively, the desire to settle scores with personal or familial rivals or to position one's self advantageously in the post-Saddam political order induced others to cooperate with the Mehdi Army, as collaboration created opportunities for enrichment and localized empowerment.
30. Thus, while both *hayys* experienced high levels of sectarian violence, the killing and forced displacement of local Sunnis was far less the by-product of simmering sectarian tensions among local residents than an instrument through which the Mehdi Army sought to weaken, and thereby ultimately overrun and displace the *hayys*' multi-sectarian communities.
31. Al-Khalidi and Tanner, "Sectarian Violence," pp. 23–4, discusses the threats faced by Christians from the various militant groups active in Iraq. Batatu, *The Old Social Classes and the Revolutionary Movements of Iraq*, (London: Saqi, 2004), p. 701, in his discussion of Christians' diminishing role in the Iraqi Communist Party during prior decades, notes the historically "exposed" position of Iraqi Christians, and identifies the roots of a communal strategy to avoid attracting attention in pursuit of survival.
32. The settlement of Shi'a families within Tujar was noted by civil society leaders from Beladiyat Proper during interviews on FOB Loyalty during March 2008.
33. On the collapsing position of Iraq's Christian community as a whole, see: Steven Lee Meyers, "With New Violence, More Christians Are Fleeing Iraq," *New York Times*, 12 December 2010.
34. The apartment towers of Beladiyat had been built during the oil-boom of the 1970s as a symbol of the Ba'th regime's commitment to the Palestinian cause. As the largest single concentration of Palestinians in the country, it emerged as a focal point for Iraq's Palestinian community as its members struggled to navigate the dangers of the post-Saddam order. Human Rights Watch, "Nowhere to Flee: The Perilous Situation of Palestinians in Iraq," Vol. 18, No. 4, September 2006, pp. 1, 8–9, estimates that there were 34,000 Palestinians in Iraq in 2003, concentrated overwhelmingly in Baghdad.
35. The relations between Iraq's resident Palestinian community and the Ba'th regime are examined in Human Rights Watch, "Nowhere to Flee"; Ayad Rahim, "Attitudes to the

West, Arabs and Fellow Iraqis," in Hazelton (ed.), CARDI, *Iraq Since the Gulf War: Prospects for Democracy*, (London: Zed Books, 1994); Makiya, *Cruelty and Silence: War, Tyranny, Uprising, and the Arab World*, (London: Jonathon Cape, 1993), pp. 266–8; and Palestine Liberation Organization, "Palestinian Refugees in Iraq," Refugees Affairs Department, 1999, accessed via Palestinian Refugee ResearchNet: http://prrn.mcgill.ca/

36. Human Rights Watch, "Nowhere to Flee," pp. 9, 15, cites Mashtal, Beladiyat, Zafaraniyyah and Baghdad al-Jadeeda as areas home to significant Palestinian clusters; references Palestine Liberation Organization (PLO) data that 63 per cent of residents enjoyed free housing (which was procured for them by the Iraqi government); and notes Palestinians resident in Mashtal whose rents increased fivefold with the fall of the regime and who faced growing hostility that ultimately compelled them to flee. Clusters of Palestinians in Baghdad al-Jadeeda, on the other hand, were evicted outright. Local Palestinians viewed this growing array of dangers with great frustration in light of their own view of the "preferential treatment" they had received in the past. For, while Saddam Hussein had been a staunch supporter of Palestinian hostilities against Israel, and Iraq's Palestinian refugee population had enjoyed special subsidies and privileges, their actual position in the country had remained deeply problematic. Prevented from obtaining citizenship and prohibited from integration into Iraqi society, Iraq's Palestinian minority had lived as hostages of the state. Housing was effectively free, yet it was often of poor quality. Basic amenities and essential commodities were provided by the state welfare system, yet economic opportunities for personal advancement were negligible. Iraq's Palestinians, however celebrated rhetorically, had been kept entirely dependent upon the regime's charity. As such, when the regime fell, and its protections and privileges disappeared, the Palestinians were left to face a wave of popular resentment that appears to have significantly outweighed the benefits accrued to them by virtue of their relationship with Saddam Hussein.
37. The difficulty encountered in fleeing Iraq is discussed further in Human Rights Watch, "Nowhere to Flee," pp. 3, 17–22, with the observation that Palestinian refugees were treated as "virtual prisoners" in the detention camps near the Iraqi border in Jordan, and that conditions were poor enough that hundreds chose to return to Iraq. The legacy of Saddam Hussein's crimes against neighboring Arab states, and his close relationship with the Palestinians (most notably, the Palestinians' overwhelming support for Saddam Hussein during Iraq's invasion of Kuwait and the ensuing Gulf War), combined to compel Jordan, Kuwait, Saudi Arabia and others to look unsympathetically upon aspiring Palestinian refugees, making flight abroad nearly impossible. Per those who remained, the Human Rights Watch report cites a Palestinian migrant interviewed at the Jordanian border, who declared "the Palestinians in al-Baladiyyat neighborhood are living like in a prison camp," p. 33.
38. Human Rights Watch, "Nowhere to Flee," pp. 13, 29, offers anecdotes from Palestinians in the Beladiyat apartments who told of "armed men" threatening them and launching attacks in the earliest days of the post-Saddam era, and references Wolf Brigade operations.
39. State persecution of Palestinians is discussed in Human Rights Watch, "Nowhere to Flee," pp. 1–2, 29–32.
40. Noted in Human Rights Watch, "Nowhere to Flee," p. 30. p. 33, which relates the account of an interviewee that, "sixteen or eighteen" Palestinians had been killed at checkpoints while attempting to reach the Interior Ministry. The very act of entering the Ministry of

Interior facility, which was a stronghold of sectarian Shi'a militarism during much of the post-Saddam era, was a danger in and of itself to the Sunni Palestinians.

41. Sistani's fatwa was issued on 30 April 2006. Cited in Human Rights Watch, "Nowhere to Flee," p. 27, pp. 24–5, which notes that the Beladiyat apartments became a focal point of violence, abductions, and murder after the Samarra bombing.
42. Human Rights Watch, "Nowhere to Flee," pp. 24–5, notes the key role of American forces in defending the Palestinian apartment complex in the aftermath of the Samarra bombing. Relations between American forces and resident Palestinians were generally positive, despite the fact that the Beladiyat apartment towers were intermittently struck by the rocket and mortar fire of Shi'a militants aiming for nearby FOB Loyalty. The nearby presence of American forces was likely vital in preventing the Palestinians' wholesale eradication from Beladiyat, as the Mehdi Army established a dominant presence across much of the rest of the district.
43. The re-establishment of security through force of arms was thus the driving force beneath early progress in Beladiyat and Mashtal. In light of prevailing sentiments among middle class and minority families, success was not a question of winning hearts and minds. Indeed, gains in security and stability progressed and solidified during the course of 2008 not because of the efficacy of development initiatives or the achievements of the Iraqi government, but as discussed further in the conclusion, despite the limited impact of either.
44. Old Habibiyyah was likewise viewed with caution by American and Iraqi forces, though it remained unclear whether this was the result of the Mehdi Army having established a coherent local presence, or whether it was due to the militia's ability to project power over and around the neighborhood from Sab'a Nissan and Sadr City.
45. The non-violent inducements of counterinsurgency that were applied in western Beladiyat included school refurbishment, micro-grant distribution to small businesses, and efforts to improve the local power supply.
46. Following the neighborhood's depopulation during the sectarian war, Mu'allemiin remained a place where outside forces battled. Mehdi Army and Special Group cells regularly targeted American patrols passing through Mu'allemiin, prompting retaliatory violence that made the neighborhood dangerous for its residents. By the late summer of 2008, however, this was beginning to change. Attacks on American patrols became increasingly rare after March Madness, and conversations with District Council politicians in September and October found that Christians were beginning to return to their former homes in western Mu'allemiin (though a significant number returned to find their homes occupied by squatters). Sunni families, on the other hand, were far slower to return to the area. Progress was thus uneven, with the side-streets of Mu'allemiin remaining barricaded with disabled cars, felled palm trees, and blocks of concrete, but the area, on the whole, experienced a notable easing of tensions on the streets and a revival of commercial activity.
47. In a pattern that was replicated by interviewees in other areas of Tisa Nissan (notably in Kamaliyah and Amin), residents of the settlement area adjacent to the District Council facility spoke freely—in private discussions in their homes, and also in front of Iraqi National Police personnel and passersby in the street—about the abuses of "the militia" while simultaneously professing Sadrist sympathies. As discussed in greater detail in the chapters that follow, by 2008 it was commonplace among many Shi'a in Tisa Nissan to speak of "the

militia" and the Sadrist movement as two distinct entities. There was thus no dissonance in proclaiming devotion to the memory of the White Lion (or, on occasion, to Muqtada al-Sadr) to an American interlocutor, while speaking contemptuously of the local manifestation of the Mehdi Army.

48. Similarly, the discordant political sympathies of the wealthier *hawasim* that established themselves along the southern tier of Beladiyat—alongside the chaotic environment in which the area's settlement took place and a resulting dearth of localized communal ties—appears to have rendered the area equally infertile for popular insurgency.
49. Fieldwork across the areas of new settlement in Beladiyat and Mashtal found nuclear families and extended families living together in individual homes, but uncovered no evidence of broader communal order in these spaces. Functioning "tribes" had not migrated into the open spaces of the two *hayys*, nor had coherent professional or communal groups of other sorts either moved intact to these areas or formed anew upon arrival. Along the southern tier of Beladiyat, migrants from Sadr City intermixed haphazardly with wealthier prospectors; the encampment to the north of the District Council facility housed families from across the country that arrived over a period of years; while even the relatively homogeneous settlement area northwest of Beladiyat Proper, which was dominated by migrants from Sadr City, appeared to lack an underpinning social order.
50. Nonetheless, echoing the defamatory narratives deployed against *al-'asima* and the *shurughis* in the 1940s and 1950s, interviewees in Beladiyat Proper and Central Mashtal (who, importantly, were seconded at times by members of the Iraqi Security Forces), spoke of the underclass development areas as bastions of criminality and loci of an array of pernicious influences. Despite evidence that the *hayys* had not been subjected to a coordinated underclass assault by the Mehdi Army and hypothetical legions of *shurughi* supporters, the narrative of the besieged middle class persisted. Reconciliation was thus rendered all the more difficult, as the defeat of the Mehdi Army and the re-establishment of law and order was viewed not as a desired end-state, but as a precursor to a return to the pre-invasion status quo via the new arrivals' eviction.

6. KAMALIYAH AND AMIN: RALLYING THE MASSES

1. An initial survey of both *hayys* was conducted by the author and R. Kent in early March 2008, in cooperation with American military personnel from 2–16 Infantry Battalion. For additional contemporary observations on conditions in the *hayys*, and the attitudes of American personnel toward them, see: Finkel, *The Good Soldiers*, (New York: Sarah Crichton Books, 2009).
2. "There can't be any poor people in Kamaliyah," responded a businessman based in the Karrada Peninsula to the suggestion that Iraqi entrepreneurs might assist American-funded development projects in Central Kamaliyah, "they stole everything in Baghdad." Interview by the author, FOB Rustamiyah, August 2008.
3. Photo by the author, May 2008.
4. Iraqi sources from central areas of Baghdad—businessmen, for example, with whom HTT personnel discussed the decrepit infrastructural condition of Kamaliyah, and government officials charged with the allocation of the city's resources for urban development—expressed

little sympathy for the *hayy's* residents. As discussed below, the area's long-standing reputation for criminality, which was forcefully reified by the role of local residents in post-invasion looting and the violence that subsequently wracked the city, rendered Kamaliyah an object of scorn more than sympathy.

5. Amin's reputation for Shi'a militarism was legion, and captured most poignantly during fieldwork by an Iraqi reporter who accompanied an American patrol through the *hayy* during October 2008. He recalled having "embedded" with Shi'a militants in Amin during 2007, observing an especially strong Iranian presence. Despite a major abatement of violence in the area during the summer of 2008, he spoke of the *hayy* with a mixture of fear and awe, remaining notably tense throughout.
6. The Muhsin al-Hakim mosque, Amin, which was a central rallying point for Shi'a militants. Photo by the author, September 2008.
7. Officers from 4–10 BCT staff, and senior elements 2–16 battalion staff interviewed in February 2008 at FOBs Loyalty and Rustamiyah respectively, raised the point that in neither *hayy* were American forces fighting against an insurgency that appeared to benefit from substantive popular participation. Likewise, initial interviews conducted in February 2008 of 2–16 personnel with extensive ground-level experience in the *hayys* found an array of views on prevailing popular sympathies toward the militia. Those tasked with operating on the streets of Amin and Kamaliyah had encountered sporadically fierce violence and displays of hostility from local civilians but, through the course of their experiences, many had come to believe that the populace was not united against them.
8. Finkel, *The Good Soldiers*, Chapter 12, details the events of March Madness in Amin and Kamaliyah, and notes that the vast bulk of the Iraqi National Police battalion responsible for the *hayys* either deserted or defected to the enemy.
9. Finkel, *The Good Soldiers*, pp. 243–24, captures the prevailing view of American military personnel during the violence of March Madness, noting "it was as if the residents of Kamaliyah and Fedaliyah and Mashtal and Amin and every other war-ruined patch of ground that the 2–16 had been trying to salvage had been waiting behind their closed doors, guns in one hand, EFPs in the other, for the chance to come out and attack."
10. Fieldwork in Amin and Kamaliyah was led by the author, in conjunction with American personnel from 1–66 Armor Battalion and the National Police Training Team attached to the Iraqi National Police Brigade overseeing Tisa Nissan, and with the additional support of J. Makeur. The investigation of Kamaliyah was conducted primarily between April and June, and that of Amin from August to October. The residents of Kamaliyah and Amin proved remarkably willing to share their personal stories, their thoughts on aspects of local history, and their perspectives on the extraordinary turbulence endured in the *hayys* since the fall of Saddam Hussein. So-called "soft knock" clearance operations in which American and Iraqi units moved house-to-house through neighborhoods to search for weapons and to assess local conditions proved particularly fruitful, as they allowed for five- to fifteen-minute conversations with an individual or family while Iraqi personnel conducted their search. Additional observations and interactions occurred with local civilians at checkpoints, in markets, and on patrols directed to observe and assess the varied sub-areas of the *hayys*, through which it was possible to interact with local residents. In light of the notoriety and suspected militia ties of prominent figures in Kamaliyah's political leadership, however, and

the wariness of Amin's representatives toward American personnel, "Key Leader Engagements" of the sort conducted in Beladiyat and Mashtal were of limited utility. Nonetheless, with joint American-Iraqi patrols occurring regularly throughout the *hayys*, it was possible to interact with and observe a broad cross-section of their populations. Drawing further upon the insights of residents of neighboring *hayys*, and also benefiting from the observations and opinions of Iraqi Security Force personnel, it was possible to examine Amin and Kamaliyah in detail: investigating aspects of local history and the circumstances surrounding the rise of the Mehdi Army, and observing popular reactions to its fall. Residents of surrounding areas of Tisa Nissan also proved notably eager to discuss the particular attributes of Kamaliyah and Amin, and their turbulent pre- and post-Saddam histories. Such interactions were frequently steeped in bias toward the Shi'a underclass, particularly in discussions of Kamaliyah, but they nonetheless provided a useful resource. Lastly, interviews and informal conversations with personnel from the Iraqi National Police took place both in Iraqi government facilities and during joint operations in the neighborhoods of Amin and Kamaliyah, wherein junior enlisted personnel (the great majority of whom were young, underclass Shi'a from Baghdad) were an especially valuable source of information.

11. Discussion of the history of Kamaliyah is drawn principally from sit-down interviews conducted by the author with local businessmen on the patrol base from which American forces administered the *hayy* in May and June 2008, supplemented by insights gathered during fieldwork. The history of Amin comes primarily from the author's interviews with long-time Sunni residents of nearby Mashtal held on FOB Loyalty in April 2008.
12. Obeidy, which developed across Highway 5 from Kamaliyah, was also heavily influenced by settlement from rural, tribal areas north of Baghdad. The modern-day *hayy* takes its name from the high number of Sunni Obeid tribesmen that established residences there, as it offered convenient transit links to their traditional tribal domain to the north. As discussed further below, connectivity with Diyala Province also lent a transient quality to Kamaliyah, as laborers moved back and forth between the city and the farmland of Diyala Province in search of seasonal employment.
13. The residents of Central Kamaliyah thus shared much in common with the traditional *kasabah*, the unskilled laborers that had long been omnipresent in Baghdad's poorest districts. Discussed in Batatu, *The Old Social Classes and the Revolutionary Movements of Iraq*, (London: Saqi, 2004), p. 18.
14. Whereas the quality of construction in Amin generally deteriorates as one progresses southwards, the purpose-built neighborhoods for veterans and the families of the wounded are of relatively high quality. These construction efforts were part of the broader campaign to placate the Iraqi people, particularly the Shi'a, during the early phase of Iraq's war with Iran. Discussed in chapters one and two, and noted further in Karsh and Rautsi, *Saddam Hussein: A Political Biography*, (New York: The Free Press, 1991), p. 153.
15. Gulick, "Village and City: Cultural Continuities in Twentieth Century Middle Eastern Cultures," in Lapidus (ed.), *Middle Eastern Cities: A Symposium on Ancient, Islamic, and Contemporary Middle Eastern Urbanism*, (Berkeley: University of California Press, 1969), pp. 138–9, notes that the Baghdad municipal government destroyed the city's red-light district in 1952–3, appropriating the area for a parking lot and bus stops, and dispersing

the prostitute population throughout the city. It would appear that with the redevelopment schemes that followed, Central Kamaliyah emerged as one of the city's premier hubs for the sex trade.

16. Information on the development of Central Kamaliyah's satellite suburbs comes from conversations with local residents. Many were adamant in making the distinction that they did not live in Central Kamaliyah, but instead in their particular sub-neighborhood. This was particularly evident in al-Bustan, where those long-time residents that remained (many had fled abroad in response to the violence that wracked the wider area during prior years) spoke contemptuously of Central Kamaliyah.
17. Recollections of the tribal "resurgence" in Amin and Kamaliyah were offered during interactions with local residents in their homes, principally as a by-product of enquiries about the potential existence of tribal leaders with legitimate social capital who might aid in the restoration of local order and supplement the (quite limited) efforts of official leadership in conjunction with the Surge. As detailed further below, this search yielded minimal results, exposing the degraded state of tribal networks in the *hayys*—and of civil society at large.
18. Interviewees engaged in the two *hayys* were commonly found to value their tribal identities, and older men in particular often recalled their origins in tribal areas of southern Iraq and the Diyala Province, yet all interviewees were unequivocal in regard to the lack of either structural coherence or geographic continuity among local "tribes." This was further supported by conversations at checkpoints along Highway 5, during which numerous interviewees recalled having moved repeatedly among different areas of Tisa Nissan, Sadr City, and areas outside of Baghdad during the course of their lives, and also by fieldwork in the residential grids of the two *hayys* that periodically found small clusters of family members residing in adjacent homes, but that failed to uncover any evidence of neighborhoods or sub-neighborhoods where members of a particular tribe resided together in a "tribal enclave" of any sort.
19. The predations of the Ba'th regime were cited as having been notably influential in the degradation of sheikhly leadership and the destruction of traditional elements of civil society. When asked about the possible existence of respected civil society figures in Tisa Nissan, particularly tribal sheikhs, whom American forces might engage to compensate for the shortcomings of poorly-regarded local government leaders, one interviewee (an elderly man from Beladiyat Proper engaged at a neighborhood Council meeting in the spring of 2008) responded succinctly: "Saddam killed all those people." The implications of this for the tribal engagement strategies of Coalition Forces were profound, and have been noted in Dodge, *Inventing Iraq: The Failure of Nation building and a History Denied*, (London: Hurst & Co., 2003), p. 161, who argues that only those with ties to the regime had been allowed to develop or sustain social capital. As such, he writes, "the 'figures of influence' that U.S. and U.K. forces are now using as intermediaries are almost certainly the very same individuals picked by Saddam Hussein to act as his eyes and ears." On the evidence of Kamaliyah and Amin, Dodge's assertion appears astute.
20. The rise of the Sadrist movement is typically discussed as having occurred by working through the tribal structures of the Shi'a underclass, with "Sadrist sheikhs" in Baghdad's slums and across southern Iraq playing key roles in giving structure to the movement. For example, see Cockburn, *Muqtada al-Sadr and the Shia insurgency in Iraq*, (London: Faber

and Faber, 2006), p. 122; Yitzhak Nakash, *Reaching for Power: The Shi'a in the Modern Arab World*, (Princeton: Princeton University Press, 2006), pp. 95–6; and International Crisis Group, "Iraq's Muqtada al-Sadr." On the evidence of Amin and Kamaliyah, however, it appears that the reverse may have been true in certain instances, and that "sheikhs" of questionable (or entirely fictive) authenticity may instead have buttressed their legitimacy and stature among their ostensible "tribesmen" by aligning themselves with the White Lion and serving as his intermediary. With respect to the pedigrees of Kamaliyah's sheikhs, long-time residents of the Riyasah suburbs, engaged by the author during patrols through the area in June 2008, expressed strong cynicism alleging that many of those whom Coalition Forces were now partnering with had previously been Ba'thist proxies.

21. As noted in the first three chapters, the fervor with which the White Lion and his emissaries were greeted cannot be accurately construed as a "revival" of Shi'ism among the Shi'a underclass, as the faith of many had been, at best, "informally" observed since their initial conversion to the sect. The rise of the Sadrist movement was thus all the more significant and remarkable, as it was an unprecedented surge not only of popular religiosity, but also of social unity within the Shi'a underclass.
22. While the rise of the Sadrist movement clearly presaged the intra-Shi'a clashes of the post-Saddam era, and was likewise instrumental in shaping Amin and Kamaliyah into welcoming terrain for the Mehdi Army, the extent to which the Sadrist movement planted localized seeds of sectarian conflict was unclear. As detailed in chapter two, Mohammed Mohammed Sadiq al-Sadr was explicitly non-sectarian, ardently espousing both Arabism and Iraqi unity. The poor to working class Sunnis of Amin and Kamaliyah that had suffered decades of neglect and oppression alongside their fellow Shi'a would thus have found much in the Sadrist message to which they might relate, and Sadrist Shi'a in Amin, Kamaliyah, and elsewhere in Tisa Nissan engaged during 2008 fieldwork were adamant regarding the compatibility of the Sadrist agenda and Iraqi nationalism. There was a strong concern regarding bias and disingenuous misrepresentation in these assertions, as sectarian partisans might naturally downplay their feelings and conceal their prior actions in encounters with American forces, yet there did appear a genuine sincerity to the impassioned assertions (particularly of men in their forties and above) regarding their non-sectarian nationalism. Sunni critics of the Sadrist trend (who had been victimized by the Mehdi Army during the post-Saddam era) were far less charitable, however, describing the White Lion as a divisive demagogue, and the Mehdi Army as an Iranian fifth column created to pull Iraq apart. Furthermore, the extent to which radical strands of Sunnism had spread throughout Amin and Kamaliyah during the 1990s could not be established, as the *hayys'* Sunni communities had been displaced from the area. Shi'a victims of Sunni persecution often castigated their former oppressors as "wahabis," but the accuracy of this (and of the extent to which Sunni militants either enjoyed substantive support from Sunni civilians in Kamaliyah or Amin, or drew significant numbers of local recruits) could not be substantiated. As such, it remained unclear to what extent the surge of popular religiosity that occurred in Amin and Kamaliyah during the sanctions era presaged the sectarian violence of the post-Saddam era.
23. Accounts of the Mehdi Army's rise in Kamaliyah were offered by local businessmen interviewed on American military facilities during May and June, by area residents engaged in

their homes during fieldwork in Central Kamaliyah and the Riyasah suburbs, and by Iraqi Security Force personnel.

24. The aggressive persecution of both groups was an early hallmark of the militia, and the Mehdi Army thereby asserted itself quickly in the *hayy*. The Mehdi Army's annihilation of the gypsy village of Qawliyah, discussed in Shadid, *Night Draws Near*, (New York: Picador, 2005), p. 437, was one of its most notorious early atrocities. Iraq's gypsies had long been associated with prostitution and other "un-Islamic" vices, making them prominent objects of social prejudice and a target of religious militants.
25. The militia's campaign in Amin was detailed by members of the Iraqi National Police battalion responsible for the *hayy* (many of whom were Shi'a Baghdadis), Baghdadi interpreters attached to Coalition Forces, displaced former Sunni residents of Mashtal interviewed on FOB Loyalty in April 2008, and further described by local residents engaged during fieldwork.
26. Conversations with American personnel from 4–10 BCT staff, and with staff and field personnel from 2–16 Infantry Battalion, emphasized the strong legacy of anti-Coalition violence in and around Amin, which featured notably high IED threats along the heavily trafficked Army Canal expressway and Highway 5 (known to American personnel as Routes "Pluto" and "Predators" respectively).
27. Fieldwork in the area of new development that emerged between the pre-invasion southern border of Amin and the Army Canal (conducted in September 2008) found many local residents who claimed roots in Sadr City. Intermixed with other new arrivals from areas of southern Iraq (Amin's position at the entry point of the main highway from the Deep South thus appears to have remained a formative influence), several spoke of Sadrist social services and local support prior to and during the sectarian war. The precise role of the militia in directing settlement into the area remained unclear, however. Rumors abounded of a coordinated re-settlement campaign involving Sadrist "realty" offices, and the militia had unquestionably established a dominant presence in the southern areas of Amin (where militia-affiliated entrepreneurs ran the small generators that supplied the area with electricity and controlled the distribution of propane and gasoline), but concrete evidence of a "colonization initiative" was elusive.
28. Local residents engaged during fieldwork in both *hayys* noted that the sectarian "cleansing" of Kamaliyah and Amin was not wholesale, and that a small Sunni minority remained scattered throughout the *hayys*.
29. Resident civilians and Iraqi National Police personnel asserted that Kamaliyah had remained deeply turbulent throughout the post-Saddam era. The common narrative constructed by interviewees featured few references to either overarching political goals among the perpetrators of violence, or the criticality of popular sectarian hatred—and far more discussion of opportunistic predation and killing.
30. This was by no means unique to Kamaliyah. Munson, *Iraq in Transition: The Legacy of Dictatorship and the Prospects for Democracy*, (Washington: Potomac Books, 2009), p. 205, observes how material concerns motivated elements of what was broadly characterized as "sectarian" violence in the upscale Mansour district of Baghdad.
31. Discussions with American intelligence officers revealed that significant numbers of those detained in Amin were from other areas of Iraq. The role of Special Group militants and

Iranian patronage in fueling violence in Amin was emphasized by American intelligence officers at Brigade and Battalion levels, and corroborated by discussions with members of the Iraqi National Police.

32. It remained unclear whether the religious leaders within these mosques, who were understood by American personnel to have incited and enabled sectarian militarism in Amin, were local figures or were imported by the militia—or, similarly, to what extent sectarian hostility blossomed in the *hayy* as a function of pre-existing sentiments, in response to Sunni atrocities, or as a result of external Shi'a agitation. Regardless, through the course of the sectarian war, Amin's mosques became infamous for their role in supplying ideological and logistical support to the operations of Shi'a militants. International Crisis Group, "Iraq's Civil War, The Sadrists and the Surge," *Middle East Report*, No. 72, February 2008, p. 19, quotes a Sadrist supporter from Amin who notes the central role of mosques in directing patterns of militia activity. During fieldwork, local residents, displaced Sunnis from Mashtal, and Iraqi National Police personnel all recalled the central role of Sadrist mosques in giving direction and velocity to sectarian violence in Amin. The so-called "mosque monitoring" programs of Coalition Forces, through which the Friday *khutbas*, or sermons, of mosques were monitored for their content, also reaffirmed that the mosques of Amin remained staunchly anti-Coalition and militantly pro-Sadrist during 2008.
33. Noted in International Crisis Group, "Iraq's Civil War, The Sadrists and the Surge," pp. 3–4. Sumedha Senanayake, "Iraq: Growing Numbers Flee Sectarian Violence," *Radio Free Europe*, 26 January 2007, quotes Sunni politician Andan al-Dulaimi's statement that Amin had been cleansed by the Mehdi Army as part of a broader campaign that was making Baghdad an increasingly Shi'a city.
34. During the course of fieldwork, no evidence was found to suggest a "Robin Hood" style aspect to the criminal-cum-militant networks active in Kamaliyah. Per the discussion raised by Juan Cole, "Marsh Arab Rebellion: Grievance, Mafias and Militias in Iraq," Fourth Wadie Jwaideh Memorial Lecture, *Department of Near Eastern Languages and Cultures, Indiana University*, 2008, Kamaliyah does not appear to have been the venue of "social banditry" *a la* Hobsbawm. As such, and as encountered elsewhere across Tisa Nissan and as noted in the previous chapter, residents of Central Kamaliyah sought to reconcile their continued affinity for the memory of the White Lion with their experience under Mehdi Army rule by differentiating between "the militia" and the Sadrist movement.
35. By early 2008, Kamaliyah's industrial park was dormant. Plagued by erratic power supplies and the threat of violence, large-scale economic activity had effectively ceased in and around Central Kamaliyah.
36. Central Kamaliyah was observed to be the most extreme example of incongruity between public disorder and private wealth in Tisa Nissan. Whereas its public spaces were in advanced states of decay, with pot-holed streets, pools of sewage flooding roads and alleys, and crumbling critical infrastructure, numerous homes were found to contain modern appliances (the utility of which were dubious, owing to the neighborhood's limited electricity supply) and substantive evidence of material wealth. Sources in the Iraqi National Police made allusion to the origins of that wealth in the looting of 2003 and the area's notorious criminality, yet this did not appear to be universally true. Instead, Central Kamaliyah appeared to be home to an assortment of families of modest means, who were focused on the preservation of order within their homes at the near-total exclusion of public life.

37. Quotation from initial survey interviews by the author with 2–16 Infantry Battalion, March 2008. American personnel from 2–16 Infantry Battalion, and their successors from 1–66 Armor Battalion, regarded Ma'mun as a central area of local militant leadership, from which senior leaders presided over the grid of Central Kamaliyah.
38. While the residents of Mu'awaqiin expressed Sadrist sympathies and were of the movement's core demographic, the residents of al-Bustan were neither. The area had been founded by far wealthier families, and while many had fled abroad (leaving caretakers to protect their homes), the area retained its pre-invasion disposition. Small local shops displayed the image of Ali al-Sistani, remaining long-time residents were found to speak English, and the neighborhood appeared to have preserved a sufficient measure of its identity to remain inhospitable to the Mehdi Army.
39. The same features that had made Kamaliyah attractive to migrants from Diyala Province in generations past continued to hold true in the aftermath of the Ba'th regime's fall, as both push and pull factors had brought families to the area. Some interviewees reported having moved to the area in an opportunistic attempt to improve their family's position in the post-Saddam order, while others had fled sectarian violence. The rise of the Awakening movement in Anbar Province drove key Iraqi al-Qaeda operatives to move to Diyala Province during 2006—creating a spike in violence against area Shi'a from late 2006 into 2007 that drove many into "safe" areas of Tisa Nissan. The effects of the influx of Sunni militants into the Diyala Province are noted in Kagan, *The Surge: A Military History*, (New York: Encounter, 2009), pp. 84–5.
40. The new settlement zone that sprawled northward from Riyasah was heavily trafficked by American forces, particularly after they relocated their local patrol base from the outskirts of Central Kamaliyah to the industrial park on the *hayy's* northern tier in the spring of 2008. The area showed little evidence of local community and appeared to be home to a collection of families that moved individually to the area in response to either security concerns in Diyala Province or the allure of free real estate in the capital.
41. Seeking to eradicate the "un-Islamic" behavior for which Kamaliyah was infamous, groups of black-clad men were recalled during fieldwork to have harassed men and women in Central Kamaliyah during 2006 and 2007. The Mehdi Army also backed a re-branding initiative that sought the abandonment of the name Kamaliyah in favor of al-Zahra (The Shining One) in a reference to the Prophet Mohammed's daughter Fatima al-Zahra. It was unclear whether the Mehdi Army had instigated the renaming scheme—civilian interviewees from Central Kamaliyah and its surrounding satellite neighborhoods repeatedly expressed their desire to transform the *hayy's* image and shed its terrible reputation—but regardless, the militia embraced the effort as part of a broader endeavor to reshape Kamaliyah. The professional-quality placards affixed to the streets of the *hayy* in support of the militia's continued offensive against American forces referred to the area as al-Zahra, exhorting the religiosity of its residents. By the time of fieldwork in 2008, however, "Kamaliyah" was still used by all those encountered (including local Sadrist politicians in the District's government).
42. Pedestrian traffic in the vicinity of the Imam Ali mosque, for example, was observed to be sparse, even on Fridays and during religious events such as Ashura—in stark contrast to mosques elsewhere in Tisa Nissan. Conversations with enlisted personnel of the Iraqi

National Police were further instructive on this point, as numerous sources asserted that it was common knowledge across much of Baghdad as to which mosques were nodes of violence and should thus be avoided.

43. As discussed further in the conclusion, the notion that the Mehdi Army's abuses against Sunni civilians enjoyed significant popular support among the Shi'a underclass at large, particularly among older generations, appeared dubious—challenging interpretations of the sectarian war as having been the outgrowth of widely-held, essentialist forces. In Amin, as elsewhere across Tisa Nissan, the abuses of militants during the sectarian war appear to have driven Shi'a civilians further into the relative safety of their homes, not out into the streets to take part in, or celebrate, the bloodshed.
44. In regard to the altered posture of the militia toward local Shi'a civilians, residents of the new development area along Amin's southern tier engaged during September 2008 spoke with evident disappointment of the cessation of service provision and the increasingly predatory actions of local fighters. The implications of the "generation gap" that divided elder supporters of the White Lion from the youths and young men that came of age in the 1990s and 2000s is detailed further below.
45. Nasr, *The Shi'a Revival; How Conflicts Within Islam will Shape the Future*, (New York: W.W. Norton, 2007), p. 110, notes the specific relationship between Muqtada and Mohammed Baqir al-Sadr.
46. Lebanon, like Iraq, has long been home to a sizable (and growing) demographic bloc of underclass Shi'a, concentrated in its rural, southern regions. The themes of class-based grievance and social prejudice at the heart of the Sadrist movement thus have parallels in the ideology of Hizbullah. Furthermore, the modern-day movement toward the empowerment of Lebanon's Shi'a underclass, spearheaded by Hizbullah and Nasrallah, was initiated in large measure by a member of the Sadr family: Musa al-Sadr, also known as "the Vanished Imam," was born and raised in Qom, Iran, educated in both Iran and Iraq, and then moved to Lebanon in 1960 where he established himself as a leading figure in the country's Shi'a community. He formed the "Supreme Islamic Shi'a Council" in an attempt to give the politically-marginalized Shi'a of southern Lebanon a stronger voice in national politics, and then later founded the "Movement of the Dispossessed," a charitable organization (with its own attached militia) that worked to further defend the interests of Lebanese Shi'a as the nation's civil war intensified. Musa al-Sadr's standing was at its peak in 1978 when he disappeared during the course of an official visit to Libya. The details of his fate have never been fully ascertained, leading to the creation of a myth—paralleling Shi'a traditions about the "hidden Imam"—that he may return at some future date.
47. Sadrist imagery displayed in a private home in Central Kamaliyah. Photo by E. Peffley, September 2008. Featuring: (left to right) Imam Hussein, Muqtada al-Sadr, Mohammed Baqir al-Sadr, and the White Lion.
48. Sadrist imagery on the street in front of the Muhsin al-Hakeem mosque, Amin. Photo by the author, October 2008. Imam Hussein at center, with (clockwise from top right) Hasan Nasrallah, Ruhollah Khomenei, the White Lion, and Muqtada al-Sadr.
49. Attitudes toward Hizbullah thus appear to mark another implication of the generational divide that characterized the Mehdi Army's campaign, with youths and young men who had no direct memory of the Iran war being far more eager to embrace Hizbullah as an

object of emulation than their elder Sadrist counterparts. Moreover, from the time of its creation, the Mehdi Army had sparked fear among Iraqis that mirrored those of many Lebanese vis-à-vis Hizbullah: not only did the existence of a heavily-armed political party independent of the state pose a serious threat to national unity and domestic stability, but Iran's role in its training, funding, and operation also rendered it all the more polarizing for its implications regarding national sovereignty. On concerns over rising Iranian influence within the Mehdi Army, see: International Crisis Group, "Iraq's Civil War, The Sadrists and the Surge," p. 15.

50. Anti-Iranian sentiments ran strong among those who endured the conflict, and anti-Iranianism had been a key element of the White Lion's rhetoric. Not only had he attacked Iranian influence in Iraq while praising the Arab virtues of Iraqi Shi'a, but he also regularly slandered his Shi'a establishment rivals (most notably Ali al-Sistani and the members of the Hakim family) by making allusions to their shameful "Persian" heritage. Disparaging references to Iran, and Iranian influence in Iraq, were encountered repeatedly during fieldwork in Amin, principally from men in their forties, fifties, and upwards.
51. In Kamaliyah, American forces commandeered an abandoned spaghetti factory on the northeastern border of Central Kamaliyah. In Amin, they moved between the District Council facility and a small compound to the north of the power station on the *hayy's* eastern edge.
52. The unilateral ceasefire that Muqtada al-Sadr imposed on the Mehdi Army in August 2007 did not lead to a cessation of fighting in Tisa Nissan—but it did produce an overall decline in violence. The main avenues of Amin's central urban grid remained treacherous with EFPs, for example, as did the stretch of Highway 5 on Kamaliyah's western edge and the Army Canal Expressway to the south of Amin. It was understood by American personnel that this reflected both the active presence of Special Group cells that were unresponsive to Muqtada's orders, and the structural incoherence of the militia in the two *hayys*, where the Mehdi Army's local affiliates pursued their own courses of action in response to the operations of American and Iraqi forces.
53. Kamaliyah was especially notorious for the caliber of its politicians. The head of the neighborhood Council in 2007, who was widely understood to have accumulated his wealth and stature by robbing banks during the 2003 looting (and who was also acknowledged to be a local partner of the Mehdi Army), was eventually removed from office on a technicality when he was found to lack the high school diploma necessary to hold office. Tellingly, in regard to local attitudes toward tribalism, a local business leader (interviewed in June 2008) asserted that this man's accumulation of wealth had "brought [him] into sheikh-hood." His successor was a relative of Muqtada al-Sadr who appeared to embody much of Kamaliyah's spirit—contradictory rumors abounded regarding the details of his past and his alleged ties to the Mehdi Army, while he transitioned seamlessly from the velour tracksuits and gold jewelry he wore on the streets of Kamaliyah to the tribal garb favored for meetings with American officers to business suits when engaged in official government business.
54. Electricity shortages would persist through 2008 in Amin, generating enormous frustration among local residents. Apart from the public health risk posed by the canals of raw sewage in Kamaliyah, several municipal workers were overcome by toxic fumes and drowned in March 2008 while attempting to drain the swimming-pool sized pits of sewage into which the canals drained.

55. The extent to which the *hayys'* populations were either sympathetic toward or actively involved in the Mehdi Army's campaign was a central point of debate among American personnel prior to the March uprising. The *hayys'* relative passivity during the late winter and early spring was seen by some as evidence of the militia's weakness and of potential popular receptiveness to the advances of the Surge, while many suspected it was merely a demonstration of strategic patience by a populace that was awaiting instruction to rise up and resume hostilities.
56. In recognition of the declining strategic position of the Mehdi Army in the wake of March Madness and the Mehdi Army's defeat in Basra, noted local militants from Kamaliyah approached American personnel offering an informal truce in May 2008. Priority targets of American forces that had been known to operate in Amin, on the other hand, but who were not local to the area, were understood by intelligence officers to have fled for southern Iraq and/or Iran.
57. The main roads remained dangerous with EFPs, and areas of Central Kamaliyah and Amin appeared hostile at times, yet both *hayys* proved largely calm during the operations undertaken during the spring and summer of 2008.
58. Market areas within Central Kamaliyah experienced a notable surge of activity as the summer of 2008 progressed, as did the large market center on Third Street in Amin. Elsewhere in the *hayys*, American forces were able to renovate schools, install local generators, and provide cash grants to individual businesses, but they lacked the resources and leverage to address the systemic problems facing the *hayys*. Local politics, on the other hand, remained business as usual. The politics of Kamaliyah remained especially sordid, with one of its Neighborhood Council representatives murdered in April 2008.
59. The HTT played a central role in this effort, which was inspired not only by the frustrations of American personnel with Tisa Nissan's official leadership, but also by prevailing trends in counterinsurgency theory that advocated engagement with civil society (especially its "traditional" manifestations) and the cultivation of civilian support. Following the success of the Awakening movement in Anbar Province, in which local tribal networks had been mobilized as allies against Iraqi al-Qaeda and used to restore stability in areas where the Iraqi government was unable to exert sufficient power, there existed strong enthusiasm within the American military to replicate its achievements and rally support along tribal lines across Iraq. For an example from the canon of counterinsurgency, see: Richard Taylor, "Tribal Alliances: Ways, Means, and Ends to Successful Strategy," *Strategic Studies Institute*, August 2005, p. 1, for the observation that "tribes are a cohesive indigenous social structure," and that "building relationships with tribes shows cultural awareness, respect for the local populace, and scores political capital that can be used over the long term." The "Sons of Iraq" program was one manifestation of this (discussed in Kagan *The Surge*, p. 155), whereby American forces sought to mobilize and arm neighborhood-watch style groups, typically through tribal frameworks. This initiative was a top priority of American forces across Baghdad yet, for reasons detailed below, it was a near-total failure in Tisa Nissan.
60. The architects of Ba'thist totalitarianism presumably understood this, having allowed the Sadrist movement to grow during the 1990s in the knowledge that the social atomization of the Shi'a underclass would greatly inhibit the translation of Sadrist enthusiasm into substantive action (a position that was validated by the failure of the *al-Sadr intifadah* in 1999).

61. This dynamic was well understood by Iraqi National Police commanders. In a June 2008 meeting at the District Council facility, a senior leader of 4–1 INP clearly expressed his view on the futility of building relationships with what he termed "good" tribal figures and members of the public—as those who were "bad" were the only ones with influence over trends in violence.
62. As introduced in chapter three, the generation gap that developed among Iraqi Shi'a was of pivotal importance in Amin in particular. In a trend that betrayed the extent to which the collapse of civil society had penetrated the nuclear family, middle-aged men from Amin (and also in Obeidy and Beladiyat) offered a remarkably similar confession during field interviews in their homes and sit-down meetings on FOB Loyalty—that they were living in fear of their children.
63. Discussions with self-identified sheikhs from Central Kamaliyah (held at the District Council facility in August 2008) and eastern Amin (held at the District Council facility in September 2008) exposed this. Kamaliyah's sheikhs were openly resigned to their inability to prevent local violence, while the inquiry of an American officer during the latter meeting as to Amin's sheikhs' ability to rally their "tribesmen" and provide neighborhood-level security in the image of the Awakening was met with a frustrated sigh: "this is Baghdad, not Anbar," one man stated simply, and in the ensuing silence of his peers conveyed the impossibility of the suggestion. After decades of stresses and pressures, sheikhs were in no position to act as battlefield commanders or as leaders of popular militias in Amin or Kamaliyah, and there did not appear to be any "tribes" that might be leveraged toward military or political objectives. The local Sons of Iraq program was thus a failure, becoming a patronage vehicle for District Council members and city bureaucrats.
64. The perceived passivity of Baghdadis and the observed dearth of popular initiative was a source of much comment and debate among American personnel, breeding pervasive frustration in the context of faltering reconstruction and governance initiatives in the *hayys*. Discussed further in the Appendix.
65. The city government itself, the *amanat*, remained plagued by its own problems of capacity and corruption, while powerful prejudices against the Shi'a underclass (specifically toward Amin and Kamaliyah as infamous venues of militarism and dysfunction respectively) meant that the *hayys*, like Tisa Nissan more broadly, were generally viewed with contempt as opposed to concern by city officials.

7. FEDALIYAH AND SHAWRA WA UMM JIDR: TRACTION IN THE REMNANTS OF TRADITION

1. Due to access constraints detailed below, it was not possible to survey either *hayy* in person prior to the violence of late March. The initial survey of Shawra wa Umm Jidr was conducted in early April 2008 by the author, R. Kent, and A. Roosendaal, in conjunction with American personnel from 2–30 Infantry Battalion, but it was only possible to inspect the Rashad neighborhood. The initial investigation of Fedaliyah was even more limited in scope, consisting primarily of discussions led by the author and R. Kent with American personnel from 4–10 BCT staff and from 2–16 Infantry Battalion (the latter of whom had been directly engaged in the administration of Fedaliyah for over a year), and drawing also upon conversa-

tions with Baghdadi interpreters and Iraqis from other areas of Tisa Nissan during March and April 2008.

2. International Crisis Group, "Iraq's Civil War, The Sadrists and the Surge," *Middle East Report*, No. 72, 7 February 2008, p. 10, emphasizes the centrality of Fedaliyah to the Mehdi Army: "A Baghdad merchant claimed that 'Fudhayliya has become the Mahdi Army's focal point. When a problem arises between Sadrist offices from different neighborhoods, the Fudhayliya office steps in to find a solution', Crisis Group interview, Baghdad, September 2007. In the words of a Baghdad student, 'Fudhayliya is the Mahdi Army's headquarters. It makes sense. Given how the *Ma'dan* fight against the Americans, they deserve it! They are very courageous and have no fear. The Americans don't come near it; they bomb it from afar', Crisis Group interview, Baghdad, May 2007." *Ma'dan* is a traditional pejorative term for the Marsh Arabs, which is still widely used. As noted in chapters one and two, and discussed further below, the Marsh Arabs had long occupied the bottom rung of southern Mesopotamia's traditional tribal order, and had been widely reviled for centuries on account of their alleged bellicosity, impiety, and general uncouthness.
3. Located on the dividing line between the regional command structures through which the American military organized its forces in and around Baghdad, Shawra and its rural environs had received little attention since 2003. This began to change as the force realignments of the Surge enabled broader and deeper coverage of Baghdad's periphery; yet in early 2008, much of the *hayy* remained uncharted territory. The implications of this were noted in Kagan, *The Surge: A Military History*, (New York: Encounter, 2009), p. 189: "The disposition of US forces in 2006 left a dramatic hole east of Baghdad," Kagan observed, "allowing Iranian weapons, secret cell leaders, and militia groups to flow freely through the area."
4. International Crisis Group, "Iraq's Civil War, The Sadrists and the Surge," p. 21, identified Fedaliyah in February 2008 as a "virtually impregnable" stronghold of the militia. Iraqi Security Force personnel were notably wary of entering Fedaliyah, which they preferred to give a wide berth. Attitudes of Iraqi policemen toward the *hayy* were laden with prejudices regarding the fearsome roughness and degenerate social norms of its residents.
5. It was common for Baghdadis to draw parallels between man and animal (with the distinction between the two often blurring) when describing the Marsh Arabs and their unique lifestyle, using the *jamoose* as an emblem of local culture and a metaphor for Marsh Arab life. The *jamoose* population of Fedaliyah was estimated at some 20,000 in Dransfield, Lynsey, "Soldiers Help Farmers Feed Water Buffalo," *Armed Forces Press Service*, 10 September 2008.
6. The *hayy's* lakes of sewage, ranging from greenish-black to bright red, were the modern-day descendants of the "lagoons of black liquids" noted in *al-'asima* by al-Madfai, "Baghdad," in Berger (ed.), *The New Metropolis in the Arab World*, (Bombay: Allied Publishers, 1963), p. 61. As observed by Finkel, *The Good Soldiers*, (New York: Sarah Crichton Books, 2009), p. 71, the uniqueness of Fedaliyah was apparent even in satellite imagery, where the *hayy* stands in stark contrast to the grey and beige of Baghdad as a brown-to-orange blotch. "Fedaliyah was the spookiest place in the AO [Area of Operations]," Finkel writes, "an area of water buffalo farms and squatter hovels, so vaguely defined that even in crystal clear satellite photos it appeared blurry and smudged, as if it existed inside of its very own sandstorm."
7. While the Marsh Arabs were exclusively Sadrist in their religious sympathies, support for Muqtada al-Sadr was not universal. Marsh Arab tribes lent political support to the Iraqi

Hizbullah (unaffiliated with the Lebanese Hizbullah, it was a tribally-defined militant group in the southern marshes that was created by a prominent Marsh Arab sheikh to fight against Saddam Hussein from the mid 1980s onwards), and also to the Fadhila Party, an offshoot of the Sadrist movement rooted in Basra that was founded by former devotees of the White Lion who did not recognize Muqtada's authority. Fedaliyah was home to an official office of the Fadhila Party, the only such facility observed in Tisa Nissan.

8. Fedaliyah sewage pit with submerged cars. Photo by the author, June 2008.
9. The importance of Shawra as a supply corridor for Shi'a militants resisting the Surge in eastern Baghdad (and, likewise, for those previously focused on prosecuting the sectarian war) was a key point of emphasis among American personnel stationed at JSS SUJ. The suspected scale of movement of Shi'a militants and Iranian weaponry, and the lack of action on the part of American or Iraqi forces to interdict either, were sufficient to prompt one American officer to suggest (only partially in jest) a deliberate conspiracy. These transit routes are noted on the map of Special Group movements provided in Cochrane, "Special Groups Regenerate," *The Institute for the Study of War*, 29 August 2008, p. 6.
10. Finkel, *The Good Soldiers*, p. 249, notes that when the Mehdi Army kidnapped the Iraqi spokesman for the Baghdad Security Plan, he was thought to have been held in Fedaliyah.
11. Hayy Nasser attracted significant attention during the summer of 2008, as the neighborhood became a fallback location for Shi'a militants driven out of other areas of Tisa Nissan. It was transformed into a barricaded fighting position, with burning tires and piles of debris blocking main access roads and militants operating openly on the streets, while local Shi'a civilians fled in large numbers. Discussions with 2–30 Infantry Battalion personnel, April 2008, JSS SUJ. Further complicating the Surge's advance across Shawra were the limited resources of the Iraqi Security Forces, which lacked the manpower and equipment (and, arguably, the sense of urgency and operational capacity) necessary to establish order across the *hayy*.
12. Operations to wall in and clear Sadr City, detailed in David Johnson, M. Wade Markel and Brian Shannon, "The 2008 Battle of Sadr City," *RAND Corporation*, 2011; and Cochrane, "Special Groups," pp. 13–5, progressed through April and May, leading Muqtada to call for a truce on 12 May. Operation Promises of Peace was then launched in June 2008 to clear the Deep South stronghold of the Maysan Province. As detailed by Cochrane, it drove Mehdi Army fighters from the area with modest resistance.
13. Fieldwork in Fedaliyah, conducted primarily from late June through August of 2008, was led by the author in conjunction with American personnel from 1–66 Armor Battalion, and with the support of J. Makeur. Owing to the fact that Fedaliyah had long been a denied area to American personnel, to the sudden nature of its transformation, and to the peculiar traits of the Marsh Arabs, examination of the *hayy* (and the place of the Mehdi Army therein) became a major source of interest for American military personnel and their various civilian support assets. The HTT's investigation of the *hayy* thus benefited significantly from the contemporary work of numerous other groups and individuals active in the *hayy* during the summer of 2008.
14. Sit-down meetings were held with the *hayy's* Neighborhood Council representative at the District Council facility and, as discussed further below, important insights were gathered from observation of interactions between local sheikhs and American and Iraqi officers

during formal meetings. Yet the investigation of Fedaliyah proceeded primarily through ground-level observation of, and interaction with, ordinary local residents. Through the duration of the summer, HTT personnel and their military counterparts spoke with residents in their homes and places of business about Fedaliyah's history, local patterns of life, and the events of the post-Saddam era—gathering a street-level view of Fedaliyah and attempting to understand its extraordinary transformation.

15. By accompanying these operations, which granted access to local residents in their homes and on the streets of Shawra's various sub-areas, and by drawing upon the growing resources and deepening insights of locally-stationed American and Iraqi units, the *hayy* was explored at ground-level. Fieldwork in Shawra was led by P. Leddy and A. Roosendaal, in conjunction with American military personnel from 2–30 Infantry Battalion between August and November 2008. The Rashad neighborhood in particular became increasingly stable during the course of autumn, enabling American personnel to survey the area and meet with local residents.
16. These reconciliation-focused meetings, overseen by Iraqi National Police commanders and involving Shi'a and Sunni tribes rooted in Shawra's northern tier, became a major point of focus in Tisa Nissan during the autumn of 2008. It was hoped that they would facilitate the return of displaced Sunnis and the reassertion of the rule of law in what had previously been an extremely dangerous, Mehdi Army-held area, and possibly serve as a model for the numerous other areas around Baghdad where the sectarian war had witnessed similar patterns of displacement.
17. Information on the history of Fedaliyah was drawn principally from conversations with Marsh Arab sheikhs from Fedaliyah that were conducted in conjunction with official meetings held at the District Council facility in August 2008, as well as sit-down interviews held on FOB Loyalty in April 2008 with Sunnis who had been displaced from Mashtal, and discussions held with the *hayy's* residents during fieldwork throughout the course of the summer.
18. As noted in Chapter One, Hilmi estimated that the Marsh Arabs comprised a mere 2 per cent of *al-'asima's* population. See: Hilmi, *Internal Migration and Regional Policy in Iraq*, Doctoral Dissertation, University of Sheffield, 1978, pp. 278–85, for a discussion of the *ma'dan* in *al-'asima*. Early population movements from the marshes appear to have occurred through a process of tribal fragmentation similar to that witnessed elsewhere across the south, in which small- to medium-sized kinship clusters moved to Baghdad, creating new micro-settlements of Marsh Arabs on the margins of the city.
19. The attention attracted, and the emotions provoked by the Marsh Arabs and their herds, was by no means universally sympathetic. The encroachment of Marsh Arabs provoked both disgust and concern among the self-consciously modern elites who were attempting to forge a new, forward-looking Iraqi culture within the heart of Baghdad during the 1950s and 1960s. The arrival of what, to them, were regarded as manifestations of the most backward and regressive elements of traditional Southern culture, marked a direct threat to their pursuit of modernity. See Hilmi, *Internal Migration*, pp. 278–85, and al-Madfai, "Baghdad," p. 61, for related observations.
20. Fedaliyah's unique ecosystem both reflected and reinforced the Marsh Arabs' distinct patterns of life. Houses, which were commonly connected to sizable pens that housed *jamoose*,

were typically built from mud bricks, and the pits from which dirt was exhumed for brick-making filled with human and animal waste, creating ponds in which the animals could cool themselves. In turn, the *jamoose* provided both income and sustenance to their owners, as their milk was famed for its health benefits and their dung was dried into cakes that were used for cooking and heating fuel. This cyclical interdependence is also noted in Cole, "Marsh Arab Rebellion: Grievance, Mafias and Militias in Iraq," Fourth Wadie Jwaideh Memorial Lecture, Department of Near Eastern Languages and Cultures, Indiana Univerisity, 2008, pp. 11–12, in reference to Marsh Arab habitats in southern Iraq.

21. Throughout the fieldwork process, it was presented as an article of faith (even by those somewhat sympathetic toward their position) that the Marsh Arabs and their *jamoose* did not belong in Baghdad, and that they should be relocated elsewhere. A duality emerged in the narratives of Baghdadis when discussing Fedaliyah: on the one hand, Marsh Arab society was said to be endemically violent, with blood feuds and killings rampant at the local level. On the other hand, however, it was noted that the people of Fedaliyah formed a coherent whole of sorts, and would fight vigorously to defend their enclave against outsiders. Furthermore, in a sign of the forces that separated Fedaliyah from the rest of Baghdad, the accumulation of wealth (which was said to reach considerable sums among the owners of *jamoose* herds) did not lead prosperous Marsh Arabs to relocate from the squalor of the *hayy*. Wealthy families instead remained in their simple homes among their animals; a habit that provoked incredulity among members of the Iraqi Police, but that appears to have been further instrumental in the maintenance of a coherent, localized social order.
22. Cole, "Marsh Arab Rebellion," suggests that the offensive against the Marsh Arabs could be construed as "genocide," "insofar as [Saddam] destroyed their way of life and cohesion as a people." For a discussion of the government offensive against the Marsh Arabs in southern Iraq, see: Nicholson and Clark (eds), *The Iraqi Marshlands: A Human and Environmental Study*, (London: Politicos Publishing, 2002). Alexander Tkachenko, "The Economy of the Marshes in the 1990s," in *The Iraqi Marshlands*, pp. 55–6, notes that Marsh Arabs had been migrating in significant numbers to Baghdad and the cities of southern Iraq since the 1970s, and the government offensive (which peaked in 1993–1994) provoked a further surge in movement. Shahristani, "The Suppression and Survival of Iraqi Shi'is," in Hazelton (ed.), CARDI, *Iraq Since the Gulf War: Prospects for Democracy*, (London: Zed Books, 1994), p. 135, notes that the marshes were largely drained by 1994, while an estimated 10,000 Marsh Arabs had fled to refugee camps in Iran.
23. Quotations from al-Khafaji, "State Terror and the Degradation of Politics," in *Iraq Since the Gulf War*, p. 20.
24. As noted in chapter two, Marsh Arab tribes were responsible for much of the violence during the so-called *al-Sadr intifadah* that occurred after the White Lion's murder. It remained unclear whether the residents of Fedaliyah contributed to the uprising, however, or the extent to which the decision to remove the Marsh Arabs from Baghdad was influenced by Marsh Arab anti-regime agitation.
25. See: Ajami, *The Foreigner's Gift: The Americans, The Arabs and the Iraqis in Iraq*, (New York: Free Press, 2006), p. 5, for discussion of urban control and encirclement strategies.
26. The development of southern Shawra comes from discussions with members of the *hayy's* neighborhood Council, conducted on JSS SUJ by A. Roosendaal and P. Leddy during September and October of 2008.

27. Long-time Shi'a residents of Rashad, engaged in their homes and in sit-down meetings on JSS SUJ during the fall of 2008, expressed nostalgia for the material quality of life enjoyed under Ba'thist rule (particularly as the area had fallen into abject disrepair with the collapse of the state), but noted that material benefits had come at the price of intense scrutiny from the security services.
28. Karsh and Rautsi, *Saddam Hussein: A Political Biography*, (New York: The Free Press, 1991), pp. 194–5, observe how the regime "celebrated" the conclusion of the war with Iran by building neighborhoods such as Hayy Nasser, absent of any true reckoning of the war's cost or the actual resources of the state.
29. Outside of the Rashad neighborhood, local residential infrastructure remained poorly developed and essential services were broadly lacking. Despite the strong local presence of the government, its representatives in southern Shawra were focused principally on the maintenance of order within Baghdad rather than the development of their immediate surroundings. The government's most significant, sustained involvement in the area was to use the area north of Hayy Nasser as a sprawling open landfill.
30. Owing to access limitations arising from the remoteness of northern Shawra, and also to the ways in which the sectarian violence and forced population movements of 2006 and 2007 made discussion of the claims of various groups to particular pieces of terrain extremely contentious, key aspects of the area's historical development remained unclear. However, as detailed further below, it was evident that both Shi'a and Sunni tribal groups had established enclaves across northern Shawra, and that those enclaves provided a measure of communal coherence and geographic cohesion not evident in Kamaliyah or Amin, for example.
31. The decision to transfer the area between Baghdad and Baquba reflected not only the indifference of both urban centers toward the marginal spaces of Shawra, but also, allegedly, the periodic desire of the Ba'th government to bolster the numbers of party loyalists within Diyala Province by reallocating the Ba'thist contingent of southern Shawra. Furthermore, the *hayy's* very name is suggestive of Baghdad's attitude toward the area, as the region from which "Shawra" takes its name is far further north, situated well beyond city limits. During the post-Saddam era, local residents desirous that the government extend essential services and improve local infrastructure would thus refer to their particular neighborhoods individually, largely eschewing the name "Shawra"—which implied the *hayy's* collective inclusion in a faraway place.
32. As noted below, the dynamics of the sectarian war offered compelling evidence of connectivity between the tribal clusters of Shawra and their counterparts elsewhere in Iraq, with local intra-Shi'a rivalries appearing to tie into tribal conflicts in the Deep South (and to the alliances forged between prominent southern tribal groups and the Mehdi Army).
33. Like Fedaliyah, the areas of Marsh Arab settlement in Basra (which grew significantly in response to the government offensive in the marshes during the 1990s) became areas of powerful support for the Mehdi Army and dangerous to Coalition Forces. Noted in Cochrane, "The Battle for Basra," *The Institute for the Study of War*, 31 May 2008, p. 3. For historical precedent, see: Wilfred Thesiger, *The Marsh Arabs* (London: Longmans, Green & Co., 1964), p. 49, on the infamy acquired by the Marsh Arabs of southern Mesopotamia during World War I, when they raided both British and Ottoman forces.

34. The aggressive role of Fedaliyah's Marsh Arabs in the sectarian war for Baghdad was emphasized by Iraqi Security Force personnel stationed at JSS al-Khansa, by Sunnis who had been displaced from Central Mashtal, and by Baghdadi interpreters attached to 1–66 Armor Battalion. The sectarian prowess of Fedaliyah's residents is also noted in International Crisis Group, "Iraq's Civil War, The Sadrists and the Surge," p. 10.
35. International Crisis Group, "Iraq's Civil War, The Sadrists and the Surge," p. 3, notes Fedaliyah as a hub of citywide sectarian operations.
36. While the migrations that brought Marsh Arab families to Baghdad were characterized by patterns of tribal unraveling similar to that of the Shi'a underclass at large, it appears that the maintenance of Fedaliyah as a small, homogeneous enclave may have not only facilitated the preservation of remaining tribal norms and bonds, but also served as an incubator of sorts, enabling the re-growth of civil society. It proved impossible to pursue this line of inquiry in depth—and the essentialist authenticity of local tribes and sheikhs remained uncertain—yet local residents engaged during fieldwork spoke openly and matter-of-factly about a legitimate local tribal order in ways not seen elsewhere in Tisa Nissan. Marsh Arab society was by no means immune to the pressures generated by modern Iraq, as noted by Christopher Mitchell, "Assault on the Marshlands," in *The Iraqi Marshlands*, p. 94, who cites communal collapse within *ma'dan* refugee communities forcibly displaced to refugee camps in Iran during the 1990s. Nonetheless, while it was a virtual certainty that Fedaliyah's appearance of having been frozen in time was deceptive in key respects, it appeared that a vibrant tribal order did exist. Furthermore, a sense of community was evident in Fedaliyah that was structured upon local families' time of settlement. The initial core of the neighborhood was known as "First Fedaliyah", arrivals of the 1960s constituted "Second Fedaliyah," and subsequent settlers "Third Fedaliyah." It was reported to be common knowledge which families belonged to which group and it appeared that a social hierarchy of sorts had formed as a result—offering further evidence of communal structure and coherence. Similarly, a local resident who claimed to have been among the first to settle in Fedaliyah in 1963 (interviewed by the author during fieldwork in July 2008) recalled how various tribal fragments had blended together to form a community in the *hayy*, emphasizing the localized nature of *ma'dan* solidarity.
37. International Crisis Group, "Iraq's Civil War, The Sadrists and the Surge," p. 10, notes that the exploits of the Marsh Arabs during the sectarian war were such as to provoke Sadrist partisans to label them "barbaric."
38. Investigation of the area of new settlement in northwestern Fedaliyah found Shi'a heads of household who claimed to have been homeowners and prosperous businessmen in their formerly mixed-sect neighborhoods of Abu Ghraib, in western Baghdad. Living in decrepit single-storey buildings on the outskirts of Fedaliyah, they expressed a unanimous desire to return to their former homes—but remained unable to do so owing to the continued threat of Sunni militants (and the lament of several interviewees that their homes and businesses had been commandeered by Sunni civilians). The plight of the displaced Shi'a living in Fedaliyah was emphasized repeatedly by the International Organization for Migration, "Anbar, Baghdad & Diyala: Governorate Profiles, Post-February 2006 IDP Needs Assessments," December 2007, accessed online: http://www.iom-iraq.net/idp.html
39. With the main east-west artery lined with EFPs, and many of the *hayy's* unpaved side-streets

too narrow for American vehicles, it remained exceedingly difficult for American forces to enter Fedaliyah, much less establish an enduring presence.

40. Rashad and Hayy Nasser were recalled to have served as fallback points for Ba'thists fleeing persecution elsewhere in Tisa Nissan, but the continuation of violence against them rendered their position in Shawra untenable.
41. Examination of the neighborhoods of southern Shawra during October and November 2008 found that elements of their pre-invasion populations remained (especially in Rashad, where long-time Shi'a residents lamented the collapse of local services that came with the fall of the regime and the sweeping phenomenon of unregulated construction that ensued), but that the area had absorbed large numbers of migrants from various areas of Iraq. Whereas initial population flows traced primarily to nearby areas of Baghdad and its immediate environs, later arrivals hailed from further afield in Diyala Province, and southern Iraq as well.
42. The eastward surge of Sadr City residents is visible in satellite imagery available online. The sprawl of these modern-day *sarifas* brought tens of thousands of new residents to Tisa Nissan, flooding Obeidy in particular, and exerting strong influence on southern Shawra as well.
43. The extent to which the militia was able to actively guide population inflows across southern Shawra was unclear. The presence of American forces on the western edge of Rashad appears to have limited its presence in that neighborhood, but the militia developed a strong contingent of support in and around Hayy Nasser. Like Sab'a Nissan, the neighborhood became a focal point of militant activity.
44. From the Taji area north of Baghdad to the so-called "Triangle of Death" south of the capital, the mixed-sect villages and towns beyond the capital's outer margins became venues of intense sectarian violence during 2006 and 2007. Fighting increased significantly in Diyala Province (in and around Baquba in particular), as the area attracted large numbers of Sunni militants fleeing the pressure created by the Awakening in Anbar Province. Discussed in Cordesman, *Iraq's Insurgency and the Road to Civil Conflict*, (Westport: Praeger Security International, 2008), Vol. 2, p. 431. The wider dynamics of violence in Diyala Province during the post-Saddam era are discussed in Kagan, *The Surge*, Chapters 4–6.
45. As was the case across much of Diyala Province, the specific nature of those alliances, and the extent to which either external militants or local actors were ultimately responsible for instigating violence, remained unclear and subject to significant controversy. On the one hand, militant groups such as the Mehdi Army and Iraqi al-Qaeda were known to make inroads into strategically important areas by positioning themselves as the protectors of their local sectarian kin, feeding on the fears and suspicions that proliferated with the escalation of sectarian violence—in essence, capitalizing on opportunities that they themselves had created. On the other hand, however, opportunistic local actors might actively invite militant networks into their neighborhoods and villages, leveraging the resources of powerful, terror-inspiring patrons in pursuit of personal or communal advantage. The particulars of northern Shawra remained unclear, though the two dominant lines of explanation encountered during fieldwork focused on the notoriously strong national-level relationship between one of the area's most prominent Sunni tribes with Iraqi al-Qaeda (not only in Diyala Province, but also in Anbar Province), and the particularly close affinity

between one prominent Shi'a tribe and the Mehdi Army (which likewise extended to the national level, with the tribe playing a key role in militia operations in the Deep South).

46. Accounts of the fighting were collected during September and October 2008 in conversations held at JSS SUJ and by telephone with the official leadership of the *hayy* (who, on the whole, claimed neutrality in the conflict), with members of the Iraqi Security Forces, and with surviving Sunnis who had been forcibly displaced from the area.
47. Sunnis were not entirely eradicated, however. During 2008, northern Shawra had a Sunni representative on the Neighborhood Council—the only Sunni official in all of Tisa Nissan beyond the Army Canal.
48. As in Fedaliyah, the essentialist authenticity of Shawra's tribal system remained unclear. Nonetheless, tribally-defined groups were observed to operate in a coherent, locally-recognized fashion not evident across much of the rest of the district. It seemed that the relative neglect and isolation of decades prior—which had fueled grievances regarding the poor quality of local services and infrastructure—had possessed benign aspects. As a small, obscure area that had, in effect, fallen between the administrative cracks between Baghdad and Baquba, civil society had survived (or, perhaps, been rehabilitated or recreated entirely) in ways not possible where the government's presence was stronger.
49. It was understood by American intelligence officers that there was a high level of connectivity between Amari and Hayy Nasser, particularly among local affiliates of the Mehdi Army.
50. The inability to capture the detailed inner workings of tribal systems in Shawra and Fedaliyah, or the specific dynamics through which they engaged the Mehdi Army, did not preclude the appreciation of their significance to the militia's overall campaign. With the limited goal of understanding how and why the militia had excelled in these two *hayys* whilst struggling in nearby areas home to legions of Sadrist Shi'a, it was sufficient to note that Fedaliyah and Shawra were places where civil society operated in an observably stronger fashion. Critical to the militia's local fortunes, not only were Fedaliyah and northern Shawra home to thousands of underclass Shi'a who ardently supported the Sadrist movement, but local residents were also organized coherently along popularly accepted lines. The resulting synergies between the cadre of the Mehdi Army, a nationally oriented militia, and the locally-rooted tribal networks of the two *hayys*, had produced an operational coherence unmatched elsewhere in Tisa Nissan.
51. From the time that 1–66 Armor Battalion replaced 2–16 Infantry Battalion (in the midst of March Madness) until the major incursion of late June, American personnel did not enter Fedaliyah. Prior to that period, the American and Iraqi Security Force presence had been light in the *hayy* for several months, leading to a *détente* of sorts whereby the forces of the Surge sought to contain Fedaliyah while avoiding the provocation of its residents.
52. Like Ba'thist security personnel who had previously been stationed in southern Shawra, Coalition Forces stationed at FOB Hope had been primarily concerned with the maintenance of order within central Baghdad, particularly in nearby Sadr City.
53. Interview with 2–16 Infantry Battalion personnel with operational experience in Fedaliyah, FOB Rustamiyah, March 2008.
54. In the words of an enlisted soldier from 1–66 Armor Battalion in the immediate aftermath of Fedaliyah's initial, uneventful clearance, it was "like someone flipped a switch" to turn off resistance. Interview by the author at JSS al-Khansa, June 2008. It stood to reason, therefore, that this "switch" might be flipped back on again.

55. In light of the cessation of price supports, local *jamoose* owners claimed that they were being compelled to sell significant portions of their herds to slaughter in order to raise the capital needed to maintain their remaining stocks. However isolated Fedaliyah's localized ecosystem may have appeared, its existence had come to rely upon the active support of the state via extensive feed subsidies. Their cessation in 2003 thus created, according to local *jamoose* owners desirous of American financial support, an economic crisis. The accuracy of these claims, and the scope of the "feed crisis" in Fedaliyah proved difficult to substantiate, yet it was raised repeatedly as a pressing concern during street-level interactions with local residents and at official meetings held at the District Council facility during the summer of 2008. American efforts to aid *jamoose* owners are detailed in Dransfield, "Soldiers Help Iraqi Farmers Feed Water Buffalo."
56. American forces sought to utilize the non-violent inducements of counterinsurgency in southern Shawra, notably by supplying otherwise unavailable clean water to local residents and attempting to remedy endemic electricity shortages. Nonetheless, the decisive changes that occurred in Shawra appeared to stem principally from the application of force against local militants (situated in a broader context of defeat and retreat by Shi'a fighters nationwide). The non-violent, positive approaches of counterinsurgency were then employed after the fact (to uncertain effect), in an effort to capitalize on the displacement of militants and to generate a measure of popular enthusiasm for the encroachment of the American military and the Iraqi government.
57. For a discussion of segmentary tribal theory, which depicts tribal networks as collections of discrete, coherent sub-components willing and able to pursue their own individual interests while nominally part of a broader coalition, see Richard Tapper, "Anthropologists, Historians, and Tribespeople on Tribe and State Formation in the Middle East," and Ernest Gellner, "Tribalism and the State in the Middle East," both in Khoury and Kostner (eds), *Tribes and State Formation in the Middle East*, (Berkeley: University of California Press, 1990).
58. In a telling reflection of local biases, and also of the limited capacity of governance in Tisa Nissan, Marsh Arab sheikhs who petitioned American commanders for economic support stated bluntly that they viewed American forces as more likely patrons than the Iraqi government. Discussions by the author with self-identified sheikhs and *jamoose* owners of Fedaliyah, held at the District Council facility, August 2008.
59. Rather than reflecting the militia's ability to mobilize popular insurgency among the new arrivals that had flooded southern Shawra, the intensity of violence in and around Hayy Nasser instead appeared more a representation of the extent to which the area's neglect in prior years (and its geographic position on the city's outskirts, offering connectivity to militant strongholds elsewhere) had enabled Shi'a militants to concentrate their forces and dig in to defend their gains.
60. As American and Iraqi forces extended their influence into northern Shawra, tribal leaders that had cooperated with the Mehdi Army expressed their intent to cease hostilities and their desire to seek reconciliation. Sporadic violence continued, however, which was attributed primarily to local youths and young men. The extent to which a generational split in fact occurred, or whether younger men were tasked with maintaining a level of violence that would be plausibly deniable, remained unclear. Hashim, *Insurgency and Counter-*

insurgency in Iraq, (Ithaca: Cornell University Press, 2006), pp. 106–7, notes that even in the rural, allegedly "tribal" areas of Iraq, "sheikhs simply no longer have control over the young men of their tribes."

8. INSURGENCY AND COUNTERINSURGENCY ON UNEVEN TERRAIN

1. As noted in chapter three, due to absent reliable census data, the exact strength of the Shi'a underclass in Baghdad, and Iraq more broadly, is unclear. Nonetheless, after the mass displacement of Sunnis from Baghdad during the sectarian war, and the exodus of middle class and minority families that began in the 1980s, accelerated dramatically in the 1990s, and then surged further in the post-Saddam era, it is a certainty that the Shi'a underclass is more demographically powerful than ever before in the history of the country and its capital—potentially comprising a majority of Baghdad's populace (based upon an overall estimate of the city's population at roughly six million, with two million underclass Shi'a in Sadr City, and at least one million more spread among Shula, Tisa Nissan, and the marginal spaces of northeast and southeast Baghdad). Moreover, it is estimated that Iraq's population has risen from approximately 23 million at the time of the US-led invasion to more than 28 million in 2010, and it is projected to explode to 56 million by 2050. Population statistics from Cordesman, "Iraq: Creating a Strategic Partnership," *CSIS*, "Third Review Draft," 2 February 2010, p. 159. The percentage of this growth attributable to the Shi'a underclass is not specifically noted but, in light of the demographic trends discussed throughout this work, one must assume that it comprises a substantial portion thereof.
2. As detailed in chapters two and three, the sustained assaults of Saddam Hussein's regime (as well as those of his proxies, which in the eyes of the establishment included the White Lion himself) had decimated Shi'ism's clerical elite, while the sanctions era had shattered the middle and upper classes and prompted a mass exodus abroad. The aspiring leaders of elite Shi'a politics were thus, overwhelmingly, returning exiles who had spent at least a decade outside of the country. As a result, not only did they have an extraordinarily limited popular base of support upon return, but the demographic cohort from which they might rally such a base was also badly degraded.
3. Drawing from the literature of international development, the implosion of the Mehdi Army could be described as an instance of "civil society failure." See: Ghazala Mansuri and Vijayendra Rao, *Localizing Development: Does Participation Work?* (Washington: The World Bank, 2013), for a description of civil society failure as "a situation in which groups that live in geographic proximity are unable to act collectively to reach a feasible and preferable outcome."
4. A comparison may be drawn between the fate of the Mehdi Army in these *hayys*, and the ultimate failure of the nebulous popular movements that emerged across the Middle East and North Africa during the Arab Spring. Many of the latter were ostensibly bound together by broadly shared political and ideological objectives (or, at the very least, shared grievances), but they lacked the necessary organizational framework of substantive social bonds rooted in a coherent civil society. In such circumstances, these mass "networks" (many of which had coalesced via social media) proved no match for politico-cum-military groups with well established organizational structures like the Muslim Brotherhood in Egypt, for example, or the tribal militias of Libya.

5. In a sign of both the socio-cultural frictions that persisted between the Marsh Arabs and their fellow Shi'a, and also the uneven quality of the Mehdi Army's "success" in cultivating broad popular support even within this *hayy*, the non-Marsh Arab Shi'a who sought refuge in Fedaliyah during the sectarian war claimed to have received little to no support from the local Sadrist operational center. Interviews by the author and J. Makeur in western Fedaliyah, July and August 2008.
6. For the approach to Counterinsurgency as "an argument" for the support of the populace that was famously advanced by General Stanley McChrystal, and noted in Filkins, "Stanley McChrystal's Long War," *The New York Times*, 14 October 2009.
7. The efforts of American and British Special Operations Forces to target leading Shi'a militants were central to this battle of attrition. The precise details of such operations in Tisa Nissan were unavailable to the author and his colleagues, but it was widely understood among conventional military personnel stationed in the district that the nocturnal targeting of "High Value Targets" was critical to the degradation of militant networks across eastern Baghdad.
8. The likely costs in casualties and collateral damage that would have arisen from an attempt to forcibly subjugate Fedaliyah (a feat from which even Saddam Hussein had abstained) appear to have been sufficient to deter frontal attack during 2007 and early 2008. Furthermore, the extremely limited potential of the non-violent inducements of counterinsurgency was widely recognized by American personnel on the ground. Owing to the Marsh Arabs' pattern of life, their terrible relationship with the Iraqi government, and their fervent devotion to the Sadrist cause, there was no prospect whatsoever of "winning hearts and minds" and prying the Marsh Arabs away from the cause of resistance with offers of material goods or services. For so long as Sadrist "resistance" remained strategically viable, the Marsh Arabs of Fedaliyah would remain among its fiercest advocates. Indeed, the financial assistance that was eventually extended to the *jamoose*-herders occurred after the Mehdi Army's collapse. This aid could be construed as an attempt to deter a reversion to violence on the part of the local population—but were the militia's overall position to have been revived somehow, it is unthinkable that this aid would have been a significant factor in the Fedaliyans' calculations.
9. The varied "non-kinetic" inducements of counterinsurgency appear to have been of only modest utility in Amin and Kamaliyah. Much has been written about the waste and fraud that plagued American attempts at nation-building in Iraq (for an example of questionable resource allocation from the district adjacent to Tisa Nissan, see: Ernesto Londoño, "Demise of Iraqi Water Park Illustrates Limitations, Abuse of US Funding Program," *The Washington Post*, 3 January 2011; and for an example of small-scale fraud by American personnel assigned to Tisa Nissan, see: Casey Grove, "Alaska-based Soldier Admits Accepting Illegal Gratuities," *Anchorage Daily News*, 2 March 2012). Regardless, the Mehdi Army's insurgent campaign in Tisa Nissan had imploded, for all intents and purposes, before American forces arrived with offers to refurbish schools and distribute micro-grants.
10. However lamentable, these woes were accurate reflections of reality in the district, where the local government's failings were less a function of the individuals involved, and more a product of the social, economic, and political environment in which the system operated (or failed to do so). The notable corruption and duplicity of certain individuals notwith-

standing, Tisa Nissan's government was representative. Beladiyat, for example, was a place that was authentically led by older men concerned foremost with their own particular neighborhood's survival, and impotent to counter the threats of Shi'a militants. Kamaliyah, likewise, was well represented by a notorious thief and self-made "sheikh" who would eventually be stripped of his position for lacking the equivalent of a high school diploma—only to be succeeded by an uncle of Muqtada al-Sadr.

11. On the nature of the killing that occurred during the sectarian war for Baghdad, and its generally personal, non-military nature, Cordesman, *Iraq's Insurgency*, Vol. 1, pp. 366–8, references documentation from the Baghdad morgue, where "the vast majority of bodies processed had been shot execution-style. Many showed signs of torture—drill holes, burns, missing eyes and limbs. Others had been strangled, beheaded, stabbed, or beaten to death." Furthermore, the evidence of Tisa Nissan does not suggest that large numbers of the forcibly displaced took to arms in search of revenge, fostering a large-scale cycle of retributive violence. Daniel Byman and Kenneth Pollack, *Things Fall Apart: Containing the Spillover from an Iraqi Civil War*, (Washington: Brookings Institution Press, 2007), pp. 6, 66, discuss the victims of sectarian violence joining up with the Mehdi Army in pursuit of vengeance, asserting "a great many of those who are fleeing their homes are not peacefully resettling in a more ethnically homogeneous region, but are joining vicious sectarian militias like Jaysh al-Mahdi in the hope of regaining their homes or at least extracting revenge on whoever drove them out." On the evidence of those who resettled in Mashtal and Beladiyat, as well as their counterparts in northwestern Fedaliyah and northern Kamaliyah, this was generally not the case in Tisa Nissan.
12. The degradation of civil society in Iraq, and its implications for Iraq's future, have long-attracted significant attention among Iraqi dissidents and intellectuals. Makiya, *Republic of Fear: The Politics of Modern Iraq*, (Berkeley: University of California Press, 1998), p. xxx, quotes from text of "Charter 91," which was an effort to formulate a new vision of political and civil society: "civil society in Iraq has been continuously violated by the state in the name of ideology. As a consequence the networks through which civility is normally produced and reproduced have been destroyed. A collapse in values in Iraq has therefore coincided with the destruction of the public realm for uncoerced human association."
13. This is noted in regard to Sunni extremism in Cordesman, *Iraq's Insurgency*, Vol. 1, p. 28, who writes, "one key reality in Iraq is that small cadres of violent extremists can do so much to drive a nation toward civil war and intimidate or dominate large elements of the local population." Similar concerns addressed in Munson, *Iraq in Transition: The Legacy of Dictatorship and the Prospects for Democracy*, (Washington: Potomac Books, 2009), p. 15, and Mark Etherington, *Revolt on the Tigris: The Al-Sadr Uprising and the Governing of Iraq*, (Ithaca: Cornell University Press, 2005), p. 147. Munson quotes Etherington's observation of "the curious absence of the majority from political debate." Munson, *Iraq in Transition*, p. 245, expresses the hope that the evident lack of cohesion and unity within identity-based blocs such as "the Shi'a" and "the Sunnis" might open the door for the formation of new, issue-based groupings (something he suggests will be "Iraq's only hope for exceeding the bounds of the confessional politics that will undoubtedly lead the nation to disaster"). Tisa Nissan offers little evidence that the underlying social structures necessary for such groupings to spread and flourish exist.

14. *Bilad al-Sham* (The Country of Syria) is a traditional term that encompasses modern-day Syria and Lebanon. This region is referred to as "the Levant", hence occasional references to ISIS as "The Islamic State in Iraq and the Levant", or ISIL.
15. For example, see: "Iraq Violence: Bomber Targets Shia Mosque in Kirkuk," *BBC Online*, 16 May 2013; "Deadly Car Bomb Blasts Hit Shia Areas of Baghdad," *BBC Online*, 17 February 2013; and Jessica Lewis, Ahmed Ali, and Kimberly Kagan, "Iraq's Sectarian Crisis Reignites as Shi'a Militias Execute Civilians and Remobilize," *Institute for the Study of War*, 31 May 2013.
16. On the persecution of Hashemi, see: W.G. Dunlop, "Al-Hashemi Death Sentence Risks Political Crisis in Iraq," *Arab News*, 11 September 2012. On the Hawijah attack, see: Patrick Cockburn, "Dozens Die as Anger Spreads Over Iraq Army Raid on Protest Camp," *The Independent* (UK), 23 April 2013. On the rehabilitation of Asaib Ahl al-Haq, see: Liz Sly, "Iranian-Backed Militant Group in Iraq is Recasting Itself as a Political Player," *The Washington Post*, 18 February 2013. Lewis et al., "Iraq's Sectarian Crisis Reignites," p. 7, further notes how Maliki's support for Asaib Ahl al-Haq was a dangerous instance of *realpolitik* by the prime minister, as he sought to undercut mainstream Sadrist influence and fragment the Shi'a underclass politically by providing support to Muqtada's far weaker yet more radical upstart rival.
17. For example, see: Borzou Daragahi, "Surge in Iraq Violence Raises Fears of Return to Sectarian Civil War," *The Financial Times*, 1 October 2013.
18. On the prospect of a return of the Mehdi Army during negotiations over the US-Iraq Status of Forces Agreement, see: "Iraqis Fear Return of the Mahdi Army," *The National*, 13 April 2011.
19. The re-branding of the rekindled Sadrist movement progressed in earnest during the summer and fall of 2008. Prominent among Muqtada's initiatives was the replacement of the Mehdi Army with is a non-violent organization dedicated to outreach and educational activities called the Mumehidoon, meaning "those who pave the way." Cordesman, "Iraq: Creating a Strategic Partnership," pp. iii-iv, 92–3, notes that, as of 2010, core elements of the rekindled Sadrist movement appeared to have remained focused on such social concerns, remaining ostensibly disassociated from militant action. In an indication that Muqtada and his associates have learned from the failings of the Mehdi Army, the loyal remnants of the militia's former core, reorganized into the Promised Day Brigades, have operated since 2010 as a narrowly-based militant network and eschewed efforts to mobilize mass participation. The origins of the group, which emerged as the successor to the Mehdi Army, are noted in Cordesman, "Iraq: Creating a Strategic Partnership," p. 109; while its campaign against withdrawing American forces during 2011 is discussed in *Associated Press*, "June the Deadliest Month for U.S. Troops in 2 Years," *USA Today*, 30 June 2011.
20. For discussion of Sadr's decision to withdraw from Iraqi politics in the run-up to the April 2014 elections, see: Jane Arraf, "Iraq's Sadr, Lion of Shiite Poor, Quits Politics. Boon for Maliki?" *The Christian Science Monitor*, 18 February 2014, and Harith al-Qarawee, "Is Muqtada al-Sadr Retiring or Repositioning?" *Al-Monitor*, 21 February 2014. Prior to Muqtada's surprise announcement, there had been widespread speculation regarding the Sadrists' electoral prospects. See Ali Abdel Sadah, "Sadr Talks Big to US Ambassador," *Al-Monitor*, 3 July 2013 for the (ultimately incorrect, but nonetheless intriguing) prediction

that "the Sadr movement will gain 70 seats in the 2014 legislative elections," which would enable the Sadrists "to take over the management of the Iraqi state." Muqtada's withdrawal sapped popular support for Sadrist candidates and undermined their performance but, provided that Sadrist candidates remain the preferred choice of Iraq's Shi'a underclass, their nation-wide political clout should grow with each successive election.

21. Discussed in Thomas Erdbrink, "In the Shadows of Shrines, Shiite Forces Are Preparing to Fight ISIS," *The New York Times*, 26 June 2014.
22. See Loveday Morris, "Shiite 'Peace Brigades' Send Signal of Aggression with Major Rally in Baghdad," *The Washington Post*, 21 June 2014. Whereas Sistani has directed his followers to directly assist the Iraqi government, Muqtada al-Sadr maintained his distance from the Maliki government and declared that the Mehdi Army will maintain operational independence.

APPENDIX: HUMAN TERRAIN MAPPING AND COUNTERINSURGENCY OPERATIONS

1. The contributions of individual team members have been noted in the footnotes of chapters five through seven. In total, this book draws upon the fieldwork of the following Human Terrain Team colleagues: J. Hubbard, R. Kent, P. Leddy, J. Makeur, and A. Roosendaal.
2. During the time frame in question, Baghdad was divided into geographic sectors that were the responsibility of individual BCTs. The BCT assigned to each sector was responsible for the day-to-day management of counterinsurgency efforts and the pursuit of security, development, and governance. For a detailed overview of the Brigade Combat Team concept, see US Army Field Manual 3–90.6, "Brigade Combat Team" is available online: http://www.globalsecurity.org/military/library/policy/army/fm/3–90–6/fm3–90–6.pdf. In regard to the overall transfer of authority to the Iraqi government, the time constraints of the Surge (which was to conclude in 2008) dictated that day-to-day operations in Tisa Nissan be handed over to the relevant elements of the Iraqi government on what was a pre-set timetable.
3. Discussion with senior BCT staff, FOB Loyalty, February 2008. As further discussed below, the HTT's work was conducted with the promise of full confidentiality for both American and Iraqi sources. To the former, confidentiality facilitated the sharing of views and opinions by American personnel that were at odds with official positions. To the latter, it protected Iraqi sources from exposure in their dealings with American personnel.
4. The use of Tisa Nissan's *hayys* as the underlying framework of analysis shared methodological commonalities with the "community study" approach of sociology, as detailed in Colin Bell and Howard Newby, *Community Studies: An Introduction to the Sociology of the Local Community*, (London: George Allen and Unwin, 1971); Robert Redfield, *The Little Community and Peasant Society and Culture*, (Chicago: University of Chicago Press, 1967); and likewise the "microsociological technique[s] of anthropology," as discussed in Dale F. Eickelman, *The Middle East: An Anthropological Approach*, (New Jersey: Pretence Hall, 1989), p. 21. The approach taken in the work of the HTT was almost entirely qualitative, eschewing the quantitative approaches (most notably, those of Social Network Analysis) that are widely favored within the defence establishment. For an overview of Social Network Analysis, see: Stanley Wasserman and Katherine Faust, *Social Network Analysis: Methods and Applications*,

(Cambridge: Cambridge University Press, 1994) and John Scott, *Social Network Analysis: A Handbook*, (London: SAGE, 2000). For examples of its use in a military/intelligence capacity, see Chapter 5 in Marc Sageman, *Understanding Terror Networks* (Philadelphia: University of Pennsylvania Press, 2004), which studies the core networks of al-Qaeda; and Brian Reed, *Formalizing the Informal: A Network Analysis of an Insurgency*, Doctoral Dissertation, University of Maryland—College Park, 2006, which details the use of social network analysis in the capture of Saddam Hussein. On efforts to quantify human terrain analysis within the intelligence community, see: Erik Eldredge and Andrew Neboshynsky, "Quantifying Human Terrain," MA Thesis, US Naval Postgraduate School, 2008, and Michael Gabbay, "Mapping the Factional Structure of the Sunni Insurgency in Iraq," *CTC Sentinel*, Vol. 1, Issue 4, March 2008, pp. 10–12. On the limitations of qualitative approaches such as the community study technique, see Redfield, *The Little Community and Peasant Society and Cultures*, (Chicago: University of Chicago Press, 1967), p. 71, who notes concerns over its "impressionistic," and thus subjective nature. Furthermore, p. 6 raises concerns as to whether the community study approach (which he discusses as related to use in rural environments) is suitable in urban areas. In the case of Baghdad, it was found to do so—in large measure because of the way in which the mechanics of the city's development (and the associated legacy of the *mahallah*) created distinctive enclaves that, in turn, influenced particular, localized patterns of violence. The legacy of the *mahallah* system on localized patterns of violence is also noted, albeit indirectly, in Munson, "What Lies Beneath: Saddam's Legacy and the Roots of Resistance in Iraq," MA Thesis, US Naval Postgraduate School, 2005, p. 29, in reference to Sunni insurgent activity in western Baghdad.

5. Oral presentations to BCT staff were paired with one- to two-page papers on relevant thematic issues thought to affect Tisa Nissan as a whole. "The Mahallah Mentality," for example, explained the dynamics beneath the city's traditional structure, and contextualized both the wide variation in conditions from one neighborhood to the next as well as proclivity of leadership figures (both in and out of government) to practice narrow habits of localism and patronage. The paper, as well as subsequent presentations on "The Unraveling of the Mahallah," and "Urban Tribalism and the Limitations of Sheikhs," addressed many of the issues detailed in Chapters One and Two of this book.
6. As a new program within the Department of Defense, Human Terrain Teams did not have operational doctrine to follow. The phased methodological approach detailed below was developed by the author and R. Kent (Team Leader of the HTT), as a way to address the particular challenges of Tisa Nissan.
7. Phase 1 interviews in Tisa Nissan were conducted by the author, R. Kent, P. Leddy, and A. Roosendaal.
8. From a methodological perspective, there was an inherent risk in structuring research around the views and opinions of the BCT. Taking the BCT's understanding of Tisa Nissan as the starting point for research had the potential to embed biases or misperceptions into the foundation of the research process. This risk was weighed against the potential benefits of gathering the information that had accumulated among the BCT's numerous constituent parts through the course of their experiences in the district, however, as by February 2008, elements of the BCT had been resident in Tisa Nissan for more than a year. Furthermore, the BCTs perspective on the district was regarded as fundamentally important to the HTT's

efforts to engage its decision-making processes. By understanding how and why the BCT saw Tisa Nissan as it did, the HTT would be better positioned to contribute to internal debates and to frame its input in a manner that would speak directly to the thoughts and perceptions of military decision-makers.

9. Deployed to Tisa Nissan in February of 2007, 2/16 IN was the first "Surge battalion" in Baghdad.
10. Maps were found to be a useful elicitation tool when interviewing military personnel with first-hand experience in the neighborhoods of the district. Asking interviewees to give a "guided tour" of the neighborhoods in which they had worked helped prompt recollections, and gave structure to discussions about the different sub-areas of each *hayy*.
11. The author conducted gap analysis during late March 2008. The author and R. Kent then created the team's research plan.
12. Furthermore, as the reconnaissance conducted during initial site visits had identified potential points of contact with the local population, the planning process sought to match information requirements with potential sources known to exist in the district in a structured collection plan. It was understood that collection efforts would require flexibility and adaptability on the part of team members, and that previously unknown or underappreciated issues would emerge and necessitate the adjustment of collection priorities, but a plan was nonetheless created to a high level of detail to provide structure and to facilitate initial collection efforts.
13. HTT personnel also worked closely with National Police Training Teams (NPTTs), the units responsible for mentoring and partnering with the 4–1 Iraqi National Police Brigade that was responsible for Tisa Nissan. This provided access not only to the resident population during joint operations, but also the opportunity to interview the policemen themselves—many of whom were underclass Shi'a from Baghdad with personal insight into the complexities of loyalty, responsibility, and culpability that affected Shi'a with Sadrist sympathies during the turmoil of the post-Saddam era.
14. Critics of the Human Terrain System have questioned the ethical practices of the program and the ability of HTT personnel to conduct legitimate research while attached to the military. For discussion of associated concerns, see: the American Anthropological Association's "AAA Commission on the Engagement of Anthropology with the US Security and Intelligence Communities, Final Report, 4 November 2007. The issue of informed consent and the complexities of conducting ethical fieldwork in a conflict environment were central themes of the training provided to HTT personnel (and, likewise, a subject of continuous and contentious extra-curricular debate among trainees). The concerns raised by the anthropological community were, in this respect, influential in setting the parameters of internal debate among academics within the program.
15. Political leaders and prominent local residents from areas generally amenable to the Surge were often comfortable meeting openly with team members at local government facilities or on American bases. After more than a year of counterinsurgency-inspired outreach efforts by Americans, such interactions were commonplace. Moreover, the subjects pursued by team members—relating to the personal stories and opinions of interviewees on a broad range of local, personal concerns (as distinct from the main focus of military personnel, which was information on the activities of militants and the progression of infrastructure projects)—were met with notable enthusiasm.

16. Residents of Central Kamaliyah and the core areas of Amin and Fedaliyah—places where the Mehdi Army had built a strong presence, and where Sadrist sympathies were near universal—proved remarkably eager, on the whole, to converse with team members within the confines of their homes. The Arabic language skills of team members were partially responsible for the rapport that was generated, but the focus of team members' inquiries (on aspects of local history and society, for example, as opposed to the insurgent-centric lines of questioning typically levied by American soldiers and Iraqi National Policemen) appeared to have been a substantially more important factor. Having spent much of the post-Saddam era hunkered down in their homes, finding few opportunities to vent their frustrations or share their feelings, the residents of Tisa Nissan proved willing to converse freely with team members—and to levy sharp condemnations of the pace of "progress" in the post-Saddam era, even when in the presence of American and Iraqi forces.
17. The decision to wear military uniforms or carry a weapon were made by individual team members in keeping with their assessment of local conditions. As a general rule, team members working in relatively secure environments and attending set meetings with established sources would dress in civilian clothes and remove armor and weapons for the interview process. When accompanying patrols through more dangerous areas, however, and engaging unknown persons in their homes and on the streets, team members would be uniformed and armed.
18. This was also a major concern facing intelligence officers, as discussed in Packer, *The Assassins' Gate: America in Iraq*, (London: Faber and Faber, 2006), pp. 230–3.
19. There was thus a distinction, and to some extent a conflict, between the role of the HTT as a research and analysis asset and its role as a facilitator of engagement between the BCT and the local populace. HTT personnel played both roles but, as far as was practicable, these functions were kept separate.
20. As evident through the course of this book, the HTT's study of Tisa Nissan amounted to the examination of the district through the prism of its violence. Civil society and the various features and fault lines of the human terrain were assessed for their relevance to the objectives and interests of the American military—creating a picture of Tisa Nissan that was by no means comprehensive. Indeed, researchers able to gain an insider's view into the communities of the district (an Iraqi sociologist of the Shi'a underclass, for example), would likely find entirely different sets of issues to examine and data points to evaluate, creating a valuable counterweight to the conflict-centric study presented in this book. Nonetheless, Anton Blok's *Honour and Violence*, (Cambridge: Polity Press, 2001), pp. 10–11 comments on the legitimacy of this practice in anthropology, where investigation may be undertaken "not to find out all about [a community], but with reference only to a limited problem stated in advance." The extraordinary stresses of the post-Saddam era proved illuminating in regard to the condition of civil society, making insurgent violence a particularly useful barometer in the qualitative measurement of communal integrity. Batatu, in *The Iraqi Revolution of 1958*, p. 211, noted similarly, in reference to Iraq, that, "it is in moments of great upheaval that societies are best studied."
21. For a pointed critique of the biases allegedly inherent in those who undertake academic research on behalf of the American government, and the assertion that any knowledge produced as a by-product of such a partnership is inevitably contaminated, see Edward

Said, *Orientalism*, (London: Penguin Books, 2007) particularly the preface, which emphasizes the centrality of motives in academic research.

22. Nicole Suveges, a Social Scientist with the Human Terrain System working in Sadr City, was killed in the bombing of a District Council facility on 24 June 2008.
23. Furthermore, there was broad understanding among American military personnel of the various motivations that might drive their "enemies" to take up arms. Statements along the lines of "if I lived here, I'd be in the militia," were commonplace among American officers and enlisted personnel alike, as the complexities and harsh realities of post-Saddam Baghdad were readily evident to those who experienced the city first hand. It was, therefore, uncontroversial to produce reporting that contextualized the motivations of Shi'a militants through reference to historical issues and contemporary politics.
24. Due to time constraints surrounding the pacing of American visits to Iraqi government facilities (which often precluded holding lengthy conversations following the conduct of official business), team members often met prospective sources at these semi-public locations, and then invited them to a follow-up interview on an American-controlled facility. This ensured privacy and security, and also that the interview would not be interrupted.
25. As such, the relevant references throughout this book do not cite the names of sources, but instead give the month and location of an encounter. In certain instances where aspects of a source's identity has bearing upon his or her opinion (the age of a source, for example, offering insight into the generation gap that developed within the rekindled Sadrist movement) the relevant details have been provided, but anonymity is maintained. More generally, however, citations throughout this work do not reference information particular to an individual source or contain direct quotations. Instead, fieldwork is cited to offer contextual support to analysis that is based on a wide pattern of observations.

BIBLIOGRAPHY

1. Hannah Batatu, *The Old Social Classes and the Revolutionary Movements of Iraq*, (London: Saqi, 2004); Faleh A. Jabar, *The Shi'ite Movement in Iraq*, (London: Saqi, 2003); Faleh Abdul-Jabar (ed.), *Ayatollahs, Sufis and Ideologues: State, Religion and Social Movements in Iraq*, (London: Saqi, 2003); Faleh A. Jabar and Hosham Dawod (eds), *Tribes and Power: Nationalism and Ethnicity in the Middle East*, (London: Saqi, 2003); Marion Farouk-Sluglett and Peter Sluglett, *Iraq Since 1958: From Revolution to Dictatorship* (London: IB Tauris, 1990); Peter Sluglett and Marion Farouk-Sluglett, "Some Reflections on the Sunni/Shi'i Question in Iraq," *British Society for Middle Eastern Studies*, Vol. 5, No. 2, 1978; Peter Sluglett and Marion Farouk-Sluglett, "The Transformation of Land Tenure and Rural Social Structure in Central and Southern Iraq, c. 1870–1958," *International Journal of Middle East Studies*, Vol. 15, No. 4, 1983; Tripp, *A History of Iraq*; Samira Haj, *The Making of Iraq, 1900–1963: Capital, Power and Ideology*, (Albany: SUNY Albany University Press, 1997); Yitzhak Nakash, *The Shi'is of Iraq*, (Princeton: Princeton University Press, 2003); Yitzhak Nakash, "The Conversion of Iraq's Tribes To Shiism," *International Journal of Middle East Studies*, Vol. 26, No. 3. August 1994.
2. W.A. Hilmi, *Internal Migration and Regional Policy in Iraq*, (University of Sheffield, Doctoral Dissertation, 1978); Doreen Warriner, *Land Reform and Development in the Middle East: A*

Study of Egypt, Syria, and Iraq, (Oxford: Oxford University Press, 1962); Doris Phillips, "Rural-to-Urban Migration in Iraq," *Economic Development and Cultural Change*, Vol. 7, No. 4, 1959; Batatu, *The Old Social Classes*.

3. Hilmi, *Internal Migration*; John Gulick, "Baghdad: Portrait of a City in Physical and Cultural Change," *Journal of the American Planning Association*, Vol. 33, No. 4, 1967; John Gulick, "Village and City: Cultural Continuities in Twentieth Century Middle Eastern Cultures," in Ira Lapidus (ed.), *Middle Eastern Cities: A Symposium on Ancient, Islamic, and Contemporary Middle Eastern Urbanism*, (Berkeley: University of California Press, 1969); Kahtan al-Madfai, "Baghdad," in Morroe Berger (ed.), *The New Metropolis in the Arab World*, (Bombay: Allied Publishers, 1963); Warriner, *Land Reform and Development*; Phillips, "Rural-to-Urban Migration"; Batatu, *The Old Social Classes*.
4. Batatu, *The Old Social Classes*; Hanna Batatu, "The Old Social Classes Revisited," in Robert Fernea & William Roger Louis (eds), *The Iraqi Revolution of 1958, The Old Social Classes Revisited*, (London: IB Tauris, 1991); Hanna Batatu, "Iraq's Shi'a, their Political Role, and the Process of their Integration into Society," in Barbara Stowasser (ed.), *The Islamic Impulse*, (London: Croom Helm, 1987); Uriel Dann, *Iraq Under Qassem: A Political History, 1958–1963*, (Jerusalem: Israel University Press, 1969); Roni Gabbay, *Communism and Agrarian Reform in Iraq*, (London: Croom Helm, 1978); Sluglett and Farouk-Sluglett, *Iraq Since 1958*; Haj, *The Making of Iraq*; Marr, *The Modern History of Iraq*.
5. Kanan Makiya, *Republic of Fear: The Politics of Modern Iraq*, (Berkely: University of California Press, 1998); Kanan Makiya, *Cruelty and Silence: War, Tyranny, Uprising, and the Arab World*, (London: Jonathan Cape, 1993); Efraim Karsh and Inari Rautsi, *Saddam Hussein: A Political Biography*, (New York: The Free Press, 1991); Hannah Batatu, "Shi'i Organizations in Iraq: al-Da'wa al-Islamiyah and al-Mujahidin," in Juan Cole and Nikki Keddie (eds), *Shi'ism and Social Protest*, (New Haven: Yale University Press, 1986); Hannah Batatu, "Iraq's Shi'a"; Hannah Batatu, "Iraq's Underground Shi'a Movements: Characteristics, Causes and Prospects," *Middle East Institute*, Vol. 35, No. 4, Autumn 1981; Jabar, *The Shi'ite Movement*; Sluglett and Farouk-Sluglett, "Some Reflections on the Sunni/Shi'i Question."
6. Marion Farouk-Sluglett and Joe Stork, "Not Quite Armageddon: The Impact of the War on Iraq," *MERIP Reports*, No. 125–126, July–September 1984; Karsh and Rautsi, *Saddam Hussein*; Abbas Alnasrawi, *The Economy of Iraq: Oil, Wars, Destruction & Development and Prospects, 1950–2010*, (London: Greenwood Press, 1994); Abbas Alnasrawi, "Economic Devastation, Underdevelopment and Outlook," in Fran Hazelton (ed.), *Iraq Since the Gulf War: Prospects for Democracy*, (London: Zed Books, 1994); Amatzia Baram, "The Ruling Political Elite in Bathi Iraq, 1968–1986: The Changing Features of a Collective Profile," *International Journal of Middle East Studies*, Vol. 21, No. 4, 1989; Patrick Clawson, "Iraq's Economy and International Sanctions," in Amatzia Baram and Barry Rubin (eds), *Iraq's Road to War*, (London: MacMillan, 1994).
7. Amatzia Baram, "Neo-Tribalism in Iraq: Saddam Hussein's Tribal Policies, 1991–1996," *International Journal of Middle East Studies*, Vol. 29, No. 1, 1997; Jabar, *The Shi'ite Movement*; Faleh A. Jabar, "Shaykhs and Ideologues: Detribalization and Retribalization in Iraq, 1968–1998," *Middle East Report*, No. 215, Summer 2001; Faleh A. Jabar, "The War Generation in Iraq: A Case of Failed Etatist Nationalism," in Lawrence Potter and Gary Sick (eds), *Iran, Iraq and the Legacies of War*, (New York: Palgrave MacMillan, 2004); Faleh A. Jabar, "Clerics,

Tribes, Ideologies and Urban Dwellers in the South of Iraq: the Potential for Rebellion," in Toby Dodge and Steven Simon (eds), *Iraq at the Crossroads: State and Society in the Shadow of Regime Change*, (Oxford: Oxford University Press, 2003); Isam al-Khafaji, "State Terror and the Degradation of Politics," in Fran Hazelton (ed.), *Iraq Since the Gulf War: Prospects for Democracy*, (London: Zed Books, 1994); Isam al-Khafaji, "A Few Days After: State and Society in a post-Saddam Iraq," in *Iraq at the Crossroads*; Jerry Long, *Saddam's War of Words: Politics, Religion, and the Iraqi Invasion of Kuwait*, (Austin: University of Texas Press, 2004); Sluglett and Farouk-Sluglett, *Iraq Since 1958*.

8. Cockburn, *Muqtada al-Sadr*; International Crisis Group, "Iraq Backgrounder: What Lies Beneath," *Middle East Report*, No. 6, 1 October 2002; International Crisis Group, "Iraq's Muqtada al-Sadr: Spoiler or Stabilizer?" *Middle East Report*, No. 55, 11 July 2006; Ali A. Allawi, *The Occupation of Iraq: Winning the War, Losing the Peace*, (New Haven: Yale University Press, 2007); Anthony Shadid, *Night Draws Near*, (New York: Picador, 2005); Fouad Ajami; *The Foreigner's Gift: The Americans, The Arabs and the Iraqis in Iraq*, (New York: Free Press, 2006).
9. Jabar, *The Shi'ite Movement*; Jabar, "The War Generation in Iraq: A Case of Failed Etatist Nationalism"; Faleh Abdul-Jabbar, "Why the *Intifada* Failed," Fatima Mohsen, "Cultural Totalitarianism," Abbas Alnasrawi, "Economic Devastation, Underdevelopment and Outlook," and Ayad Rahim, "Attitudes to the West, Arabs and Fellow Iraqis," all in *Iraq Since the Gulf War*; Al-Khafaji, "A Few Days After: State and Society in a post-Saddam Iraq," and Jabar, "Clerics, Tribes, Ideologies and Urban Dwellers in the South of Iraq: the Potential for Rebellion"; Kenneth M. Pollack, *The Threatening Storm: The Case for Invading Iraq*, (New York: Random House, 2002); Peter Munson, *Iraq in Transition: The Legacy of Dictatorship and the Prospects for Democracy*, (Washington: Potomac Books, 2009); Peter Munson, "What Lies Beneath: Saddam's Legacy and the Roots of Resistance in Iraq," M.A. Thesis, US Naval Postgraduate School, December 2005; Makiya, *Republic of Fear*; Makiya, *Cruelty and Silence*; Sarah Graham-Brown, "Sanctioning Iraq: A Failed Policy," *Middle East Report*, No. 215, Summer 2000.
10. International Crisis Group, "Shiite Politics in Iraq"; International Crisis Group, "Iraq's Muqtada al-Sadr"; International Crisis Group, "The Next Iraqi War? Sectarianism and Civil Conflict," *Middle East Report*, No. 52, 27 February 2006; International Crisis Group, "Iraq's Civil War, The Sadrists and the Surge"; Cochrane, "Special Groups"; Cochrane, "The Battle for Basra"; Cochrane, "The Fragmentation of the Sadrist Movement."
11. Allawi, *The Occupation of Iraq*; Cockburn, *Muqtada al-Sadr*; Shadid, *Night Draws Near*; Kagan, *The Surge*; Ahmed Hashim, *Insurgency and Counter-Insurgency in Iraq*, (Ithaca: Cornell University Press, 2006); Cordesman, "Sadr and the Mahdi Army"; Anthony Cordesman and Emma Davies, *Iraq's Insurgency and the Road to Civil Conflict*, Vols 1 & 2, (Westport: Praeger Security International, 2008); Anthony Cordesman, "Iraq: Creating a Strategic Partnership," *CSIS*, "Third Review Draft," 2 February 2010; Munson, *Iraq in Transition*; Kilcullen, *The Accidental Guerilla*; Ashraf al-Khalidi and Victor Tanner, "Sectarian Violence: Radical Groups Drive Displacement," *The Brookings Institution—University of Bern Project on International Displacement*, October 2006; Jamille Bigio and Jen Scott, "Internal Displacement in Iraq: The Process of Working Toward Durable Solutions," *The Brookings Institution—University of Bern Project on International Displacement*, June 2009.

12. Contextual and methodological concerns relating to the conduct of fieldwork that is utilized in these chapters are presented in Appendix A, while issues particular to specific areas or circumstances are detailed in footnotes within each chapter.
13. David Finkel, *The Good Soldiers*, (New York: Sarah Crichton Books, 2009); International Crisis Group, "Iraq's Civil War, the Sadrists and the Surge"; Cochrane, "The Fragmentation of the Sadrist Movement"; Cochrane, "Special Groups."
14. Hilmi, *Internal Migration*; Batatu, *The Old Social Classes*; Gulick, "Baghdad: Portrait of a City."

BIBLIOGRAPHY

The first two chapters of this book are based upon academic sources from a variety of disciplines. Chapter one's discussion of Ottoman-ruled Mesopotamia and early Iraqi history draws from the historical scholarship of Hanna Batatu, Faleh Abdul Jabar, Peter Sluglett and Marion Farouk-Sluglett, Charles Tripp, and Samira Haj; while treatment of the mass-conversions to Shi'ism that took place during the late nineteenth and early twentieth centuries also benefits from the work of Yitzhak Nakash.[1] The ensuing study of the sweeping rural-to-urban migrations of the twentieth century builds principally from the voluminous doctoral dissertation of W.A. Hilmi, supported by the writings of Doreen Warriner, Doris Phillips, and Batatu.[2] Hilmi's work is likewise central to the discussion of Baghdad at mid century, supplemented by the urban studies-centric insights of John Gulick, Kahtan al-Madfai, Warriner, and Phillips, as well as the historical observations of Batatu.[3] For contextual information on Iraqi politics during the middle decades of the twentieth century and the dynamics of the 1958 revolution and its aftermath, the works of Batatu, Uriel Dann, Haj, the Slugletts, Roni Gabbay, and Phebe Marr are used most prominently.[4] Concluding chapter one, discussion of Ba'th Party rule and its implications for Iraqi society relies most heavily on the work of Kanan Makiya and Efraim Karsh; while treatment of the Ba'th regime's posture toward its Shi'a subjects is based largely upon the work of Jabar, the Slugletts, and Batatu.[5]

Chapter two's survey of the Iraqi state's declining fortunes from the late 1980s draws from an array of authors, including the Slugletts, Karsh, Abbas Alnasrawi, Amatzia Baram, and Patrick Clawson.[6] The ensuing discussion of the changes that swept Iraqi society as a result of the state's contraction (principally via the rise of tribalism, popular religiosity, and efforts of the state to manipulate and control both) relies heavily on the work of Baram and Jabar, benefiting also from the insights of Isam al-Khafaji, Jerry Long, and the Slugletts.[7] The discussion of Mohammed Mohammed Sadiq al-Sadr's career is built principally from Patrick Cockburn's biography of Muqtada al-Sadr, the post-Saddam era reporting of the International Crisis Group, and a variety of non-academic works on post-Saddam Iraq such as those of Ali Allawi, Anthony Shadid, and Fouad Ajami.[8] Lastly, analysis of the hardships of the sanctions era and their impact on Iraqi society draws from numerous authors, including Jabar, Kenneth Pollack, Peter Munson, Makiya, and Sarah Graham-Brown.[9]

Chapter three's account of the Mehdi Army's rise and fall builds from the observations and experiences of the author, while also relying heavily upon a fairly narrow range of sources—

reflecting the limited and often duplicative nature of much of the literature of post-Saddam Iraq. Most useful, and most widely cited, were the publications of the International Crisis Group and the Institute for the Study of War.[10] The former provided balanced insights into macro- and micro-level political and social developments, while the latter offered a quasi-official account of American efforts that benefits from the principal authors' close ties to the American military. Press accounts and non-academic works on post-Saddam Iraq such as those of Allawi, Cockburn, and Shadid are used intermittently; while the works of authors affiliated with the American defense establishment (some of whom participated in the conflict) such as Kimberly Kagan, Ahmed Hashim, Anthony Cordesman, Munson and David Kilcullen are cited along with material disseminated by think-tanks such as the Brookings Institution.[11]

From chapter four through to the end of the book, analysis is based largely on primary research conducted in Baghdad. The observations and experiences of the author, his colleagues on a Human Terrain Team (HTT), and those of the American military personnel whom the HTT supported during 2008 provide the core source material from which analysis is conducted.[12] Secondary sources are also used to further substantiate observations and analysis, most notably David Finkel's account of 2–16 Infantry Battalion's deployment to eastern Tisa Nissan during the Surge, the reporting of the International Crisis Group on events in Baghdad (which contain footnotes that offer invaluable local specificity), and the Institute for the Study of War's writings on American military operations and the dynamics of Shi'a violence.[13] Assorted supplementary sources from policy organizations are also used, along with historical insights from Hilmi, Batatu, Gulick and others.[14]

Books

Aburish, Said K., *Saddam Hussein: Politics of Revenge*, (London: Bloomsbury, 2000).
Ajami, Fouad, *The Arab Predicament*, (Cambridge: Cambridge University Press, 1999).
Ajami, Fouad, *The Foreigner's Gift: The Americans, The Arabs and the Iraqis in Iraq*, (New York: Free Press, 2006).
Ali, Hassan Mohammed, *Land Reclamation and Settlement in Iraq*, (Baghdad: Baghdad Printing Press, 1955).
Allawi, Ali, *The Occupation of Iraq: Winning the War, Losing the Peace*, (New Haven: Yale University Press, 2007).
Alnasrawi, Abbas, *The Economy of Iraq: Oil, Wars, Destruction & Development and Prospects, 1950–2010*, (London: Greenwood Press, 1994).
Anderson, Benedict, *Imagined Communities: Reflections on the Origin and Spread of Nationalism*, (London: Verso, 2006).
Arendt, Hannah, *The Origins of Totalitarianism*, (San Diego: Harcourt Brace, 1973).
Arnove, Anthony (ed.), *Iraq Under Siege: The Deadly Impact of Sanctions and War*, (London: Pluto Press, 2000).
al-Arif, Ismael, *Iraq Reborn: A Firsthand Account of the July 1958 Revolution and After*, (New York: Vantage Press, 1982).
Atiyyah, Ghassan, *Iraq: 1908–1921*, (Beirut: The Arab Institute for Research and Publishing, 1973).
Axelgard, Frederick, *A New Iraq? The Gulf War and Implications for US Policy*, (New York: Praeger, 1988).

BIBLIOGRAPHY

Baali, Fuad, *Society, State, and Urbanism: Ibn Khaldun's Sociological Thought*, (Albany: SUNY Albany Press, 1988).

Baram, Amatzia and Barry Rubin (eds), *Iraq's Road to War*, (London: MacMillan, 1994).

Batatu, Hanna, *The Old Social Classes and the Revolutionary Movements of Iraq*, (London: Saqi, 2004).

Bell, Colin and Howard Newby, *Community Studies: An Introduction to the Sociology of the Local Community*, (London: George Allen and Unwin, 1971).

Bengio, Ofra, *Saddam's Word: Political Discourse in Iraq*, (Oxford: Oxford University Press, 1998).

Berger, Morroe (ed.), *The New Metropolis in the Arab World*, (Bombay: Allied Publishers, 1963).

Blake, G.H. and R.I. Lawless (eds), *The Changing Middle Eastern City*, (London: Croom Helm, 1980).

Blok, Anton, *Honour and Violence*, (Cambridge: Polity Press, 2001).

Bonine, Michael E. (ed.), *Population, Poverty, and Politics in Middle Eastern Cities*, (Gainsville: U Florida Press, 1997).

Bremer, L. Paul III and Malcolm McConnell, *My Year in Iraq: The Struggle to Build a Future of Hope*, (New York: Simon & Schuster, 2006).

Buzzell, Colby, *My War: Killing Time in Iraq*, (London: Penguin, 2005).

Byman, Daniel and Kenneth Pollack, *Things Fall Apart: Containing the Spillover from an Iraqi Civil War*, (Washington: Brookings Institution Press, 2007).

CARDRI, *Saddam's Iraq: Revolution or Reaction?* (London: Zed Books, 1989).

Casper, Gretchen, *Fragile Democracies: The Legacies of Authoritarian Rule*, (Pittsburgh: Pittsburgh University Press, 1996).

Chandraseskaran, Rajiv, *Imperial Life in the Emerald City: Inside Iraq's Green Zone*, (New York: Knopf, 2006).

Cleveland, William, *The Making of An Arab Nationalist: Ottomanism and Arabism in the Life and Thought of Sati' al-Husri*, (Princeton: Princeton University Press, 1971).

Cockburn, Patrick, *Muqtada al-Sadr and the Shia Insurgency in Iraq*, (London: Faber and Faber, 2009).

Cole, Juan, *Sacred Space and Holy War: The Politics, Culture and History of Shi'ite Islam*, (London: IB Tauris, 2005).

Cole, Juan and Nikkie Keddie (eds), *Shi'ism and Social Protest*, (New Haven: Yale University Press, 1986).

Cordesman, Anthony and Emma Davies, *Iraq's Insurgency and the Road to Civil Conflict*, Vols 1 & 2, (Westport: Praeger Security International, 2008).

Cortright, David and George Lopez, *The Sanctions Decade: Assessing UN Strategies in the 1990s*, (Boulder: Lynne Riener, 2000).

Dann, Uriel, *Iraq Under Qassim: A Political History, 1958–1963*, (Jerusalem: Israel University Press, 1969).

Della Porta, Donna and Mario Diani, *Social Movements: An Introduction*, (Oxford: Blackwell, 1999).

Diamond, Larry and Marc Plattner (eds), *Nationalism, Ethnic Conflict, and Democracy*, (Baltimore: Johns Hopkins University Press, 1994).

Dodge, Toby, *Inventing Iraq: The Failure of Nation Building and a History Denied*, (London: Hurst & Co., 2003).

Dodge, Toby and Steven Simon (eds), *Iraq at the Crossroads: State and Society in the Shadow of Regime Change*, (Oxford: Oxford University Press, 2003).
Eickelman, Dale F., *The Middle East: An Anthropological Approach*, (New Jersey: Pretence Hall, 1989).
Esfandiari, Haleh and A.L. Udovitch (eds), *The Economic Dimensions of Middle Eastern History: Essays in Honor of Charles Issawi*, (Princeton: The Darwin Press, 1990).
Etherington, Mark, *Revolt on the Tigris: The Al-Sadr Uprising and the Governing of Iraq*, (Ithaca: Cornell University Press, 2005).
Fernea, Elizabeth W., *Guests of the Sheik: An Ethnography of an Iraqi Village*, (London: Robert Hale, 1968).
Fernea, Robert, *Shaykh and Effendi: Changing Patterns of Authority Among the el Shabana of Southern Iraq*, (Cambridge: Harvard University Press, 1970).
Fernea, Robert and William Roger Louis (eds), *The Iraqi Revolution of 1958, The Old Social Classes Revisited*, (London: IB Tauris, 1991).
Freedman, Lawrence and Efraim Karsh *The Gulf Conflict 1990–1991: Diplomacy and War in the New World Order*, (Princeton: Princeton University Press, 1993).
Filkins, Dexter, *The Forever War* (New York: Vintage Books, 2009).
Finkel, David, *The Good Soldiers*, (New York: Sarah Crichton Books, 2009).
Fukuyama, Francis, *Trust: The Social Virtues and the Creation of Prosperity*, (New York: The Free Press, 1995).
Gabbay, Roni, *Communism and Agrarian Reform in Iraq*, (London: Croom Helm, 1978).
Galula, David, *Counterinsurgency Warfare: Theory and Practice*, (London: Praeger Security International, 2006).
Gordon, Michael and Bernard Trainor, *Cobra II: The Inside Story of the Invasion and Occupation of Iraq*, (London: Atlantic Books, 2006).
Graham, Steven (ed.), *Cities, War, and Terrorism: Towards an Urban Geopolitics*, (Oxford: Blackwell, 2004).
Guha, Ranajit and Gayatri Chakravorty (eds), Selected Subaltern Studies, (Oxford: Oxford University Press, 1988).
Hagedorn, John (ed.), *Gangs in the Global City: Alternatives to Traditional Criminology*, (Urbana: University of Illinois Press, 2007).
Haj, Samira, *The Making of Iraq, 1900–1963: Capital, Power and Ideology*, (Albany: SUNY Albany University Press, 1997).
Halpern, Manfred, *The Politics of Social Change in the Middle East and North Africa*, (Princeton: Princeton University Press, 1963).
Hashim, Ahmed, *Insurgency and Counter-Insurgency in Iraq*, (Ithaca: Cornell University Press, 2006).
Hazelton, Fran (ed.), CARDRI, *Iraq Since the Gulf War: Prospects for Democracy*, (London: Zed Books, 1994).
Herring, Eric and Glen Rangwala, *Iraq in Fragments: The Occupation and its Legacy*, (Ithaca: Cornell University Press, 2006).
Hiro, Dilip, *The Longest War: The Iran-Iraq Military Conflict*, (New York: Routledge, 1991).
Hobsbawm, Eric, *Bandits*, (London: Weidenfeld & Nicolson, 2000).
Ismael, Tareq, *The Rise and Fall of the Communist Party of Iraq*, (Cambridge: Cambridge University Press, 2007).

Jabar, Faleh A., *The Shi'ite Movement in Iraq*, (London: Saqi, 2003).
Jabar, Faleh, A. and Hosham Dawood (eds), *Tribes and Power: Nationalism and Ethnicity in the Middle East*, (London: Saqi, 2003).
Jabar, Faleh A. (ed.), *Ayatollahs, Sufis and Ideologues: State, Religion and Social Movements in Iraq*, (London: Saqi, 2002).
Jalal, Ferhang, *The Role of Government in the Industrialization of Iraq 1950–1965*, (London: Frank Cass, 1972).
Jankowski, James and Israel Gershoni (eds), *Rethinking Nationalism in the Arab, Middle East* (New York: Columbia University Press, 1997).
Kagan, Kimberly, *The Surge: A Military History*, (New York: Encounter, 2009).
Karsh, Efraim, *Essential Histories: The Iran Iraq War, 1980–1988*, (London: Osprey Publishing, 2002).
Karsh, Efraim and Inari Rautsi, *Saddam Hussein: A Political Biography*, (New York: The Free Press, 1991).
Kelidar, Abbas (ed.), *The Integration of Modern Iraq*, (London: Croom Helm, 1979).
Khadduri, Majid, *Republican Iraq: A Study in Iraqi Politics Since the Revolution of 1958*, (London: Oxford University Press, 1969).
Khoury, Philip and Joseph Kostiner (eds), *Tribes and State Formation in the Middle East*, (Berkeley: University of California Press, 1990).
Kilcullen, David, *The Accidental Guerilla: Fighting Small Wars in the Midst of a Big One*, (London: Hurst & Co., 2009).
Lapidus, Ira (ed.), *Middle Eastern Cities: A Symposium on Ancient, Islamic, and Contemporary Middle Eastern Urbanism*, (Berkeley: University of California Press, 1969).
Long, Jerry, *Saddam's War of Words: Politics, Religion, and the Iraqi Invasion of Kuwait*, (Austin: University of Texas Press, 2004).
Mahdi, Kamil (ed.), *Iraq's Economic Predicament*, (Reading: Ithaca Press, 2002).
Makiya, Kanan, *Republic of Fear: The Politics of Modern Iraq*, (Berkely: University of California Press, 1998).
——— *Cruelty and Silence: War, Tyranny, Uprising, and the Arab World*, (London: Jonathan Cape, 1993).
Mansoor, Peter, *Baghdad at Sunrise: A Brigade Commander's War in Iraq*, (New Haven: Yale University Press, 2008).
Marr, Phebe, *The Modern History of Iraq*, (Boulder: Westview Press, 2004).
Marston, Daniel and Carter Malkasian (eds), *Counterinsurgency in Modern Warfare*, (Oxford: Osprey, 2008).
Matar, Fuad, *Saddam Hussein: A Biographical and Ideological Account of His Leadership Style and Crisis Management*, (London: Highlight Production, 1990).
Munson, Peter, *Iraq in Transition: The Legacy of Dictatorship and the Prospects for Democracy*, (Washington: Potomac Books, 2009).
Nagl, John A., *Learning to Eat Soup with a Knife: Counterinsurgency Lessons from Malaya to Vietnam*, (Chicago: University of Chicago Press, 2005).
Nakash, Yitzhak, *The Shi'is of Iraq*, (Princeton: Princeton University Press, 2003).
——— *Reaching for Power: The Shi'a in the Modern Arab World*, (Princeton: Princeton University Press, 2006).

Nasr, Vali, *The Shi'a Revival: How Conflicts Within Islam Will Shape the Future*, (New York: W.W. Norton, 2007).

Nicholson, Emma and Peter Clark (eds), *The Iraqi Marshlands: A Human and Environmental Study*, (London: Politicos Publishing, 2002).

Packer, George, *The Assassins' Gate: America in Iraq*, (London: Faber and Faber, 2006).

Penrose, Edith and E.F., *Iraq: International Relations and National Development*, (London: Ernest Benn, 1978).

Pollack, Kenneth M., *The Threatening Storm: The Case for Invading Iraq*, (New York: Random House, 2002).

Potter, Lawrence and Gary Sick (eds), *Iran, Iraq and the Legacies of War*, (New York: Palgrave MacMillan, 2004).

Qubain, Fahim, *The Reconstruction of Iraq: 1950–1957*, (New York: Frederick A. Praeger, 1958).

Redfield, Robert, *The Little Community and Peasant Society and Culture*, (Chicago: University of Chicago Press, 1967).

Ricks, Thomas, *Fiasco: The American Military Adventure in Iraq*, (London: Penguin Books, 2006).

Riverbend, *Baghdad Burning: Girl Blog from Iraq*, (London: Marion Boyers, 2005).

Robinson, Linda, *Tell Me How This Ends: General David Petraeus and the Search for a Way Out of Iraq*, (New York: PublicAffairs, 2008).

Sageman, Marc, *Understanding Terror Networks*, (Philadelphia: University of Pennsylvania Press, 2004).

Said, Edward, *Orientalism*, (London: Penguin Books, 2007).

Salzman, Philip Carl, *Culture and Conflict in the Middle East*, (Amherst: Humanity Books, 2008).

Sassoon, Joseph, *The Iraqi Refugees: The New Crisis in the Middle East*, (London: IB Tauris, 2011).

——— *Saddam Hussein's Bath Party: Inside an Authoritarian Regime*, (Cambridge: Cambridge University Press, 2012).

Scott, John, *Social Network Analysis: A Handbook*, (London: SAGE, 2000).

Schwedler, Jillian (ed.), *Toward Civil Society in the Middle East?* (London: Lynne Rienner, 1995).

Seligman, Adam, *The Problem of Trust*, (Princeton: Princeton University Press, 1997).

Shadid, Anthony, *Night Draws Near*, (New York: Picador, 2005).

Simmel, Georg (trans. Rienhard Bendix), *The Web of Group Affiliations*, (New York: The Free Press, 1955).

Simmel, Georg (trans. Kurt Wolff), *Conflict*, (New York: The Free Press, 1955).

Simons, Geoff, *Iraq: From Sumer to Post-Saddam*, (Hampshire: Palgrave Macmillan, 2004).

Sluglett, Peter, *Britain in Iraq: 1914–1932*, (London: Ithaca Press, 1976).

Sluglett, Peter, and Marion Farouk-Sluglett, *Iraq Since 1958: From Revolution to Dictatorship*, (London: IB Tauris, 1990).

Stansfield, Gareth, *Iraq: People, History, Politics*, (Cambridge: Polity, 2007).

Stewart, Rory, *The Prince of the Marshes and other Occupational Hazards of a Year in Iraq*, (Orlando: Harcourt, 2006).

Stowasser, Barbara (ed.), *The Islamic Impulse*, (London: Croom Helm, 1987).

Tarbush, Mohammed, *The Role of the Military in Politics: A Case Study of Iraq to 1941*, (London: Keegan Paul, 1982).

Thesiger, Wilfred, *The Marsh Arabs*, (London: Longmans, Green & Co., 1964).

Tripp, Charles, *A History of Iraq*, (Cambridge: Cambridge University Press, 2007).
Tse-tung, Mao (trans. Samuel B. Griffith), *On Guerilla Warfare*, (BN Publishing, 2007).
Warriner, Doreen, *Land Reform and Development in the Middle East: A Study of Egypt, Syria, and Iraq*, (Oxford: Oxford University Press, 1962).
Wasserman, Stanley and Katherine Faust, *Social Network Analysis: Methods and Applications*, (Cambridge: Cambridge University Press, 1994).
Weatherford, Jack, *Genghis Khan and the Making of the Modern World*, (New York: Crown Publishers, 2004).
West, Bing, *The Strongest Tribe: War, Politics, and the Endgame in Iraq*, (New York: Random House, 2008).
Workman, W. Thom, *The Social Origins of the Iran-Iraq War*, (London: Lynn & Rienner Publishing, 1994).

Chapters

Alnasrawi, Abbas, "Economic Devastation, Underdevelopment and Outlook," in Hazelton, Fran (ed.), CARDRI, *Iraq Since the Gulf War: Prospects for Democracy*, (London: Zed Books, 1994).
Alwan, Arif, "Charter 91," in Hazelton, Fran (ed.), CARDRI, *Iraq Since the Gulf War: Prospects for Democracy*, (London: Zed Books, 1994).
Baram, Amatzia and Barry Rubin, "Introduction," in Baram, Amatzia and Barry Rubin (eds), *Iraq's Road to War*, (London: MacMillan, 1994).
——— "The Iraqi Invasion of Kuwait: Decision-making in Baghdad," in Baram, Amatzia and Barry Rubin (eds), *Iraq's Road to War*, (London: MacMillan, 1994).
Batatu, Hanna, "Shi'i Organizations in Iraq: al-Da'wa al-Islamiyah and al-Mujahidin," in Cole, Juan and Nikkie Keddie (eds), *Shi'ism and Social Protest*, (New Haven: Yale University Press, 1986).
——— "Iraq's Shi'a, their Political Role, and the Process of their Integration into Society," in Stowasser, Barbara (ed.), *The Islamic Impulse*, (London: Croom Helm, 1987).
——— "The Old Social Classes Revisited," in Fernea, Robert and William Roger Louis (eds), *The Iraqi Revolution of 1958, The Old Social Classes Revisited*, (London: IB Tauris, 1991).
al-Bayati, Hamid, "Destruction of the Southern Marshes," in Hazelton, Fran (ed.), CARDRI, *Iraq Since the Gulf War: Prospects for Democracy*, (London: Zed Books, 1994).
Bengio, Ofra, "Iraq's Shi'a and Kurdish Communities: From Resentment to Revolt," in Baram, Amatzia and Barry Rubin (eds), *Iraq's Road to War*, (London: MacMillan, 1994).
Blake, G.H., and R.I. Lawless, "The Urban Future," in Blake, G.H. and R.I. Lawless (eds), *The Changing Middle Eastern City*, (London: Croom Helm, 1980).
Bonine, Michael E., "Population, Poverty, and Politics: Contemporary Middle East Cities in Crisis," in Bonine, Michael E. (ed.), *Population, Poverty, and Politics in Middle Eastern Cities*, (Gainsville: U Florida Press, 1997).
Bonte, Pierre, "Ibn Khaldun and Contemporary Anthropology: Cycles and Factional Alliances of Tribe and State in the Maghreb," in Jabar, Faleh, A. and Hosham Dawod (eds), *Tribes and Power: Nationalism and Ethnicity in the Middle East*, (London: Saqi, 2003).
Bowman, Kirk S. and Jerrold D. Green, "Urbanization and Political Instability in the Middle East," in Bonine, Michael E. (ed.), *Population, Poverty, and Politics in Middle Eastern Cities*, (Gainsville: U Florida Press, 1997).

Brotherton, David C., "Toward the Gang as a Social Movement," in Hagedorn, John (ed.), *Gangs in the Global City: Alternatives to Traditional Criminology*, (Urbana: University of Illinois Press, 2007).

Caton, Steven, "Anthropological Theories of Tribe and State Formation in the Middle East: Ideology and the Semiotics of Power," in Khoury, Philip and Joseph Kostiner (eds), *Tribes and State Formation in the Middle East*, (Berkeley: University of California Press, 1990).

Chaudhry, Kiren Aziz "Consuming Interests: Market Failure and the Social Foundations of Iraqi Etatisme," in Mahdi, Kamil (ed.), *Iraq's Economic Predicament*, (Reading: Ithaca Press, 2002).

Clawson, Patrick, "Iraq's Economy and International Sanctions," in Baram, Amatzia and Barry Rubin (eds), *Iraq's Road to War*, (London: MacMillan, 1994).

Cole, Juan and Nikkie Keddie, "Introduction," in Cole, Juan and Nikkie Keddie (eds), *Shi'ism and Social Protest*, (New Haven: Yale University Press, 1986).

Conte, Edouard, "Agnatic Illusions: The Element of Choice in Arab Kinship," in Jabar, Faleh, A. and Hosham Dawod (eds), *Tribes and Power: Nationalism and Ethnicity in the Middle East*, (London: Saqi, 2003).

Dawood, Hosham, "The 'State-ization' of the Tribe and the Tribalization of the State: the Case of Iraq," in Jabar, Faleh, A. and Hosham Dawood (eds), *Tribes and Power: Nationalism and Ethnicity in the Middle East*, (London: Saqi, 2003).

Dodge, Toby, "The Social Ontology of Late Colonialism: Tribes and the Mandated State in Iraq," in Jabar, Faleh, A. and Hosham Dawod (eds), *Tribes and Power: Nationalism and Ethnicity in the Middle East*, (London: Saqi, 2003).

Farouk-Sluglett, Marion and Peter Sluglett, "Iraqi Ba'thism: Nationalism, Socialism and National Socialism," in CARDRI, *Saddam's Iraq: Revolution or Reaction?* (London: Zed Books, 1989).

——— "The Social Classes and the Origins of the Revolution," in Fernea, Robert and William Roger Louis (eds), *The Iraqi Revolution of 1958, The Old Social Classes Revisited*, (London: IB Tauris, 1991).

Fernea, Robert, "State and Tribe in Southern Iraq: The struggle for Hegemony before the 1958 Revolution," in Fernea, Robert and William Roger Louis (eds), *The Iraqi Revolution of 1958, The Old Social Classes Revisited*, (London: IB Tauris, 1991).

Gazder, Haris and Athar Hussein, "Crisis and Response: A Study of the Impact of Economic Sanctions in Iraq," in Mahdi, Kamil (ed.), *Iraq's Economic Predicament*, (Reading: Ithaca Press, 2002).

Gellner, Ernest, "Tribalism and the State in the Middle East," in Khoury, Philip and Joseph Kostiner (eds), *Tribes and State Formation in the Middle East*, (Berkeley: University of California Press, 1990).

Gershoni, Israel, "Rethinking the Formation of Arab Nationalism in the Middle East, 1920–1945: Old and New Narratives," in Jankowski, James and Israel Gershoni (eds), *Rethinking Nationalism in the Arab Middle East*, (New York: Columbia University Press, 1997).

Graham, Steven, "Cities as Strategic Sites: Place Annihilation and Urban Geopolitics," in Graham, Steven (ed.), *Cities, War, and Terrorism: Towards and Urban Geopolitics*, (Oxford: Blackwell, 2004).

Greenshields, T.H., "'Quarters' and Ethnicity," in Blake, G.H. and R.I. Lawless (eds), *The Changing Middle Eastern City*, (London: Croom Helm, 1980).

Guha, Ranajit, "The Prose of Counter-Insurgency," in Guha, Ranajit and Gayatri Chakravorty (eds), Selected Subaltern Studies, (Oxford: Oxford University Press, 1988).
Gulick, John, "Village and City: Cultural Continuities in Twentieth Century Middle Eastern Cultures," in Lapidus, Ira (ed.), *Middle Eastern Cities: A Symposium on Ancient, Islamic, and Contemporary Middle Eastern Urbanism*, (Berkeley: University of California Press, 1969).
Heine, Peter, "Zghurt and Shmurt: Aspects of Traditional Shi'i Society," in Jabar, Faleh Abdul (ed.), *Ayatollahs, Sufis and Ideologues: State, Religion and Social Movements in Iraq*, (London: Saqi, 2002).
Heller, Mark A., "Iraq's Army: Military Weakness, Political Utility," in Baram, Amatzia and Barry Rubin (eds), *Iraq's Road to War*, (London: MacMillan, 1994).
Horowitz, David, "Democracy in Divided Societies," in Diamond, Larry and Marc Plattner (eds), *Nationalism, Ethnic Conflict, and Democracy*, (Baltimore: Johns Hopkins University Press, 1994).
Hourani, Albert, "Conclusion: Tribes and States in Islamic History," in Khoury, Philip and Joseph Kostiner (eds), *Tribes and State Formation in the Middle East*, (Berkeley: University of California Press, 1990).
Humadi, Zuhair, "Civil Society Under the Ba'th in Iraq," in Schwedler, Jillian (ed.), *Toward Civil Society in the Middle East?* (London: Lynne Rienner, 1995).
Issawi, Charles, "Economic Change and Urbanization in the Middle East," in Lapidus, Ira (ed.), *Middle Eastern Cities: A Symposium on Ancient, Islamic, and Contemporary Middle Eastern Urbanism*, (Berkeley: University of California Press, 1969).
Jabar, Faleh A., "Why the *Intifada* Failed," in Hazelton, Fran (ed.), CARDRI, *Iraq Since the Gulf War: Prospects for Democracy*, (London: Zed Books, 1994).
——— "The Genesis and Development of Marja'ism versus the State," in Jabar, Faleh Abdul (ed.), *Ayatollahs, Sufis and Ideologues: State, Religion and Social Movements in Iraq*, (London: Saqi, 2002).
——— "Sheikhs and Ideologues: Deconstruction and Reconstruction of Tribes under Patrimonial Totalitarianism in Iraq, 1968–1998," in Jabar, Faleh, A. and Hosham Dawod (eds), *Tribes and Power: Nationalism and Ethnicity in the Middle East* (London: Saqi, 2003).
——— "The Iraqi Army and Anti-Army: Some Reflections on the Role of the Military," in Dodge, Toby and Steven Simon (eds), *Iraq at the Crossroads: State and Society in the Shadow of Regime Change* (Oxford: Oxford University Press, 2003).
——— "Clerics, Tribes, Ideologies and Urban Dwellers in the South of Iraq: the Potential for Rebellion," in Dodge, Toby and Steven Simon (eds), *Iraq at the Crossroads: State and Society in the Shadow of Regime Change*, (Oxford: Oxford University Press, 2003).
——— "The War Generation in Iraq: A Case of Failed Etatist Nationalism," in Potter, Lawrence and Gary Sick (eds), *Iran, Iraq and the Legacies of War*, (New York: Palgrave MacMillan, 2004).
al-Jaza'iri, Zuhair, "Ba'thist Ideology and Practice," in Hazelton, Fran (ed.), CARDRI, *Iraq Since the Gulf War: Prospects for Democracy*, (London: Zed Books, 1994).
al-Jomard, Atheel, "Internal Migration in Iraq," in Kelidar, Abbas (ed.), *The Integration of Modern Iraq*, (London: Croom Helm, 1979).
Karim, Thair, "Tribes and Nationalism: Tribal Political Culture and Behavior in Iraq, 1914–20," in Jabar, Faleh, A. and Hosham Dawod (eds), *Tribes and Power: Nationalism and Ethnicity in the Middle East*, (London: Saqi, 2003).

al-Khafaji, Isam, "The Parasitic Base of the Ba'thist Regime," in CARDRI, *Saddam's Iraq: Revolution or Reaction?* (London: Zed Books, 1989).

——— "State Terror and the Degradation of Politics," in Hazelton, Fran (ed.), CARDRI, *Iraq Since the Gulf War: Prospects for Democracy*, (London: Zed Books, 1994).

——— "A Few Days After: State and Society in a post-Saddam Iraq," in Dodge, Toby and Steven Simon (eds), *Iraq at the Crossroads: State and Society in the Shadow of Regime Change*, (Oxford: Oxford University Press, 2003).

Khoury, Philip and Joseph Kostiner, "Introduction: Tribes and the Complexities of State Formation in the Middle East," in Khoury, Philip and Joseph Kostiner (eds), *Tribes and State Formation in the Middle East*, (Berkeley: University of California Press, 1990).

al-Khudayri, Tariq, "Iraq's Manufacturing Industry: Status and Prospects for Rehabilitation and Reform," in Mahdi, Kamil (ed.), *Iraq's Economic Predicament*, (Reading: Ithaca Press, 2002).

Kubba, Laith, "Iraqi Shi'i Politics," in Potter, Lawrence and Gary Sick (eds), *Iran, Iraq and the Legacies of War*, (New York: Palgrave MacMillan, 2004).

Lapidus, Ira, "Tribes and State Formation in Islamic History," in Khoury, Philip and Joseph Kostiner (eds), *Tribes and State Formation in the Middle East*, (Berkeley: University of California Press, 1990).

Louis, William Roger, "The British and the Origins of the Iraqi Revolution," in Fernea, Robert and William Roger Louis (eds), *The Iraqi Revolution of 1958, The Old Social Classes Revisited*, (London: IB Tauris, 1991).

al-Madfai, Khatan H.J., "Baghdad," in Berger, Morroe (ed.), *The New Metropolis in the Arab World*, (Bombay: Allied Publishers, 1963).

Makiya, Kanan, "Intolerance and Identity," in Hazelton, Fran (ed.), CARDRI, *Iraq Since the Gulf War: Prospects for Democracy*, (London: Zed Books, 1994).

Malkasian, Carter, "Counterinsurgency in Iraq: May 2003–January 2010," in Marston, Daniel and Carter Malkasian (eds), *Counterinsurgency in Modern Warfare*, (Oxford: Osprey, 2008).

McLachlan, Keith, "Iraq: Problems of Regional Development," in Kelidar, Abbas (ed.), *The Integration of Modern Iraq*, (London: Croom Helm, 1979).

Mitchell, Christopher, "Assault on the Marshlands," in Nicholson, Emma and Peter Clark (eds), *The Iraqi Marshlands: A Human and Environmental Study*, (London: Politicos Publishing, 2002).

Mohsen, Fatima, "Cultural Totalitarianism," in Hazelton, Fran (ed.), CARDRI, *Iraq Since the Gulf War: Prospects for Democracy*, (London: Zed Books, 1994).

Nakash, Yitzhak, "The Nature of Shi'ism in Iraq," in Jabar, Faleh Abdul (ed.), *Ayatollahs, Sufis and Ideologues: State, Religion and Social Movements in Iraq*, (London: Saqi, 2002).

Penrose, Edith, "Industrial Policy and Performance in Iraq," in Kelidar, Abbas (ed.), *The Integration of Modern Iraq*, (London: Croom Helm, 1979).

Pool, David, "From Elite to Class: The Transformation of Iraqi Political Leadership," in Kelidar, Abbas (ed.), *The Integration of Modern Iraq*, (London: Croom Helm, 1979).

Rahim, Ayad, "Attitudes to the West, Arabs and Fellow Iraqis," in Hazelton, Fran (ed.), CARDRI, *Iraq Since the Gulf War: Prospects for Democracy*, (London: Zed Books, 1994).

al-Ruhaini, Abdul Halim "The Da'wa Islamic Party: Origins, Actors, and Ideology," in Jabar, Faleh A. (ed.), *Ayatollahs, Sufis and Ideologues: State, Religion and Social Movements in Iraq*, (London: Saqi, 2002).

Sakai, Keiko, "Tribalization as a Tool of State Control in Iraq: Observations on the Army, the Cabinets and the National Assembly," in Jabar, Faleh, A. and Hosham Dawod (eds), *Tribes and Power: Nationalism and Ethnicity in the Middle East*, (London: Saqi, 2003).

Schwedler, Jillian, "Introduction," in Schwedler, Jillian (ed.), *Toward Civil Society in the Middle East?* (London: Lynne Rienner, 1995).

al-Shahristani, Hussain, "The Suppression and Survival of Iraqi Shi'is," in Hazelton, Fran (ed.), CARDRI, *Iraq Since the Gulf War: Prospects for Democracy*, (London: Zed Books, 1994).

Shaw, Martin, "New Wars of the City: Relationships of 'Urbicide' and 'Genocide'," in Graham, Steven (ed.), *Cities, War, and Terrorism: Towards and Urban Geopolitics*, (Oxford: Blackwell, 2004).

Simon, Reeva S., "The Imposition of Nationalism on a Non-Nation State: The Case of Iraq During the Interwar Period, 1921–1941," in Jankowski, James and Israel Gershoni (eds), *Rethinking Nationalism in the Arab Middle East*, (New York: Columbia University Press, 1997).

Sluglett, Peter, "The International Context of Iraq from 1980 to the Present," in Nicholson, Emma and Peter Clark (eds), *The Iraqi Marshlands: A Human and Environmental Study*, (London: Politicos Publishing, 2002).

Tapper, Richard, "Anthropologists, Historians, and Tribespeople on Tribe and State Formation in the Middle East," in Khoury, Philip and Joseph Kostiner (eds), *Tribes and State Formation in the Middle East*, (Berkeley: University of California Press, 1990).

Thatcher, Nicholas G., "Reflections on US Foreign Policy towards Iraq in the 1950s," in Fernea, Robert and William Roger Louis (eds), *The Iraqi Revolution of 1958, The Old Social Classes Revisited*, (London: IB Tauris, 1991).

Tibi, Bassam, "The Simultaneity of the Unsimultaneous: Old Tribes and Imposed Nation-States in the Modern Middle East," in Khoury, Philip and Joseph Kostiner (eds), *Tribes and State Formation in the Middle East*, (Berkeley: University of California Press, 1990).

Tkachenko, Alexander, "The Economy of the Marshes in the 1990s," in Nicholson, Emma and Peter Clark (eds), *The Iraqi Marshlands: A Human and Environmental Study*, (London: Politicos Publishing, 2002).

Vasile, Elizabeth, "Devotion as Distinction, Piety as Power: Religious Revival and the Transformation of Space in the Illegal Settlements of Tunis," in Bonine, Michael E. (ed.), *Population, Poverty, and Politics in Middle Eastern Cities*, (Gainsville: U Florida Press, 1997).

Voices in the Wilderness, "Myths and Realities Regarding Iraq and Sanctions," in Arnove, Anthony (ed.), *Iraq Under Siege: The Deadly Impact of Sanctions and War*, (London: Pluto Press, 2000).

Wacquant, Loic J.D., "Three Pernicious Premises in the Study of the American Ghetto," in Hagedorn, John (ed.), *Gangs in the Global City: Alternatives to Traditional Criminology*, (Urbana: University of Illinois Press, 2007).

Waterbury, John, "The Growth of Public Sector Enterprise in the Middle East," in Esfandiari, Haleh and A.L. Udovitch (eds), *The Economic Dimensions of Middle Eastern History: Essays in Honor of Charles Issawi*, (Princeton: The Darwin Press, 1990).

Young, Jock, "Globalization and Social Exclusion: Sociology of Vindictiveness and the Criminology of Transgression," in Hagedorn, John (ed.), *Gangs in the Global City: Alternatives to Traditional Criminology*, (Urbana: University of Illinois Press, 2007).

Yousif, Abdul-Salam, "The Struggle for Cultural Hegemony during the Iraqi Revolution," Fernea, Robert and William Roger Louis (eds), *The Iraqi Revolution of 1958, The Old Social Classes Revisited*, (London: IB Tauris, 1991).

Zaher, U., "Political Developments in Iraq 1963–1980," in CARDRI, *Saddam's Iraq: Revolution or Reaction?* (London: Zed Books, 1989).

Zubaida, Sami, "Community, Class and Minorities in Iraqi Politics," in Fernea, Robert and William Roger Louis (eds), *The Iraqi Revolution of 1958, The Old Social Classes Revisited*, (London: IB Tauris, 1991).

Journal Articles

Adams, Warren, "Reflections on Recent Land Reform Experience in Iraq," *Land Economics*, Vol. 39, No. 2, May 1963.

Ali, Mohammed, John Blacker and Gareth Jones, "Annual Mortality Rates and Excess Deaths of Children under-Five in Iraq, 1991–1998," *Population Studies*, Vol. 57, No. 2, July 2003.

Alnasrawi, Abbas, "The Economic Consequences of the Iran-Iraq War," *Third World Quarterly*, Vol. 8, July 1986.

Baali, Fuad, "Social Factors in Iraqi Rural-Urban Migration," *American Journal of Economics and Sociology*, Vol. 25, No. 4, October 1966.

Baer, Gabriel, "Agrarian Problems in Iraq," *Middle Eastern Affairs*, December 1952.

Baram, Amatzia, "The Ruling Political Elite in Bathi Iraq, 1968–1986: The Changing Features of a Collective Profile," *International Journal of Middle East Studies*, Vol. 21, No. 4, 1989.

Baram, Amatzia, "Neo-Tribalism in Iraq: Saddam Hussein's Tribal Policies, 1991–1996," *International Journal of Middle East Studies*, Vol. 29, No. 1, 1997.

——— "The Effect of Iraqi Sanctions: Statistical Pitfalls and Responsibility," *Middle East Journal*, Vol. 54, No. 2, Spring 2000.

Batatu, Hanna, "Iraq's Underground Shi'a Movements: Characteristics, Causes and Prospects," *Middle East Institute*, Vol. 35, No. 4, Autumn 1981.

——— "State and Capitalism in Iraq: A Comment," *MERIP Middle East Report*, No. 142, September–October 1986.

Chaudhry, Kiren Aziz, "On the Way to Market: Economic Liberalization and Iraq's Invasion of Kuwait," *Middle East Report*, No. 170, May–June 1991.

——— "Economic Liberalization and the Lineages of the Rentier State," *Comparative Politics*, Vol. 27, No. 1, October 1994.

Cole, Juan and Moojan Momen, "Mafia, Mob and Shiism in Iraq: The Rebellion of Ottoman Karbala 1824–1823," *Past and Present*, No. 112, August 1986.

De Sanstisteban, Agustin Velloso, "Sanctions, War, Occupation, and the De-development of Education in Iraq," *International Review of Education*, Vol. 51, No. 1, 2005.

Fearon, James and David Laitin, "Ethnicity, Insurgency, and Civil War," *American Political Science Review*, Vol. 97, No. 1, February 2003.

Graham-Brown, Sarah, "Sanctioning Iraq: A Failed Policy," *Middle East Report*, No. 215, Summer 2000.

Gulick, John, "Baghdad: Portrait of a City in Physical and Cultural Change," *Journal of the American Planning Association*, Vol. 33, No. 4, 1967.

Hancock, Michael, "Scourges of God: A General Comparison of Tamerlane and Hulagu in the History of Baghdad," undated, accessed via www.academia.edu

Ibrahim, Saad, "Over-urbanization and Under-urbanism: The Case of the Arab World," *International Journal of Middle East Studies*, Vol. 6, No. 1, January 1975.
Inglehart, Ronald, Mansoor Moaddel and Mark Tessler, "Xenophobia and In-Group Solidarity in Iraq: A Natural Experiment on the Impact of Insecurity," *Perspectives on Politics*, Vol. 4, No. 3, September 2006.
Jabar, Faleh A., "Why the Uprisings Failed," *Middle East Report*, No. 22, May–June 1992.
——— "Shaykhs and Ideologues: Detribalization and Retribalization in Iraq, 1968–1998," *Middle East Report*, No. 215, Summer 2001.
——— "The Worldly Roots of Religiosity in Post-Saddam Iraq," *Middle East Report*, No. 227, Summer 2003.
al-Khafaji, Isam, "Iraq's Seventh Year: Saddam's Quart d'Heure?" *Middle East Report*, No. 151, March–April 1988.
Luizard, Pierre-Jean and Joe Stork, "The Iraq Question from the Inside," *Middle East Report*, No. 193, March–April 1995.
Nakash, Yitzhak, "The Conversion of Iraq's Tribes To Shiism," *International Journal of Middle East Studies*, Vol. 26, No. 3. August 1994.
Phillips, Doris, "Rural-to-Urban Migration in Iraq," *Economic Development and Cultural Change*, Vol. 7, No. 4, 1959.
Rubin, Michael, "The Future of Iraq: Democracy, Civil War, or Chaos?" *Middle East Review of International Affairs*, Middle East Forum, September 2005.
Sluglett, Peter and Marion Farouk-Sluglett, "Iraq Since 1986: The Strengthening of Saddam," *Middle East Report*, No. 167, November–December 1990.
——— "Some Reflections on the Sunni/Shi'i Question in Iraq," *British Society for Middle Eastern Studies*, Vol. 5, No. 2, 1978.
——— "The Transformation of Land Tenure and Rural Social Structure in Central and Southern Iraq, c. 1870–1958," *International Journal of Middle East Studies*, Vol. 15, No. 4, 1983.
Sluglett, Peter, Marion Farouk-Sluglett and Joe Stork, "Not Quite Armageddon: The Impact of the War on Iraq," *MERIP Reports*, No. 125/126, July–September 1984.
Springborg, Robert, "Iraq's Agrarian Infitah," *MERIP Middle East Report*, No. 145, March–April 1987.
Tilly, Charles, "Terror, Terrorism, Terrorists," *Sociological Theory*, Vol. 22, No. 1, March 2004.
Tripp, Charles, "After Saddam," *Survival*, Vol. 44, No. 4, Winter 2002–03.

Academic Manuscripts

Berman, Eli, Jacob Shapiro and Joseph Felter, "Can Hearts and Minds Be Bought? The Economics of Counterinsurgency in Iraq," draft manuscript dated March 2011, to be published in *Journal of Political Economy* (available online via University of California, San Diego, Department of Economics: http://econ.ucsd.edu/~elib/ham.pdf).
Cole, Juan, "Marsh Arab Rebellion: Grievance, Mafias and Militias in Iraq," Fourth Wadie Jwaideh Memorial Lecture, Department of Near Eastern Languages and Cultures, Indiana University, 2008.
Eldredge, Erik and Andrew Neboshynsky, "Quantifying Human Terrain," MA Thesis, US Naval Postgraduate School, 2008.
Haussler, Nicholas, "Third Generation Gangs Revisited: The Iraq Insurgency," MA Thesis, US Naval Postgraduate School, 2005.

Hilmi, W.A., *Internal Migration and Regional Policy in Iraq*, Doctoral Dissertation, University of Sheffield, 1978.

Munson, Peter, "What Lies Beneath: Saddam's Legacy and the Roots of Resistance in Iraq," MA Thesis, US Naval Postgraduate School, 2005.

Reed, Brian, *Formalizing the Informal: A Network Analysis of an Insurgency*, Doctoral Dissertation, University of Maryland—College Park, 2006.

Shervington, M.W., "Small Wars and Counter-Insurgency Warfare: Lessons From Iraq," MA Thesis, Cranfield University, Department of Defence Management and Security Analysis, 2005.

Policy Institutes & Think Tanks

Abedin, Mahan, "The Sadrist Movement," *Middle East Intelligence Bulletin*, Vol. 5, No. 7, July 2003.

Beckett, Ian, "Insurgency in Iraq: An Historical Perspective," *Strategic Studies Institute*, January 2005.

Bigio, Jamille and Jen Scott, "Internal Displacement in Iraq: The Process of Working Toward Durable Solutions," *The Brookings Institution—University of Bern Project on International Displacement*, June 2009.

Byman, Daniel, "An Autopsy of the Iraq Debacle: Policy Failure or a Bridge Too Far?" *Security Studies*, Vol. 17, 2008.

Cochrane, Marisa, "The Battle for Basra," *The Institute for the Study of War*, 31 May 2008.

——— "Special Groups Regenerate," *The Institute for the Study of War*, 29 August 2008.

——— "The Fragmentation of the Sadrist Movement," *The Institute for the Study of War*, January 2009.

Cordesman, Anthony, "Sadr and the Mahdi Army: Evolution, Capabilities, and a New Direction," *CSIS*, 4 August 2008.

——— "Iraq: Creating a Strategic Partnership," *CSIS*, "Third Review Draft," 2 February 2010.

Foote, Christopher, William Block, Keith Crane, and Simon Gray, "Economic Policy and Prospects in Iraq," *Federal Reserve Bank of Boston*, Public Policy Discussion Paper 04–1, 4 May 2004.

Gabbay, Michael, "Mapping the Factional Structure of the Sunni Insurgency in Iraq," *CTC Sentinel*, Vol. 1, Issue 4, March 2008.

Gentile, Gian, "Freeing the Army from the Counterinsurgency Straightjacket," *Joint Forces Quarterly*, Issue 58, 2010.

Goodman, Adam, "Informal Networks and Insurgency in Iraq," *Defence Academy of the United Kingdom: Advanced Research & Assessment Group*, April 2008.

Hashim, Ahmed, "Understanding the Roots of the Shi'a Insurgency in Iraq," *Terrorism Monitor*, Vol. 2, No. 13, 2004.

Hendrickson, David and Robert Tucker, "Revisions in Need of Revising: What Went Wrong in the Iraq War," *Strategic Studies Institute*, December 2005.

Hoffman, Bruce, "Insurgency and Counterinsurgency in Iraq," *RAND Corporation*, 2004.

Human Rights Watch, "Endless Torment: The 1991 Uprising in Iraq and its Aftermath," June 1992, accessed online: http://www.hrw.org/reports/1992/Iraq926.htm

——— "Nowhere to Flee: The Perilous Situation of Palestinians in Iraq," September 2006, accessed online: http://www.hrw.org/sites/default/files/reports/iraq0706web.pdf

International Crisis Group, "Iraq Backgrounder: What Lies Beneath," *Middle East Report*, No. 6, 1 October 2002.

——— "Iraq's Shi'ites Under Occupation," *Middle East Briefing*, 9 September 2003.

——— "Unmaking Iraq: A Constitutional Process Gone Awry," *Middle East Briefing*, No. 19, 26 September 2005.

——— "The Next Iraqi War? Sectarianism and Civil Conflict," *Middle East Report*, No. 52, 27 February 2006.

——— "Iraq's Muqtada al-Sadr: Spoiler or Stabilizer?" *Middle East Report*, No. 55, 11 July 2006.

——— "Shiite Politics in Iraq," *Middle East Report*, No. 70, 15 November 2007.

——— "Iraq's Civil War, The Sadrists and the Surge," *Middle East Report*, No. 72, 7 February 2008.

International Organization for Migration, "Anbar, Baghdad & Diyala: Governorate Profiles, Post-February 2006 IDP Needs Assessments," December 2007, accessed online: http://www.iom-iraq.net/idp.html

Johnson, David, M. Wade Markel and Brian Shannon, "The 2008 Battle of Sadr City," *RAND Corporation*, 2011.

al-Khalidi, Ashraf and Victor Tanner, "Sectarian Violence: Radical Groups Drive Displacement," *The Brookings Institution—University of Bern Project on International Displacement*, October 2006.

Kilcullen, David, "Countering Global Insurgency," *Journal of Strategic Studies*, Vol. 28, August 2005.

Kramer, Martin, "Ivory Towers on Sand: The Failure of Middle East Studies in America," *The Washington Institute for Near East Policy*, 2001.

Lamborn, G.L., "The People in Arms: A Practitioner's Guide to Understanding Insurgency and Dealing with it Effectively," *Small Wars Journal*, June 2009.

Lewis, Jessica, Ahmed Ali and Kimberly Kagan, "Iraq's Sectarian Crisis Reignites as Shi'a Militias Execute Civilians and Remobilize," *Institute for the Study of War*, 31 May 2013.

Mansuri, Ghazala and Vijayendra Rao, "Localizing Development: Does Participation Work?" *The World Bank*, 2013.

Manwaring, Max, "Street Gangs: The New Urban Insurgency," *Strategic Studies Institute*, March 2005.

——— "Shadows of Things Past and Images of the Future: Lessons for the Insurgencies in Our Midst," *Strategic Studies Institute*, November 2004.

McFate, Montgomery, "Anthropology and Counterinsurgency: The Strange Story of their Curious Relationship," *Military Review*, March–April 2005.

McFate, Montgomery and Steve Fondacaro, "Reflections on the Human Terrain System During the First 4 Years," *PRISM*, Vol. 2, No. 4, September 2011.

Metz, Steven, "Insurgency and Counterinsurgency in Iraq," *The Washington Quarterly*, Vol. 27, No. 1, Winter 2003–2004.

Morrow, Jonathan, "Iraq's Constitutional Process II: An Opportunity Lost," *United States Institute of Peace*, Special Report 155, November 2005.

Ollivant, Douglas, "Countering the New Orthodoxy: Reinterpreting Counterinsurgency in Iraq," *New America Foundation*, June 2011.

Palestine Liberation Organization, "Palestinian Refugees in Iraq," *Refugees Affairs Department*, 1999, accessed via Palestinian Refugee ResearchNet: http://prrn.mcgill.ca

Paul, Christopher, Colin Clarke and Beth Grill, "Victory Has a Thousand Fathers: Sources of Success in Counterinsurgency," *RAND Corporation*, 2010.

Petraeus, David, "Learning Counterinsurgency: Observations From Soldiering in Iraq," *Military Review*, Vol. 86, January–February 2006.

Ronfeldt, David, "In Search of How Societies Work: Tribes—The First and Forever Form," *RAND Corporation*, 2006.

Sepp, Kalev, "From 'Shock and Awe' to 'Hearts and Minds': The Fall and Rise of US Counterinsurgency Capability in Iraq," *Third World Quarterly*, Vol. 28, No. 2, 2007.

Stancati, Bernard, "Tribal Dynamics and the Iraq Surge," *Strategic Studies Quarterly*, Summer 2010.

Strakes, Jason E. "Fourth Generation Conflict? Local Social Formations and Insurgencies in Post-Ba'ath Iraq," *Journal of Third World Studies*, Vol. 24, Fall 2007.

Taylor, Richard, "Tribal Alliances: Ways, Means, and Ends to Successful Strategy," *Strategic Studies Institute*, August 2005.

Terrell, Andrew W., "Nationalism, Sectarianism, and the Future of the US Presence in Post-Saddam Iraq," *Strategic Studies Institute*, July 2003.

Ucko, David, "Militias, Tribes and Insurgents: The Challenge of Political Reintegration in Iraq," *Conflict, Security & Development*, Vol. 8, No. 3, October 2008.

Media Reports

Associated Press, "June the Deadliest Month for U.S. Troops in 2 Years," *USA Today*, 30 June 2011.

Barnes, Fred, "How Bush Decided on the Surge," *The Weekly Standard*, Vol. 13, No. 20, 4 February 2008.

Bowman, Tom, "As the Iraq War Ends, Reassessing the Surge," *NPR*, 16 December 2011.

Dransfield, Lyndsey, "Soldiers Help Iraqi Farmers Feed Water Buffalo," *American Forces Press Services*, 10 September 2008.

The Economist, "Abdul Majid al-Khoei," 17 April 2003.

Filkins, Dexter, "Stanley McChrystal's Long War," *The New York Times*, 14 October 2009.

Frazier Ian, "Invaders: Destroying Baghdad," *The New Yorker*, 25 April 2005.

Gisik, Michael, "Troops Arrest Eight Iraqi Police Officers," *Stars and Stripes*, 17 May 2008.

Grove, Casey, "Alaska-based Soldier Admits Accepting Illegal Gratuities," *Anchorage Daily News*, 2 March 2012.

Henry, Ed, "Obama Not Planning to Credit Bush over Iraq 'Surge,'" *CNN*, 31 August 2010.

Karatas, Nilgun, "Turkish Contractors to Rebuild Sadr City," *Hurriyet Daily News*, 10 December 2010.

Londoño, Ernesto, "Demise of Iraqi Water Park Illustrates Limitations, Abuse of US Funding Program," *The Washington Post*, 3 January 2011.

Murphy, Dan, "The Iraq War Death Toll? At least 162,000 and Counting," *Christian Science Monitor*, 2 January 2012.

Meyers, Steven Lee, "With New Violence, More Christians Are Fleeing Iraq," *New York Times*, 12 December 2010.

Packer, George, "Obama's Iraq Problem," *The New Yorker*, 7 July 2008.
Roggio, Bill, "Mahdi Army Decimated During Recent Fighting," *Long War Journal*, 26 June 2008.
Rovner, Joshua and Tim Hoyt, "There is No Checklist for Counterinsurgency," *Foreign Policy—The AfPak Channel*, 18 November 2010.
Susman, Tina, "Security Crackdown Widens to Shiite Slum," *Los Angeles Times*, 5 March 2007.
Sabrina Tavernise, "A Shiite Militia in Baghdad Sees its Power Wane," *The New York Times*, 27 July 2008.
Senanayake, Sumedha, "Iraq: Growing Numbers Flee Sectarian Violence," *Radio Free Europe*, 26 January 2007.
Ward, Celeste, "Countering the Military's Latest Fad: Counterinsurgency," *The Washington Post*, 17 May 2009.
Wood, Michael, "Abdul Majid al-Khoei," *The Guardian*, 12 April 2003.
Zubaida, Sami, "The Rise and Fall of Civil Society in Iraq," *Open Democracy*, 5 February 2003.

Official Documents & Manuals

Peacock, James, Robert Albro, Carolyn Fluehr-Lobban, Kerry Fosher, Laura McNamara, Monica Heller, George Marcus, David Price and Alan Goodman, "AAA Commission on the Engagement of Anthropology with the US Security and Intelligence Communities," Final Report, 4 November 2007, available online via the American Anthropological Association: http://www.aaanet.org/pdf/FINAL_Report_Complete.pdf
US Army Field Manual 3–24, *Counterinsurgency*, (Washington DC: Department of the Army, 2006).
US Army Field Manual 3–90.6, *Brigade Combat Team*, (Washington DC: Department of the Army, 2010).

Online Databases

Brookings Institute Iraq Index: http://www.brookings.edu/about/centers/saban/iraq-index
Columbia University's "Gulf 2000" Mapping Project: http://gulf2000.columbia.edu/maps.shtml
Institute for the Study of War Map Catalogue: http://www.understandingwar.org/publications
Iraq Body Count: http://www.iraqbodycount.org/
University of Texas Perry-Castañeda Iraq Map Library: http://www.lib.utexas.edu/maps/iraq.html